PROPERTY TAX MANUAL:
Strategies and Techniques For Reduction and Control

PROPERTY TAX MANUAL:
Strategies and Techniques For Reduction and Control

Jerrold F. Janata

Prentice-Hall, Inc.
Englewood Cliffs, N.J.

Prentice Hall International, Inc., *London*
Prentice-Hall of Australia, Pty. Ltd., *Sydney*
Prentice-Hall of Canada, Ltd., *Toronto*
Prentice-Hall of India Private Ltd., *New Delhi*
Prentice-Hall of Japan, Inc., *Tokyo*
Prentice-Hall of Southeast Asia Pte. Ltd., *Singapore*
Whitehall Books, Ltd., Wellington, *New Zealand*

"This publication is designed to provide accurate and authoritative information in regard to the subject matter covered. It is sold with the understanding that the publisher is not engaged in rendering legal, accounting, or other professional service. If legal advice or other expert assistance is required, the service of a competent professional person should be sought.

. . . *From the Declaration of Principles jointly adopted by a Committee of the American Bar Association and a Committee of Publishers and Associations.*"

Library of Congress Cataloging in Publication Data

Janata, Jerrold F
Property tax manual.

Includes bibliographical references and index.
1. Property tax--United States. I. Title.
HJ4120.J32 352'.13 78-26324
ISBN 0-13-731000-5

Printed in the United States of America

About the Author

Jerrold F. Janata is President of International Appraisal Company, a firm specializing in property tax appeals and control programs. He was Property Tax Manager for F.W. Woolworth and I.T.T. Continental Baking Company, handling all property tax matters in those multi-state corporations. He has directed property tax control efforts at more than 200 corporations in every state and in Canada. Mr. Janata is a Senior Member of the American Society of Appraisers and he has lectured before the Tax Executives Institute, American Institute of Certified Public Accountants, National Tax Association, and the International Association of Assessing Officers. He has received awards from the I.A.A.O. for his lectures and publications. Mr. Janata holds a B.A. in Political Science, a J.D. from Fordham Law School and an M.B.A. in Finance from Iona College. He has been admitted to the New York and Federal Bars.

This book is dedicated with love to my wife, Madelyn, whose energy, enthusiasm, friendship, support, and understanding made its writing possible.

ACKNOWLEDGMENTS

I would like to acknowledge the assistance of International Appraisal Company, Inc., of Paramus, New Jersey, whose resources were made available to me during the preparation of this manuscript.

I also made extensive use of "The Assessment and Valuation Legal Reporter" published by the International Association of Assessing Officers, Chicago, Illinois.

I gratefully acknowledge the assistance, guidance and contribution of colleagues whose time and advice were given freely. They include Messrs. Alexander L. Hazen, Paul D. Roberts, John L. Piropato, Leon A. Klein, Edward H. Fowler, James Prevost and Jack Jacksen.

I also wish to thank all those property tax men and assessors who shared the experiences set forth in this manual with me. I trust they will not be too critical of my side of the story.

With deep appreciation I thank Helene Fischer for typing, editing and physically preparing the manual.

Lastly, and with pride, I thank my daughter, Gloria, who assisted with much of the research for this book.

How This Book Will Help You to Reduce and Control Property Taxes

This book gives you court-sanctioned property tax assessment reduction techniques that can be applied to real and personal property by any taxpayer, large or small, anywhere in the United States.

All of these techniques are organized into a logical presentation that will enable you to analyze the fairness of a property assessment; determine the best strategy to use in pursuing a reduction; and bring an appeal to a successful conclusion.

You will be equipped to swiftly and effectively reduce and control property taxes.

Tax practitioners and practical businessmen have long been aware of the negative impact an excessive property tax has on the profitability of a real estate operation. The property tax is the largest single expense item, excluding financing, on any income producing real estate. The continued existence of a shopping center with property taxes in excess of \$1.00 per square foot is virtually threatened. Property taxes in excess of 20% of the gross income of an apartment house or office building can seriously affect the bottom line profit picture. Property taxes that exceed 4% of the fair market value of a property are considered to be confiscatory.

And yet, shopping center property taxes do exceed \$1.00 per square foot, apartment and office building property taxes do exceed 20% of gross, and property taxes do exceed 4% of fair market value in several major cities.

What can you do about it? Well, U. S. taxpayers achieved property tax savings in the past year in excess of \$2 billion. There is no secret involved in this result. Homeowners secure reductions because their basements flood. Shopping center developers reduce taxes because of inadequate parking. Apartment operators argue value loss because of deteriorating neighborhoods. Industrial real estate and machinery and equipment are granted assessment reductions because of functional obsolescence. The reasons are as varied as the properties themselves.

SYSTEMATIC TAX SAVINGS

These techniques work and the payoffs are significant. Your present property tax obligation can be reduced from 10% to 35%. Sometimes 50% reductions can be achieved. Here are some actual savings as set forth in this book:

Project	Savings
10-year assessment reduction effort through negotiations, board of review hearing, additional construction and revaluation saves:	\$830,000

Project	Savings
Taxpayer challenge of speculative land assessment based on remote possibility of zoning changes results in tax savings of:	$150,000
Taxpayer refused to accept assessor's use of contract rent to value retail store. Court held economic rent should be used.	$340,000
Taxpayer rejected assessor's income projection for 1,000-unit hotel and submitted actual income figures to Board. Board reduced assessment by $2.4 million, with annual savings of:	$100,000
A properly presented apartment house income and expense statement reflecting economic obsolescence resulted in annual tax savings of:	$ 30,000
Successful presentation of functional and economic obsolescence in an "old" industrial plant gave taxpayer annual tax savings of:	$150,000
Sale price of "new" industrial plant prevailed over assessor's valuation at cost. Annual tax savings:	$300,000
Proper presentation led to personal property tax audit adjustments for out-of-state inventory, interest and penalty adjustments, statutory definition of "inventory," and economic obsolescence of:	$245,000
Taxpayer challenged a state promulgated depreciation schedule resulting in a shorter useful life for machinery and equipment. This, coupled with proper application of functional and economic obsolescence, resulted in personal property tax savings of:	$320,000
Initial negotiations with assessor and revaluation firm, supported by detailed taxpayer's position letter documenting economic problems, resulted in tax savings of:	$120,000
The assessor considered an industrial property a specialty and used only the cost approach. Taxpayer showed it was a general purpose facility and presented income and market data evidence. Board decision in taxpayer's favor reduced assessment by $2.7 million. Tax savings:	$105,000

Throughout the text are many case studies and examples. Some of these include:

- Assessor disregarded current zoning constraints in assessing land. Court held this was speculative and unfair to taxpayer. $150,000 was refunded to taxpayer.
- Taxpayer admitted that his 68 acres of land would be worth $2.5 million if developed for hotel or apartment use. However, because he was growing coconuts, his $54,312 agricultural assessment was upheld by the Court, despite the fact that he was losing money each year and the coconuts could have been grown on only five acres.
- Downtown retail store assessment reduced on precedent-setting decision when Court recognized economic obsolescence due to shopping center competition.
- Assessment reductions achieved when taxpayer challenged assessor's use of projected income figures vis-a-vis the actual experience of the hotel.
- Monumental office building valued on cost new and incremental rental value in promoting economic interests of owner. Dissent in this 4-3 decision rejected both these concepts in favor of capitalization of actual income. Unfortunately, this 4-3 difference of opinion caused taxpayer to lose, but later cases place greater reliance on standard income approach.
- Design shortcomings (saw-tooth roof, steel sash window walls, low ceilings, small bays, no room for expansion) resulted in a 25% assessment reduction on one of the oldest primary metal plants in the United States.

• Arm's-length sale of a relatively new industrial facility resulted in a 40% reduction in assessor's cost approach assessment.

• Taxpayer challenged statutory definition of inventory which did not include "work-in-process." Court held tax statutes should be strictly construed and held "work-in-process" not taxable.

• Taxpayer presented evidence which caused the state promulgated useful life schedule to be disregarded by State Board. Application of taxpayer's shorter life schedule plus functional/technological obsolescence resulted in substantial assessment reduction and tax savings.

• Taxpayer, after assessor refused to consider a sale of the property, went over the assessor's head to the mayor, and assessment reduction to the purchase price was obtained.

HOW THIS BOOK IS ORGANIZED

This is not an old-fashioned textbook steeped in academic rhetoric. It is a practical how-to-do-it guide with actual examples (many involving the author's participation) focusing on the latest and best techniques for property tax savings.

1. This book will enable you to quickly identify the easiest areas for large property tax reductions.

2. It will tell you how and where to get help; check lists, leading cases, cost manuals, recognized source material, and local practice are cited throughout.

3. The breadth of the book covers everything from simple residential appeals to complex industrial and commercial appeals; from informal negotiations with the local assessor to appeals carried to the Supreme Court of the United States.

4. Throughout the book, case studies are given illustrating how actual taxpayers have saved *millions* of dollars in property taxes.

HIGHLIGHTING THE BENEFITS

How to develop and implement a property tax reduction and control plan. Are market value assessments attainable and for how long? How to isolate the inherent weakness in mass-produced assessments. Do you have to know somebody? (See Chapter 1.)

How to examine the key issues of market value and equalization. Rules of thumb to establish market value. Dealing with the equalization rate issue. The significance of the classification issue in our tax revolt society. (See Chapter 2.)

How to use an appraisal report to achieve property tax savings. Basic elements. Comparison between standard and ad valorem format. Effective presentation. When to call an appraiser and how to measure appraisal fees to be sure you get your money's worth. (See Chapter 3.)

How to challenge a land assessment. Valuation techniques. Classification and transitional issues. When is machinery and equipment land? How should mineral, air, water and timber rights be assessed? (See Chapter 4.)

How to appeal a residential assessment at minimum cost. Exemptions, classification, and deductions. Mobile homes. Eight questions most often asked by assessor in negotiations. How to complete an application for assessment review. How to present a residential appeal to a Board of Review. Advantages of a class action. (See Chapter 5.)

How to use economic obsolescence, economic rent and comparable sales to win downtown retail store assessment appeals. How to use cost, income and comparable sales to reduce shopping center assessments. Assessment problems of the net lessee. (See Chapter 6.)

Achieving property tax savings goals in large and small hotel/motel assessment appeals. How to use the income approach and gross and net income multipliers. Successful restaurant appeals. (See Chapter 7.)

How to successfully appeal assessments levied against office buildings, apartment houses, condominiums and cooperatives. Cost vs. income: the Seagram's case. How to reconstruct an income and expense statement for presentation to the assessor. (See Chapter 8.)

How to use physical, functional/technological and economic obsolescence arguments to achieve industrial plant assessment reductions. How to present cost, income and market data to support your value conclusions. How to use excess operating costs and "existing vs. new" plant comparisons to prove obsolescence. Are out-of-state comparables admissible? When is an industrial plant a "specialty"? (See Chapter 9.)

How to search out unique "unit-in-use" value measures to handle assessment problems on special purpose properties: gasoline service stations, bowling centers, country clubs and golf courses, motion picture theaters and drive-ins. When is a special purpose property not a special purpose property? (See Chapter 10.)

Techniques for establishing equitable personal property assessments. What is personal property? How to determine situs. Exemptions. Tips on minimizing liability through tax compliance practice. Actual case example of audit and appeal to local and state levels. (See Chapter 11.)

How to use gray area subtleties to your tax advantage when distinguishing between real and personal property. Definitions and guidelines. "Used in business" and "common law" concepts. The "and then some" rules in California and New York. (See Chapter 12.)

How to qualify for an exempt category status and pay no property tax at all. Government, religious, educational, charitable, and homeowners' exemptions. Issues concerning lessors and lessees dealing with exempt entitites. "Unwritten" exemptions. "In lieu of" tax payments. (See Chapter 13.)

How to plan effective initial negotiations with the assessor to set the stage for the best tax savings result. Overvaluation, equalization and "local" grounds for appeal. Actual case history of meeting and follow-up including a taxpayer's position letter. (See Chapter 14.)

How to present appeals to a Board of Assessment Review. The application: timeliness, proper information and service. Examples of Board of Assessment Review hearings. (See Chapter 15.)

Appeal to Court—the culmination of your effort toward equitable assessments. Tips on procedural steps to avoid fatal defects. Example of typical legal papers necessary to bring action to court. How to use pre-trial meetings and information exchanges to your advantage. Example of a typical trial. (See Chapter 16.)

Jerrold F. Janata

Table of Contents

Part III: TECHNIQUES AND METHODS IN SUCCESSFUL PROPERTY TAX APPEAL PRACTICE

Part I

Opportunities, Analysis, Strategies, and Techniques To Reduce and Control Property Taxes

1
How to Develop a Property Tax Reduction And Control Plan

The Plan and How It Works

- Know the Property
- Know How the Property Is Assessed
- Know the Property's Market Value
- Know the Equalization Rate
- Know the Appeal Calendar
- Develop an Attitude
- Implement the Plan

Are Market Value Assessments Attainable?

- What Is an Acceptable Ad Valorem Tax Value Assessment—for a Given Period—Under the Circumstances?

How to Isolate the Inherent Weakness in Mass-Produced Assessments

Do You Have to Know Somebody?

1

The importance of a property tax reduction and control plan cannot be overstated. The real property tax is the largest single expense item, excluding financing, charged against income producing real estate. The personal property tax is also a substantial dollar burden to the taxpayer.

The assessments that form the basis for this tax levy are, in the main, mass produced via formulas from cost manuals or taxing authorities. In general, very little attention is given to the unique characteristics of the subject property. In many instances, proper consideration of these unique characteristics, such as severe physical depreciation or functional and economic obsolescence, results in assessment reductions and property tax savings.

All too often the experienced tax practitioner accepts these machine produced assessments without thorough investigation. This is unacceptable in our sophisticated tax society.

The concerned tax practitioner can no longer assume that he is properly representing his client by checking to see if last year's assessment was the same as this year's assessment. To properly and professionally serve his client, he must examine the equitableness of that assessment each year and, where warranted, initiate action to reduce taxes by implementing modern techniques of property tax reduction and control.

In addition, it is no longer acceptable for the professional to wait until the problem is presented by the client. Property tax reduction and control requires planning. Just as steps are recommended to achieve tax savings through proper income or estate tax planning—or to take advantage of investment tax credit qualifying property—so too must steps be recommended to develop a continuous program of property tax reduction and control.

The taxpayer-client has every right to minimize his tax obligation as long as he acts within the law. And since he pays the bills, he should insist on this ongoing property tax control effort. Anything short of this type of program is *not* proper representation.

THE PLAN AND HOW IT WORKS

The elements of a property tax reduction and control plan are:

- know the property
- know how the property is assessed
- know the property's market value
- know the equalization rate
- know the appeal calendar
- develop an attitude
- implement the plan

As subsequent chapters will show, there are several essential ingredients that go into a successful property tax reduction and control effort.

Know the Property

A basic knowledge of the subject property or properties is absolutely necessary. You should be familiar with the following:

> *Real Estate*—land area; survey or plot plan; square footage of building; floor plan; date and cost of construction and additions, date of purchase and purchase price; lease information, if any; and income statements for three to five years for income producing property.
>
> *Personal Property*—a complete inventory of the assets. An asset listing should show asset number, identification/description, and original cost. You should also obtain copies of the personal property returns.

Know How the Property Is Assessed

This requires complete familiarity with local practice and procedures. The key element in the establishment of an assessment is often the ''unwritten'' local custom which may have existed for years in a given jurisdiction. A semblance of uniformity may have been achieved by the assessor through this effort. But, if the assessment cannot stand the scrutiny of modern day valuation principles, it must yield!

The assessor's property record card and the tax bill must be reviewed. Assessors' manuals, statutes, and case law are also prime sources of data indispensable to your understanding of your assessment. Copies of these items should be obtained and studied.

Several cases cited in this manual show the importance of proper review of these sources to develop supportive arguments for the taxpayer's valuation position.

Know the Property's Market Value

The first major issue in a property tax case is the market value of the subject property.

Follow the method of the entrepreneur in this effort. How do these experts arrive at investment decisions? Certain value rules of thumb may be followed. They will not make you an overnight appraiser, but you will be able to arrive at some broad preliminary value conclusions against which to compare the assessment.

Detailed development of these rules of thumb will be presented in Chapter 2 to assist in arriving at preliminary value ranges. In addition, Chapters 4 through 11 will present valuation examples of land, residential, retail, hotel/motel, office/apartment, industrial, special purpose and personal property.

Know the Equalization Rate

The second major issue in a property tax case is the equalization issue. This is the percentage of market value at which the property is assessed.

The issue of equalization is a critical factor in achieving equitable property tax assessments. The best presented valuation case resulting in a substantial assessment reduction can be neutralized by a discriminatory equalization scheme.

The properly prepared property tax practitioner must, therefore, be aware of this issue in order to avoid losing all that has been gained in the market value portion of the case.

The equalization issue will also be presented in detail in Chapter 2.

Know the Appeal Calendar

It is essential that you be familiar with the appeal calendar in the jurisdiction where the subject property is located. This enables you to establish a timetable to be properly prepared for:

- review of property data
- review of assessment data
- preliminary meeting with assessor
- negotiation session with assessor
- exchange of information with assessor
- appeal to the local Board of Review
- appeal to State Board of Review
- appeal to Court

It is also essential that you watch the calendar for the second year of appeal while you are still working on the first year's appeal. Crowded calendars and other delays often require that a second year be appealed before the first year's valuation issue is resolved. Just be sure that the second year's appeal timetable is not forgotten.

Develop an Attitude

The thrust of this manual is to challenge complacent acceptance of inequitable assessments. The attitude of the tax practitioner must center around the fact that assessments are no more than an opinion of value.

True, the assessor's opinion has some weight behind it. The assessment is often based on state promulgated schedules and theories—strong because it is part of a value measurement system that stands up year after year—weak because it does not always take an in-depth look at the individual property.

It also has strength because the assessment is presumptively correct and a board of review or court may adopt it even if no evidence is introduced to substantiate it. Taxpayer must overcome the presumption of correctness and if he does not prove that the assessment was improperly arrived at, it will not be disturbed.[1]

This manual will show numerous examples of court cases involving every type of property where the taxpayer did overcome the presumptive correctness of an assessment. In effect, taxpayer's opinion of value prevailed over the assessor's opinion of value.

This property tax manual is *not* an indictment of the assessor's opinion. This property tax manual *is* an indictment of complacent acceptance of inequitable assessments. It is a call for a thorough and in-depth testing of assessments to establish equity.

You may be surprised to find that your worthy adversary, the assessor, is pursuing equity with equal vigor. This mutual energy, clashing at the negotiation table, before a Board of Review or in Court, is the stuff that equitable assessments are made of.

The results may not be what either the taxpayer or the assessor wants to see as the final assessment. But it is the best we have in an imperfect system. And the vigorous pursuit of equitable assessments assures us of a healthy property tax capable of sustaining our local governmental system.

---

[1]*State ex rel. North Shore Development Co., et al. v. Axtell,* 216 Wis. 153, 256 N.W. 622 (1934).

It is the author's experience—and this may be a surprise—that today's professional assessor will react with sincere fairness to a taxpayer's complaint. Unfortunately, the equitableness of the assessment issue is often lost in the complex problems facing the assessor. These include a requirement for continuity of his value measurement system, a continuing erosion of his tax base through loss of ratables and increase in exemptions, and declining property values. He is concerned about the school budget, the problems of the elderly, urban blight, and his own reelection or reappointment. You may present a perfectly logical valuation argument to an assessor who cannot respond due to more demanding practical and political constraints.

Thus, you must plead your case to a Board of Review or a Court. Do these august bodies have the valuation answer?

Perhaps Marshall G. Kaplan, President of the Tax Commission of the City of New York, said it best:

> Reviewing assessments is neither an art nor a science. It is no more precise than the evaluation of personal injuries or the computation of prison sentences. It is less likely to lend itself to formal findings of fact and conclusions of law than any other field. The reported decisions generally teach little and have fleeting value as precedents.[2]

Clearly then, Board and Court decisions are just another opinion. Several cases cited in this manual include dissenting opinions dividing the court rendering the decision. Often, if one of the judges voted a different way, the case would result in exactly the opposite conclusion.

These facts illustrate why the tax practitioner cannot complacently accept the assessor's opinion of value. It must be tested and challenged, where warranted.

Implement the Plan

All of the key elements of a successful property tax reduction and control plan have been listed in the preceding sections. But a plan is only as good as its implementation.

Obtain and review the data necessary to know the property and how it is assessed. Follow the rules of thumb (Chapter 2) and specific valuation examples (Chapters 4 through 11) to estimate the property's market value. Seek out the sources of equalization rates as outlined in Chapter 2. Record the dates essential to a timely appeal effort. And, finally, challenge the assessor's opinion of value where warranted!

The plan should be pursued with vigor, and its ultimate goal should be the establishment of a market value assessment.

ARE MARKET VALUE ASSESSMENTS ATTAINABLE?

The basic reference point for the assessor's opinion of true value or full cash value is "market value." The definition of market value is set forth in Chapter 3 on appraisals. It is the "willing buyer-willing seller" concept. Market value is the highest price in terms of money that a property will bring in an open and competitive market where both the buyer and seller are aware of all the facts and each acts prudently. The selling price established is,

---

[2] "Assessing Partially Completed Problem Properties," *Real Estate Review*, spring 1977, Vol. 7, No. 1, the Real Estate Institute of New York University.

under these circumstances, based on an "arm's-length" transaction as opposed to an "inside" deal involving family, intracorporate, or other entanglements.

The term "fair market value" as used in ad valorem (according to value)[3] matters means the same as market value. The word "fair" seems to have been added to emphasize the taxpayer's continual plea for equity.

Can you expect to establish an assessment that represents fair market value?[4] The answer is: probably not!

What you can expect to achieve is: *"an acceptable ad valorem tax value assessment–for a given period–under the circumstances."*

What Is an Acceptable Ad Valorem Tax Value Assessment—for a Given Period—Under the Circumstances?

An assessment may be considered to be acceptable when informal negotiations or formal administrative and legal remedies have been exhausted. This assumes that the case was properly prepared and presented.

The possible values range from the ideal for the taxpayer (his opinion of value) to the ideal for the assessor (the assessment as levied). In between is a compromise value which may bear little relationship to fair market value from an investor's point of view.

For example, if an assessment is levied at $1,500,000 and taxpayer believes the property is worth only $1,000,000 on the open market, it may be prudent to accept an assessment of $1,250,000 if offered during negotiations with the assessor.

If the tax rate is 2.5%, $6,250 in tax savings is immediately obtained, taxpayer cannot be absolutely sure that the assessment will be reduced to $1,000,000 on appeal, and the cost of further appeal may offset the additional $6,250 in tax savings that might be achieved.

Thus, the $1,250,000 is an *acceptable ad valorem tax value assessment,* even though the taxpayer is quite sure that a knowledgeable investor would pay only $1,000,000 for the property.

The given period is the time during which you can expect to maintain an acceptable assessment. This can range from one year to several years.

In a negotiated settlement, it is generally dictated by agreement of the parties to leave the assessment as fixed for two or more years into the future. This, of course, is subject to new construction or demolition at the subject property, or a revaluation in the taxing jurisdiction. Finally, changing market conditions often result in property value adjustment requirements.

Assume an income producing property (shopping center, apartment or office building, hotel or leased industrial) with the following assessment data:

Assessment:	$8,000,000
Equalization Rate:	100%
Assessor's Market Value:	$8,000,000

[3]Duties are either *ad valorem* or *specific:* the former when the duty is laid in the form of a percentage on the value of the property; the latter where it is imposed as a fixed sum on each article of a class without regard to its value. The term *ad valorem* tax means a tax or duty upon the value of the article or thing subject to taxation. Arthur v. Johnston, 185 S.C. 324, 194 S.E. 151, 154 (1937), Black's Law Dictionary, West Publishing Co., St. Paul, Minn.

[4]Equalization rates (the percentage of market value at which assessments are levied) will be covered in Chapter 2. For purposes of this discussion, assume assessments are levied at 100% of market value.

Tax Rate: 2½% or \$2.50/100—Assume a rate increase of 10% per year
Annual Taxes: \$200,000

A typical history of a series of given periods might be as follows (please refer to the chart at the end of this section):

Year

1 Assessment is appealed. Negotiations with assessor are fruitless. Crowded calendar prevents an immediate Board hearing.

2 Assessment is appealed for the second year. First-year appeal finally goes on calendar for hearing.

Both years are consolidated. Negotiations take place. Taxpayer agrees to withdraw first year's appeal. He accepts a 20% reduction in assessment for second year and agrees not to appeal in third year. Assessment is reduced to \$6,400,000.

Perhaps, in this example, the taxpayer might have obtained a greater reduction if he *won* an appeal. Still, it might be wiser to accept a 20% reduction (which is reasonably substantial) as a "sure thing." This eliminates the risk of receiving no reduction from a Board or Court. By taking the 20% reduction, the "gravy" was eliminated from the assessment. This initial reduction begins to generate tax savings which, in effect, pay for the appeal effort. And, there are always future years to appeal where additional reductions can be achieved without jeopardizing the initial assessment reduction.

Of utmost importance is the fact that it is a lot more palatable for an assessor or a Board to grant a 20% reduction than it is to grant a 40% reduction.

The reduction achieved establishes *an acceptable ad valorem tax value assessment* for this *given period* of three years.

Year

3. No action per agreement.

Thus, the three-year effort to date has produced \$92,480 (\$44,000 + \$48,480) in tax savings. The *ongoing* movement toward an acceptable assessment has begun. Now it is time to take another good hard look at the assessment.

Year

4 Another look. Assessment is now \$6,400,000. Taxes are \$213,120 (\$6,400,000 × \$3.33) due to tax rate increases. This is higher than they were in the first appeal year (\$8,000,000 × \$2.50=\$200,000)—despite the assessment reduction of 20%. Some construction has taken place. Portions of the structures have been demolished. Some recent comparable sales indicate that the assessment is still high.

Assessment is appealed. Negotiations break down. Crowded calendar delays hearing.

5 Assessment is appealed. Year 4 comes up for hearing. Years 4 and 5 are consolidated. Board hearing is held and taxpayer wins a 20% reduction to \$5,120,000.

6 No action.

Note that another *acceptable ad volorem tax value assessment* was achieved for the *given period:* Years 4-5-6.

Year

7 \$1 million in additional construction takes place at property. Assessor increases assessment by \$1 million to \$6,120,000. Taxpayer takes issue with increase and appeals. Crowded calendar delays hearing.

8 Assessment is appealed. Year 7 comes up for hearing. Taxpayer loses and assessor's increase is upheld.

9 No action.

Unfortunately for the taxpayer, this *given period,* years 7-8-9, was not as favorable as the preceding periods. Nevertheless, as the chart at the end of this section will show, tax savings generated by the original reduction are still being received by the taxpayer.

Year

10 A jurisdiction-wide revaluation takes place. Start all over again!

The above example is not hypothetical. It is based on actual experience. It illustrates most clearly the requirement for an *ongoing and continuous property tax control program.*

The chart in Figure 1–1 shows the full impact of a long-range property tax control effort. Total cumulative tax savings over a ten-year period exceeds $830,000. Do the property tax obligation locations you are responsible for have a ten-year plan?

-1- Year	-2- Assessment	-3- If No Appeal Action, Assmt. Would Have Been	-4- Tax Rate per $100	-5- Taxes Payable Col. 2 × Col. 4	-6- If No Appeal Action, Taxes Would Have Been Col. 3 × Col. 4	-7- Cumulative Year's Tax Savings
1	$8,000,000	$8,000,000	$2.50	$200,000	$200,000	-0-
2	6,400,000	8,000,000	2.75	176,000	220,000	$ 44,000
3	6,400,000	8,000,000	3.03	193,920	242,400	48,480
4	5,120,000	8,000,000	3.33	170,496	266,400	95,904
5	5,120,000	8,000,000	3.67	187,904	293,600	105,696
6	5,120,000	8,000,000	4.03	206,336	322,400	116,064
7	6,120,000	9,000,000	4.44	271,728	399,600	127,872
8	6,120,000	9,000,000	4.88	298,656	439,200	140,544
9	6,120,000	9,000,000	5.37	328,644	483,300	154,656
10	Revaluation New Assessment	?	5.90	?	?	?
					TOTAL:	$833,216

FIGURE 1-1

HOW TO ISOLATE THE INHERENT WEAKNESS IN MASS-PRODUCED ASSESSMENTS

Assessments in the United States are, of necessity, mass produced. Assessing offices simply do not have the budgets, manpower, or wherewithall to do otherwise. Mass appraisal firms are hired to revalue entire jurisdictions. Methods are formulated to measure value based on standards developed from cost manuals.

In varying degrees, the best cost approach job that can be done is done. However, there is one serious shortcoming. This is the lack of individuality in the assessment. The property is described on the assessor's property record card and guideline cost and depreciation measures are applied. But it is very rare that proper adjustment is made to recognize the unique individual characteristics of the property. These factors, often in the form of severe physical or functional and economic obsolescence, have a negative effect on the value of the property. Common sense dictates that the assessor, pressed for time and under budget constraints, will not direct his energies toward uncovering obsolescence factors concerning your property.

It is also very rare to find that the income and market data approaches to value have been used to develop the assessment. Only vague references are made to the fact that the cost approach conclusion was checked against income and market data information.

A property tax control program begins by being sure that individual treatment is given to the development of the subject property's assessment. It is, therefore, an absolute necessity that the assessor be made aware of those factors that have a bearing on value.

In subsequent chapters, example after example will show how to successfully present data on depreciation, obsolescence, and the income and market data approaches to value to the assessor. The proper presentation of this evidence and the ability to support it are key elements in a property tax control program.

DO YOU HAVE TO KNOW SOMEBODY?

Folklore has it that the magic or mystery in obtaining property tax reductions is that you have to "know somebody." It is the author's experience—and this might be thought of as naive in some circles—that you need only know the strength of your case and be able to present it properly!

Forget who the assessor is! Forget who the members of the Board are! With the exception of a couple of big city jurisdictions, and a few "hanging" boards and judges (where there is no rhyme or reason for decisions), you can win substantial reductions by presenting the best possible valuation argument. The cases set forth in this manual will show this time and again with specific case examples.

In Chapter 2 we will cover the fundamentals necessary to properly prepare and present the market value and equalization rate issues in a property tax case.

2
How to Examine the Key Issues: Market Value and Equalization

How to Develop Rules of Thumb to Establish Market Value

- Land
- Residential
- Retail Stores
- Hotels and Motels
- Office Buildings and Apartment Houses
- Industrial
- Personal Property

How to Deal with the Equalization Rate Issue

- Discrimination
- How to Prove Ratio

A Third Important Issue–Classification

- *de jure* System
- *de facto* System
- Significance of the Issue

2

There are two basic questions which must be answered before a meaningful property tax reduction and control plan can be implemented. They are:

1. What is the market value of the subject property?
2. What is the prevailing equalization rate in the subject jurisdiction?

Once the assessor has established market value, he applies the equalization rate (the percentage of market value at which he assesses property) to arrive at the assessment. The average equalization rate or ratio in the United States is about one-third. Thus:

Assessor's Market Value	Equalization Rate	Assessed Value
$300,000	33-1/3%	$100,000

The goal of this chapter will be to provide the reader with some rules of thumb to use as a guide in arriving at market value. It will also examine pertinent equalization rate issues and illustrate through court decisions how taxpayers are coping with discriminatory assessments.

HOW TO DEVELOP RULES OF THUMB TO ESTABLISH MARKET VALUE

It is not the purpose of this section to make the reader an overnight appraiser. It will merely provide a starting point for the valuation of several different properties.

Chapter 3, ''How to Use an Appraisal Report to Achieve Property Tax Savings,'' should be read in detail with regard to the basic elements that make up an appraisal. The reader will immediately realize that there can be no substitute for a detailed, professional opinion of value.

Nevertheless, we are looking for a starting point to measure market value. Let us begin the way the assessor approaches the market value issue. In general, he:

1. Measures land value by examining sales of comparable land.
2. Values buildings by arriving at cost new less depreciation.
3. Values personal property as follows: inventory—by auditing the accounting records of the taxpayer; machinery and equipment—by trending the original cost to cost new and then applying depreciation.

Land

There are *no* rules of thumb for land value. Value can range anywhere from a few hundred dollars an acre for farmland to downtown values of several hundred dollars per square foot which converts to several million dollars per acre. Industrial land can range from $1,200 per acre in Montana, to $100,000 per acre on the east and west coasts: the Meadowlands of New Jersey and the industrial parks of California.

The immediate measure available to you is comparable sales of similarly zoned land near the subject. Size similarities, amount of frontage, access to major arteries and topography are all factors which have a bearing on the land's value.

Chapter 4 on "How to Challenge a Land Assessment" will show what the courts have said concerning land value measures. It will also set forth in detail the market data and land residual approaches to land value.

For the purposes of the remainder of our rule-of-thumb valuation exercise, we will assume that the assessor's land market value as indicated on the tax bill is correct. This assumption is, of course, in lieu of a recent arm's-length purchase price or data on comparable sales of similar parcels.

Preliminary reviews of assessments where we can apply rules of thumb usually involve "desk top" investigations and do not involve "field work" or inspection of the property. Thus, we will want to use data that is immediately on hand. Therefore, in lieu of a sale or market data, we will use the assessor's land market value as a simple "in-house" reference point to begin our search for value via rules of thumb.

Of course, if the initial inquiry indicates that the assessment is excessive, the land value investigation must begin in earnest. No assumptions can be made until comparable land sales are thoroughly analyzed.

Residential

Cost: Chapter 5 shows a square-foot cost range for residential construction as follows:

Low	Average	Good	Excellent
$16.06	$20.10	$24.32	$37.45

Income: The income approach is not generally used in the valuation of residences.

Market Data: The market data section of Chapter 5 makes reference to the average price of a new home as slightly in excess of $50,000. In many areas, the average price is $75,000.

These ranges are, of course, too broad to lead to any conclusions. The best source of value rules of thumb comes from comparing the subject residence to similar homes that have sold recently. This information can be obtained from local residential real estate brokers.

The sales data on neighborhood homes should be gathered. This data should be compared to the subject and adjustments should be made for such items as size, location, age, date of sale and condition. A value conclusion should be reached for the subject home and compared to the assessor's market value. If the assessment is excessive, it should be challenged.

Retail Stores

Downtown and Department Stores; Free-Standing and Discount Houses; Shopping Centers

Retail stores in the broad categories listed above are covered in detail in Chapter 6. For the purposes of our rule-of-thumb study, we will use a new 100,000-square-foot retail store that could fall into any of the above types of retail operations.

Land Value: Assume a 4-to-1 land to building ratio. There are two and a half acres ± under roof. This works out to ten acres of land for parking. (If you are downtown, the land area would be much less.)

Assume that the assessor has $100,000 per acre as his land market value. You have not yet completed a comparable land sales study, so we will use the assessor's land value of $1,000,000 as the land value starting point.

Cost Approach: Construction cost for retail stores can range from $12.00 per square foot to $50.00 per square foot, with additional adjustments for extras. Our rule-of-thumb average cost is $30.00 per square foot. Thus: 100,000 square feet × $30.00 per square foot = $3,000,000.

The current original cost of this retail store investment is:

Land	$1,000,000
Building	$3,000,000
Total	$4,000,000

Let us further assume that the assessor's market value is also $4 million.

The taxpayer must look to the income and market data approaches to value to challenge the assessor's reliance on the cost approach.

If the cost, income and market data approaches to value are in equilibrium—each indicating the same market value—the taxpayer will be hard pressed to convincingly challenge the assessor. Let us examine those valuation factors which are necessary to equilibrium.

Income Approach: Rental ranges are as varied as construction costs. However, in order to support the investment costs, the property would have to produce a net rent as follows:

Gross Rent	= $6.66/sq. ft.	$666,000	
Expenses	= $2.66/sq. ft.	266,000	40%
Net Rent	= $4.00/sq ft.	$400,000	

Net Rental Income: $400,000 ($100,000 × $4.00/sq. ft.)
Capitalization Rate: 10%
Capitalized Value via Income approach: $4,000,000 (400,000 ÷ 10%)

If real estate taxes are 3% of the $4,000,000 market value, they are $120,000 or $1.20 per square foot. They also amount to 18% of the gross income and 45% of the total expenses.

To equal the investment, the property would have to sell at about six times gross:

Gross Rent $666,000 × (gross rent multiplier) = $3,996,000.

Market Data: To support the cost and income approaches to value, comparable sales data would have to be introduced to show that this type of retail store would sell for $40.00 per square foot land and building:

100,000 sq. ft. × $40 per square foot = $4,000,000.

Summary Comment: The retail store examples of interrelated financial and value factors show value in equilibrium for each of the three approaches. It is the job of the property tax practitioner to isolate those variables which are out of equilibrium and support an argument for assessment reduction. For example, the cost to construct might be lower; net rent might only be $3.00 per square foot; or, due to greater risk factors, the proper capitalization rate might be 12% rather than 10%. The proper identification and presentation of these issues is the basis of successful assessment appeal. Several examples are set forth in Chapter 6.

Hotels and Motels

For our rule-of-thumb study, we will use a new 500-room motor hotel with 300,000 square feet of building on ten acres of land.

Land Value: Assume that the tax bill indicates an assessor's market value for the land of $550,000 per acre or $5,500,000. Since we have not yet investigated comparable land sales in the vicinity of subject, we will use the assessor's land value as our starting point.

Cost Approach: Assume the 500-room or unit motor hotel has a building unit cost of $25,000 or a total cost of $12,500,000. This works out to $41.66 per square foot.

500 units × $25,000 = $12,500,000
$41.66 × 300,000 square feet = $12,498,000

The original cost of this investment:

Land	$ 5,500,000
Building	12,500,000
Total	$18,000,000

Note that if property taxes are 3% of this original investment cost, they would equal $540,000 per year or $1,080 per unit:

$18,000,000 × .03 = $540,000
500 units × $1,080 = $540,000

Income Approach: If the assessor uses the cost approach to value the property, the taxpayer must look to the income and market data approaches to value to counter the assessor's value position.

One rule-of-thumb income approach to valuing a hotel/motel is as follows:

1.	500 rooms × 365 days	=	182,500 rooms per year
2.	Occupancy rate		75%
3.	Rooms sold per year		136,875
4.	Average daily rate		$40
5.	Gross Room Sales		$5,475,000
6.	Ratio of Food & Beverage Sales		80%
7.	Food & Beverage Sales		$4,380,000
8.	Gross Sales		$9,855,000[1]

It is the practice in the industry to lease the real property (land and building) of a hotel/motel at a percentage of room, food and beverage sales. If this rental income is capitalized into value, it can be an excellent valuation reference. For example:

Room Sales $5,475,000 @ 25% =	$ 1,368,750
Food & Beverage $4,380,000 @ 10% =	438,000
Net Rental Income	$ 1,806,750
Capitalized @ 10%	$18,067,500
Say	$18,000,000

This result shows the factors of income necessary to support the investment of $18,000,000 cited in the cost approach. The 25% room sales factor and the 10% (6% is also

[1]The property taxes of $540,000 equal 5.5% of the gross sales.

commonly used) food and beverage factor are industry rules of thumb that can be used to isolate that portion of the income attributable to land and building.

Market Data Approach: In order for the market data approach to be in equilibrium with the cost and income approaches, the hotel/motel would have to sell for $36,000 per unit, or a gross income multiplier of about 1.8.

500 rooms × $36,000/unit	=	$18,000,000
$9,855,000 gross sales × 1.8	=	$17,739,000

Summary Comment: Chapter 7 sets forth examples of hotel/motel property tax appeals. There are several arguments that the taxpayer can present to support his valuation conclusion.

Perhaps the occupancy rate or the room rental rate is lower than indicated in our rule-of-thumb example; perhaps the risk factor warrants a higher capitalization rate. All variables must be examined carefully to present the strongest case.

Office Buildings and Apartment Houses

Office building and apartment house property tax issues are set forth in detail in Chapter 8. Let us apply our rule-of-thumb study to a 100,000 square foot office building on ten acres of land.

Office Building

Land: Assume an assessor's land value of $1,000,000. We have not yet completed an in-depth study of land value, so we will use the assessor's land market value as our starting point.

Cost Approach: Assume a new office building cost of $30.00 per square foot to build new. Thus, the total investment is as follows:

Land	$1,000,000
Building	$3,000,000
Total	$4,000,000

Income Approach: Assume the following income and expense situation:

1. Gross Rental Income (8.00 per sq. ft. × 100,000 sq. ft.)	$ 800,000
2. Expenses at 50%	400,000
3. Net Income	$ 400,000
4. Capitalization Rate: 10%	
5. Capitalized Value ($400,000 ÷ .10) =	$4,000,000

Note: If taxes are 3% of the market value of $4,000,000, they equal $120,000 or 15% of gross. The taxes are also 30% of the total expenses.

In one New England city, it is the assessor's rule of thumb to use 16% of the gross income as his real estate tax figure. Thus, the assessment is only arrived at after the tax figure is fixed at 16% of gross.

Market Data Approach: To maintain equilibrium among the cost, income and market data approaches to value, the property would have to sell at $4,000,000 or $40.00 per square foot land and building. The selling price would also work out to five times gross:

$40.00 × 100,000 sq. ft. = $4,000,000
5 × $800,000 = $4,000,000

Apartment House

Land: Assume that the assessor's market value for land is $250,000 or $2,500 per unit for a new 100-unit garden apartment.

Cost Approach: The construction cost for the 100 units is $20,000 per unit or $2,000,000. Assume this is a 100,000-square-foot building costing $20.00 per square foot. Thus, the total investment is:

Land:	$ 250,000
Building:	2,000,000
Total:	$2,250,000

Income Approach: If the operation produces $300 per unit per month, the gross annual income is $360,000:

1. $300 per unit per month × 100 units =		
$30,000 per unit × 12 months	=	$ 360,000
2. Assume expenses are 40% of gross		144,000
3. Net income		$ 216,000
4. Capitalize at 10% ($216,000 ÷ .10)	=	$2,160,000

Note: If real estate taxes are 3% of the original investment, they equal $67,500 or 19% ± of gross. They are also 47% of the total expenses.

Market Data Approach: In order for the three approaches to value to be in reasonable equilibrium, the property would have to sell at $22,500 per unit or about six times gross:

$22,500 per unit × 100 units = $2,250,000
6 × $360,000 = $2,160,000

In Pennsylvania the assessors use the following rule of thumb:

> A first-class apartment building may be said to be worth, say, 12 times its gross income. A run-down building in a deteriorating neighborhood may be said to be worth six times its gross.[2]

Summary Comment: Chapter 8 will show office building and apartment house examples of how taxpayers and assessors presented arguments to challenge or support these variable valuation measures. In one case, the assessor convinced the court to attribute a higher gross income figure to the office building property. In another case, the taxpayer showed that he was entitled to an apartment house assessment reduction because of a severe decline in his rental income. These are the kinds of arguments that must be researched and properly presented to win property tax reductions.

Industrial

Assume a new 250,000-square-foot industrial property on 20 acres of land. We will now apply our rule-of-thumb valuation measures.

---

[2]*Assessor's Handbook*, Commonwealth of Pennsylvania, Third Edition, Harrisburg, August 1976, p. 36.

Land: Assume the 20 acres are assessed at a market value of 10,000 per acre or \$200,000. The land to building ratio is 3 to 1, which is acceptable for an industrial property. There are about 6 acres under roof (250,000 square feet ÷43,560 square feet per acre = 5.7 acres).

Cost Approach: Assume the building cost \$20.00 per square foot or \$5,000,000. Thus, the total investment is:

Land:	\$ 200,000
Building:	5,000,000
Total:	\$5,200,000

Note: If property taxes are 3% of this investment, they equal \$156,000 or 62¢ per square foot.

Income Approach: In order for the property to warrant this investment, it would have to throw off a net income of \$2.00 per square foot.

1. Net income \$2.00 × 250,000 sq. ft. = \$ 500,000
2. Capitalized at 10% (\$500,000 ÷ .10) = \$5,000,000

Market Data Approach: To keep the three approaches to value in equilibrium, the property would have to sell for \$20.80 per square foot land and building.

250,000 square feet × \$20.80 per sq. ft. = \$5,200,000

Summary Comment: Chapter 9 on industrial plant assessment appeals will show how to isolate and present arguments to support your valuation position. It will highlight methods of measuring physical depreciation and functional and economic obsolescence. It will show the relevancy of the income and market data approaches to the market value of industrial plants.

Personal Property

Our rules of thumb valuation comments will be limited to inventory, machinery and equipment (M&E) and furniture and fixtures (F&F).

Audit Appraisal: The assessor will generally be working with the figures reported to him on the taxpayer's annual rendition of personal property. He will seldom conduct a physical appraisal.

Inventory: The assessor must be sure that taxpayer's books reflect the following:

(1) Inventory is physically complete
(2) Proper trade level (valued according to stage of production)
(3) Present day pricing.

Taxpayer must be sure that:

(1) Obsolescence, damaged and distressed merchandise are reflected
(2) Goods in transit are not included
(3) Adjustments between lien date and inventory date are reflected
(4) Exclusions are properly reflected for general administrative costs, central office overhead, selling and research and development charges.

Machinery and Equipment (M&E) and Furniture and Fixtures (F&F): The assessor generally values M&E and F&F by trending the original cost of the assets (provided by the taxpayer on his annual rendition) to current value. He applies a trending factor obtained from cost manuals and other sources to the original cost by year of acquisition.

He then applies a depreciation factor to the trended original cost to arrive at his depreciated cost or "market value."

Original Cost of a 5-Year-Old Item of M&E or F&F	Trending Factor	=	Trended Original Cost	Depreciation Factor	Market Value
$10,000	1.50		$15,000	50%	$7,500

Summary Comment: Chapter 10 will show actual case examples where this method was challenged by the taxpayer. This resulted in the application of functional and economic obsolescence, thereby reducing the assessments.

HOW TO DEAL WITH THE EQUALIZATION RATE ISSUE

An equalization rate or ratio is the percentage of market value at which the property is assessed. Several states assess at 100% of market value.

In ratio states, assessors are required to value all property at fair market value and then set the property in the assessment roll at a *uniform* percentage of value. Failure to do this results in discrimination against the individual or group of taxpayers.

Discrimination

The taxpayer's right to be free from discriminatory assessments is mandated by the equal protection clause of the 14th Amendment of the United States Constitution. No less an august body than the U. S. Supreme Court so held in the 1923 *Sioux City Bridge* case.[3]

This case had everything: an assessment increase after appeal; a jurisdictional problem (74% of the bridge was in Nebraska and 26% was in Iowa); a claim of functional obsolescence (the bridge was too light for modern traffic); a ratio study; and a reversal of Nebraska's highest court!

The *Sioux City Bridge* case involved a railroad bridge across the Missouri River to Iowa. 74% was in Dakota County, Nebraska, and 26% was in Iowa. The assessor levied a $600,000-assessment and on appeal to the Board of Equalization, the assessment was *increased* to $700,000.

A tax commissioner of a railroad that leased the bridge "testified that from an examination of the sales of real estate as shown by deeds of record in Nebraska and in Dakota County and the tax list, the acre property in Dakota County was assessed at 55.70 per cent of its value, that improvements in city property were assessed at 49.29 per cent of their selling value, and had been so assessed for seven years."[4]

The Nebraska Supreme Court held that ". . . when property is assessed at its true value, and other property in the district is assessed below its true value, the proper remedy is to have the property assessed below its true value raised, rather than to have property assessed at its true value reduced."[5]

---

[3]*Sioux City Bridge Co. v. Dakota County,* 260 U.S. 441, 43 S. Ct. 190, 67 L. Ed. 340 (1923).
[4]Ibid @ 443.
[5]Ibid @ 444.

The U. S. Supreme Court held that this would "deny the injured taxpayer any remedy at all because it is utterly impossible for him by any judicial proceeding to secure an increase in the assessment of the great mass of underassessed property in the taxing district. This Court holds that the right of the taxpayer whose property alone is taxed at 100 per cent of its true value is to have his assessment reduced to the percentage of that value at which others are taxed even though this is a departure from the requirement of statute."[6]

The conclusion is based on the principle that where it is impossible to secure both the standard of the true value, and the uniformity and equality required by law, the latter requirement is to be preferred as the just and ultimate purpose of the law.

The Nebraska Supreme Court decision was reversed and the case was remanded for further hearing on the issue of uniformity. The Court called for something more than mere errors of judgment to support a claim of discrimination. It called for the taxpayer to show something more—". . . an intentional violation of the essential principle of practical uniformity."[7]

This theme was further developed in *Hillsborough v. Cromwell* in 1946, where the United States Supreme Court again said:

> The equal protection clause of the Fourteenth Amendment protects the individual from state action which selects him out for discriminatory treatment by subjecting him to taxes not imposed on others of the same class. The right is the right to equal treatment.[8]

Taxpayers began fighting the ratio issue in earnest back in 1957 when the highest court in New Jersey held the entire tax roll of Middletown was invalid due to discrimination.[9] The court cited the statutory 100% level of assessment requirement and gave Middletown two years (until 1959) to correct the tax roll and to levy market value assessments. Subsequent statutory changes introduced "taxable value" codifying local option fractional assessment.[10]

Later, in 1961, another New Jersey taxpayer tried to show the prevailing level of assessment but found there was no uniform equalization rate in effect. Residential property was assessed at from 4.13% to 86% of market value; vacant land, from 2.25% to 88%; and other property from 5.13% to 79.88%.

When the taxpayer complained, the municipality argued that the situation was too chaotic to permit any relief. The highest court in New Jersey said, "It would be a sad reflection on the judiciary and indeed upon all government if the rights of the taxpayer were to be diminished in proportion to the violence of the assault upon them." The court accepted evidence adequate to prove a fair approximation of the ratio and reduced the assessment to that level.[11]

In 1961 there was also significant ratio action in Massachusetts. In the Bettigole[12] case the assessor admitted to assessing different classes of real property at different percentages of market value: residential—50%; industrial and commercial—85%. The court held that equitable relief would be granted if such a scheme is proven. In 1965 in the *Shoppers' World* case, the assessor did *not* admit to any ratio. Taxpayer sought to prove a "scheme" by showing the assessor intentionally levied assessments in a disproportionate manner. The assessor objected on the grounds that the taxpayer could only argue the overvaluation issue.

The highest court in Massachusetts reversed a position maintained for 71 years and

---

[6]Ibid @ 446.
[7]Ibid @ 447.
[8]*Township of Hillsborough v. Cromwell,* 326 U.S. 620, 623, 66 S. Ct. 53, 90 L. Ed. 358 (1946).
[9]*Switz v. Township of Middletown,* 23 N.J. 580, 130 A.2d 15 (1957).
[10]N.J.S.A 54: A.2.25 (Supp. 1975).
[11]*In the Matter of Kents,* 34 N.J. 21, 166A.2d 763 (1971).
[12]*Bettigole v. Assessors of Springfield,* 343 Mass. 223, 178 N.E. 2d 10 (1961).

permitted proof of any such "scheme" to be presented to the Massachusetts Appellate Tax Board.[13]

There has been a long line of decisions on the equalization issue handed down by the highest courts in several states. All the courts concur in not permitting discriminatory assessment practices.[14]

How to Prove Ratio

The taxpayer has several sources available to him to help in proving the prevailing equalization rate in his jurisdiction.

1. Statutory rates published throughout the jurisdiction or state, such as 25% in California or 33⅓% in Indiana. This is an immediate reference point and the assessment can be easily converted to a market value figure.

2. Figures published by State Equalization Boards.

The National Commission on Urban Problems urges that these studies be published on a regular basis and that the Federal Government give financial assistance in their completion. Such studies are carried on in over half the states. They use three basic approaches in comparing assessed valuation with (A) sales data; (B) appraisal data; or (C) both sales and appraisal data.[15]

The National Commission on Urban Problems also recommended that the taxpayer be permitted to introduce these studies as evidence as proof of the level of assessment on appeal.[16]

The *Guth* case in New York[17] found that the state equalization rate was objectively and expertly arrived at. The taxpayer could rely solely on the rate as evidence of the general level of assessment in the subject jurisdiction.

The 1976 *Executive Towers*[18] case expanded *Guth* with reference to whether the state equalization rate applied to other jurisdictions and other years. *Executive Towers* held that *Guth* (A) applied statewide; (B) the state rate and its applicability could be proven by the testimony of expert witnesses without petitioner offering testimony of officials of the State

---

[13]*Shoppers' World, Inc. v. Board of Assessors of Framingham,* 348 Mass. 366, 203 N.E. 2d 811 (1965).

[14]*Lerner Shops of Connecticut, Inc. v. Town of Waterbury,* 151 Conn. 79, 193 A. 2d 472 (1964).

In re Petition of Hamm v. State, 255 Minn. 64, 95 N.W. 2d 649 (1959).

Dulton Reality, Inc. v. Minn., 270 Minn. 1, 132 N.W. 2d 394 (1964).

Deitch Co. v. Bd. of Property Assess., 417 Pa. 213, 209 A. 2d 397 (1965). *McKnight S. Cen. v. Bd. of Property Assess.,* 417 Pa. 234, 209 A. 2d 389 (1965). *Pgh. Mir. Mile S. Cen. v. Bd. of Property Assess.,* 417 Pa. 243, 209 A. 2d 394 (1965). *Rieck Ice Cream Co. Appeal,* 417 Pa. 249, 209 A. 2d 383 (1965).

Louisville and Nashville Railway Company v. State Board of Equalization, 249 F. Supp. 894 (1966).

McNayr v. State, Fla. 166 So. 2d 142 (1964); *Walter v. Schuler,* Fla. 176 So. 2d 81 (1965), and *Dade County v. DuPont Plaza,* Fla. 117 So. 2d 849.

Russman v. Luckett, Ky. 391 S.W. 2d 694 (1965).

State v. Board of Tax Appeals, 175 Ohio 450, 195 N.E. 2d 908 (1964).

Michaels v. Watson, 40 Cal. Rep. 464 (1964).

Hellerstein v. Assessor of Islip, 37 N.Y. 2d 1 (1975).

Town of Sudbury v. Comm. of Corporations and Taxation, 366 Mass. 558, 321 N.E. 2d 641 (1974).

Jordan Marsh Company v. Board of Assessors of Quincy, 331 N.E. 2d 61 (1975).

E. Ingraham Co. v. Town & City of Bristol, 144 Conn. 374 (1957).

Southern Railway v. Clement, 57 Tenn. App. 54 (1967).

For further discussion see also Jerrold F. Janata, "Property Taxes in the U.S and the Equalization Problem," *Assessors Journal,* Vol. 5, No. 4, January 1971, pp. 13–32.

[15]*Assessors News Letter* (February and March 1969), Vol. 35, Nos. 2 and 3, pp. 23-26 and 47-52, respectively. Recommendation 6 (d) and e.

[16]Id.

[17]*Ed Guth Reality, Inc. v. Gingold,* 34 N.Y. 2d 440, 358 N.Y.S. 2d 367, 315 N.E. 2d 441 (1974).

[18]*860 Executive Towers, Inc. v. Board of Assessors,* 385 N.Y.S. 2d 604, 53 App. Div. 2d 463 (2nd Dept. 1976).

Board of Equalization, as had been done in *Guth*; (C) once the rate was established, the taxing jurisdiction was estopped from contesting these issues brought by other taxpayers.

3. Admissions by the assessor specifying his method of approach in applying equalization rates.

4. Stipulation. Another method of establishing an equalization rate is through stipulation with the assessor. It may be in your best interest to establish a stipulated ratio rather than going through the expense of a ratio study. True, you may have to agree to a higher figure, but you must weigh this loss in tax savings against the cost of the ratio study.

For example:

The assessor is willing to stipulate to an equalization rate of 50%.

You believe you can prove 33⅓%.

Assume the trial results in a market value figure of $1,000,000, and there is a tax rate of $100/1,000.

		Rate	Taxes
Market Value	$1,000,000		
50% Assessment	500,000	100	$50,000
33⅓% Assessment	333,333	100	$33,333

The difference in taxes is $16,667, and this must be weighed against the cost of a ratio study. It would probably not be practical in this example. If, however, there were multiple years under appeal, or many different taxpayers involved, it would then be practical and even necessary.

The stipulation referred to above contemplates that both sides agree to a figure that is then established as the ratio.

In one case, the assessor showed up at the trial with no evidence of ratio at all. Taxpayer did not want to endure another long delay. He stipulated to the fact that *if* the assessor had presented an expert with a ratio study, it would have come in at 15%. The trial court accepted the 15% figure! On appeal, it was held that the trial court was within its discretion in accepting the "phantom expert's" 15% figure.[19]

Thus, we see that the taxpayer in this instance stipulated himself out of the ratio trial.

5. Ratio Study. This is where the taxpayer hires an expert to prepare a comparison, on a sampling basis, of the sales prices of sold parcels with their assessed valuations, and application of statistical procedures to determine assessment levels and measure nonuniformity of assessment.

Several ratio studies have been used successfully in court and settlement efforts. A ratio study in Boston showed that residential property was assessed at from 25 to 30% below city-wide averages.[20]

Summary Comment: In summary, we see that the courts will not permit discriminatory assessment practices. Assessments may be levied at 100% of market value or a fraction thereof as long as *all* property is treated in a *uniform* fashion.

In establishing the equalization rate on appeal the taxpayer may: use statutes, figures published by state equalization boards, admissions by the assessor, stipulation, or have a ratio study conducted to compare sales prices of sold properties to their assessments.

---

[19] *Westinghouse Electric v. Delaware County*, 30 Pa. 264, 373 A. 2d 766 (1977).

[20] Oliver Oldman and Henry Aaron, "Assessment Sales Ratio Under the Boston Property Tax," *The National Tax Journal* (March 1965), Vol. XVIII, No. 1, p 41.

These procedures will enable the taxpayer to present a supportable equalization rate or ratio to the court. The hope is that it reflects the average rates prevailing in the jurisdiction and it will be applied to the market value of the subject property to arrive at an equitable assessment.

A THIRD IMPORTANT ISSUE: CLASSIFICATION

In the previous section we learned that ". . . the equal protection clause of the 14th Amendment protects the individual from state action which selects him out for discriminatory treatment subjecting him to taxes not imposed on others of the same class."

However, the United States Supreme Court has also said: ". . . states may classify property for taxation; may set up different modes of assessment, valuation and collection; may tax some kinds of property at higher rates than others; . . . may treat railroads and other utilities with that separateness which their distinctive characteristics and functions in society make appropriate—these are among the commonplaces of taxation and of constitutional law."[21]

These two statements appear to be in conflict with each other. On the one hand, the Court calls for uniform treatment. On the other hand, the principle of jurisdictional uniformity is dramatically modified by allowing different classes of property to be taxed differently by different levels of assessment or different rates of taxation.

The classification (dividing a given category into a number of smaller groups or classes having certain common characteristics) can be based solely on the use of the property. Thus, commercial and industrial property in Tennessee is assessed at 40% of market value, while residential property is assessed at only 25% of market value.[22]

What then are the rights of the property taxpayer? Are there avenues of challenge open to him or must he silently accept "classification" despite the possibility of special interest group influence on legislation? There are several cases with which the tax practitioner should be familiar.[23]

De jure System

A *de jure* system of classification exists pursuant to statute and through administrative implementation of the statutory standard. The *Browning* case said that if the classification is reasonable (not obviously discriminatory), challenge to its constitutionality would be frivolous.

However, the taxpayer can challenge the "reasonableness" of such statutes as violating uniformity and due process clauses of the State and Federal Constitution, and perhaps as an undue burden on interstate commerce. These were the issues raised in an Arizona case where properties are classified at a percentage of market value as follows:

Class One	—railroad property	—60%
Class Two	—telephone and utility	—40%
Class Three	—commercial and industrial	—25%
Class Four	—agricultural and all other (including residential)	—18%

[21]*Nashville, Chattanooga & St. Louis Railway v. Browning,* 310 U.S. 362, 368, 60 S. Ct. 968, 972, 84 L. Ed. 1254, 1258 (1940).

[22]T.C.A., §67-601 (Supp. 1974).

[23]For an excellent in-depth study of this subject see Beebe and Sinnott, "In the Wake of Hellerstein: Whither New York?" *State of New York, Division of Equalization and Assessment, Office of Special Studies, Empire State Plaza, Albany, New York 12223 (June 1, 1977).*

The State Court upheld the classification and the U. S. Supreme Court refused to review the matter.[24]

The Arizona Court cited another U. S. Supreme Court case which says:

> The power of the State to classify according to occupation for the purpose of taxation is broad. Equal protection does not require identity of treatment. It only requires that classification rest on real and not feigned differences, that the distinction have some relevance to the purpose for which the classification is made, and that the different treatments be not so disparate, relative to the difference in classification, as to be wholly arbitrary.[25]

Thus we see the broad power of the state to pursue a reasonable *de jure* classification system. Perhaps *Browning* is right when it says that a challenge against such a system is frivolous.

De facto System

A *de facto* system of classification is one which exists in fact but which is not sanctioned by statute. *De facto* systems of classification which discriminate against commercial and industrial taxpayers in favor of residential taxpayers exist in every state and *are* subject to challenge. The system creates arbitrary and systematic discrimination in the assessment process and cannot withstand scrutiny under the Fourteenth Amendment of the U. S. Constitution and many state constitutions.[26] See the Classification section in Chapter 4 on land for additional cases.

Significance of the Issue

With the success of the Jarvis-Gann Proposition 13, Californians voted themselves a $6 to $7 billion dollar, 57% cut in property taxes. All property taxpayers in California appear to benefit. Homeowners save $2.3 billion; rented residential property, $1.2 billion; and commercial and industrial, $2.9 billion.[27]

It does not seem practical that California lawmakers will permit commercial and industrial taxpayers to enjoy this unsolicited benefit for too long. Voters reacted to inflationary residential assessment increases and high tax rates. The movement was strictly a residential one.

Thus, a very inviting option is open to California legislators. They can simply change their *de facto* system to a *de jure* system and classify real property into different groups and assess commercial and industrial property at a higher rate than residential.

The California "tax revolt" movement appears to be gaining momentum on a nationwide scale. Classification will become an inviting alternative in other states and the tax practitioner must be prepared to cope with this issue. Jurisdictions that convert *de facto* systems to *de jure* systems reduce their vulnerability to challenge and can continue to tax commercial and industrial properties at a 3% of market value rate.

---

[24]*Apache County v. Atchison, Topeka & Santa Fe Ry. Co.* 106 Ariz. 356, 476 P. 2d 657 (1970), app. dsmd. 401 U.S. 1005, 91 S. Ct. 1257, 28 L. Ed. 2d 542 (1971).

[25]*Walters v. City of St. Louis,* 347 U.S. 231, 237, 74 S. Ct. 505, 509, 98 L. Ed. 660 (1954).

[26]*Louisville and Nashville Railroad Company v. Public Service Commission of Tennessee,* 249 F. Supp. 894 (M.D. Tenn. 1966) aff'd., 389 F. 2d 247 (6th Cir. 1968)

[27]*Time Magazine,* "Sound and Fury Over Taxes," June 19, 1978 at Page 15.

3
How to Use an Appraisal Report To Achieve Property Tax Savings

3

An ad valorem tax appraisal is different from a standard market value appraisal. The basic components are the same, but there are many unique characteristics peculiar to a property tax appeal appraisal. It is the proper presentation of these unique factors that wins in negotiations with an assessor or in appearances before Boards of Review or Courts. Indeed, the appraisal is the most important instrument in the orchestration of a property tax appeal.

The thrust of the ad valorem tax appraisal must be toward testimony presentation by an expert witness. In addition to standard valuation techniques, the appraiser must be cognizant of statutes, court decisions, assessors' guidelines and local assessment practice. With these constraints in mind, the appraisal report must flow logically toward a reasonable and convincing value conclusion. And above all, it must stand up to in-depth and sometimes devastating cross-examination.

It is the job of the property tax practitioner to see to it that his appraiser's opinion of market value is the strongest and best presented in order to win property tax reductions.

You must know exactly what you want in order to instruct the appraiser concerning what specific items must be emphasized in the appraisal report. If there is severe functional obsolescence in a property, the appraiser should be made aware of that fact and the obsolescence should be presented with all supportive documentation available.

This is no way means that you should attempt to influence the appraiser regarding his method of approach or value conclusion. It is simply good practice to establish areas of understanding at the outset to assure a compatibility of attitude and mutuality of direction in the appraisal assignment. It should be noted that it would be unethical for an appraiser to suppress facts, data or opinions adverse to the case his client is trying to establish or to become an advocate of his client's cause.[1]

But it is good appraisal practice to uncover all pertinent characteristics of a property which contribute or detract from value.[2]

Thus, your appraiser must objectively report the results of his findings. You can help by making sure the appropriate data is made available to him.

WHAT ARE THE BASIC ELEMENTS OF AN APPRAISAL?

For our purposes, an appraisal is a written opinion of value. The value conclusion is usually developed by reference to the cost, income and market data approaches to value.

The Cost Approach

The cost approach consists of four basic steps.

[1]The Principles of Appraisal Practice and Code of Ethics of the American Society of Appraisers, Sections 4.3 and 7.4.
[2]Ibid., Section 6.9.

1. First there is an estimate of the land's value as if vacant. This is usually done by reviewing comparable land sales or through a land residual valuation exercise.[3]

2. The second step in the cost approach consists of arriving at a reproduction cost of the existing structure that is the subject of the appraisal. The appraiser refers to a "cost manual" to develop his reproduction cost figures.

A simplified example follows:

> The subject of the appraisal is a restaurant. The appraiser refers to the nationally known Marshall Valuation Service[4] and chooses to use the calculator method of costing the improvements. He turns to the restaurant section which is reproduced here.
>
> He selects a class and type that fits the description of subject. A class "B" "average" type construction indicates a cost per square foot of $37.44. Adjustments, as warranted, are made per the instructions below the class listings. Adjustments may also be made for time and location. Yard improvements (paving, lighting, etc.) must also be included here.

3. Depreciation from all sources must now be considered. This includes physical, functional and economic depreciation or obsolescence.

Physical depreciation is loss in value due to deterioration resulting from age and the elements. Note that the page from the *Marshall Valuation Service* (Figure 3-1) indicates a typical life expectancy of 40 years. Thus, if the restaurant is ten years old, it is 25% physically depreciated.

Functional obsolescence is loss in value due to lack of utility or desirability inherent in the property. If the subject restaurant did not have an adequate parking facility, it would suffer from functional obsolescence.

Economic obsolescence is loss in value from causes not inherent in, but from without, the property. I represented Howard Johnson's at one restaurant where a new freeway ramp all but eliminated vehicle traffic in front of the property. The Board of Review accepted this argument as a form of economic obsolescence.

4. The appropriate consideration of all these factors combines to permit the appraiser to arrive at a depreciated cost for the structure. To this figure, the appraiser adds the land value.

A typical cost approach exercise, in simplified form, looks like Figure 3-2.

The Income Approach

In the income approach to value, the appraiser's task is to develop a value which the property's net earning power will support.[5] The net income stream is converted into a value through the use of a capitalization rate.

The development of an appropriate capitalization rate comes from several sources. It can be developed directly from the marketplace if you find comparable sales with net rentals. An example of this would be the following:

Assume an apartment house has a net income of $37,100 and it sells on the open market for $371,000. The capitalization rate developed from the market is 10%. ($37,100 ÷ $371,000 = 10%.)

---

[3]See Valuation Techniques section in Chapter 4 on Land.

[4]Marshall and Swift Publication Company, 1617 Beverly Blvd., Los Angeles, CA 90026.

[5]See the apartment house example of the development of net income in Chapter 8.

RESTAURANTS

CLASS	TYPE	EXTERIOR WALLS	INTERIOR	LIGHTING, PLUMBING AND MECHANICAL	HEAT	COST Cu. Ft.	COST Sq. Ft.
A	Good	Metal or stone panels, good brick, usually part of a building	Plaster, with enamel or vinyl, carpet and vinyl flooring, decorated interior	Good lighting and outlets, good plumbing	Complete H.V.A.C.	$4.28	$51.33
	Average	Brick or concrete, usually part of a building	Plaster or drywall, acoustic tile, rubber or vinyl asbestos tile	Adequate lighting and outlets, adequate plumbing	Complete H.V.A.C.	3.28	39.40
B	Good	Concrete or stone panels, good brick, usually part of a building	Plaster, with enamel or vinyl, carpet and vinyl flooring, decorated interior	Good lighting and outlets, good plumbing	Complete H.V.A.C.	4.11	49.29
	Average	Brick or concrete, usually part of a building	Plaster or drywall, acoustic tile, rubber or vinyl asbestos tile	Adequate lighting and outlets, adequate plumbing	Complete H.V.A.C.	3.12	37.44
C	Excellent	†Individual design, highly ornamental exterior	High quality detail, best acoustics, carpeted, deluxe quality	Special lighting effects, tiled restrooms, good fixtures	Complete H.V.A.C.	5.36	64.37
	Very Good	†Individual design, brick and good metal, ornamentation	Typically, best chain restaurants, carpeted lounge and dining room	Good lighting and restrooms with standard fixtures	Complete H.V.A.C.	4.17	50.00
	Good	†Brick, concrete or metal panels, ornamentation	Typical chain restaurant or coffee shop, vinyl floors	Good lighting and service outlets, plain restrooms	Complete H.V.A.C.	3.24	38.84
	Average	†Brick, block, tilt-up, plain building, stock plans	Typical neighborhood restaurant, vinyl asbestos, small kitchen	Adequate lighting and outlets, small restrooms	Complete H.V.A.C.	2.53	30.40
	Low Cost	†Cheap brick or block, very plain, low cost front	Low cost short order cafe, minimum finish, asphalt tile	Minimum lighting and outlets, minimum plumbing	Forced air	1.85	22.19
D	Excellent	†Individual design, highly ornamental exterior	High quality detail, best acoustics, carpeted, deluxe quality	Special lighting effects, tiled restrooms, good fixtures	Complete H.V.A.C.	4.82	57.79
	Very Good	†Individual design, brick and good metal, ornamentation	Typically, best chain restaurants, carpeted lounge and dining room	Good fixtures, good restrooms with standard fixtures	Complete H.V.A.C.	3.74	44.85
	Good	†Stucco or siding, metal and glass, some ornamentation	Typical chain restaurant or coffee shop, vinyl floors	Good lighting and service outlets, small restrooms	Complete H.V.A.C.	2.90	34.81
	Average	†Stucco or siding, plain front and building, stock plans	Typical neighborhood restaurant, vinyl asbestos, small kitchen	Adequate lighting and outlets, small restrooms	Complete H.V.A.C.	2.27	27.25
	Low Cost	†Cheap stucco or siding, very plain construction	Low cost short order cafe, minimum finish, asphalt tile	Minimum lighting and outlets, minimum plumbing	Forced air	1.64	19.72

HEATING, COOLING, AND AIR CONDITIONING

Costs for restaurant mechanical items are listed separately from those for other buildings in this section because of the special requirements. Costs listed below are averages. Moderate climate costs are included in the base costs above.

COMPLETE H.V.A.C		WARM CLIMATE Down to 30° F	MODERATE CLIMATE Down to 0° F	COLD CLIMATE Down to −30° F
Class A & B	Good	$5.25	$6.40	$7.75
	Average	4.15	5.05	6.20
Class C & D	Excellent	$6.65	$8.05	$9.70
	Very good	5.30	6.40	7.70
	Good	4.20	5.10	6.15
	Average	3.45	4.20	5.05
	Low cost	1.40	1.85	2.40

(Low cost prices are for forced air heat and ventilation only)

DRIVE-IN RESTAURANTS

†Add 10% to the base restaurant costs for drive-in restaurants, without seating.

ELEVATORS

For buildings on this page, add elevator costs from Section 58.

MULTISTORY BUILDINGS

Add .6% for each story over three, above ground, to all base costs, excluding mezzanines.

SPRINKLERS

Add for sprinkler systems from Section 43.

TYPICAL LIFE EXPECTANCIES

These life expectancy studies do not include cases of mortality from economic obsolescence or poor business management.

QUALITY	CLASS A	B	C	D
Excellent and Very good	45	45	40	35
Good and Average	40	40	35	30
Low cost	----	----	30	25

FIGURE 3-1

Cost Approach

Subject:	Restaurant		
Class:	B		
Quality:	Average		
Stories:	One		
Height:	11 Feet		
Floor Area:	5,000 square feet		
Base Square Foot Cost			$37.44
Square Foot Adjustments		Assume	-0-
Height and Size Adjustments		Assume	-0-
Final Adjustments			
Current Cost Multipler		—1.02	
Local Multiplier		—1.03	
Final Square Foot Cost			$ 39.33
Replacement Cost ($39.33 × 5,000 sq. ft.)			$196,650
Depreciation:	Physical	25%	
	Functional	10%*	
	Economic	10%*	
Depreciation Amount			88,493
Depreciated Cost			$108,157
Add Land Value			30,000
Total Value—Cost Approach			$138,157

*These percentages depend on the severity of the problems mentioned in the preceding paragraphs.

FIGURE 3-2

Another method of developing a capitalization rate is the band of investment technique. This method requires an investigation of the mortgage market. Assume: a bank will lend 70% of the property's value at 9½%; you want a 12% return on your 30% equity position:

Mortgage	70% × 9.50 = 6.65	
Equity	30% × 12.00 = 3.60	
	10.25	Say: 10%

There are a number of other techniques in use for the development of capitalization rates. Just be very sure that your appraiser has strong supportive material for his conclusion.

The Market Data Approach

In the market data approach, the appraiser looks to sales of comparable properties and the price that a willing seller will sell to a willing buyer. Factors that must be examined include sale price, factors influencing the sale, location and degree of comparability. This investigation must encompass size, shape, layout, land area, zoning, age and condition.

An ideal comparable is presented later in this chapter.

EFFECTIVE PRESENTATION OF UNIQUE ASPECTS OF AN AD VALOREM APPRAISAL IS THE KEY TO SUCCESS

The following comments will follow the ad valorem format outlined in Figure 3-3 and highlight the points that must be emphasized to win property tax appeals.

Comparison Between Standard And Ad Valorem Appraisal Format[6]

Standard Format

Part I Introduction
1. Title page
2. Table of Contents
3. Letter of Transmittal
4. Photographs
5. Statement of Limiting Conditions and assumptions
6. References

Part II Factual Data
7. Purpose of the Appraisal
8. Legal description
9. Area, city and neighborhood data
10. Property data
    a. Site
    b. Improvements
    c. Equipment
    d. History
    e. Assessed value and annual tax load
    f. Zoning

Part III Analyses and Conclusions
11. Analysis of highest and best use
12. Land value
13. Value estimate by cost approach
14. Value estimate by income approach
15. Value estimate by comparative (market) approach
16. Interpretation and correlation of estimates
17. Certification

Part IV Exhibits and Addenda
18. Location map
19. Comparative map data
20. Details of the comparative data
21. Plot plan
22. Floor plans
23. Other pertinent exhibits
24. Qualifications

Ad Valorem Format

Part I Introduction
1. Letter of Transmittal
2. Summary of Important Data and Conclusions
3. Table of Contents
4. Photo (aerial or exterior, interior)
5. Location map
6. Plot plan
7. Floor plan
8. Process flow (M&E) diagram
9. Statement of Limiting Conditions and assumptions

Part II Factual Data
10. Purpose of the Appraisal
11. Legal description
12. Area, city and neighborhood data
13. Property data
    a. Site
    b. Improvements
    c. Equipment
    d. History
    e. Assessed value and annual tax load
    f. Zoning

Part III Analyses and Conclusions
14. Analysis of highest and best use
15. Land value
    a. Description of comparables
    b. Photo/Plot plan
    c. Comparative map data
16. Value estimate by cost approach
    a. Source of cost data
    b. Supportive data for depreciation and obsolescence allocation
    c. Photos to make specific points
17. Value estimate by income approach
    a. Description of comparables
    b. Photos/Floor plans
    c. Comparative map data
    d. Supportive data for capitalization rate
18. Value estimate by comparative (market) approach
    a. Description of comparables
    b. Photos/Floor plans
    c. Comparative map data
    d. Specific references of comparability—including photos
19. Interpretation and correlation of estimates
20. Market value allocation to assessment parcels
21. Certification

Part IV Addenda
22. Qualifications
    a. Emphasize appraiser's specific appraisal expertise with property similar to subject

FIGURE 3-3

[6]General Services Administration Form 1241A

In General

The ad valorem format is designed for testimony presentation. You will have only a limited time to get your story across to a Board of Review (where the vast majority of these cases are resolved) and you must be able to make your points quickly and decisively.

Note that all supportive data (photos, plot plans, maps) are presented in the appraisal report itself rather than in the addenda. This avoids the necessity of continually referring to the back of the appraisal. The proper and most effective method is to have the supportive data in its logical sequence of presentation. This permits the appraiser/witness to present his narrative evenly, smoothly, page after page, and without delays caused by the inability of a Board member to find a particular reference.

In that regard, it is absolutely necessary that each member of a hearing body have a copy of the appraisal and that all pages be numbered for easy reference.

Part I. Introduction

1. Letter of Transmittal

Date

Mr. xxxxxxxxxxxxxxxx
xxxxxxxxxxxxxxxxxxxx
xxxxxxxxxxxxxxxxxxxxx

Subject: (Identification)

Dear Mr. xxxxxxxxxxx

Attached is an appraisal of the subject property. The report, including exhibits, fully describes our method of approach and contains all pertinent data gathered in our investigation.

After careful consideration, we have concluded that the market value of the subject property as of ____________________ is:
(DATE)

FIVE HUNDRED THOUSAND DOLLARS
($500,000)

Reviewed and Approved by: Respectfully submitted,

____________________ ____________________
XXXXXXXXXX XXXXXXXXXXXXX

The letter of transmittal is a working tool of introduction. It should clearly identify the subject property being appraised. It should state the appraiser's opinion of market value as of a particular date.

The "as of" date is important and should coincide with the jurisdiction's assessment date. This can get complicated if more than one year is involved in the appeal. If multiple years are involved, you must decide if you want separate appraisals for each year. This may be necessary if a specific change occurred that would have significant impact on value. Examples of such changes are substantial additional construction, fire damage, and eminent domain taking.

On the other hand, if no significant changes in the property or market conditions have occurred, an appraiser may arrive at the same value conclusion for a two- or three-year period. The cost approach should be reviewed to allow for cost index increases and depreciation. This may result in minor adjustments in the cost approach value conclusion. If market conditions are stable, the income and market data approaches should not be substantially affected.

Sometimes you get to a hearing or trial and you find that you have two or more years under appeal and both sides' appraisals refer to only one year. An easy way out is to stipulate that the appraiser's value conclusions apply to all years under appeal.

Note that the signature portion of the letter allows for two appraisers to sign. The appraisal is often completed many months, and even years, before testimony is required. By having two appraisers sign the appraisal, you can avoid the problems that sometimes occur if death, illness or employment changes occur prior to the hearing of your case. This assumes, of course, that both appraisers actually worked on this assignment and can testify accordingly.

Finally, be sure that the appraiser you choose is an experienced witness with past exposure to the type of cross-examination he is likely to encounter at your hearing or trial.

2. *Summary of Important Data and Conclusions*

Headings	*Conclusion*	*Page Reference*
Purpose of the Appraisal	Market Value	
Date of Value Estimate		
Property Rights Appraised	Unencumbered fee simple interest	
City		
Neighborhood		
Land Size		
Taxes: City, County, School	$	
Highest and Best Use		
Size	square feet	
Age of Improvements		
Indicated Land Value	$	
Estimates of Value		
Cost Approach	$	
Income Approach	$	
Market Data Approach	$	
Indicated Market Value	$	
Assessments	City: $	
	County: $	
	School: $	
Market Value Comparison		
Assessor: Land	$	
Land Value per this Appraisal	$	
Difference	$	
Assessor: Improvements	$	
Improvements Value per this Appraisal	$	
Difference	$	
Assessor: Land and Improvements	$	
Land and Improvements per this Appraisal	$	
Difference	$	

The purpose of this page is to set forth in synopsis fashion such items as land area, square footage of building, market value conclusions, and comparison to the assessment.

It presents the basic elements that make up the subject property and permits the Board, at a glance, to come to grips with the difference in value between the parties.

3. Table of Contents

Do not overlook the importance of the table of contents. It is essentially the same as the ad valorem format presented here. It should establish the logical outline of the appraisal presentation.

The important overview here is that one section of the report should not contradict another, and that references and figures should be consistent throughout.

4–8. Photo (Aerial, Exterior, Interior), Location Map, Plot and Floor Plan, Process Flow (M&E) Diagram

The remaining items listed in the introduction part of the appraisal should now be presented. Their purpose is to fully acquaint the Board with the subject property. (See Figures 3-4, 3-5, 3-6 and 3-7).

The front view of subject (Figure 3-4) should be one of several exterior photographs aimed at fully acquainting a Board or Court with the subject property. The location map (Figure 3-5) should clearly illustrate ''where'' the subject is located in relation to major geographical reference points.

The plot plan (Figure 3-6) of the subject property should show the buildings, boundary lines and major arteries. Be sure that the building identification numbers tie in to the building descriptions in the body of the appraisal report. Note the contour lines showing the uneven topography of this site. This was included as part of a land value issue to show that hilly terrain was worth less per acre than the flat land.

FIGURE 3-4

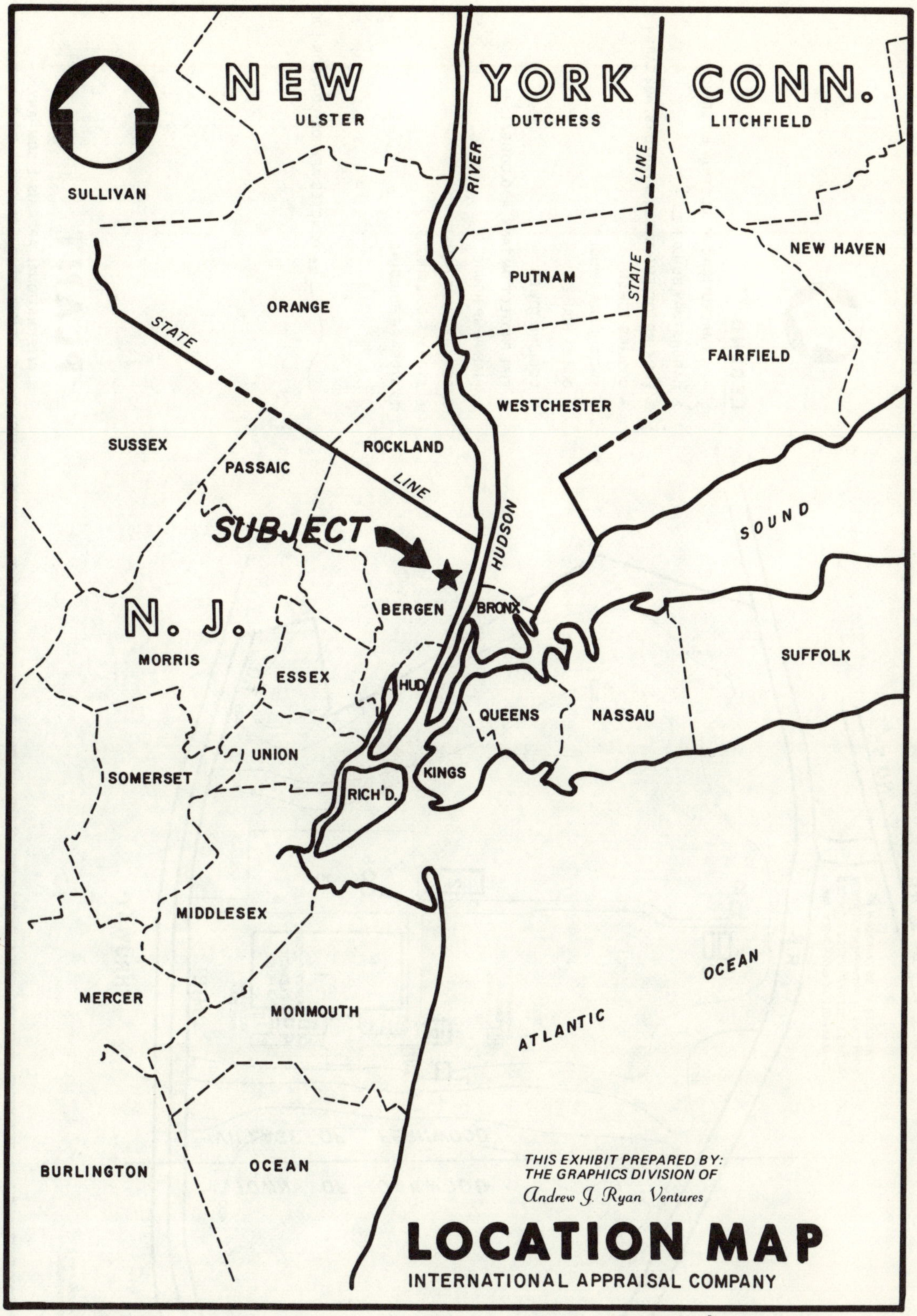
NEW YORK
CONN.
ULSTER
DUTCHESS
LITCHFIELD
SULLIVAN
RIVER
LINE
NEW HAVEN
PUTNAM
STATE
ORANGE
STATE
FAIRFIELD
WESTCHESTER
SUSSEX
ROCKLAND
PASSAIC
LINE
HUDSON
SOUND
SUBJECT
BERGEN
BRONX
N. J.
MORRIS
ESSEX
SUFFOLK
HUD
QUEENS
NASSAU
UNION
SOMERSET
KINGS
RICH'D.
MIDDLESEX
OCEAN
MERCER
MONMOUTH
ATLANTIC
BURLINGTON
OCEAN
THIS EXHIBIT PREPARED BY:
THE GRAPHICS DIVISION OF
Andrew J. Ryan Ventures
LOCATION MAP
INTERNATIONAL APPRAISAL COMPANY

FIGURE 3-5

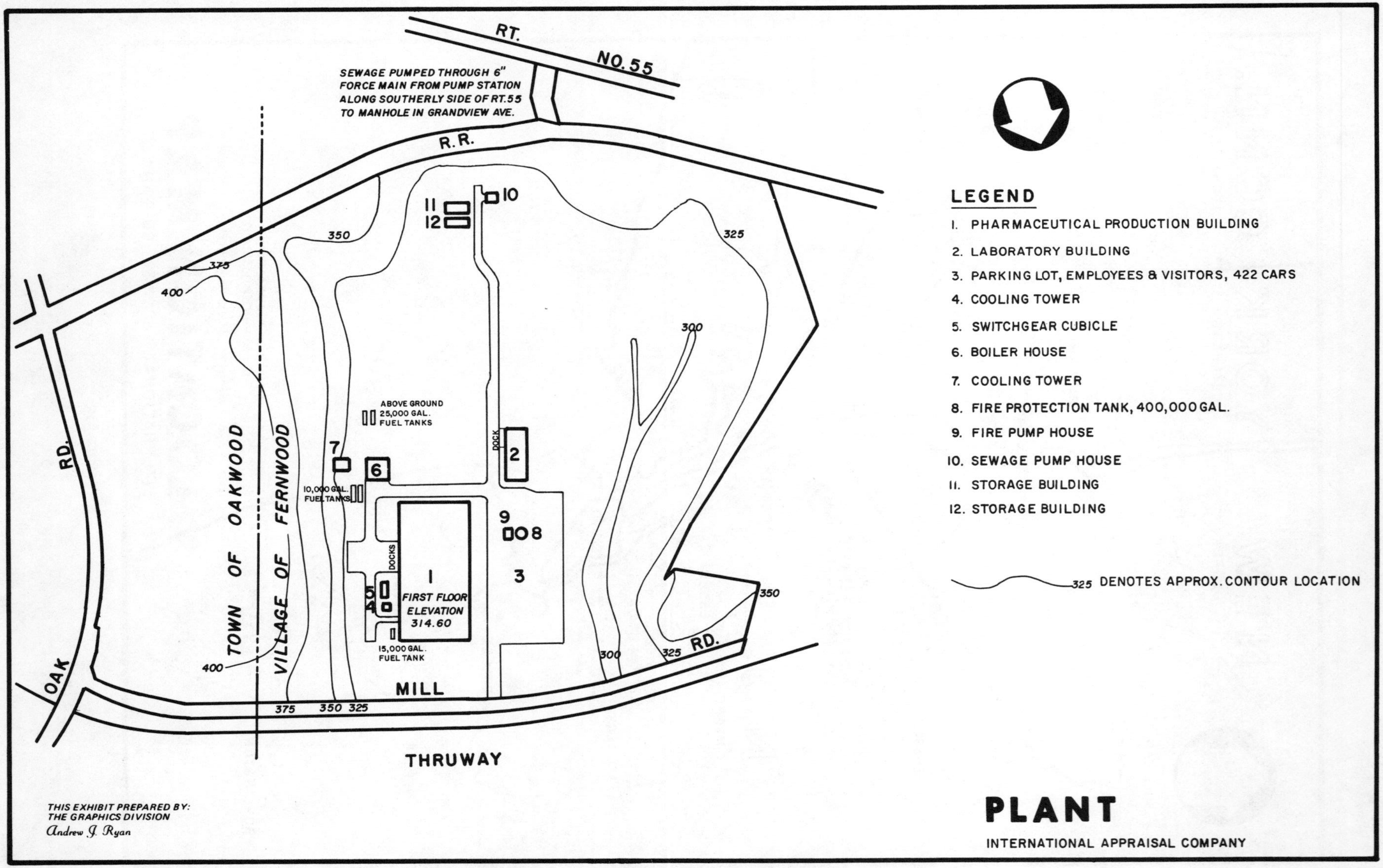
RT. NO. 55
SEWAGE PUMPED THROUGH 6" FORCE MAIN FROM PUMP STATION ALONG SOUTHERLY SIDE OF RT.55 TO MANHOLE IN GRANDVIEW AVE.
R.R.
TOWN OF OAKWOOD
VILLAGE OF FERNWOOD
OAK RD.
MILL RD.
THRUWAY
ABOVE GROUND 25,000 GAL. FUEL TANKS
10,000 GAL. FUEL TANKS
15,000 GAL. FUEL TANK
FIRST FLOOR ELEVATION 314.60
DOCKS
DOCK
LEGEND
1. PHARMACEUTICAL PRODUCTION BUILDING
2. LABORATORY BUILDING
3. PARKING LOT, EMPLOYEES & VISITORS, 422 CARS
4. COOLING TOWER
5. SWITCHGEAR CUBICLE
6. BOILER HOUSE
7. COOLING TOWER
8. FIRE PROTECTION TANK, 400,000 GAL.
9. FIRE PUMP HOUSE
10. SEWAGE PUMP HOUSE
11. STORAGE BUILDING
12. STORAGE BUILDING
325 DENOTES APPROX. CONTOUR LOCATION
THIS EXHIBIT PREPARED BY: THE GRAPHICS DIVISION
Andrew J. Ryan
PLANT
INTERNATIONAL APPRAISAL COMPANY

FIGURE 3-6

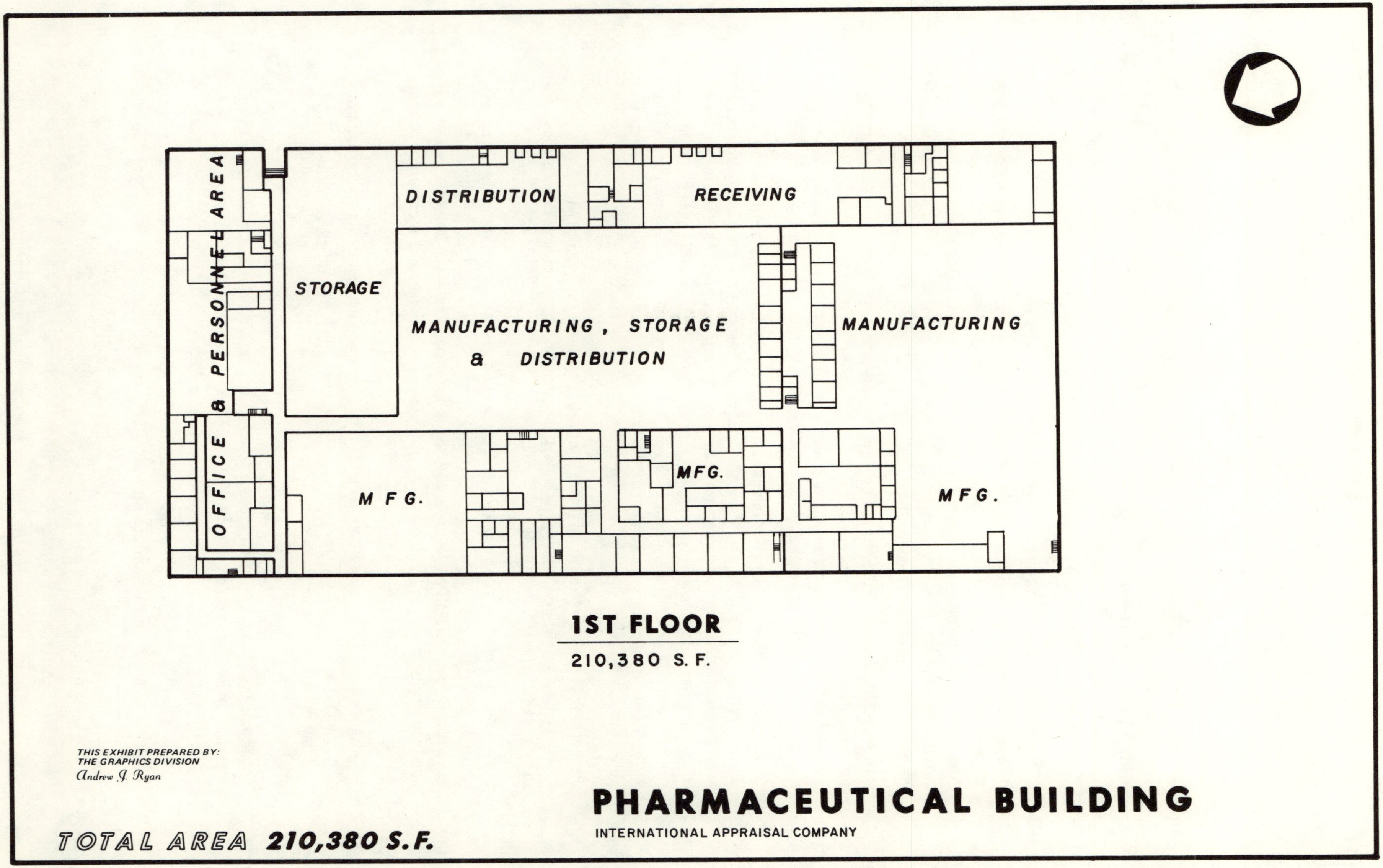
OFFICE & PERSONNEL AREA
STORAGE
DISTRIBUTION
RECEIVING
MANUFACTURING, STORAGE & DISTRIBUTION
MANUFACTURING
M F G.
MFG.
MFG.
1ST FLOOR
210,380 S. F.
THIS EXHIBIT PREPARED BY:
THE GRAPHICS DIVISION
Andrew J. Ryan
PHARMACEUTICAL BUILDING
INTERNATIONAL APPRAISAL COMPANY
TOTAL AREA 210,380 S.F.

FIGURE 3-7

Floor plans of the subject property's major structures should be presented (Figure 3-7). This is a good reference point when the witness describes building use and work-flow procedures. This leads to a further understanding on the part of Board or Court as to exactly what type of property is involved in the appeal.

When this portion of your presentation is completed, there should be no doubt in the mind of the trier of the fact concerning what the property looks like and where it is.

See the personal property appraisal section of this chapter for an example of a Process Flow (M&E) Diagram (Figure 3-23).

9. Statement of Limiting Conditions and Assumptions

CONTINGENT AND LIMITING CONDITIONS

The appraisers assume no responsibility for matters legal in character, nor render any opinion as to the title, which is assumed to be good. The legal description, if any furnished, is assumed to be correct. All existing liens and encumbrances have been disregarded and the property is appraised as though free and clear under responsible ownership and competent management.

Areas and dimensions of the properties were not physically measured but were furnished by the principal, or from plot plans furnished by the principal. Maps or sketches, if any included in this report, are to assist the reader in visualizing the property. We have made no survey of the property and assume no responsibility for its accuracy.

Verification of factual matters contained in this report has been made to the extent deemed practicable. The appraisers certify that to the best of their knowledge and belief, such factual matters are true and correct, and that no important factors affecting the value of this property were knowingly overlooked or withheld. Market data has been taken from sources deemed to be reliable, but which could not be verified in all cases. The resultant estimate of market value is predicated on the financial structure prevailing as of the date of value.

This appraisal report sets forth all of the limiting conditions (imposed by the terms of the assignment or by the undersigned) affecting the analysis, opinions and conclusions contained in this report.

Possession of this report, or a copy thereof, does not carry with it the right of publication, nor may all or any part of the contents of this report be conveyed to the public through advertising, public relations, news, sales or other media, without written consent and approval of the authors, particularly as to value conclusions, and the identity of the appraisers or firm with which they are connected.

The distribution of the total valuation in this report between land and improvement applies only under the existing program of utilization. The separate valuations for land and building must not be used in conjunction with any other appraisal and are invalid if so used.

The appraisers shall not be required to give testimony or appear in court by reason of this appraisal, unless specific arrangements for these services are otherwise arranged.

This is a standard set of limiting conditions promulgated by appraisal societies to set forth the constraints within which the appraisal was completed. Just make sure the appraiser doesn't limit himself out of the courtroom with the wording in this section.

Part II. Factual Data

10. Purpose of the Appraisal

PURPOSE OF APPRAISAL

The appraisal was made for the purpose of estimating the market value of the subject property, including land and improvements, as of ____________________ .

PROPERTY RIGHTS APPRAISED

The property rights appraised are all rights existing in fee simple as of the appraisal date. These rights are the legal and economic properties of the owner that may rightfully be exchanged for money or equivalent goods. Property rights inherent in the ownership of tangible personal property, and intangible benefits of the property itself, are not the subject of this report.

MARKET VALUE

Market value is ''the highest price in terms of money which a property will bring in a competitive and open market under all conditions requisite to a fair sale, the buyer and seller, each acting prudently, knowledgeably, and assuming the price is not affected by undue stimulus.

Implicit in this definition is the consummation of a sale as of a specified date and the passing of title from seller to buyer under conditions whereby:

1. buyer and seller are typically motivated;
2. both parties are well-informed or well-advised, and each acting in what he considers his own best interest;
3. a reasonable time is allowed for exposure in the open market;
4. payment is made in cash or its equivalent;
5. financing, if any, is on terms generally available in the community at the specified date and typical for the property type in its locale;
6. the price represents a normal consideration for the property sold unaffected by special financing amounts and/or terms, services, fees, costs, or credits incurred in the transaction.''[7]

The purpose of the appraisal is to estimate the market value of the subject property. It is good practice to tie ''market value'' into ''full value'' or whatever the statutory wording is in a given jurisdiction.

For example, the New York State Constitution Article XVI, Section 2 says: ''Assessment shall in no case exceed full value.''

Full value means market value or what a willing purchaser will pay to a willing seller.[8]

11–13. Area and Property Data

These are standard entries in appraisal reports to give necessary factual data on the subject property. Be sure that the data obtained by the appraiser from the Chambers of Commerce doesn't call the city the greatest in the country if you are claiming a great deal of economic obsolescence.

---

[7]The American Institute of Real Estate Appraisers and The Society of Real Estate Appraisers, *Real Estate Appraisal Terminology*, Cambridge, Massachusetts, c. 1975, p. 137.

[8]*Beeman v. Pawelek*, 96 N.Y.S. 2d 204, Affd. 276 A.D. 1057, 96 N.Y.S. 2d 312 (1950).

13. e. Assessed Value and Annual Tax Load

This section is important because it ties the tax bills/assessment parcels into the appraisal by specific reference. This section should also be tied in to Section 20 of the format which is the market value allocation to the assessed parcels.

13. f. Zoning

This is important because the zoning of all the comparables should be similar to the zoning regulations that apply to subject.

Part III. Analyses and Conclusions

In the Introduction and Factual Data parts of the ad valorem format, we have dealt primarily with facts and not opinions. The only opinion expressed was the fair market value conclusion set forth in the cover letter. This is as it should be. This allows the undisputed facts to be clearly placed before the trier of the fact, uncluttered by random opinions carelessly sprinkled about.

Part III, Analyses and Conclusions, is a different story. This is where the appraiser expresses and supports his opinion.

14. Analysis of Highest and Best Use

Many layman Boards of Review believe it to be contradictory to say that an asset is at its highest and best use if you are going to penalize the property with obsolescence. Therefore, it is good practice, in order to avoid this misunderstanding, to lightly qualify your statement that the property is at its highest and best use by referring to your most serious problems.

This is easily done because "highest and best use" involves concepts of most profitable or most economic use.

For example:

> This appraiser believes that the present heavy industrial use of the subject site is its highest and best use. However, the age of the structures, type of construction and plant layout detract from its optimum profitable use.

15. Land Value

I believe that for testimony purposes, the most effective way to present land sales is with the descriptions, photographs, plot plans and comparative map data all in the land section. This enables the appraiser to refer to these items one page after another rather than turning to the addenda in back of the appraisal.

The comparable sales should be near the subject and similar in zoning, size and shape. If such land sales are not available, then a range of sales activity should be presented with adjustments to show the appraiser's reasoning in arriving at his land value.

16. Value Estimate by Cost Approach

As stated earlier, the first step in the cost approach is to develop the reproduction cost of the subject property. A reproduction cost figure is developed from a cost manual based upon the structural components that make up the buildings.

You must be sure that the appraiser has the supportive data to show exactly how he arrived at his reproduction cost conclusion. Let him show you his worksheets and the specific pages in a specific cost manual that he used in his calculations. If you do not, your case may be in trouble when your appraiser is cross-examined.

This same rule of supportive data requirement holds true for depreciation. Make sure the physical depreciation allocation makes sense logically and that it is mathematically correct as applied. Functional and economic obsolescence allocations should be proven by some acceptable method. It is simply not enough to rely solely on the appraiser's opinion.

In this regard, photographs are essential:

If the roof or parking lot condition creates a severe maintenance problem, illustrate this physical depreciation with photographs (Figures 3-8 and 3-9).

FIGURE 3-8

FIGURE 3-9

FIGURE 3-10

If the roof was designed incorrectly, with not enough pitch to permit water to drain properly, show the functional obsolescence problem in a photograph (Figure 3-10).

FIGURE 3-11

If design shortcomings, such as low ceilings and 10′ × 10′ bays, hamper material handling, emphasize the functional obsolescence problem with a photograph (Figure 3-11).

FIGURE 3-12

If your machinery and equipment ruined 17,000 loaves of bread because it was not technologically current, let the Board see what this means (Figure 3-12).

Photographs permit the Board members to develop their own impressions of the problems. This has much more impact than relying on your witness to convey his impressions to the Board.

17. Value Estimate by the Income Approach

Effective comparables will be near to subject and similar in size, shape, and general usage. The leases used will be dated reasonably close to the appraisal date. Again, all descriptive data, floor plans and photos should be set forth at this point so that the Board can see for themselves just how comparable the leased properties are to subject.

The net income developed from these comparables and attributed to subject must be capitalized. The development of your appraiser's capitalization rate should be gone into in detail with much supportive data appearing in the appraisal report.

As stated earlier, one of the best sources of these capitalization rates is the market itself if you can learn the rental income and sales price of a property that is comparable to the subject.

Figure 3-13 is an example of a summary of Comparable Rentals for easy reference. The individual data relating to each property would, of course, precede this comparison.

Also shown (Figure 3-14) is an example of how to include your basic capitalization rate source directly in the report. There are always cross-examination questions on how the capitalization rate was developed. Including the basic source in the report adds credibility to the witness.

18. Value Estimate by Comparative (Market) Approach

As in land and income, comparable sales must be near to subject and similar in size and use. The sale date must be reasonably close to the appraisal date.

Comparable Rentals

No.	Address	Date	Term	Size SF	Annual Rental Net Net	Annual Rental SF Net Net	Comments
1.	900 Central Ave. Yonkers, New York	December 19	20 years	150,000	$360,000	$2.40	An excellent comparable with high quality construction.
2.	900 Central Ave. Yonkers, N.Y.	December 19	5 years	150,000	373,500	2.49	Same comment as above; very comparable.
3.	900 Kee Drive Mahwah, N.J.	March, 19	15 years	169,187	355,340	2.10	Excellent comparable in close proximity to the subject. Rental would equate to $2.50.
4.	950 Kee Drive Mahwah, N.J.	December, 19	10 years	122,400	226,400	1.85	Excellent technology facility, in close proximity to subject. Rental would equate to $2.40.
5.	975 Franklin Avenue Mahwah, N.J.	September, 19	10 years	108,000	297,000	2.75	A prime example of good industrial office, research, testing labs, and light manufacturing areas.
6.	985 Franklin Avenue Mahway, N.J.	Current	5 to 10 years	208,000	520,000	2.50*	A fine available industrial facility, very adaptable. Good quality construction, been exposed to the market for over 2 years.

This includes extensive interior finish for office and research areas.

FIGURE 3-13

Descriptions of comparables should highlight those items that are the same. Photographs, including interior shots, should convince the trier of the fact that the comparable is a good indication of what subject would sell for if exposed to the open market.

Note the striking similarity between subject and comparable sale No. 1, as set forth in Figures 3-15 and 3-16.

25 points of comparison are presented in Figure 3-17. They include:

	Subject	Comparable No. 1
Land Area	25 acres	22 acres
Building Area	366,308 sq. ft.	289,384 sq. ft.
Construction Date	1964 & 71	1962 & 69

The laboratory buildings are almost identical in size: Subject—65,897 square feet; Comparable No. 1—65,230 square feet. In subject photo (Figure 3-15), the lab is detached from the main plant and is to the right of the water tank. Comparable No. 1 photo (Figure 3-16) shows the lab attached to the main plant on the right.

If the subject plant's lab were moved to the left of the water tank and attached to the main plant, you would have two buildings that are almost identical.

Interior photos can be used very effectively to show comparability between the subject and another property. The photos in Figures 3-18 and 3-19 show similarity in basic construction, ceiling height, bay width and crane service.

Keep in mind that you cannot overdo points of comparability when trying to convince a Board or Judge that your market data comparisons are valid.

The comparables map (Figure 3-20) should show the subject property and the location of the comparables. Note the five-mile radius circles to show distance from the subject. Note also that subject is in New York and several of the comparables are in New Jersey. These

YIELDS ON SELECTED SECURITIES

AVERAGES OF DAILY RATES ENDED FRIDAY

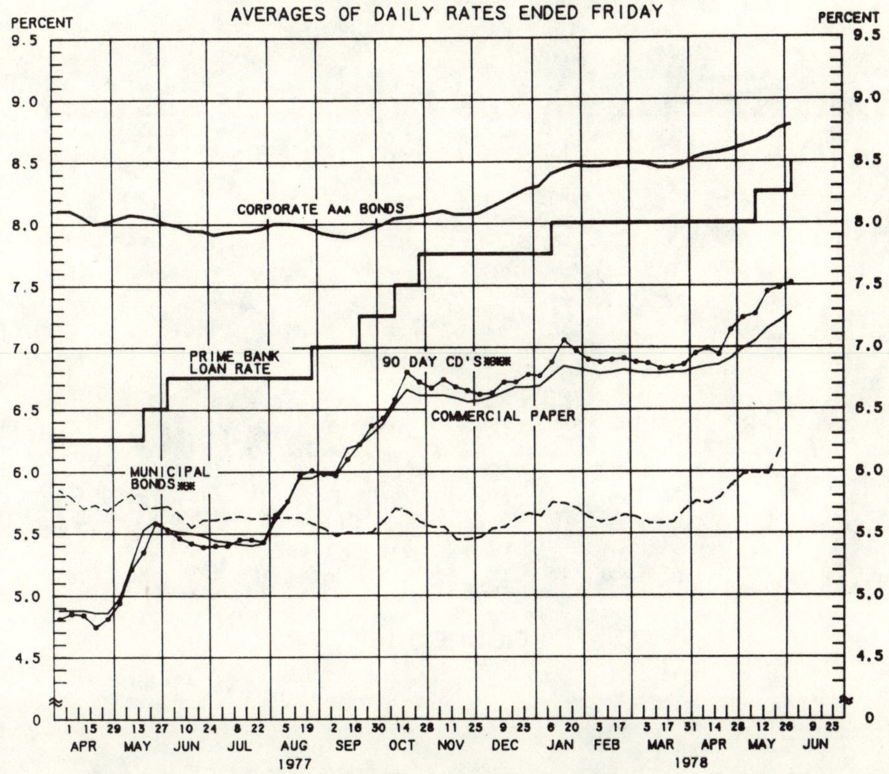

LATEST DATA PLOTTED ARE AVERAGES OF RATES AVAILABLE FOR THE WEEK ENDING: JUNE 2, 1978

1978	90 DAY CD'S ***	PRIME COMMERCIAL PAPER 4-6 MONTH	PRIME BANKERS' ACCEPTANCES	CORPORATE AAA BONDS	MUNICIPAL BONDS **
APR. 7	6.95	6.83	6.85	8.53	5.76
14	6.99	6.85	6.84	8.56	5.74
21	6.94	6.86	6.92	8.57	5.79
28	7.14	6.91	7.06	8.59	5.89
MAY 5	7.24	6.99	7.18	8.62	5.98
12	7.27	7.05	7.27	8.65	5.99
19	7.45	7.15	7.35	8.69	5.98
26	7.48	7.21	7.45	8.76	6.18
JUNE 2 *	7.52	7.28	7.50	8.79	N.A.
9					
16					
23					
30					

* AVERAGES OF RATES AVAILABLE.
** BOND BUYER'S AVERAGE INDEX OF 20 MUNICIPAL BONDS, THURSDAY DATA.
*** SEVEN-DAY AVERAGES OF SECONDARY MARKET RATES FOR THE WEEK ENDING WEDNESDAY TWO DAYS EARLIER THAN DATES SHOWN. CURRENT DATA APPEAR IN THE BOARD OF GOVERNORS' H.9 RELEASE.
N.A. - NOT AVAILABLE

PREPARED BY FEDERAL RESERVE BANK OF ST. LOUIS

FIGURE 3-14

FIGURE 3-15

FIGURE 3-16

MARKET DATA APPROACH

Comparable Grid

Statistical Data	Comparable No. 1	Subject Property
1) Location	Smith Street Wayne, New Jersey	Hemion Road & New York Thruway, Town of Newton
2) Land Area	22 Acres	Required—25 Acres (3:1)
3) Total Building Area	289,384 Square Feet	366,308 Square Feet
4) Oldest Construction	1962	1964
5) Newest Construction	1969	1971
6) Kitchens & Full Cafeteria	Yes	Yes
7) Built-in Laboratory Facilities W/Hoods	Yes	Yes
8) Explosion Proof Roof	Yes	No
9) Finished Product	Identical	Identical
10) Rail Siding	Yes	No
11) All Utilities	Yes	Yes
12) Office Areas— Air Conditioned, Carpeted	Yes	Partially Carpeted
13) Sprinkler System	Yes	Yes
14) Main Plant	202,880 Square Feet	210,380 Square Feet
15) Boiler House	In Main Plant	9,215 Square Feet
16) Office Building	26,496 Square Feet	25,040 Square Feet
17) Laboratory	65,230 Square Feet	65,897 Square Feet
18) Mezzanines	None	Yes
19) Fuel Pump House	Yes	Yes
20) Sewer Pump Station	None, Gravity Feed	Yes
21) Storage Building "A"	None Included in Main Plant Area	Yes
21A) Storage Building "B"	None Included in Main	Yes
22) Transportation	New Jersey Turnpike; U.S. 80 & 280 U.S. Highway No. 287; U.S. Highway No. 23; Garden State Parkway; Others; Superior to the Subject	New York Thruway; Highway No. 17 Inferior to the Comparable
23) Access to Sophisticated Labor Market	Excellent	Good
24) Tax Assessor's 1976	$8,207,817 (28.20/SF)	$15,784,536 − 2,310,000 Surplus Land $13,474,536 ($36.78/SF)
25) Actual Fair Market Value as per 7/30/76 Sale Plus Improvements Added	$6,650,000 ($22.98/SF)	Fair Market Value Less Surplus Land per This Appraisal $8,058,776 ($22.00/SF)

FIGURE 3-17

FIGURE 3-18

FIGURE 3-19

SUBJECT
5mi
10mi
15mi
20mi
25mi
30mi
35mi
40mi
45mi
② DENOTES IMPROVED SALE
COMPARABLES MAP
INTERNATIONAL APPRAISAL COMPANY
THIS EXHIBIT PREPARED BY:
THE GRAPHICS DIVISION
Andrew J. Ryan

FIGURE 3-20

out-of-state comparables are admissible in New York. See *A&P Tea Co. v. Kiernan,* 42 N.Y. 2d 236, 397 N.Y.S. 2d 718, 366 N.E. 2d 808 (1977).

The comparable analysis graph is an excellent addition to the income and market data sections of the appraisal report. The market data graph illustrated in Figure 3-21 shows the sales prices and adjustments of comparables resulting in a value range per square foot for subject.

This format has immediate visual impact on the trier of the fact. There can be no doubt that the value range is between $21.00 and $23.00 per square foot, supporting the appraiser's conclusion that the property has a market value of $22.00 per square foot.

The graph is an ideal supplement to the Summary of Comparable Rentals Chart shown earlier. It would follow a Summary of Comparable Improved Sales Chart in the market data section of the report.

19. Interpretation and Correlation of Estimates

This is the section of the report where the appraiser reviews the value conclusions he arrived at in the cost, income and market data approaches, and selects the approach which he finds most reliable as his final value judgment.

20. Market Value Allocation to Assessment Parcels

In multi-parcel appeals, it is often difficult to allocate your appraiser's market value figures to each of the parcels being appraised. Your appraiser should make the allocation in this section. It is a way to make life simpler for a Board of Review. If the Board decides in your favor they should have an immediate reference for establishing the new assessments so there will be no delay if they wish to grant you a reduction on the spot.

I have seen a number of hearings come to a standstill when no one could figure out how to convert the market value figures into assessment figures on the various parcels under appeal.

This section should, of course, tie into the Section 13e of the format, Assessed Value and Annual Tax Load.

21. Certification

It is required that an appraiser state in his appraisal report that "he has no present or contemplated future interest in the subject property or any other interest which might tend to prevent his making a fair and unbiased appraisal. . . ."[9]

Part IV. Addenda

22. Qualifications

An appraiser's qualifications are usually preprinted pages setting forth the appraiser's credentials. But you should not stop there. Seek out what special expertise this appraiser has with regard to your particular type of property. Try to show what similar properties he has appraised.

You must continually try to show that your appraiser knows more about this particular area of appraising and, therefore, he is the expert whose value judgment should be relied upon.

Photographs of major items of machinery and equipment should be included in the appraisal report. A photo like this aluminum pot line (Figure 3-22) helps a Board or Judge to better understand the type of asset that is the subject of appeal.

[9]The Principles of Appraisal Practice and Code of Ethics of the American Society of Appraisers, Section 8.5.

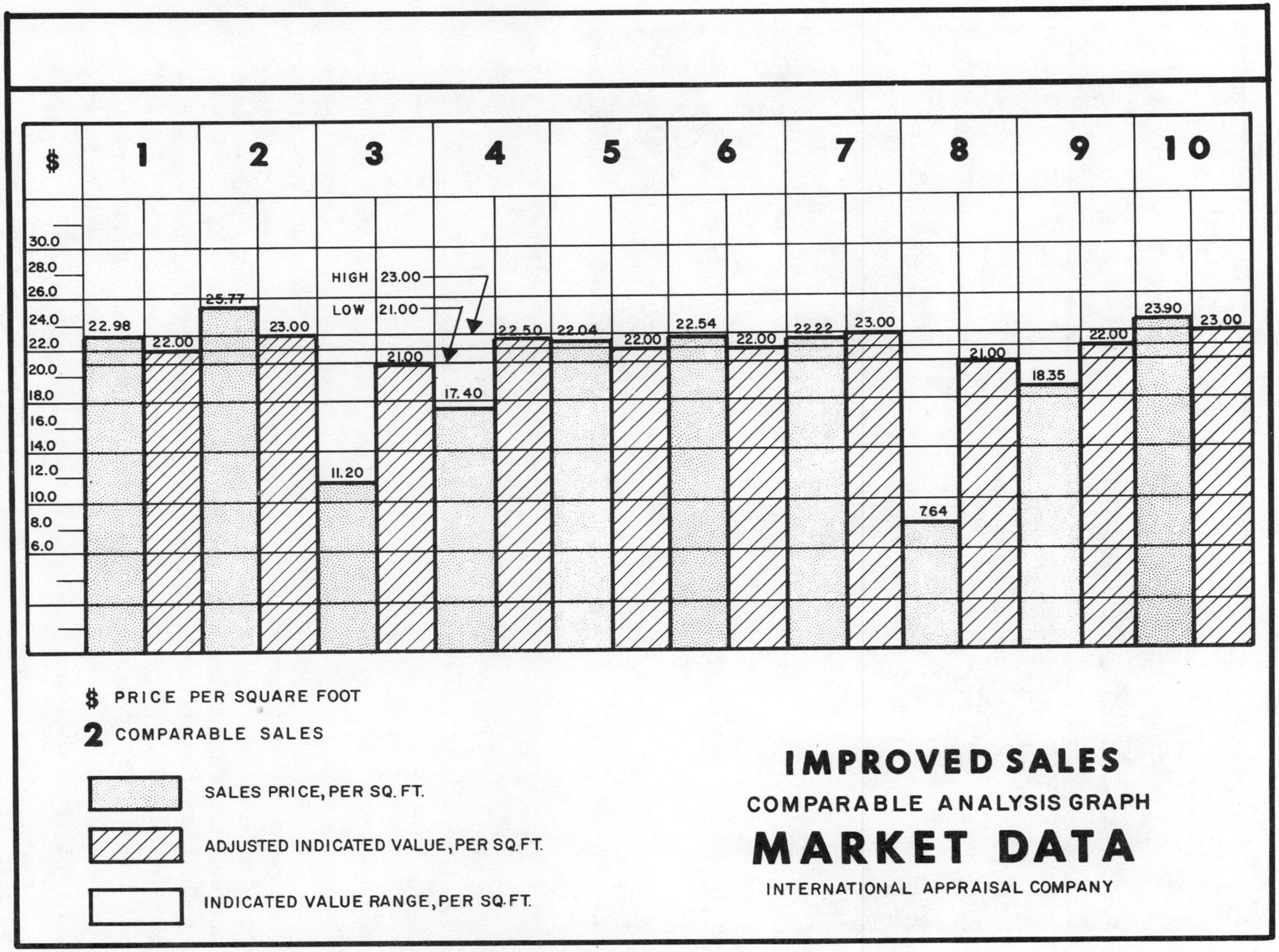
$
1
2
3
4
5
6
7
8
9
10
30.0
28.0
26.0
24.0
22.0
20.0
18.0
16.0
14.0
12.0
10.0
8.0
6.0
22.98
22.00
25.77
23.00
HIGH 23.00
LOW 21.00
11.20
21.00
17.40
22.50
22.04
22.00
22.54
22.00
22.22
23.00
7.64
21.00
18.35
22.00
23.90
23.00
$ PRICE PER SQUARE FOOT
2 COMPARABLE SALES
SALES PRICE, PER SQ. FT.
ADJUSTED INDICATED VALUE, PER SQ.FT.
INDICATED VALUE RANGE, PER SQ.FT.
IMPROVED SALES
COMPARABLE ANALYSIS GRAPH
MARKET DATA
INTERNATIONAL APPRAISAL COMPANY

FIGURE 3-21

FIGURE 3-22

THESE SAME BASIC PRINCIPLES APPLY TO PERSONAL PROPERTY APPRAISALS

Personal property ad valorem valuation issues center around inventory and machinery and equipment.[10] I have been involved in several major machinery and equipment valuation appeals.

The assessor uses a mass appraisal technique similar to real estate. Broad valuation measures are applied to property values as reported by the taxpayer. Original cost figures are trended to current cost. State promulgated depreciation schedules are applied to arrive at depreciated cost which is the basis of the assessment.

This is a cost approach technique and because of a lack of an organized market there is usually no income or market data reference easily available.

Non-use of the ''market data'' approach can be explained as follows:

The word ''market'' connotes a more or less organized body of competing buyers and sellers in a fairly well-organized trading environment.

> Many of the types of property which courts have occasion to value, such as the fixed assets of a business enterprise, or real estate, are not dealt in on an organized exchange and can be sold, if at all, only by special negotiations with one or more prospective

[10] See Chapter 9 for more detail on these specific items.

purchasers. To say that the sales of these forms of property indicate their *market* value, would be inconsistent with the popular concept as to the nature of a market.[11]

It has, therefore, become the practice in the United States to value machinery and equipment via the ''cost approach'' to value for property tax purposes. This is generally done by ascertaining the original cost of the assets, establishing current cost, and then applying appropriate amounts of physical, functional/technological and economic obsolescence and depreciation. This is the actual practice of some 42 states and the District of Columbia that levy a personal property tax.

An actual case involving appraisal testimony is set forth in Chapter 9. It includes the cost approach described above and also presents the taxpayer's experience with sales of similar machinery and equipment. It also involves testimony as to functional and economic obsolescence.

A typical product flow chart is set forth in Figure 3-23. This type of chart can be used to describe the manufacturing procedures carried on at the subject plant. Don't be afraid to bring along an example of the product manufactured. Again, your job is to familiarize the Board or Court with the equipment, how it operates, and what it produces. Then you are ready to present your valuation evidence.

Be sure that your product flow drawing shows the major items of equipment. Then doublecheck to be sure that the major items are accounted for in your description of the assets and photographs. Nothing hurts your case more than to find that your expert is unable to tie together his listing of assets, product flow chart, and photographs.

WHEN SHOULD YOU CALL AN APPRAISER?

Obviously the best way to achieve a property tax reduction is for you and you alone to talk an assessor into giving you one. Unfortunately, most assessors require support for your value conclusions in the form of an objective appraisal.

It would probably not be prudent for you to merely go out and buy an appraisal report if you suspect that a property is over-assessed. You may pay a substantial appraisal fee only to find you have no case at all and you should not appeal the assessment.

A practical method is to ask an appraiser to do a preliminary study in an attempt to develop a value range for the subject property. This would not be an appraisal. It would be a preliminary value estimate based on one or two days' work to give you some idea of what value conclusion would be reached as the result of a full narrative appraisal report.

The benefit of this effort is that, for a minimal per diem fee, you are presented with an excellent reference to judge the fairness of your present assessment.

Assuming that the preliminary study shows the assessment to be excessive, it is in your best interest to make your request for the appraisal as soon as possible. The appraiser has the same scheduling problems that you have, and early notice allows for realistic completion dates well in advance of hearings.

Keep in mind that there may be occasions when two appraisals are required. It is often good practice to introduce a local appraiser (familiar with the local color and history of the area) and a national appraisal firm (familiar with special features of a given property).

Be sure to establish at the outset the number of copies of the appraisal report you will

---

[11]James C. Bonbright, *The Valuation of Property,* Vol. I (1st ed., Charlottesville, Va., the Michie Company, 1975), p. 42.

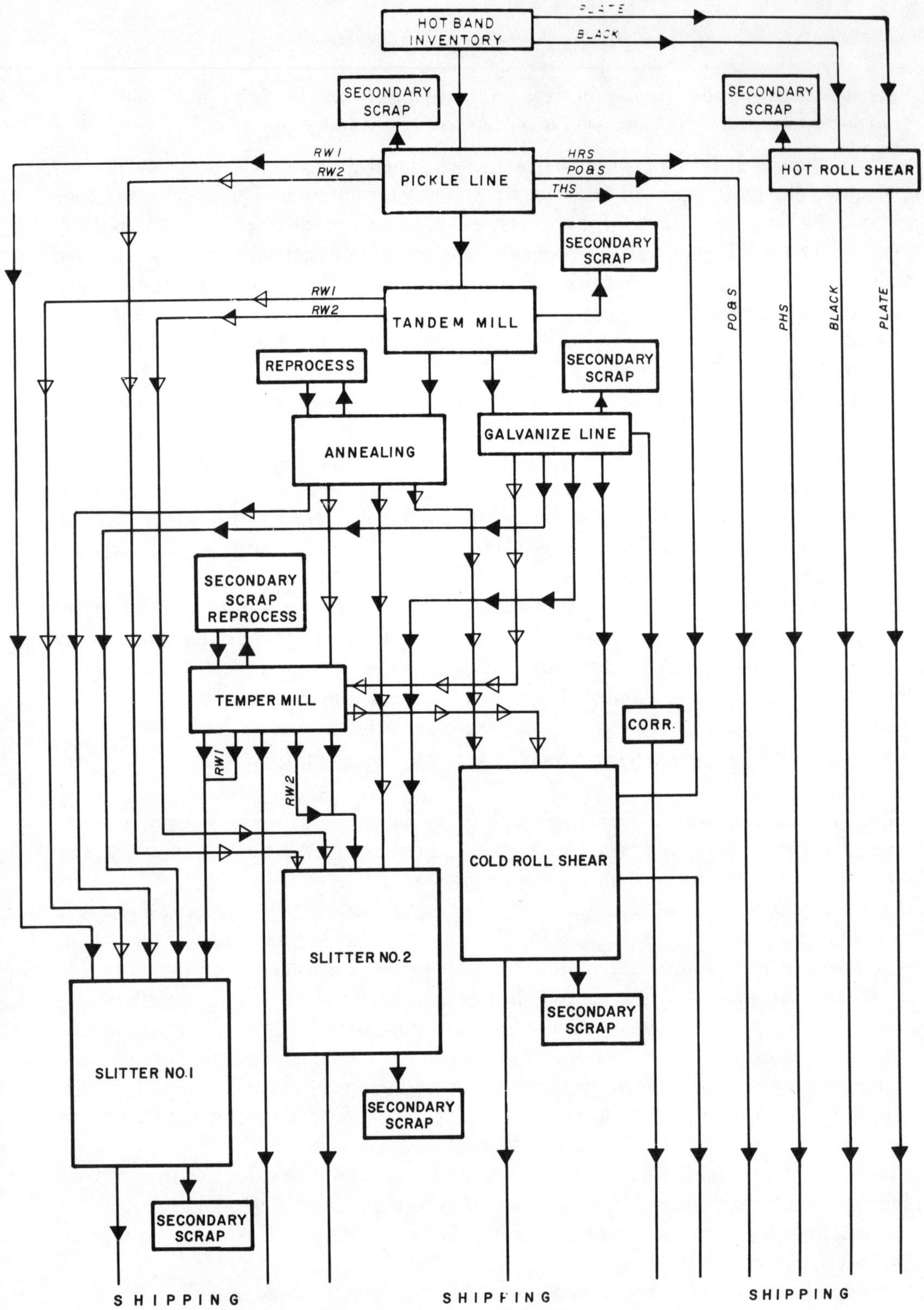

PRODUCT FLOW

INTERNATIONAL APPRAISAL COMPANY

FIGURE 3-23

require. Many times, six or more copies are needed for distribution to you, your attorney, Board members, the assessor and his attorney.

APPRAISAL FEES: MAKE SURE YOU GET YOUR MONEY'S WORTH

An appraisal firm is a professional service organization whose principles of operation are similar to those of a law firm, CPA firm, engineering or consulting firm. Broadly speaking, one-third of the volume is paid out in salaries, one-third in other expenses, and the remaining one-third is profit.

Fee quotes are based on such factors as the complexity of the assignment, the experience and background of the individuals working on the job, the speed with which the appraisal is needed, and the number of man-days necessary to complete the job.

Fees, of course, fluctuate from appraisal company to appraisal company and from one part of the country to another. A median range might be $50 per hour or $400 per day, with or without expenses. Using this reference as a general rule of thumb, you can estimate the number of days that an appraiser anticipates is necessary to complete the appraisal report.

You should be sure that the final appraisal report reflects the time that you paid for.

Part II

Methods and Approaches To be Applied In Establishing More Equitable Property Tax Assessments

4
How to Challenge a Land Assessment: Proper Valuation and Classification Are Key Factors in Effecting Property Tax Savings

4

In real estate assessment appeals you are almost always dealing with land valuation considerations. You may not always pursue a land assessment appeal, but you should be aware of certain basic facts and factors to enable you to make proper judgments.

This chapter will review the facts you must assemble in order to fully acquaint you with the subject land. Valuation techniques will be explained to enable you to draw valuation conclusions from the pertinent data you have collected.

Since so much land is valued by the assessor according to statutory classification definition, these classification categories will be examined to acquaint you with the prerequisites necessary to a favorable classification for your land.

Finally, various land valuation problems, including transitional land value and taxable interests related to the land, will be presented to highlight those areas in which an informed taxpayer can achieve favorable results in the form of assessment reductions and property tax savings.

ASSEMBLING PERTINENT DATA

Before you can consider the question of a land assessment appeal, you must be completely familiar with the subject land.

Size and Shape

You should obtain size and shape particulars directly from primary sources of information such as the deed and survey. It is most important to precisely identify the subject property at the outset in order to avoid complications due to error later on.

A land map showing the tract should be available. If not, you can probably obtain one from the assessor's office.

Topography

This is an important factor to be considered because multi-level elevations can help or hinder the property's value, depending on its use. I recently completed a land valuation appraisal assignment on industrial land located on a mountainside in Montana. The original turn-of-the-century plant was constructed on several levels of the mountainside due to gravity flow requirements of certain manufacturing processes. Technological advances over the years eliminated the gravity flow requirements. At the time of my appraisal, the multi-level and steep grades served no manufacturing purpose and, in fact, hindered material handling.

Thus, the terraced land was of no value as industrial land, except for the fact that an industrial plant was operating on it. I valued it by using sales of more desirable flat industrial land. In comparing this level industrial land to the subject, I penalized the subject due to its mountainside topography.

You must also consider any land fill requirements necessary to make the land usable or salable. You can be sure that an alert assessor will be adding these costs to the purchase price of the land when he works up his land value assessment. Land fill and other land improvements can sometimes exceed the basic cost of the land itself. Thus, it is very important to be aware of this expense factor and its impact on the value of the subject tract.

Soil

The richness of the soil is most important in farmland appraising. Characteristics of surface soil and subsoil are generally available from state sources and these ratings should be reviewed with regard to texture, color, fertility and nitrogen content. Availability of water is also a primary factor of concern in the ability of soil to produce merchantable products. Complete familiarity with these details is a must in farmland-appraising practices.

The weight-bearing capacity of your soil can be very important if construction of a substantial structure is contemplated. Piling jobs are very expensive. For example, 100 creosoted wood pilings each 50' long by 14'' in diameter cost in the area of $40,000. It should be pointed out to the assessor that any prudent investor would deduct that cost from his offering price for your land.

Yard Improvements

In dealing with land valuation you may encounter ''yard improvements'' that the assessor carries as part of his land assessment. You should be basically familiar with the cost of such items as these: *paving:* 3'' asphalt on 2'' base: $.40—$.45 per square foot; 3'' concrete unreinforced *sidewalks:* $.50—$.65 per square foot; *fences:* chain link galvanized steel, 8' height: $6.00 per lineal foot; *overhead street lights:* $700 each; *water main:* 6'' cast iron: $11.00 per lineal foot; *gas mains:* 3'': $6.00 per lineal foot. Current cost data on these items is available in standard cost manuals.

Landscaping

This can be an important valuation factor depending on the use of the land. A resort hotel must invest substantially in grass, shrubbery, and trees to properly appoint its setting. Trees and shrubbery plantings that have grown into beautiful specimens greatly enhance the value of residential lots and should be considered in your valuation inquiry.

Location

Location is of primary importance in the valuation of land. Depending on use, such factors as egress and ingress, and access to major highways, water routes, airports and population centers have significant impact on land value.

If your land or portions of it are located in a designated flood plain, you should be sure that the assessor is aware of this fact. Land value is reduced sharply when subject to this type of encumbrance and this problem should be brought to the assessor's attention in every case.

Zoning

Zoning is legislative regulation defining the use to which certain land within designated areas may be put. Zoning restrictions or the lack thereof may play a key role in the value of land for taxation purposes.

I participated in a land appeal in which current zoning was the crucial factor. The subject property was some of the last privately owned ocean-front land in California. It was just north of Santa Cruz and zoned for agricultural development or one house per ten acres of land. (See Figures 4–1 and 4–2.)

Investors purchased the land and sought zoning changes allowing for a community development with high-rise hotel, marina, and many single-family and multiple dwellings.

Ecology-minded individuals, spearheaded by students and faculty from the University of California at Santa Cruz, pressed for and caused the implementation of legislation fixing a moratorium on any possible changes in present zoning of ocean-front land. This development freeze is in keeping with California's sweeping land use control measures to protect its prime agricultural land (first-class farmland in terms of soil, climate and topography) from indiscriminate urban encroachment. California has recently taken over most of the subject land for a state park.

Scene is of subject land looking west toward the Pacific Ocean at the very top of the photo. Rough topography of cattle-grazing land in center makes value minimal under current zoning. Dark area in upper portion of photo shows Brussels sprouts growing area.

FIGURE 4-1

Scene is typical of subject ocean-front land. The keen interest of both developer and ecologist is understandable.

FIGURE 4-2

On assessment day, the land was unimproved except for a few homes. Its primary use was to grow Brussels sprouts and to graze cattle. Nevertheless, the assessor levied values on the future sale of land as if the land were developed. Superior Court Judge Charles Franich said that the assessor had failed to follow the ''market data approach'' to value. An assessment based on the future sale of land as if it could be developed into a residential use, despite current zoning constraints, was speculative and unfair to the taxpayer. Santa Cruz County was ordered to refund $150,000 in property taxes to the complaining taxpayers.[1]

The case stands for the general rule that when future zoning changes are remote, it is speculative to base value on the possibility of such changes. But the taxpayer cannot expect every judge to disregard the reasonable future use of land.

In a Minnesota case, the judge agreed with the taxpayer that R-1 Zoning (single-family residential use) restricted the value of the land. He held, however, that there was a trend that indicated subject land would not be developed under R-1 zoning classification. He also held that the zoning changes assumed by the assessor were ''remote.'' He found value at $12,000 per acre—somewhere between taxpayer's $4,500 and assessor's $35,600 per acre values.[2]

Easements

You should become familiar with any easements which affect the value of your site. These might include water, mineral or air rights, railroad rights of way, electric transmission

---

[1]Decision not reported.

[2]*Hedberg & Sons, Co. v. County of Hennepin,* 305 Minn. 80, 232 N.W. 2d 743 (1975).

lines and pipelines. Public or private restrictions—housing acts, pollution codes—should also be thoroughly researched.

Remember, easements can work both ways with regard to land value. A 25-foot strip can have no value for tax purposes because of an easement. However, if the rest of the property benefits from the easement, an additional value can be added.[3]

Utilities

The status of your land in relation to water, gas and sewer mains and electricity should be examined carefully. You must determine if they are immediately available to the site or if they will be in the future. A lack of these amenities can have a serious negative effect on the value of your land and the assessor should be made aware of this problem if it exists.

If you do have a problem, be sure to show that the lack of the utility in question does in fact affect the land value. One taxpayer lost 50% in assessment reductions (granted by the County Appeal Tax Court and the Maryland Tax Court) on appeal because of failure to show what effect ''sewer moratorium'' (making sewer service unavailable until 1979) had on the market value of the subject property.[4]

Tax Bills

You should obtain copies of the latest tax bills on the subject land. Often there are several, and each one describes a small portion of the entire tract. You must be sure that the tax bills tie in precisely with the information you have already obtained from deeds, surveys and land maps.

The tax bills are important because they furnish you with the assessment, tax rate, block and lot or other identification number and, usually, a brief metes and bounds description.

Assessment Data

You should determine the basis for the assessor's land value. He will generally have some sort of schedule or land value map depicting valuation entries. These may be front foot or square foot values downtown, or acre value in industrial or rural areas. There may also be combinations of these measurement factors on the same parcel, e.g., front foot value for the land along a lake to a certain depth and per acre value for the rear land.

Figures 4–3 and 4–4 are typical examples of urban and rural tax maps.

Assessors use all types of schedules to value land. For example, in Windham County, Vermont, the following schedule was used:

Westminister Land Schedule
1969

Categories	1	2	3	4
Site (1st acre)	500	1,500	2,000	2,500
Next 4 acres	200	300	400	600
Next 20 acres	100	150	300	500
Balance	25	50	75	280

[3]*People ex rel. News Syndcate Co. v. Sexton, et al.*, N.Y.L.J., December 9, 1939, p. 2057.

[4]*County Executive for Montgomery County v. Supervisor of Assessments*, 275 Md. 64, 337 A. 2d 682 (1975).

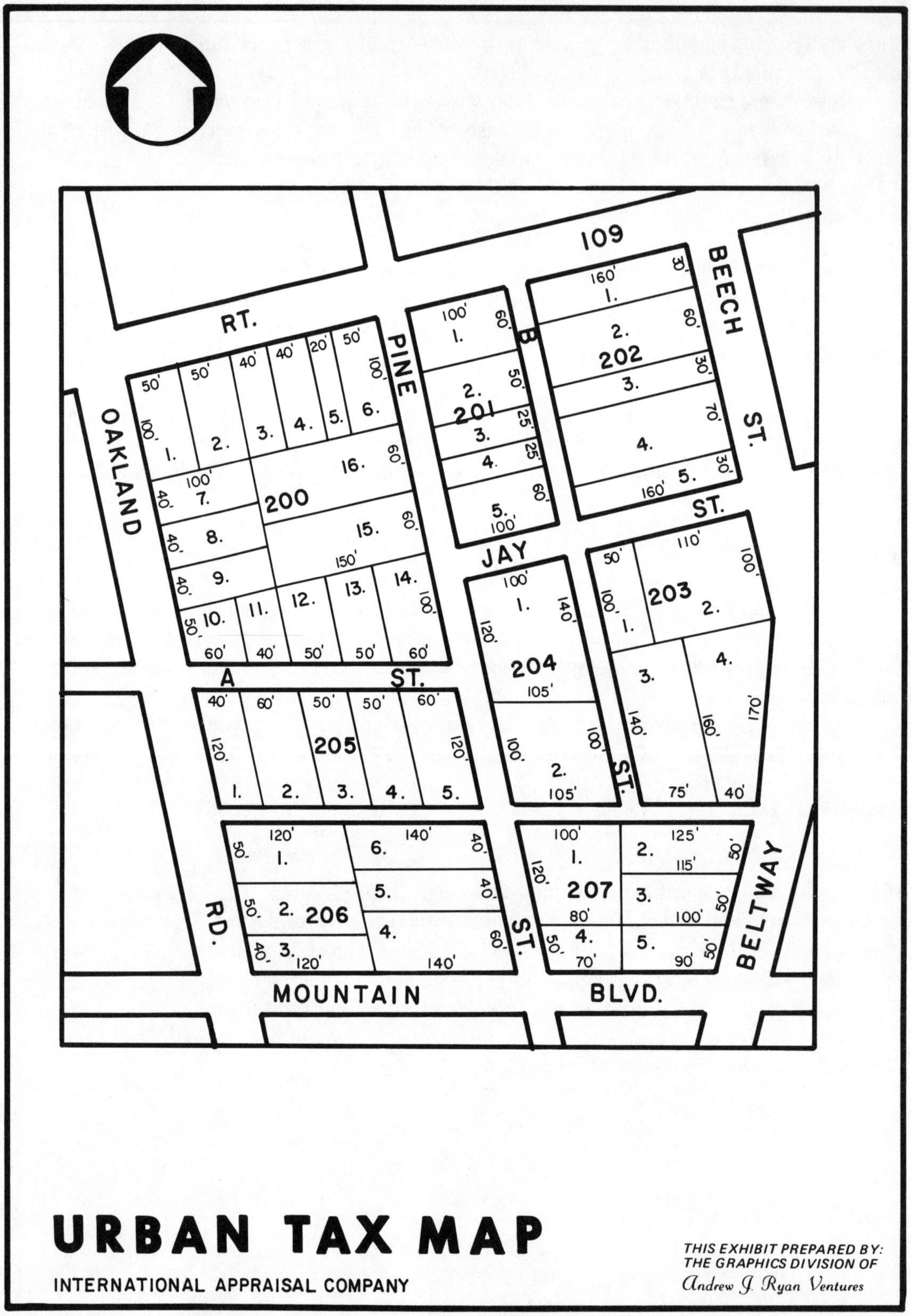

RT. 109
OAKLAND RD.
PINE ST.
B
BEECH ST.
JAY ST.
A ST.
BELTWAY
MOUNTAIN BLVD.
200
201
202
203
204
205
206
207
URBAN TAX MAP
INTERNATIONAL APPRAISAL COMPANY
THIS EXHIBIT PREPARED BY:
THE GRAPHICS DIVISION OF
Andrew J. Ryan Ventures

FIGURE 4-3

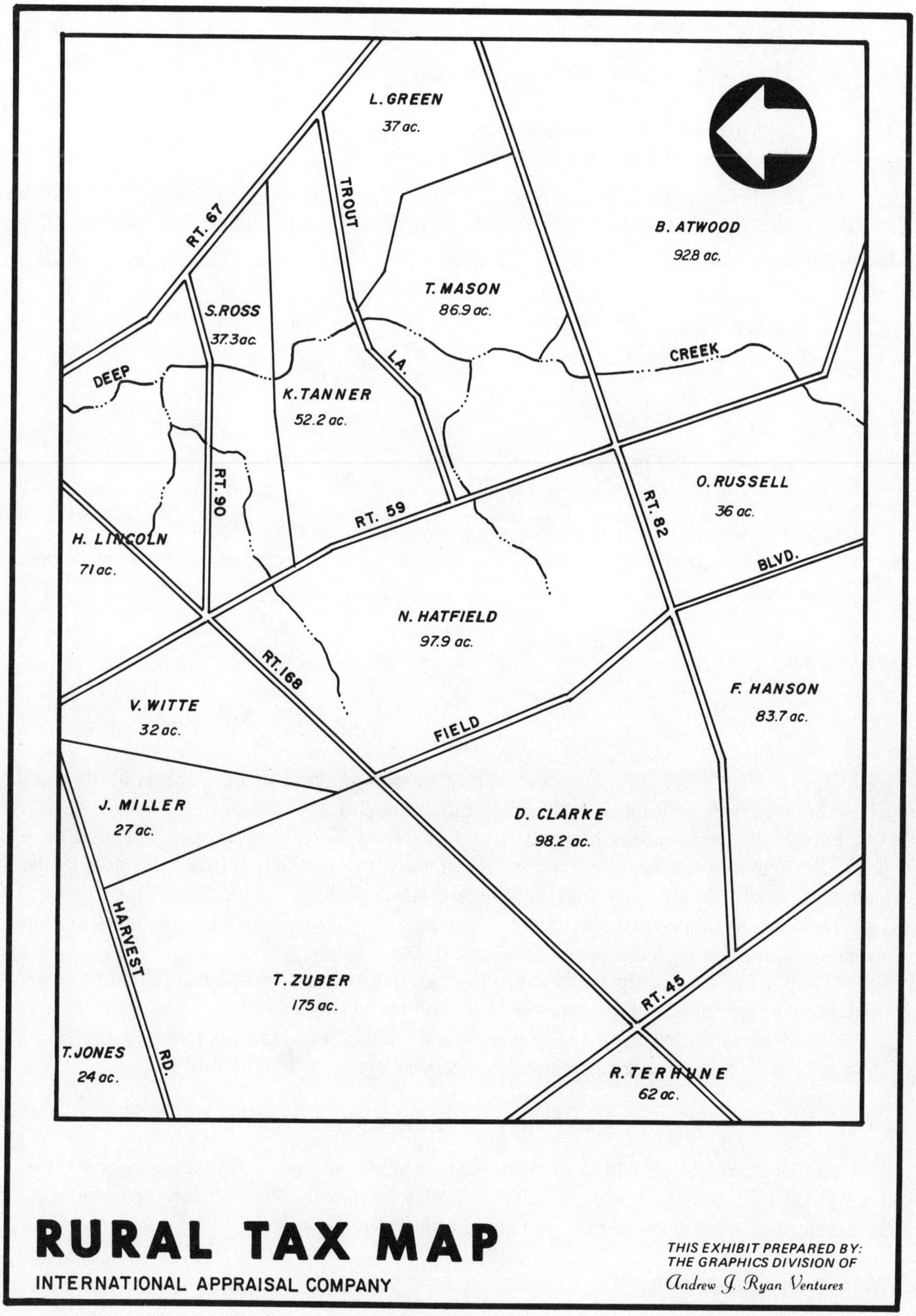
L. GREEN
37 ac.
B. ATWOOD
92.8 ac.
T. MASON
86.9 ac.
S. ROSS
37.3 ac.
K. TANNER
52.2 ac.
O. RUSSELL
36 ac.
H. LINCOLN
71 ac.
N. HATFIELD
97.9 ac.
F. HANSON
83.7 ac.
V. WITTE
32 ac.
J. MILLER
27 ac.
D. CLARKE
98.2 ac.
T. ZUBER
175 ac.
T. JONES
24 ac.
R. TERHUNE
62 ac.
RT. 67
TROUT
LA.
DEEP
CREEK
RT. 90
RT. 59
RT. 82
BLVD.
RT. 168
FIELD
HARVEST
RD.
RT. 45
RURAL TAX MAP
INTERNATIONAL APPRAISAL COMPANY
THIS EXHIBIT PREPARED BY:
THE GRAPHICS DIVISION OF
Andrew J. Ryan Ventures

FIGURE 4-4

Categories
1. Poorer land (inaccessible or landlocked).
2. Average land on a road.
3. Above average (developed).
4. Extraordinary land along Connecticut River Valley, tillage land

The plaintiff taxpayer's land was classified 4, "most valuable." The assessor added $25,000 to the above schedule conclusions to allow for a one-mile road and electricity to the house site:

Assessor's Valuation		
First acre	$ 2,500	
Next 4 acres ($600)	2,400	
Next 20 acres ($500)	10,000	
Remaining 200 acres ($280)	56,000	
Total		$70,900
Estimated cost of road and electricity to site	$25,000	
Grand Total		$95,900

Taxpayer had purchased the 225 acres three years before for $54,000.

Taxpayer developed and introduced the following data based on the assessments levied on similar land:

Property	Acreage	Category 4 Value
X	129	$44,120
Y	116	21,380
Z	53	24,940
Taxpayer	225	70,900

This, in the Court's opinion, "establishes beyond question that the appraisal of plaintiff's land was decidedly much higher than other lands in the area."

Further, the comparables had access to public roads and since taxpayer's land already was in the highest category under the formula, it was unwarranted to inflate that figure by the estimated cost of the road and electricity to the site.[5]

This case illustrates that a taxpayer can overcome presumptions of correctness of land valuation forumulas, if the proper homework is done.

You must also ascertain the equalization rate that prevails in the jurisdiction to determine at what percentage of fair market value you are assessed.

And, be sure to determine under what classification your land is carried on the assessor's books. This issue will be covered in detail in a later section of this chapter.

VALUATION TECHNIQUES

For our purposes, we will examine the two generally accepted approaches to land value: the Market Data Approach and the Land Residual Technique. We will also consider other land valuation approaches as they pertain to property tax issues.

Market Data Approach

This generally preferred approach involves gathering, recording and comparing sales data on comparable sites.

---

[5]*Bookstaver v. Town of Westminster,* 131 Vt. 133, 300 A. 2d 891 (1973).

Data on sales of similar parcels may be obtained from the principals, brokers, assessors and public records. The following data should be obtained: grantor and grantee, date of sale, sale price, mortgage or other considerations affecting the price, legal description, size and encumbrances, if any.

Properly done, this exercise will relate the comparable sale to the subject and indicate value after adjustment for time, location, size, shape and other variables.

A simple market data comparison exercise is as follows:

Assume that subject parcel is a 10,000 square foot rectangular lot 50' × 200' fronting on Main Street, downtown.

Comparable 1: The parcel next to subject; also 50' × 200'. Sold within a few months of the appraisal date for $.90 per square foot. There would be no adjustments for time, location or size, and you have an excellent indication of the value of subject.

Comparable 2: This lot is 40' × 200', one block north of subject, on the same side of the street, and sold for $.80 per square foot two years ago. Adjustment for time: +10%; location: +10% (closer to primary shopping area); size: −5%; total adjustment: +15% or $.92 per square foot.

Comparable 3: A corner property across the street with 50' of frontage on Main Street and 200' on Side Street, sold last year for $.75 per square foot. Adjustments: Time: +5%; Location: +15% for corner influence; size: no adjustment; total adjustment: +20% or $.90 per square foot.

		Adjustments			
		Time	Location	Size	Subject's Indicated Value per Sq. Ft. as Adjusted
Comparables					
1	$.90/sq. ft.	None	None	None	$.90
2	.80/sq. ft.	+ 10%	+ 10%	− 5%	.92
3	.75/sq. ft.	+ 5%	+ 15%	None	.90

Concluded Value for Subject: $.90/sq. ft.

Properly documented comparable sales have long been accepted as evidence of market value. Of course, the best evidence is a sale of the subject land itself.

The sale price of a parcel of land between a willing seller and a willing buyer is one of the most important elements in fixing land value.[6]

Land value by use of comparable sales is "the best information of market value after an actual sale of the property itself."[7]

But, comparable sales must be adjusted for such factors as time, location, distance from subject, marketability and topography.[8]

And, prices paid are *not* the controlling factor. All factors must be considered.[9]

---

[6]*Minnesota Entertainment Enterprises, Inc. v. State of Minnesota,* 235 N.W. 2d 390 (1975). This case involved an allocation of land value because six drive-in theaters were also sold.

[7]*State ex rel. Park Plaza Shopping Center, Inc. v. O'Malley, et al.,* 59 Wash. 2d 217, 207 N.W. 2d 622 (1973).

[8]*John W. Merrithew, et al. v. State of New York,* 329 NYS 2d 476, 38 A.D. 2d 996 (1972).

[9]*Cardinal Federal Savings & Loan Assn. vs. Cuyahoga County Board of Revision,* 336 N.E. 2d 433 (1975). This Ohio case involved urban renewal land.

Land Residual Technique

If comparable sales data described in the preceding section is not available, the value of the site may be arrived at through the use of the land residual technique of the income approach.

This technique involves the estimation of the total net income which the land will produce if developed to its highest and best use. A fair interest return and a provision for recapture are subtracted from the net income to allow for the improvements. The residual net income is attributable to the land and the land value is arrived at after capitalization at a reasonable risk rate.

Assume that the highest and best use of a site is an apartment house which will produce $25,000 in annual net income. Assume the improvements cost $200,000 and a fair return and provision for recapture is 10%; $20,000 of the annual net income is attributable to the improvements: ($200,000 × 10% = $20,000).

The residual $5,000 of the total net income of $25,000 is then attributable to the land. If an appropriate capitalization rate is 8%, the value of the land is $62,500: ($5,000 ÷ 8% = $62,500).

Other Land Valuation Approaches

We have now reviewed the basic land valuation techniques of market data and land residual. Several combinations and variations of these techniques are constantly in use and many have been the subject of litigation.

In Nebraska, an appraiser from the revaluation firm who increased taxpayer's farmland value for tax purposes from $69,025 to $147,525 proved his case by using six sales of similar parcels, an income capitalization approach using a 5.5% capitalization rate, and a "summation or cost approach" classifying each tract and assigning a value per acre from an analysis of market data.[10]

Here we find a combination of the market data approach and an income capitalization approach using the farmland's productivity to arrive at net income to be capitalized. It is a well-settled rule that actual or potential income from real property may be considered in determining its value for tax purposes. Thus, it was proper for an assessor to consider what farmland could produce annually in wheat and other crops.[11]

Where land is unique and there is an absence of market data, income alone can establish value. This was the situation with regard to the valuation of the Sea Lion Caves in Oregon where income was derived from the tourist trade.[12]

The real differences of opinion in these cases center around how much weight is to be given to the element of income or earnings.

In a Maryland case, the Court disagreed with the taxpayer and held that his vacant lot, adjacent to a used car lot, should be assessed in accordance with its income-producing potential. The assessor was correct in using the income approach as the controlling factor in establishing value.[13]

---

[10]*Sam R. Cheedomelka vs. Board of Equalization of Dodge County,* 192 N.W. 2d 403 (1971). The Court used the words "summation or cost approach." It looks more like a variation of the market data approach to me.

[11]*Bennett v. Board of Review,* 234 Iowa 800, 13 N.W. 2d 351 (1944), 96 A.L.R. 2d 661.

[12]*Donavan G. Houghton et al. v. Department of Revenue,* 4 Oregon Tax Court 451 (1971), aff'd. Ore. Sup. Ct. 495 P. 2d 715 (1972).

[13]*Easter v. Dept. of Assessments,* 288 Md. 547, 180 A.2d 700 (1962).

However, in an Oregon case, the effects of a long-term land lease were disregarded in favor of comparable sales. Some leases had remaining terms of 30 years and taxpayer argued that the leases should be the controlling factor in setting value. The Court upheld the assessor who used land sales of $1.70 to $3.70 per square foot from a busy shopping center area across the street from the subject to establish value at $1.00 per square foot.[14]

To understand these cases, a brief review of the nature of lease interests is necessary. The owner or lessor has the right to receive rent over the period of the lease and the right to the reversion of the real estate at the end of the lease. The tenant or lessee has the right to the use and occupancy of the real estate over the term of the lease.

When the assessor addresses himself to a leased land valuation situation he is concerned with uniformity of assessments dictated by current economics. This concern must prevail over contractual arrangements between lessor and lessee. Of course, if the land is currently leased at its fair rental value, economic rent and contract rent are the same. This is not usually the case, however, due to continually changing economic conditions.

The courts in the last two cases cited are upholding the assessor's use of current economic conditions to value the real estate.

It should be noted that the land would be sold in the real estate market subject to the lease and the investor would be purchasing the lease income. In a condemnation case, therefore, the court could not simply ignore the lease in awarding proper damages.[15] It was held that the owner was entitled to have awarded to him the present value of the right to receive rents over the period of the lease, together with whatever the reversion may be.

The valuation of this interest is computed in the following example:

Annual net rental for 20 yrs. = ground rent of: (land currently worth $100,000 @ 8%)	$ 8,000
Present value of contract rent for 20 yrs. discounted at an interest rate of 8% per year—$8,000 = 9.818147*	78,545
Present value of anticipated reversion of land at end of lease discounted @ 8% per year—$100,000 = .214548**	21,455
Total Value of Leased Fee	$100,000

* Present worth one per period
**Present worth of one
See any compound interest and annuity table 20-year period @ 8%.

Finally, where sales are infrequent, courts will look to measures of value in common use in the area of the subject land. In Oregon where local practice was to sell large ranches based on "cow or animal units" (say 8,500 average cow units at $350 per unit), it was held that this was the best approach to value. The assessment was reduced from $3.4 million to $2.6 million. It should be noted that a comparable sale (same size, 60 miles away) was introduced on a "cow unit" basis. Also, the sale of the 64,000-acre subject ranch two years earlier at over $6 million (including livestock and equipment) was introduced.[16]

---

[14]*Swan Lake Moulding Co. v. Dept. of Revenue,* 478 P. 2d 393 (1970), 30 A.L.R. 361.
[15]*City of Atlanta v. Harriet L. McLucas, et al,* 187 S.E. 2d 560 (1972).
[16]*Lake County Board of Equalization vs. Dept. of Revenue and ZX Ranch, Inc.,* 478 P. 2d 377 (1970).

CLASSIFICATION

Now that you have completed your inquiry into the pertinent facts regarding the subject land, and have applied the valuation techniques described above, it is time to determine the proper classification of your land for property tax purposes. This is most important because, if you meet various prerequisites, you may be entitled to a particular classification category which will result in a reduced assessment and lower taxes.

Many jurisdictions have placed land in different categories for assessment purposes. The distinctions are usually dependent on land use and spelled out in statutes. This type of distinction is well within the statutory authority of the legislature, provided such classification is uniform, reasonable and natural.

Types of Classification

The more common special land uses that have been granted lower assessments are (1) *agricultural land:* to preserve farmland and maintain a readily available source of food; (2) *open space land:* to preserve our natural resources; (3) *wild land:* so as not to interfere with New Hampshire's natural ecological process; (4) *homesteads:* to ease the property tax burden of the homeowner; (5) *recreational land/seasonal residences:*[17] to give a tax break to those who occupy homes for only a portion of the year; and (6) other land uses such as rural land, parking ramps and refineries.

Constitutionality

Not every assessor will sit still and accept this type of legislation. In Minnesota an assessor challenged a law granting special assessment treatment to land used for agriculture on the grounds that it was an illegal exemption. The Court held that this "Green Acre Statute" was constitutional because use of land is a proper basis for classification and it was not unreasonable, arbitrary or capricious. The Court said that the legislature had recognized the hardships of a farmer no longer financially able to continue the agricultural use of the land because of high property taxes.[18]

Meeting the Prerequisites

In this case, the taxpayer qualified for preferential treatment because he met all the prerequisites listed in the Minnesota statute.[19] " . . . 10 acres or more . . . timely application . . . 33%1/3% of the total family income is derived therefrom. . . ." You must meet all the prerequisites set forth in the statute; and be careful—if you do not make timely application you do not get relief.[20]

As always, the burden is on the taxpayer to show that his use of the land comes within the legislative intent of the statute. In Connecticut, an assessor denied a preferential farmland assessment to a nursery arguing that the statute's sole purpose was to encourage food production. The Court looked beyond food production to the legislative intent to conserve

---

[17] *Otis Lodge, Inc. v. Comm. of Taxation,* 206 N.W. 2d 3 (1973).
[18] *Elwell v. County of Hennepin,* 221 N.W. 2d 538 (1974).
[19] Minnesota Agricultural Property Tax Law, Minnesota Statutes 273.111.
[20] *Campion v. County of Hennepin,* 221 N.W. 2d 549 (1974).

natural resources. It was held that taxpayer's 11 acres of cultivated nursery land of plants, trees, bushes and shrubs were entitled to "farmland" classification.[21]

The issues are never black and white. And the gray areas can go either way. In Florida, land was acquired for the primary purpose of subdividing it and selling it as lots. The Court said that any agricultural use was "clearly incidental" to this primary purpose and the land did not qualify for the favorable agricultural classification.[22]

However, in the famous Key Biscayne Coconut Caper, the taxpayer admitted that if his 68 acres were developed to their highest and best use (hotels, motels or apartments), the land would be worth almost $2.5 million. He nevertheless argued that he should be granted an agricultural assessment of $54,312 because he was growing coconut trees on the land—a bona fide agricultural use. The Third District Court of Appeal of Florida agreed, despite the fact that the coconut plantation had been losing money for several years and all the coconuts could be grown on about five acres. The Court said: "There is nothing in the law that requires a person to operate a business efficiently or at a profit." The deciding factor: the land was actually producing coconuts, and therefore was entitled to agricultural classification. Claims of obvious sham were not heard by the Court.[23]

Each case must stand on its own set of facts subject to the wording of the various statutes. Planting Christmas trees is not enough to create a forest land classification in Oregon,[24] but planting Christmas trees in Maryland will qualify for agricultural classification.[25]

Maintaining Favorable Classification

Once he has achieved it, the taxpayer must be vigilant to maintain his favorable classification. In Arizona, a taxpayer was granted a "grazing land" classification at $7.00 per acre after appeals to the county and state boards. Subsequently, the assessor, because there was also a home and store on the land, changed the classification to "commercial use" and "property held for further development." The Superior Court of Yavapi County granted summary judgment saying it was improper for the assessor to reclassify the same land without showing a change in circumstance. The point is: once you get your favorable classification—be sure to protect it.[26]

Limitations on Classification

The right to classify is not a blanket one. A Florida statute said: " . . . platted land unsold as lots shall be valued for tax assessment purposes on the same basis as any unplatted acreage of similar character until 60% of such lands included in one plat have been sold as individual lots." The intent was to give developers a tax break by treating unsold lots as unplatted until 60% of the tract was sold. Purchasers of the individual lots did not receive this preferential treatment and the Florida Supreme Court found the statute to be unconstitutional. It was held that ownership of lots was *not* valid criterion for classification.[27]

---

[21]*Helmer Johnson et al. v. Board of Tax Review of the Town of Fairfield,* 273 A.2d 706 (1970).
[22]*Firstamerica Development Corp. v. County of Volusia,* 298 So. 2d 191 (1974).
[23]*Matheson v. Elcook,* 173 So. 2d 164 (1965).
[24]*Masters v. Department of Revenue,* 5 Oregon Tax Court 134 (1972).
[25]*Stieger v. Supervisor of Assessments of Howard County,* Maryland Tax Court, Case No. 35 (1973).
[26]*Yavapi County v. Wilkinson,* 534 P. 2d 735 (1975).
[27]*Interlachen Lakes Estates, Inc. v. Snyder,* 304 So.2d 433 (1974).

TRANSITIONAL LAND AND ROLL-BACK TAXES

When a city community begins to spread into the country, both land use and land value are in transition. This situation poses difficult valuation and equity problems for the assessor. Consider the problem of the farmer caught between increased land values because of urban growth on one side of his farm and increased land value due to shopping center development on the other side of his farm. To assess the farm at the increased value would, in effect, put the farmer out of business. Classification as farmland, which we discussed in the preceding section, will solve this immediate problem. But what happens when the farmer finally sells his farm at the higher per acre value and the use is changed?

New Jersey has sought to recapture some of the taxes which would have been paid by this land if it had been taxed on the same basis of all other property.[28] The Farmland Assessment Act of 1964 provides for "roll-back taxes" to be collected for the year in which the use change takes place and the two previous years. The roll-back taxes are computed by arriving at the full and fair value of the land and subtracting the special treatment assessment. The appropriate tax rates for the three years are applied to the difference.

As a practical matter, the farmer usually benefits completely because the new owner, generally a developer, will agree to pay any roll-back taxes as part of the purchase price. Thus, the assessor does equity to the farmer (who continues the use of the family farm) and collects roll-back taxes when that use is changed.

TAXABLE INTERESTS RELATED TO THE LAND

The broad legal definition of land embraces the surface of the earth and everything under or over it—to an indefinite extent upward and downward. The definition includes not only the soil but also things permanently affixed by nature: water, trees, growing crops, minerals under the land; things permanently affixed by man—buildings, fixtures, fences, bridges, dikes, canals;[29] and the use of air space or air rights.

When Does Vacant Land Become Subject to Taxation as Improved Land?

When improvements to your land are in the process of construction on assessment day, you should be completely familiar with statutes and local practice concerning "partial assessments." The issue is: how can you maintain your unimproved status?

Many jurisdictions base the improvement assessments on the portion of the final value which is present on assessment day. Other jurisdictions tax land as unimproved until improvements in progress are substantially complete. In Florida, for example, if the improvements in progress are not substantially complete, the land shall be assessed as unimproved.[30] The Florida courts have interpreted "substantially complete" as follows: ready for occupancy except for finishing touches is deemed substantially complete; a large portion of the premises occupied although additional labor and materials are necessary for final completion is presumed substantially complete.[31]

In still other jurisdictions, the matter is one of local practice to be decided through negotiations on partial assessments with the assessor. This initial issue is most important

[28] *New Jersey Statutes Annotated 54:4*–23.1 *et seq.*

[29] *Reynard v. City of Caldwell,* 55 Idaho 342, 42 P.2d 292, 296 (1935); *Gas Products Co. v. Rankin,* 63 Mont. 372, 207 P. 993, 997 (1922), 24 A.L.R. 294.

[30] *Florida Statutes Annotated* 103.11(4)

[31] *William Markham, Tax Assessor of Broward County v. Sherwood Park, Ltd.,* 244 So. 2d 129 (1971).

because you have the opportunity to establish the basis for the equitable future assessment of your property.

When Are Machinery and Equipment "Land?"

When the New Hampshire Courts say so! It has been held that a ski lift is an "integrated whole which cannot be readily segregated into its component parts. . . . intimately intertwined with the primary use of the land itself." The Court held that only factor machinery is excepted from the legislative definition of real estate.[32]

Oregon has held that an elevator shaft to the underground Sea Lion Caves is land, and thereby disallowed any depreciation allowances for the shaft.[33]

You must be familiar with the statutes and their interpretation in order to be aware of the fine distinctions drawn between what is and is not real estate. This topic will be covered in detail in Chapter 12.

Mineral Rights

Mineral or subsurface rights include the use and profits derived from the extraction of oil, gas, coal or minerals from underground portions of a designated area of land.

Mineral rights interests are usually valued by assessors through the use of state promulgated formulas which include such variables as ore reserves, mining costs and profits, financial requirements and future prospects.

The taxpayer has the burden of showing these valuation formulas to be incorrect. In a Wyoming case, the taxpayer failed to prove lack of uniformity and failure to consider certain costs in a state formula involving gross production, sales prices less cost and royalties and a method for determining mining costs.[34]

But where an assessor ignored the probable life of oil and taxpayer proved they were short-lived wells, the Court found the assessment to be arbitrary and invalid.[35]

And Kaiser Steel was successful in New Mexico in arguing that coal produced from a "captive mine" to provide raw material for its own steel mill could not be valued based on small amounts sold to other steel mills. Only 4% and 9% of the total production was sold at $8.50 per ton and the Court held that the small sales were insufficient to support a valuation.[36]

Even a recent sale price of mineral rights can be rebutted if there were changes in value between the sale date and assessment date. The assessment was based on the sale price of $24.7 million. Subsequent geological data indicated a fair cash value of only $5.4 million. The Kentucky Court held the sale price could no longer be considered as the best evidence.[37]

Air Rights

If you can breathe it, it's taxable. This right to undisturbed use and control of a designated air space within the perimeter of a stated land area and within stated elevations has not escaped from the assessor.

---

[32]*King Ridge, Inc. vs. Town of Sutton,* 340 A2d 106 (1975).
[33]See Footnote 12, supra.
[34]*Hillard v. Big Horn Coal Company,* 549 P. 2d 293 (1976).
[35]*Angle v. Board of County Commissioners,* (Kansas), 522 P. 2d 347 (1974).
[36]*Kaiser Steel Corporation v. Property Appraisal Department,* 490 P. 2d 968 (1971).
[37]*Allied Chemical Corporation v. Union County Board of Supervisors,* 511 S.W. 2d 196 (1974).

In Maryland, taxpayer signed a long-term lease specifically agreeing not to build above his existing small structure to allow for light and air to a neighboring building. This was in return for a rental arrangement. The Court held "air rights acquire value on their utilization," are assessable as air rights only and taxpayer was bound by the value disclosed in the lease.[38]

But, in Connecticut, an electric company's 100-foot right-of-way below its power lines was held not to be included under a statute allowing for taxation easements to use air space. The Court said that if the legislature wants to tax such interests, it will have to enact appropriate laws.[39]

An interesting air rights case was recently decided by the United States Supreme Court.

New York City designated Grand Central Terminal, one of the city's "most famous buildings and a magnificent example of the French Beaux Arts style," as a historic landmark.

Penn Central was refused permission to build a 50-story office tower above the terminal. It was argued that Penn Central's airspace was appropriated for government use and this "taking" of the air space requires "just compensation" under the Fifth Amendment.

The Justices held, in a six-to-three decision, that New York did not have to make compensation: New York's action was similar to a zoning law. This simply prohibits the use of certain features of the space while it allows gainful use of the remainder. The Court said the station itself "must be regarded as capable of earning a reasonable rate of return."[40]

Water Rights

Even assessing jurisdictions squabble over the taxability of this riparian right to use and enjoy water flowing across or along your land.

The assessor of Fallsburg, New York, placed the riparian rights only of New York City on his tax rolls. Even Archie Schwartz couldn't win this one. The Court held that although riparian rights are an interest in real property, they are not "land itself" and not real property for taxing purposes. The riparian rights could have been assessed, however, along with land to which it was connected.[41]

Riparian rights interests may affect land value quite substantially. In a New Jersey tidelands case involving land on the Hackensack River, the parties agreed that the 2½-acre property was worth about $90,000 but the purchase price was only $35,500 because title was clouded by tideland or riparian rights that might be claimed by New Jersey. The Division of Tax Appeals agreed but the Court reversed and set value at $90,000, saying this was what a willing buyer would pay a willing seller. There was no evidence that New Jersey owned an interest and there could be no reduction based on a state exemption.[42]

Timber Rights

In California, uncut timber is treated as part of the land and valued as bare land, disregarding the timber. Value is derived from sales of comparable bare land or by allocating

---

[38]*Department of Assessments of Baltimore City v. Macht,* Maryland Tax Court No. 637 (1971); *Macht v. Department of Assessments of Baltimore City,* Court of Appeals of Maryland, No. 16, September Term (1972).

[39]*Hartford Electric Light Company v. Town of Wethersfield,* Supreme Court, June Term, 1973.

[40]*Penn Central Transp. Co. v. City of New York,*—U.S.—, —S.Ct.—, —L. Ed.—(1978), 42 N.Y. 2d 334, 397 N.Y.S. 2d 914, 366 N.E. 2d 1271 (1977), 50 App. Div. 2d 265, 377 N.Y.S. 2d 20 (1975).

[41]*City of New York v. Archie Schwartz, et al., Assessors of Town of Fallsburg,* 320 N.Y.S. 2d 983, 36 App. Dir. 2d 402 (1971).

[42]*Town of Secaucus v. Damsil, Inc. et al.,* 120 N.J. Super. 470, 295 A.2d 8 (1972).

to land a portion of the total value of land and timber. A voluminous assessor's handbook on "the Appraisal of Timber Property" has been issued by the State Board of Equalization. State promulgated guides or schedules are the usual valuation reference for the assessor.

In a Florida case, Weyerhaeuser was successful in reducing a forest land assessment from $9.7 to $6.3 million because the assessor substituted his judgment for Department of Revenue schedules in valuing 54,000 acres.[43] The state guidelines are presumed correct unless the assessor can show his rates are better.[44]

Standing timber should be valued at its market value on assessment day. Taxpayer's bid and subsequent sale price was much higher than market value on assessment day. The Board favored using average prices paid for standing timber for two months on either side of assessment day to establish a true value.[45]

These cases illustrate that the alert taxpayer can challenge unreasonable action by the assessor and win assessment reductions.

---

[43]*Weyerhaeuser Company v. Del Pettit, Assessor,* Board of Tax Appeals Docket Nos. 5835 and 5460 (1973).

[44]*Container Corporation of America, et al., v. Rutherford, Etc., et al.,* 293 So. 2d 379 (1974).

[45]*Fort Vancouver Plywood Company, et al., v. Assessors of Colwitz and Jefferson Counties,* Washington Board of Tax Appeals Dockets #1102, # 971 and #972 (1971).

5
How to Properly Prepare Residential Assessment Appeals In Order to Achieve Substantial Reductions at Minimum Cost

5

Residential taxpayers are mad! They are tax revolt/Proposition 13 mad! They are getting property tax limitation and circuit breaker legislation passed. They are refusing to vote for tax increases for public education, causing schools to shut down.

They are being ordained en masse as ministers in Hardenburg, New York. By using this mail order church method, they can declare their homes church property and evade the tax.

In Bucks County, Pennsylvania, they are even madder. A crowd of mostly middle-aged and elderly residents threatened county commissioners with tarring and feathering after a property tax increase of 126% was proposed.

But, a word of caution is necessary here. As an advisor to a residential property taxpayer, you must be sure of what he is mad at. One taxpayer bought his house 15 years ago for $50,000 and paid a property tax of $800. It was assessed in the mid-1960's at a market value of $65,560 and the taxes in 1976 were $2,238. In 1977, the assessment rose to $157,900 with an indicated tax of $5,180.

The taxpayer, who had hoped to live in his house all his life, posted signs on the lawn: "For Sale Soon Thanks to Big Spenders."

What is important is that the taxpayer says: "I don't argue with the *assessment*; it's the big spenders who caused this."[1]

The taxpayer is saying that the $157,900 assessment is realistic. It indicates the fair market value of the residence. He is mad at the tax rate which is levied against that assessment. Thus, he is not arguing value; he is arguing tax dollars.

This is not to say that residential assessments are never excessive. The point made here is that you must establish at the outset just who the residential taxpayer is mad at. Is he mad at the assessor because the assessment is too high? Or is he mad at the municipal supervisors and school board who establish the jurisdiction's budget and spend his tax dollars?

The remainder of this chapter is designed to assist you in advising the taxpayer who is mad because his assessment is too high.

If he is a taxpayer who is mad because his tax rate is too high, his remedy lies elsewhere. You should advise him to direct his attention to:

- attending municipal and school board budget meetings.
- writing his legislators.
- joining a tax group whose goals are tax reform.

PRELIMINARY CONSIDERATIONS

Before considering the equitableness of a residential taxpayer's assessment, be sure that he is taking advantage of exemptions he is entitled to.

[1] *The Wall Street Journal,* September 7, 1977, at pg. 1, column 1.

Homeowners' Exemptions

As stated in Chapter 12 on exemptions, the purpose of this benefit is to preserve owner-occupied residential property. Apparently the idea is working pretty well because almost two out of every three American families own their own homes.

Florida, for example, provides a general homestead exemption of $5,000 for all homeowners.

The homeowner's exemption is created by statute and the benefit will not always extend itself as one might logically conclude. In Georgia, the homestead exemption was *not* granted to occupants of cooperatives. The thinking of the court centered on the cooperative's landlord-tenant relationship which imposed certain restrictions on the buyer. The Georgia constitution granted the exemption to *owners* of property only, and the court would not extend the exemption beyond that unrestricted definition.[2]

Circuit Breaker Relief

Many states have enacted circuit breaker legislation.[3] The qualified taxpayer's tax load is cut off or reduced when his property tax becomes too high a percentage of the family's household income.

The statutes generally provide that if the taxpayer is over a certain age (say 62), and his income did not exceed a certain amount (say $10,000) in the preceding year, he may qualify for circuit breaker relief.

Veteran's Exemption

A residential taxpayer may qualify for a veteran's exemption. This usually means that if he served in the armed forces during a particular period, he is entitled to a reduction in his property tax bill.

Classification

It is possible that residential property can be classified incorrectly. For example, if the residence is 30 miles from a lake, there may be no reason for it to be classified *recreational* which results in a higher assessment.[4]

You may find that your client's home is located in an area designed as a *flood plain*. Perhaps the assessor gives special treatment to land values so designated. Be sure to test this or any similar classification benefit.

But be reasonable. A home in a city used only for weekend gardening and relaxation did not qualify for seasonal residential recreational classification in Minnesota. The dissent said it should be based on use. The majority held that the legislature did not intend all part-time residents to get a tax break.[5]

Classification benefits may also be dictated by the use of the property. If the land is used for farming or horticulture, it may be entitled to *Agricultural Act Benefits*.

---

[2] *Brandywine Townhouses, Inc., et al v. Joint City-County Board of Tax Assessors,* 231 Ga. 585, 203 S.E. 2d 222 (1974).

[3] See Ronald E. Gettel, *You Can Get Your Real Estate Taxes Reduced,* McGraw-Hill Book Company, New York, 1977, for a summary of relief and exemption statutes.

[4] Harry Rogers, *Home Owner's Way to Lower Taxes,* Self-Help Publications, Carmel, Cal., 1975, page 8.

[5] *Lilja v. County of Wright,* 307 Minn. 276, 239 N.W. 2d 465 (1976).

Twenty miles west of Boston, a taxpayer lives on and farms 16 acres of land on Route 2A in Acton. The assessment held for many years at $26,000 with taxes of $1,600 per year. A recent revaluation (Court ordered to 100%) increased the assessment to $600,000 and the annual taxes to $15,000.

There were simply not enough pumpkins and butternut squash to pay the taxes. Taxpayers appealed to the Acton Board of Assessors who reclassified the land from business to farming under the Agricultural and Horticultural Act.

This brought the tax back down to the original level. If, however, the use of the land should change, so will the tax. The higher tax would be levied retroactively for four years.[6]

Damage Relief

If a home was damaged by flood, fire, windstorm, or some other natural calamity, it may be entitled to property tax relief.

For example, in California, property tax relief was granted to taxpayers whose property was damaged by earthquake.

But not all jurisdictions are so kind. In Massachusetts, assessments are fixed on January 1. On January 14th, taxpayer's home was damaged by fire. By September, repairs were completed. The Court would not consider the temporary reduction in value as a basis for reducing the assessment.[7]

Solar Energy Deduction

A home may be entitled to an assessment deduction if it is equipped with a solar energy heating and cooling system. Indiana and New Hampshire provide such exemptions.

Highest and Best Use

There may be a basis for a reduction if the property is not being used at its highest and best use. Taxpayer's valuation experts argued that the subject property, a home near the University of Oregon campus, should be an eight-apartment multiple dwelling unit. The Court agreed that the home did not add value to the land and reduced the assessment from $26,430 to $20,000.[8]

Partially Complete Homes, Additions and Improvements

Check with the assessor to see how he treats these various categories of property condition in his assessment procedures. When, for example, does a new home go on the assessment roll? Is it recorded in its incomplete stage or does it first go on after occupancy?

Tennessee law required that improvements were completed when occupied or sold. Incomplete improvements were to be assessed as personal property based on the market value of the materials used.[9]

Similarly, in San Francisco items such as new furnace, ceiling, floor surface, roof, fire escape, fence and several other items will not increase a home assessment. A combination of

---

[6] *The Boston Herald American*, December 15, 1977 at 30, Column 1. See Chapter 4 for comment on a similar statute in the transitional land and roll-back taxes section. *Massachusetts General Law, Ann.*, Ch. 61A Sect. 3 (1932), amended 1975.

[7] *Sarris v. Board of Assessors of Swampscott*, 315 N.E. 2d 892 (1974).

[8] *Agate v. Department of Revenue*, 5 Oregon Tax Court 25 (1972).

[9] *State ex rel. Russell v. LaManna*, 498 S.W. 2d 891 (1973).

these items may, but in general the assessment will not be affected by these additions and improvements. You should consult with the assessor to see if he has a similar program in the jurisdiction where the subject residence is located.

Is a "Mobile Home" Real Estate Subject to a Property Tax?

There are basic statutes in your state that define real estate. See Chapter 12 for a detailed discussion of the difference between real and personal property. Courts generally look at how an item is annexed to the realty (will the item be damaged if it is removed?); the intention of the party (was it intended that the item remain permanently?); and the adaptation of the item to the land (is it intimately intertwined with the primary use of the land?).

In the case of a houseboat, the New York Board of Equalization reviewed the above factors and called the houseboat realty. An analogy was made to lunch wagons and mobile homes. Great attention was given to the permanency of utility connections.[10]

Mobile homes have become a major part of residential housing in the United States. Between five and six million Americans live in mobile homes of all types. Many are firmly rooted in glorified trailer parks with swimming pools, laundries, stores and utility hookups. They are taxed as vehicles or personal property in several states. They have also been held to be real estate or housing by assessors on the search for additional ratables against which to levy a real property tax.

A former Los Angeles County assessor said: "If it looks, walks and quacks like a duck then it should be assessed like a duck."

The situation can get tricky. For example, the landowner of a mobile home park paid real estate taxes on the land and the cement slab foundations for the mobile homes. The assessor tried to increase the assessments to reflect accessories owned by tenants, such as carports and patio covers. Colorado, however, has a graduated annual specific ownership tax on mobile homes and the assessor had no right to levy on the accessories which are part of the mobile home.[11]

Thus, we see that mobile homes may be subject to forms of taxation other than the real property tax.

In Illinois, for example, there is a 15¢ per square foot privilege tax and mobile homes on permanent foundations do not have to pay a real estate tax.[12]

In Ohio, there is a mobile home tax (which is not a real property tax) and the mobile home was not entitled to a homestead exemption. The taxpayer did not stop there, however. He argued that the statute said a homestead was a dwelling occupied as a home, including the land around it. The Ohio Attorney General agreed that the statute did not require the dwelling to be taxed as real estate and granted the homestead exemption to the land.[13]

A Massachusetts taxpayer was not as lucky. A prefabricated home was moved along a highway to a mobile home park. It was classified as a permanent conventional home and did not qualify for an exemption as movable living quarters.[14]

Procedure

Don't expect any help from the assessor. You must see to it that the residential taxpayer takes advantage of an exemption or other relief he is entitled to.

---

[10]5 Op. Counsel State Board of Equalization and Assessment, No. 27 (1975).

[11]*M.H.C. Realty Corporation v. Board of County Commissioners,* 31 Colo. 564, 506 P. 2d 762 (1973).

[12]*Berry v. Costello,* 62 Ill. 2d 342, 341 N.E. 2d 709 (1976).

[13]State of Ohio, Attorney General Opinion, No. 73-003 (1973).

[14]*Ellis et al. v. Board of Assessors of Acushnet,* 265 N.E. 2d 491 (1970).

Visit the local assessor's office and ask questions. Pick up any printed material explaining the exemptions, benefits, or classification requirements.

If the taxpayer qualifies, certain procedural steps are necessary to perfect his rights. Usually a specific form must be filed with the assessor on or before a fixed date.

Be sure to comply with all filing procedures.

And don't forget to check that proper credit or adjustment is reflected on the tax bill. There are breakdowns in communication between the assessor and the tax collector. Be sure that the benefit was conveyed to the collector for incorporation into the tax bill because the tax bill is the bottom line.

ASSEMBLING PERTINENT DATA

Tax Bill

Become familiar with the information set forth on the tax bill. This usually includes identification of property and owner, assessment (sometimes market value), tax rate, taxes and payment dates.

Purchase Price in Recent Sales Contract

If the home was recently purchased, the contract of sale should be reviewed. This is important evidence regarding the market value of the home. If the assessor's market value is greatly in excess of the purchase price, there may be a very good case. The assessor will argue that values have increased since the purchase date. If that argument can be offset, a reduction can be attained.

If the purchase price included items of personal property, be sure that this can be documented with the contract of sale or some other formal record. The statement that your client paid $2,500 for personal property will not be enough for a Board or Court to rely on.[15]

Survey

See if there is a survey of the lot and the structure. If there have been no additions since the survey was made, it will be a good point of reference regarding measurements.

Important Dates

Establish the calendar of events early to avoid last-minute rush decisions. Try to leave plenty of time to investigate the equitableness of the assessment. Most assessment appeals must be filed in writing by a specific date. If you do not meet the deadline, you must wait another year to appeal.

Call the assessor's office and ask about the appeal date deadlines. Allow for at least 30 days of preparation to ready the case.

Investigation at the Assessor's Office

As a first step in the investigation you should ask to see the assessor's *property record card* pertaining to the property.

It should identify the property and owner. It should correspond to the details of the tax bill.

---

[15]*Appeal of King County Assessor,* Washington Board of Tax Appeals, Docket 13763 (1976).

The land value computations should be examined. Has the lot been measured properly? The property record card usually shows frontage and depth measurements with a unit value, say $50 per front foot. A depth factor may also be considered here. If all similar lots are 100′ deep and the subject is 110′ deep, the depth factor would be +10%. Thus the calculation:

Frontage	Depth	Unit Value	Deoth Factor	Actual Value	True Cash Value
50	110	50	110%	55	2,750

The property record card may also show conversion from true cash value to assessed value. Be sure the proper equalization rate was applied and doublecheck the mathematics.

See Chapter 2 for sources of equalization rates.

You may also come across a *building permit record entry*. Be sure that the data entered there is correct.

On the reverse side of the card you can usually find the details of the assessor's cost approach. Be sure all entries reflect what is actually on the property. Is there a full basement? Attic? Garage? Check to see that the drawing truly depicts the building.

The unit costs come from the assessor's manual which may be State promulgated. You should ask to have certain of the entries explained to you and you should request that the source of these entries be identified. Try to get a copy of the pertinent sections of the manual to see if a lower cost factor could have been applied to the home.

For example, the source of a unit price of $21 per square foot for the basic dwelling should be shown to you so that you can compare the structural details in the manual to the subject home.

Remember, the assessor will be able to show you his source with little or no problem. The trick is to see if he had other options in applying that amount.

While you are reviewing your property record card, ask if you can see those of neighborhood homes that you feel are comparable to the subject. Check and compare the entries on the cards to see if any of the properties have received different treatment. If so, find out why.

Pick up copies of the appropriate appeal forms. Look them over and ask any questions you might have about properly completing the form. Be sure to verify the filing date deadline to permit enough time for preparation of the case.

PREPARING FOR A NEGOTIATING SESSION WITH THE ASSESSOR

Basic Strategy

Contrary to popular belief, the assessor, his staff, or the revaluation firm do a conscientious job in valuing residential property. There is logical reasoning behind their decisions and they are able to support those decisions with back-up material that must stand up before a Board or Court.

In addition, they have heard questions and arguments on residential assessments hundreds or even thousands of times before. They will have two or three very reasonable answers for each question. You will be at a disadvantage because you will probably be hearing their questions and answers for the first time.

Therefore, your job of preparation is twofold: (1) You must prepare a set of questions critiquing the assessor's valuation approach and you must anticipate his answers. (2) At the same time, you must prepare yourself to answer the questions he will ask you.

Land Value Issue

The assessor's property record card indicated his opinion of land value at a basic unit price of $50 per front foot. In order to counter this argument, it is necessary to develop a valuation position based on sales prices of comparable land.

Perhaps a nearby lot sold recently or is for sale. Check on the sale or asking price and divide by the front footage (allow for any depth differences) to see how the land assessment stands up.

If there are no such lots nearby, ask local real estate brokers where residential land is selling within a reasonable distance from the subject—and for what front foot price.

Examination of several nearby land sales and offerings may indicate that the assessor's front foot value cannot be substantiated. The assessor should be able to explain why he did not use these sales, or if he did use them, how they are reflected in his value conclusion.

The assessor will say something like: "Land prices have multiplied six times in the past twenty years and now account for an unprecedented 25% of builders' costs. In Dade County, for example, a 100 × 75 foot lot that sold for $3,500 ten years ago now sells for over $20,000." He will then be quick to show you the comparable land sales that he relied on.

This will usually bring the issue to a standstill. Decide who has the better comparables and weigh this in the decision to appeal further.

And you can win. In one case, the taxpayer introduced comparable land sales which were less than half the value per acre used by the assessor. The court found these comparables relevant and the assessment was corrected accordingly.[16]

Cost Approach Issue

The property record card shows the assessor's cost approach. The primary judgment factor here is his unit price of $21 per square foot.

Any cost manual will show a residential cost range as follows:

Excellent, best brick, special fixtures, air conditioning	$37.45/square foot
Good, brick, good lighting and outlets, forced air	24.32/square foot
Average, brick, drywall, forced air	20.10/square foot
Low cost, block, drywall, minimal lighting, wall furnace	16.06/square foot[17]

There are many variables and all involve judgment as to cost.

If research shows the assessor's costs to be high, try to use data from his assessor's manual to show costs that are more applicable to the subject residence.

The assessor will say something like this: "In 1950, the typical new house was only 894

[16]*Louise S. Bookstaver v. Town of Westminster,* 131 Vt. 133, 300 A. 2d 891 (1973).

[17]*Marshall Valuation Service,* Section 12, page 9, July 1977, Marshall & Swift Publication Co., Los Angeles, Calif. See also *Boeckh Building Valuation Manual,* Volume 1, Residential and Agricultural, American Appraisal Company, Milwaukee, Wisconsin.

square feet. Now a new house has 1,590 square feet. Half of today's new homes have central air conditioning, up from a little more than one-third in 1971.

"Builders pay as much as $400 for 1,000 feet of lumber that cost $100 ten years ago. The price of cement has risen about 60% over the past five years, in part because it is dried in kilns that require costly energy. Labor charges in building are $12.20 an hour.

"Ten years ago, many builders paid only 5% or 6% on construction loans. Now they are charged 9% to 9½%. Mortgage rates average around 9% nationwide vs. about 5½% a dozen years ago. This is a 65% rise and when stretched out over the 360 monthly payments made in 30 years, it adds $23,000 to the cost of paying off a $30,000 mortgage.

"Builders claim that zoning restrictions and other minutely detailed regulations, mostly local, can increase builders' costs to 20% of a $50,000 house.

"With all of these increased costs of construction, how can I use less than $21 per square foot on this house?"

Market Data Issue

If it can be shown that several similar homes have sold at a price below the subject assessment, you have a very good case. Again, a local realtor is a primary source of this information.

If the assessor can show you several sales of similar homes at prices higher than the subject assessment, he has a very good case.

He will usually say something like this: "There is an enormous amount of market data available on residential properties. Some three million existing single-family homes change hands annually at an average sale price for used housing in the area of $40,000.[18]

"The Federal Home Loan Bank Board reported that the average price of a new home bought with a conventional mortgage was now slightly in excess of $50,000. Ten years ago, the average price was $30,000.[19] In southern California and other urban areas, the average price is $75,000. Some 1.45 million single-family homes were built in 1977.[20]

"In pleasant, but by no means luxurious, residential areas in the northeast, midwest and west, $50,000 to $60,000 houses are almost non-existent. $75,000 to $80,000 and up are standard.

"In mid-'77, average prices were:

Chicago	—	$62,100
Washington, D.C.	—	$67,700
Los Angeles	—	$72,100[21]

"In view of these prices, how can I possibly reduce your assessment?"

If your comparables are better than his, you should get a reduction, but it is not easy. The comparables must be similar to the subject, and require little adjustment. One court held that comparable sales requiring 20% adjustments were meaningless.[22]

The adjustments involve judgment concerning the impact on sales price of size, shape, extras, time and location.

Location is, of course, of utmost importance. A private street or cul de sac is more conducive to peaceful home ownership than is a home on a heavily trafficked road or

---

[18]*The Wall Street Journal,* April 5, 1976 at page 1, column 6, citing the National Association of Realtors.

[19]*The New York Times,* October 24, 1976 at page 39.

[20]*Ibid.,* December 4, 1977, Section 3, Business and Finance at page 1, column 5.

[21]*Time* magazine, September 12, 1977, "Housing: It's Outa Sight," at page 50.

[22]*Wunschel v. Board of Review,* 217 N.W. 2d 576 (1974).

freeway. But you cannot expect to obtain a reduction by simply walking into the assessor's office and telling him or the Board of Review that the subject residence is 400 yards from a freeway toll plaza.[23] You must document the effect that this condition has on value. You must show that comparable sales prove your point because the toll plaza homes sell at less per square foot than the cul de sac homes.

Comparison to Other Assessments

The subject assessment is the only one at issue, so it is not technically correct to bring in other individual assessments.

In one interesting case the taxpayer introduced the assessments of the mayor and a councilman to show that he was receiving unfair treatment. As a result, the mayor and councilman had their assessments increased! However, the taxpayer did *not* get a reduction! He did not satisfy the burden of proof in Minnesota by showing that his assessment was inequitable due to a systematic, arbitrary, or intentional undervaluation scheme on the part of the assessor.[24]

Similarly, a group of taxpayers got together and alleged lack of uniformity in their assessments, all of which were in the same subdivision. Again, a Maryland court required the taxpayers to prove a systematic, intentional, arbitrary and fraudulent procedure on the part of the assessor. The assessment of one parcel at a lower portion of value than another parcel was not enough. And mere errors in judgment on the part of the assessor were not enough either.[25]

The issue is the market value of the *subject* property.

MEETING WITH THE ASSESSOR

Now that you are properly prepared and you have anticipated what the assessor will say, you should arrange for an informal conference with the assessor or his representative. See Chapter 14 for detailed coverage of initial negotiations.

Eight Questions Most Often Asked by the Assessor

1. Would your client be willing to sell his house for the market value indicated by the assessment?
2. What did he pay for the property and when did he buy it?
3. What was the original amount of the mortgage?
4. What is the home insured for?
5. Have any recent improvements been made to the house? When and how much did they cost? Who was the contractor?
6. Are you familiar with such-and-such house in the neighborhood? Are you aware that it just sold for $$$? Do you think it is reasonably comparable to the subject home?
7. Are any rooms rented out in the house? For how much annual rent?
8. Have any parcels of land been sold lately (off the home tract)? When and for how much?

You should pursue the line of questioning developed during your investigation at the assessor's office. If no compromise can be reached, you must seriously consider appealing the assessment to the Board of Review.

---

[23] *Appeal of King County Assessor,* Board of Tax Appeals, Docket No. 14025 (1977).

[24] *Ploetz v. County of Hennepin,* 301 Minn. 410, 223 N.W. 2d 761 (1974).

[25] *Hilland et al. v. Montgomery County,* Nos. 345-349, Maryland Tax Court (1972).

Application for Assessment Review

The protest form usually requires the appropriate identification of the property, the submission of an opinion of value vs. that of the assessor, the raising of the overvaluation and equalization issues, and signature and notarization. See Chapter 15 for in-depth comments on the application for assessment review.

A RESIDENTIAL ASSESSMENT APPEAL

Presenting a Case to a Board of Review

In general, the property is identified and the assessor indicates his opinion of value. There is a presumption that he is correct and the burden of proof is on the taxpayer to present evidence to show why the assessment is excessive. At this point, the taxpayer must go forward and present valuation arguments.

If possible, try to attend some of these public hearings beforehand to get a feel for what goes on and what the procedures are.

I have witnessed many hundreds of residential appeals and I have never known a Board to give a residential taxpayer a particularly hard time. They are usually attentive and accommodating, receptive and understanding. This does not always mean the taxpayer will get a reduction, but they will certainly give him his "day in court."

The assessor should respond to your evidence in your presence and in the presence of the Board. It is improper for the Board to go into closed session where the assessor may criticize your comparables. In Wisconsin, at least, it is improper for an administrative agency to base its decision on evidence obtained without notice to or in the presence of the interested party.[26]

When the assessor begins introducing his comparables, ask to see the data he is relying on. There should be a photograph, a location map, an indication of size and type of construction.

And the Board can't simply get away with saying they "relied on comparables." In at least one case, a court said that the Board has an affirmative duty to make specific findings concerning values of comparables.[27] The Board must address itself to the comparability of the market data that is introduced by the assessor.

You may be surprised to receive a decision right on the spot, or the Board may withhold judgment until they have an opportunity to deliberate and issue a written opinion.

It is important that you obtain the appropriate set of local rules and regulations so that you are sure to comply with all the prerequisites in properly presenting an appeal to a Board of Review. See Chapter 15 for examples of informal and formal Board of Review hearings.

Appeal to Court

If you are not successful before the Board of Review, and your case is strong enough, you can appeal to the courts. One taxpayer went all the way to the Oregon Tax Court. He purchased his home for $36,000. The following year it was assessed at $41,230. Taxpayer argued a $36,500 value. An appeal to the Board of Equalization reduced the assessment to

---

[26] *Dolphin v. Board of Review,* 70 Wis. 2d 403, 234 N.W. 2d 277 (1975).

[27] *Schweizer v. Town of Pomfret,* 134 Vt. 436, 365 A. 2d 134 (1976).

$39,850. This figure was affirmed by the court.[28] Although the taxpayer did not receive a further reduction on his appeal to court, he had the satisfaction of knowing that he pursued the matter as far as he could.

It is not easy. If you fail to adequately compare properties and offer no evidence to support allegations of excessive assessments, you will not prevail. So held the Iowa Supreme Court.[29]

Class Action

If several neighbors are upset about their assessments, a class action suit may be organized. This involves a group of complainants with generally the same condition or mutual interest in a given legal circumstance.

This may be very beneficial to all because it can defray expenses for legal and appraisal services over a large group of individuals.[30]

See Chapter 16 for more on appeal to Court.

Is There a Possibility of an Assessment Increase? Yes!

Although it usually doesn't happen, there is a chance that as a result of an appeal, the assessment will be increased. This is the point I made at the beginning of this chapter. Be sure you know what your client is mad at. If he does not have a case regarding the value of the property, then you should *not* appeal. If an error on this basic issue is made, you could find that the appeal effort has resulted in an increased assessment.

[28]*Price v. Department of Revenue,* 7 Oregon Tax Court 18 (1977).
[29]*Power v. Regis,* 220 N.W. 2d 587 (1974).
[30]*People ex rel. Thompson v. Property Tax Appeal Board,* 22 Ill. App. 3d 316, 317 N.E. 2d 121 (1974).

6

Strategy and Techniques in Successful Assessment Appeals of Downtown Retail And Department Store, Free-Standing and Discount Houses, and Shopping Centers

6

The opportunity for assessment reduction on retail property varies with the location and type of stores you are dealing with. The wide use of the automobile after WWII began the population movement to the suburbs. The shopping center soon developed to meet the retail needs of these new areas.

Fresh and modern designed shopping centers became instant competition for the older retail outlets in the downtown central business district (CBD). Ease of traffic access and unlimited free parking won out over traffic congestion and inadequate parking. Urban retail decline set in. Sales volume fell off and retail real estate values fell accordingly.

Downward assessment adjustments did not follow as quickly as the value decline. The assessor had to protect his core of ratables and, in general, refused to recognize this economic obsolescence. The major retail chains, as well as local store owners, challenged these assessments and, to date, are continually winning substantial assessment reductions.

The discount house materialized to compete with both the CBD and the shopping center. This market was soon saturated, resulting in an excess of discount operations, declining sales volumes, lower rentals, and lower real estate values—all good grounds for assessment appeal.

To come full cycle, we find the older shopping centers now being challenged by the more modern regional enclosed mall centers. The decline in business and property value which plagues the downtown CBD now challenges the continued economic existence of many of our older shopping centers. Again, grounds for assessment appeal.

ASSEMBLING PERTINENT DATA

In order to begin your review of a retail real estate assessment, you will need a copy of the *tax bill*. This identifies the property and sets forth the assessment. You will then have to make a determination as to the local *ratio or equalization rate* to establish the relationship between the assessed value and the assessor's opinion of fair market value. You should also review the assessor's *property record cards* in order to understand his basis for value. (See Chapter 2 for detailed treatment of these items.)

The next item to look at is the *land*. How much is there? When was it purchased and for how much? Is it adequate to your needs? Shopping centers, for example, need land which is four times the building area in order to provide adequate parking. What is comparable land selling for?

Location is most important. Is there accesss to main arteries? Is there good egress and ingress?

What is the type and style of *construction*? Is it modern or outdated? When was the structure built and at what cost? What is the extent of depreciation? What would it cost today to build? What is the square footage of the building? How much of that is sales area? Is there a mezzanine?

Is the property leased? What is the rental and terms of the lease? You should obtain a *copy of the lease*. What are other similar properties renting for today? By sampling current similar rentals, you can determine *economic rent* which may be different from your *contract rent*.

Another method of determining economic rent is to ascertain what percentage of sales volume is ordinarily paid in rent in your industry. There are sources available to give you this information in addition to your own experience.[1] Assume your contract rent calls for $50,000 in annual rent for twenty years and the lease was negotiated in 1970. At that time, your sales were $1 million and the industry median of rent as a percentage of sales was 5%. But, six years later, due to adverse economic trends, your sales had fallen to 50% of what they once were or $500,000 per year. Since the rent percentage factor had remained the same, you could only afford to pay $25,000. It can be argued that this is your economic rent. Several major assessing jurisdictions will consider this argument as valid.

The purpose in developing this economic rent is, of course, to capitalize it into value. The contrast is striking and simply recognizes economic obsolescence which would influence a potential purchaser with regard to what he would be willing to pay for the property.

$50,000 contract rent capitalized @ 12% =	$416,666
$25,000 economic rent capitalized @ 12% =	$208,333

The assessor will, of course, argue that the purchaser is buying a lease or an annuity since there are still several years to run on the lease. The basic rule in assessing, however, is uniformity. Uniform assessments cannot be levied on the basis of the negotiating abilities of real estate agents who created this lease a number of years ago.

If your figures accurately reflect economic rent, they should be the basis for the assessment from the income point of view.

In the case of a shopping center, you must review three-to-five-year *operating statements* and the entire *rent roll*. This will show the true strength of the center. If it has strong AAA anchor tenants and healthy long-term leases, the center is strong economically. If anchor tenants are not AAA and leases are short term, you may soon find vacancies, reduced rentals, and a decline in the value of this real estate. Certainly the assessor should be told about this situation.

Finally, *arm's-length sales* transactions in the open market should also be reviewed. This would give a value indication from the comparable sales point of view.

The following examples will illustrate the above comments.

HOW TO USE ECONOMIC OBSOLESCENCE, ECONOMIC RENT, AND COMPARABLE SALES TO WIN DOWNTOWN RETAIL STORE ASSESSMENT APPEALS

One of the most important ingredients of a successful real estate assessment appeal is the attitude of the taxpayer. If a taxpayer has a case, he must be willing to pursue the matter into the courts in order to correct the overassessment. The idea of not going to court because of the time and expense involved, should, of course, be weighed against the potential tax savings attainable. But the taxpayer must be willing to seek his relief beyond the assessor, beyond the Board of Review at the local and state levels, into the courts, and to see the issue through to the highest court in the state, if necessary, to achieve his result. And, along the way, the taxpayer may be required to "make some law."

---

[1]See for example, *Percentage Leases*, National Institute of Real Estate Brokers, Chicago, Illinois, and *Dollars & Cents of Shopping Centers*, 1978, The Urban Land Institute, Washington, D.C.

I was involved in just such a case in the good State of North Carolina. The appraisal assignment was to establish the fair market value of a typical downtown F. W. Woolworth store.

Example #1: Pertinent Data

The two-story and basement store was located in the Central Business District (CBD) of Winston-Salem. It had 14,900 square feet of first floor retail area. The second floor of 9,000 square feet was vacant and not in use. The basement was partially used for storage. Approximately one-third of the CBD retail space was vacant. Four major shopping centers had opened to the north, south, east and west, resulting in a severe decline in CBD retail business. Subject store's sales were off 20% when compared to the period prior to the opening of the shopping centers. CBD parking was limited.

The lease was for $42,500/year fully net requiring Woolworth to pay the real estate taxes. The lease began in 1955 and ran for 40 years through 1996.

The Forsyth County Assessor used a cost approach and capitalized the contract rent to arrive at his fair market value of $479,560.

Fact Situation: Standard CBD Problem

This statement of facts is a typical example of a downtown retail store assessment problem: vacant second floor space was not able to be leased; many vacant stores in the CBD; shopping centers draining pedestrian traffic; sales volume decline and lack of parking; a long-term net lease negotiated prior to the impact of shopping centers on the CBD was realized; and a property tax assessment which did not consider these facts of economic obsolescence.

Appeal Procedure

The first step was to meet with the local assessor to acquaint him with the fact situation and to request an assessment reduction. He refused to budge from his cost approach/contract rent position. The matter was appealed to the Forsyth County Board of Equalization and Review where the assessor's market value of $479,560 was confirmed.

This decision was appealed to the North Carolina State Department of Assessment. That body recognized that CBD economic obsolescence resulted in an economic rent for subject property below the contract rent and granted a 14% reduction to $411,690. The County appealed the decision to Superior Court, arguing that there was no precedent in North Carolina law for such a decision. The Superior Court upheld the State Board's reduction. The County appealed to the Supreme Court, the highest court in North Carolina.

Cost and Contract Rent vs. Economic Rent

Justice I. Beverly Lake wrote the decision and held that the State Board reduction was well founded on the evidence presented by Woolworth. The Board was correct in taking notice of judicially cognizable facts and it is a "matter of common knowledge" that in recent years (this was a 1972 decision) downtown metropolitan areas have suffered severely from shopping center competition. In addition, the County's argument that the cost approach should prevail because 90,000 other properties were valued by the same method in the recent revaluation is erroneous. The County should have considered economic rent based on current comparable rentals in the CBD. The economic rent presented by Woolworth of $28,500 was developed in that way and it was a valid reference for the State Board to use.

Thus, the State Board reduction was upheld by the highest Court in North Carolina and some "new law" was made: the Court took judicial notice of the plight of the CBD suffering from shopping center competition; reliance on the cost approach by the assessor was error; and the assessor should have considered economic rent with regard to the income producing capacity of the subject property in setting Woolworth's assessment.[2]

Example #2: Pertinent Data

In another actual case involving a similar downtown retail store property tax appeal in a northeastern city, the assessor relied on an annuity capitalization of the contract rent to support his assessment. I submitted appraisal data on comparable rentals and sales to support the taxpayer's position.

The property involved in this appeal was a three-story and basement structure with 8,000 square feet of ground floor area for retail sales on the main street in the CBD. Again, the basement was only partially used for storage and the upper two floors were completely vacant and not in use. Shopping centers on the outskirts of the city limits had drawn pedestrian traffic away from downtown. In addition, a new enclosed-mall downtown shopping plaza/office building/hotel complex opened about two blocks north of the subject property. The result of this was to move the 100% prime shopping area of the CBD from in front of the subject property to the enclosed mall two blocks north.

The property was leased by an AAA national variety retail chain in 1930 for 50 years through 1980 on a net basis for $60,000 per year. In 1953, due to declining sales volume and severe losses, the variety store was closed and the property was sublet to two subtenants for $44,000 on a gross basis. This meant that the original AAA tenant taxpayer paid $60,000 per year in rent plus $40,000 per year in real estate taxes. He only received $44,000 per year in subtenant rental income for an annual loss of $56,000. And this would go on until 1980!

The assessor carried the property on the assessment rolls at a fair market value of $900,000. The taxpayer argued that the property was worth $300,000.

After negotiations with the local assessor and an appeal to the local Board of Review failed to result in anything other than a token reduction offer, the matter was appealed into the courts and a special referee was appointed to hear the case.

Economic Rent and Comparable Sales vs. Annuity Capitalization of Contract Rent

Taxpayer presented the 1953 sublease as an indication of economic rent. Additional current rentals from nearby and adjacent stores were also introduced. Taxpayer also introduced arm's-length sales of similar type retail store buildings on either side of the subject store. All of these items supported taxpayer's value of $300,000.

The assessor presented land sales on which 26- and 30-story office buildings were to be constructed by a local bank and a local trust company. Leases from the enclosed downtown mall were also submitted as indications of current rentals supporting the use of the subject's original contract rent as its economic rent.

The downtown street presented in Figure 6-1 plan shows the locations of the various comparables relied on by taxpayer (left side of street) and assessor (right side of street). Note especially the close proximity of taxpayer's comparables to subject.

---

[2]*In re Property in Forsyth County,* 191 S.E. 2d 692 (1972).

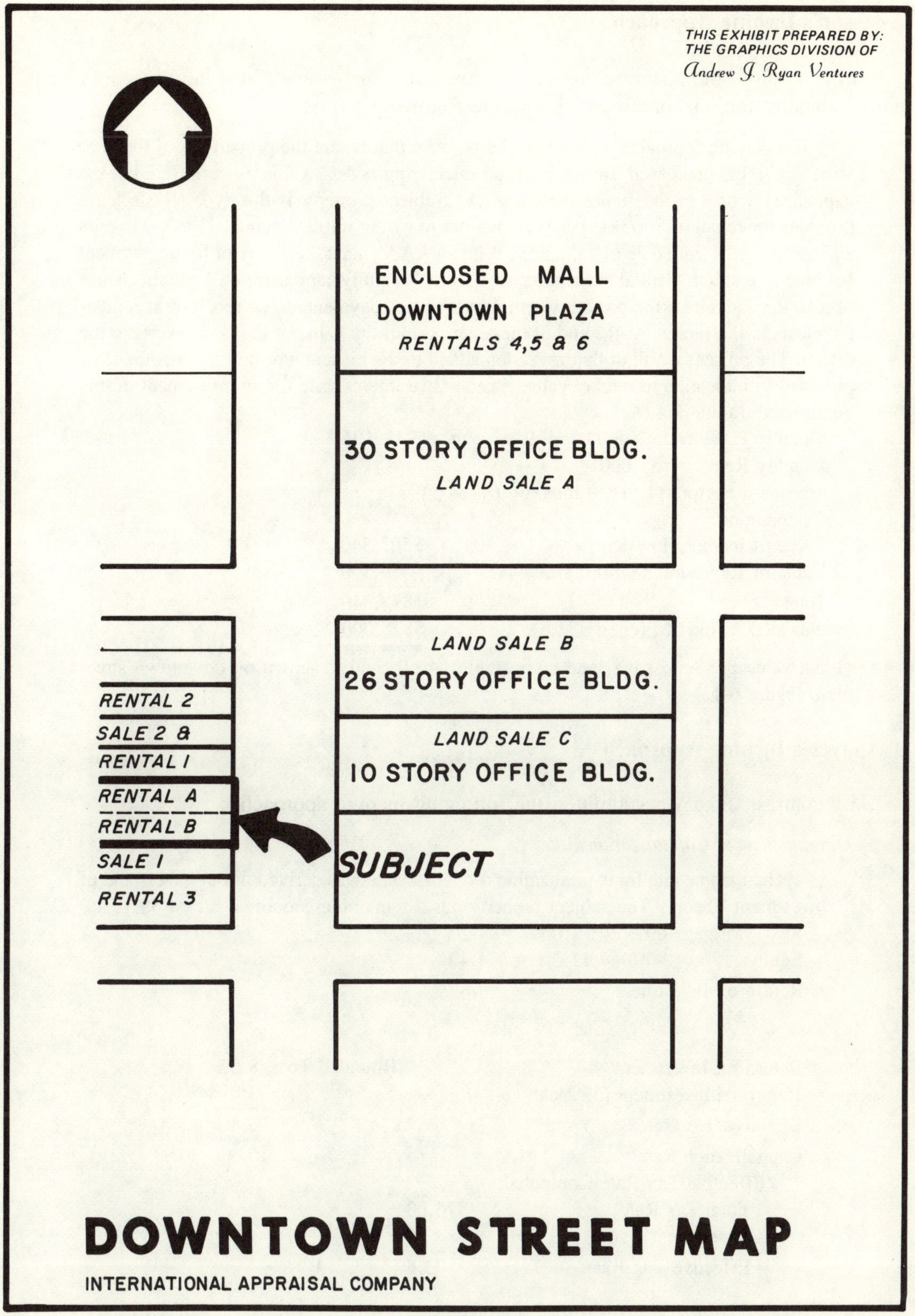
THIS EXHIBIT PREPARED BY:
THE GRAPHICS DIVISION OF
Andrew J. Ryan Ventures
ENCLOSED MALL
DOWNTOWN PLAZA
RENTALS 4,5 & 6
30 STORY OFFICE BLDG.
LAND SALE A
LAND SALE B
26 STORY OFFICE BLDG.
LAND SALE C
10 STORY OFFICE BLDG.
RENTAL 2
SALE 2 &
RENTAL 1
RENTAL A
RENTAL B
SALE 1
RENTAL 3
SUBJECT
DOWNTOWN STREET MAP
INTERNATIONAL APPRAISAL COMPANY

FIGURE 6-1

Assessor's Income Approach

In addition to the above referenced comparables, the assessor also introduced an "annuity capitalization" income approach in the following terms:

> The income approach is based on the premise that where the property is of the type which will be purchased for income producing purposes, value is reflected by the capitalized worth of the future income flow. Subject property is this type. Basic lease provides for rental of $60,000 per year, net-net to owner until March 31, 1980, 11 years and nine months from date of valuation. With an AAA tenant, certainty of future payment is virtually assured. Capitalization process used is "annuity capitalization" which, by use of a factor, calculates the present worth of a series of payments to be received at regular payments in the future. At the end of the lease period, the value of the land reverts to the owner. The present worth of that reversion added to the present worth of the income flow provides an indication to market value. Speculative interest rate for an investment of this quality and duration is 6%.
>
> Monthly P.W. factor for 11 yrs. 9 mos. @ 6% − 101.508
> Monthly Rental = $5,000
> Reversion Factor, 11 yrs. 9 mos. @ 6% = .495
> Computation:
>
> | | |
> |---|---|
> | Value of income flow $5,000 × 101.508 = | $507,540 |
> | Value of Reversion *$740,000 × .495 = | 366,300 |
> | Total | $873,840 |
> | Indicated Value of Property | $875,000 |
>
> *Land value per Assessor's land comparables A, B, and C shown on downtown street plan, Figure 6-1.

Taxpayer's Income Approach

By contrast, taxpayer submitted the following income approach:

Development of Capitalization Rate:

The income rate for capitalization of Net Income was derived through the Band of Investment Theory. The subject property has a remaining economic life of 33 years.

First Mortgage	60%	@ 7.00% =	4.2%
Equity	40%	@ 11.0% =	4.4%
Return on Investment			8.6%

Return on Investment	Rounded To:	8.5%
Return of Investment (33 Years)		3.0%
Effective Tax Rate*		3.8%
Capitalization Rate[3]		15.3%

*Effective Tax Rate Computed:

Total Tax Rate	$76.00
Assessment Ratio	50%
Effective Tax Rate	3.8%

[3]The capitalization rate is not excessive for a downtown location. See *Northwestern Mutual Life Insurance vs. Board of Review,* 225 N.W. 2d 317 (1975) where 12.8% was used on a downtown J.C Penney store in Dubuque, Iowa.

Capitalization of Income:

Estimated Gross Income		$ 44,000	
Vacancy and Rent Loss		2,200	
Effective Income		$ 41,800	
Expenses			
Management	$2,090		
Reserve for Replacement	125		
Insurance	950		
Total Expenses			$ 3,165
Net Income Before Recapture			$ 38,635
Income Attributable to Land ($205,000 × 12.3%)			$ 25,215
Income Attributable to Improvements			$ 13,420
Improvement Value $13,420 ÷ 15.3%)			$ 87,712
Land Value			$205,000
Indicated Value—Income Approach			$292,712
		Rounded to:	$295,000

Court Decision

The referee who heard this case decided that the best evidence of value was the capitalization of the economic rent indicated by subject property's sublease and by the arm's-length leases and sales of similar real estate directly next door to and on either side of subject. He believed that the land sales across the street from subject were speculative assemblage plottage by the local bank and the local trust company. He further believed that the enclosed mall rentals offered by the assessor were not indicative of the rental market situation in the immediate vicinity of subject property. Finally, he rejected the annuity capitalization of the contract rent in favor of the capitalization of economic rental income as presented by taxpayer. His decision was to reduce the assessment from $900,000 to $450,000. This 50% reduction in value resulted in $100,000 in tax refunds plus $20,000 per year in tax savings over the remaining 12 years of the lease.[4]

Example #3: Sale Price vs. Standard of Valuation Measurement on Stores Similarly Situated

In the two cases just described, the assessor was understandably reluctant to grant sweeping assessment reductions in his CBD. After all, the CBD had long been the strength of the assessment roll and the major source of his property tax revenue. Over the years a standard of measurement grows up with regard to these properties. To adjust one assessment, the assessor runs the risk of having to adjust all assessments. This would undermine the strongest portion of his ratables. Thus, relying on arguments of "standard of valuation measurement" or "uniformity of assessments," the assessor will often refuse to make downward adjustments. This is true despite even arm's-length sales transactions indicating values below his assessments.

[4]For a reconstructed mock trial of this case see: Jerrold F. Janata, "Mock Trial Depicting Ad Valorem Property Tax Assessment Appeal," *Proceedings of the 65th Annual Conference of the National Tax Association,* Washington, D.C. (1972), pp. 142-173.

In Virginia a downtown W. T. Grant store sold for $7.50 per square foot in an arm's-length transaction. The assessor refused to reduce his $29.00 per square foot value because that was his fixed standard of valuation measurement which he applied to similar stores. The Supreme Court of Appeals of Virginia held that the arm's-length sale truly reflected the fair market value of the store.[5]

This case illustrates that while the taxpayer may feel sympathy for the problems of the assessor in coping with downtown assessment levels, he cannot, in good conscience, accept rules of "standard measures" which are only uniform in that they are uniformly high.

The CBD in General

The property tax problems facing the CBD taxpayer are clearly illustrated by the preceding case examples. I appeared on behalf of several national chain variety and department store retailers in most major cities in the United States and Canada through the early sixties to the present time. Always the problems were the same: the high cost of CBD land; inadequate and restricted sites; more red tape, more complicated engineering and architectural work; pedestrian traffic drawn away by shopping centers; declining sales volume and, therefore, a lack of interest by the retailer to locate in the CBD. Finally, there is the lack of impact, appeal and excitement that are so important to the retailer.

To the retailer, impact, appeal and excitement are aimed at getting people walking downtown pushing baby buggies. Hartford, Connecticut is attempting this in its CBD. A $70-million Civic Center with convention and exhibit halls has been constructed. Attached is a 22-story hotel and an enclosed shopping mall with 53 retail tenants. This is exciting and pedestrian traffic is good.

Another example of excitement in the CBD is the 463,000 square foot Sanger-Harris Department Store in the center of Dallas. Its six-story facade features Roman arches with slender white marble piers that frame a mural of Italian glass tiles and provide a sheltered walkway. Federated Department Stores, Inc., decided to stay in downtown Dallas because it provided everything a regional shopping center provides: 2.5 million people in the Dallas-Fort Worth Metroplex and anchor tenants Neiman-Marcus and Titche's to lend drawing power. The imaginative Roman arch design caused the sacrifice of several thousand square feet of selling space to make this a spectacular centerpiece to attract more customers.

The real estate assessment has been levied on this property from the cost point of view. This is the method of approach generally followed by assessors in Texas. In order to overcome this cost method of approach presumption the taxpayer would have to present extremely convincing evidence to the assessor. The evidence would, of necessity, involve the income and market data arguments set forth in the court cases previously cited. But there is no substantial precedent in Texas law for the use of these approaches so the judgment decision lies almost entirely with the assessor. The taxpayer is at a distinct disadvantage in this type of situation.

It would seem then, that impact, appeal and excitement do not offset the problems of the downtown retail property taxpayer. This fact, and the other difficulties referenced above, will continue to plague the central city and will not easily permit economic recovery to a level that once was enjoyed in the CBD.

---

[5]*City of Harrisonburg vs. Grace Taubman, et al.*, 181 S.E. 2d 654 (1971).

FREE-STANDING STORES AND DISCOUNT HOUSES ASSESSMENTS CAN BE REDUCED

Somewhere between the CBD and the shopping center is the free-standing store and the discount house. These two types of individual style retail operations generally are not a part of CBD frontage and are not a part of a shopping center.

Free-Standing Supermarket Example

One very effective assessment reduction argument I have used with regard to free-standing supermarkets is that they represent an older generation of stores that have become obsolete because of their size. They generally occupy some 8,000 to 12,000 square feet of selling space. The typical new supermarkets now being built are 19,000 square feet and in some shopping centers they exceed 40,000 square feet.

I show the assessor that the practice in the industry is to lease twice the space that a free-standing store has in order to achieve an acceptable and competitive profit margin. I emphasize the negative aspects of the free-standing store with regard to parking, egress and ingress, and that it has to draw pedestrian traffic by itself because it is not part of a CBD or shopping center.

The assessor will, of course, want to see actual contract rent figures, comparable rents to prove economic rent and, possibly, sales volume figures. He might want to apply, say, a 1% factor to the sales volume figure to develop an economic rent. Be careful here because some supermarket chains sell a great deal more merchandise per square foot of selling area than others. Be sure you are aware of industry averages before you go along with this type of exercise.

Discount House Example: Sales vs. Vacancy

When a discount house is in normal economic circumstances, it lends itself nicely to the cost, income, and market data approaches to value. This is the standard valuation reference measure for both the taxpayer and the assessor. However, when there is an overabundance of discount houses in a given retail area, valuation measurement is not so easy.

In one actual case example, a midwest corporation acquired a string of a dozen 120,000 square foot discount houses located in several different cities in California. Of the twelve, only two remained profitable over the next two years and ten were closed due to losses. I appealed two of these, vacant and in the same county, to the assessor and then to the County Board of Review. How could I lose? The stores were vacant due to lack of sales volume, a clear indication of economic obsolescence. They had been on the market with an active broker for a year with no buyers, a clear indication that the market for this type of property was saturated.

Unfortunately, the assessor came up with eight comparable sales of discount houses in the county which supported his assessment. The Board held that these sales were an indication of what the subject properties would sell for, eventually. The mere fact that they were vacant at the time of the appeal was only an interim consideration.

The point of this example is that these 120,000 square foot general purpose buildings were being absorbed into the general real estate market for other than retail use. This would include light industry, light assembly or warehouse distribution. The Board indicated that it might have considered economic obsolescence arguments if the building's only use were as a discount house.

HOW TO USE COST, INCOME, AND COMPARABLE SALES TO REDUCE SHOPPING CENTER ASSESSMENTS

We now consider assessment reduction on the new CBD, the shopping center. They come in all shapes and sizes:

Neighborhood: GLA (Gross Leasable Area) between 25,000 and 100,000 square feet;
Community: GLA between 80,000 and 270,000 square feet with a junior department store;
Regional (a small city CBD): one or two department stores of 100,000 square feet +, GLA between 300,000 and 850,000 square feet;
Super-Regional Centers (major area CBD): three department stores of 100,000 square feet + GLA between 700,000 and 1,300,000 square feet.[6]

The draw is, of course, adequate off-street parking, one-stop shopping, modern shops and department stores, and weather controlled malls.

In General

During initial negotiations with an assessor, you might want to refer to the general argument that you have created a small city with numerous amenities at no expense to the taxing jurisdiction in which you are located. You have your own sidewalks, street lighting, refuse disposal, street cleaning, security protection, landscaping, benches, and pedestrian mall with music and art. All of these items are generally paid for by the community with property tax dollars.

In addition, since you require about 5.5 parking spaces for every 1,000 square feet of GLA, you can also argue that 75% of your property is non-income producing parking.

These comments make for a nice opening statement to an assessor, but I have not found them to result in substantial assessment reductions. There is no substitute for hard factual data that fits the law of the jurisdiction involved and supports your valuation conclusion.

Fact Situation: Shopping Center

Assume a 500,000 square foot GLA enclosed mall regional shopping center on 50 acres of land. (Assume for the purposes of this example that GLA = gross square footage.)

Cost:	Land 50 Acres @ $40,000/acre	= $2,000,000
	Buildings 500,000 sq. ft. @ $35/sq. ft.	= 17,500,000
	Total Cost	$19,500,000

Ratio is 100%.
Effective Tax Rate is 3%.

Example #1: Projected Income vs. Cost

The assessor, in levying his initial assessment, projects:

Operating Receipts: $7.50/sq. ft. × 500,000 sq. ft.	= $3,750,000
Operating Expenses: $3.00/sq. ft. × 500,000 sq. ft.	= 1,500,000
Net Income: $4.50/sq. ft. × 500,000 sq. ft.	= $2,250,000

[6] *Dollars & Cents of Shopping Centers: 1975,* the Urban Land Institute, Washington, D.C.

Capitalization Rate = 9%
Fair Market Value Per Assessor's Income Approach
$2,250,000 ÷ 9%) $25,000,000
Ratio is 100%.
Real Estate Taxes are 3% of $25,000,000 or $750,000 = $1.50 per square foot of GLA.

In this type of situation, the new regional Valley River Center successfully argued that an income approach projection was grossly premature and there was a need to wait for experience. The court agreed and relied on detailed and accurate cost data.[7]

Result, assessment is reduced to $19,500,000:

Old Assessed Value	New Assessed Value	Difference	Tax Rate	Annual Tax Savings
$25,000,000	$19,500,000	$5,500,000	3%	$165,000

Real Estate taxes are 3% of $19,500,000 or $585,000 = $1.17/sq. ft.

Example #2: Cost vs. Actual Income

Three years later you have a shopping center that is on its way to becoming a mature operation. The assessment has remained at $19,500,000.

Your actual experience reflects the following:

3-Year stabilized picture:	
Operating Receipts: $5.50/sq. ft. × 500,000 sq. ft.	= $2,750,000
Operating Expenses: $3.00/sq. ft. × 500,000 sq. ft.	1,500,000
Net Income: $2.50/sq. Ft. × 500,000 sq. ft.	= $1,250,000
Assume your capitalization rate is 10%. Your income approach to value indicates a fair market value of ($1,250,000 ÷ 10%)	$12,500,000

The assessor argues that his cost approach based on cost manuals promulgated by the state should be used to fix the assessment. You argue that the income approach should prevail.

An Arkansas Court agrees with you. Cost less depreciation is only a guide to the assessor and should not be substituted for good judgment.[8]

Results: The Court reduces your assessed value as follows:

Old Assessed Value	New Assessed Value	Difference	Tax Rate	Annual Tax Savings
$19,500,000	$16,000,000	$3,500,000	3%	$105,000

Real Estate Taxes are 3% of $16,000,000 or $480,000 = $.96 per square foot GLA.

Example #3: Income vs. Sale Price

Three years later your gross rent has stabilized at $5.00 per square foot × 500,000 square feet = $2,500,000.

You sell the shopping center for six times the gross rent, or $15,000,000, in an arm's-length transaction.

---

[7] *W. H. Shields, et al. vs. Department of Revenue,* 5 Oregon Tax Court 160 (1972).

[8] *Board of Equalization vs. Evelyn Hills Shopping Center et al.,* 476 S.W. 2d 376 (1971).

The assessor continues to apply the income approach and the valuation remains at $16,000,000.

The new owner appeals to court. *Held*: Where a market exists for a shopping center, the property should be valued by the market data approach. The Supreme Court of Oregon found that this ''genuine arm's-length sale'' fairly represented the market value of the shopping center.[9]

Result:

Old Assessed Value	New Assessed Value	Difference	Tax Rate	Annual Tax Savings
$16,000,000	$15,000,000	$1,000,000	3%	$30,000

Real estate taxes are 3% of $15,000,000 or $450,000 × $.90 per square foot.

Shopping Center Examples Summary

The fact situations set forth in the three preceding examples are hypothetical. The court cases cited are actual decisions rendered on a similar set of circumstances. Again, the deciding factor is which *opinion* of the proper valuation approach will be adopted by the court to most accurately measure fair market value. In each of the three cases cited, the taxpayer's approach and method prevailed.

ASSESSMENT PROBLEMS OF THE SHOPPING CENTER NET LESSEE

It is not unusual for the typical shopping center net lessee to find himself in the following situation. He, in accordance with his lease, pays real estate taxes based on the square feet he occupies as a percentage of the entire shopping center square footage. In a 1,000,000 square foot shopping center, a 10,000 square foot tenant pays 1% of the property tax levied on the entire shopping center.

As only a 1% interested party, he does not carry a lot of weight. However, if taxes are $1.00 per square foot, he pays $10,000 a year in real estate taxes and must simply hope that the shopping center owner is protecting his interests by doing everything necessary to keep the assessment at an equitable level.

He must always be alert for abuses. In one case, land owned by Henshaw was assessed at $3.37 per square foot vs. $1.00 per square foot for land owned in the shopping center name. All land was an integral part of the shopping center and the court held that Henshaw was singled out for assessment at a much higher value.[10]

The problem of the net lessee is similar. He must guard against arbitrary assessed valuations levied against that portion of the shopping center for which he has agreed to assume the real estate tax burden.

He usually finds that the major department stores in the center are assessed separately, leaving himself and the other smaller net lessees to fend for themselves. One movement gaining some momentum in the United States is for the national chain net lessees to band together to either appeal unfavorable shopping center assessments, or to demand that the shopping center owner appeal to achieve equity.

---

[9]*Equity Land Resources, Inc. vs. Department of Revenue,* 521 P. 2d 324 (1974).

[10]*Henshaw vs. Department of Revenue,* 5 Oregon Tax Court 263 (1973).

CHECK LISTS

Downtown

( ) Economic rent of subject.
( ) Comparable sales of similar properties.
( ) Vacant second story.
( ) CBD vacancies.
( ) Parking.
( ) Sales volume and income and expense statement for 3-5 years to show trends.
( ) Shopping center competitors.
( ) What is assessor's method of approach?

Free-Standing and Discount Houses

( ) Parking.
( ) Egress and ingress.
( ) Ability of free-standing store to draw customers without benefit of CBD frontage or shopping center amenities.
( ) Size considerations—has industry practice increased size of stores, rendering older store obsolete?
( ) Can building be used for other than retail purposes? This broadens its marketability.

Shopping Centers

( ) Cost.
( ) Actual income experience—income and expense statement for 3-5 years.
( ) Projected income—economic rent.
( ) Sale price.
( ) Net lessee—equitableness of overall shopping center assessment.

7
Achieving Property Tax Savings Goals in Hotel/Motel and Restaurant Appeals

Assembling Pertinent Data

- Land
- Location
- Zoning
- Building
- Other Improvements
- Cost of Furnishings
- Income and Expenses
- Lease
- Hospitality Industry
- Real Estate Assessment
- Personal Property Assessment

Example #1: Typical 100-Unit Motel

- Cost
- Income Approach
- Gross Income Multiplier
- Capitalization of Rental Income
- Net Income Multiplier
- Raise All Issues to Influence Opinion

Example #2: Larger (488-Unit) Resort Type Motor Lodge with Banquet Facilities

- Basic Facts
- Valuation Methods of Approach
- Comparative Income and Expense Statement
- Income Attributable to Furnishings and Equipment
- Assessor's Capitalization Rate
- Assessor's Value Per the Income Approach
- Taxpayer's Income Valuation
- The Board's Decision
- Additional Example (1,000-Room Major Hotel)

Example #3: Downtown Hotel

- Tax Relief Possibilities
- Downtown Hotel Fact Situation

Restaurant Example

Check List

7

Newer hotels/motels are similar in design to office buildings and apartment houses with steel or concrete frames and exterior walls of masonry, metal or glass panels. But the comparison stops there. A hotel/motel is a business enterprise involving tangible real estate and furnishings and intangible assets: management ability and goodwill. This creates a valuation problem. How much value should be allocated to the land, to the building, furnishings, management ability, goodwill? And, depending on this allocation, what is the value subject to property taxes?

The highest court in the State of New York, in dealing with a 19-story New York City hotel, discussed the fact that the sales price and income reflected the value of the real estate as well as the worth of management, goodwill, hotel furniture and hotel services. The court said that a hotel, unlike an apartment house or office building, produces income only in combination with the business conducted upon it.[1]

Throughout this chapter, we will address ourselves to this income produced by a combination of real estate and the business conducted upon it. We will show the primary methods in use to accurately reflect the value of the land, buildings and personalty vis-a-vis the business entrepreneur's efforts. It should be remembered at the outset that *only* the real estate should be subject to a real estate tax and *only* the value of the personalty should be subject to a personal property tax.

Since so many hotel/motel operations include food and beverage services, restaurant appeals will also be included in this chapter.

ASSEMBLING PERTINENT DATA

Hotels and motels come in all shapes and sizes. We will consider what data is necessary in general to all. This includes the standard 100-unit Holiday or Ramada Inn type motel, the larger resort-type 500- and 1,000-unit motor hotels with ballroom facilities, and the typical central city ''downtown'' hotel. Specific examples involving each of these types will follow this section.

The first step in gathering data is to obtain the essentials on the property itself.

Land

What is the *land* area involved? How many square feet or acres are we dealing with? A site plan survey-type drawing is necessary to get the overall view. You should determine if there are easements, sewer lines or anything else that helps or hinders the use of the property. What did the land cost and when was it purchased? If the land is leased, what are the details of that lease? A copy of same should be studied.

---

[1]*Peo. ex rel. Hotel Paramount Corp. v. Chambers,* 298 N.Y. 372, 83 N.E. 2d 839 (1949).

Location

Is there easy access from a main traffic artery, airport or train or bus terminal to facilitate traffic flow to the operation?

Zoning

What is the *zoning*? Does it enhance the setting or is there a chance for incongruous use that would spoil views or result in inacceptable noise or odors from industry?

Building

What is the basic construction of the *building*? What is its square footage? What did it cost to build and when was it built? Today, hotel construction costs range from $20 to $50 per square foot. Motels would cost something less per square foot. Have there been any additions? How many units or rooms are there? A copy of the descriptive brochure usually available in the lobby is a helpful reference.

Other Improvements

Are there *other improvements* such as a pool, tennis courts, covered walkways and large indoor or outdoor parking areas?

Cost of Furnishings

We are also interested in *cost of furnishings*. This will become important in our valuation analysis. It is also important in those states where a personal property tax is levied on these items.

What does it cost to furnish the average hotel/motel room? The above-average room? You must consider the cost of carpets, draperies, furniture, color TV and art work (if any); linen, china, silverware, restaurant equipment, office machines and office furniture.

Income and Expenses

A *five-year income and expense statement* should be reviewed in detail to understand the trend of the business operation. Five years gives a proper perspective and offsets any one-year aberrations which should not have a bearing on a properly levied assessment. This item will be handled in detail in the examples that follow.

Lease

Since many hotel/motels are *leased,* it is most important to obtain a copy of the lease for detailed analysis. Most valuation experts agree that hotels/motels are special purpose, income producing operations that can best be valued via the income approach.

The typical lease covers real estate only, is absolutely net, and provides for rents (often with a guaranteed minimum) based on a percentage of room, food and beverage sales. The average leasing percentages that I have been exposed to are 25% of room sales and from 5% to 10% of food and beverage sales.[2]

---

[2]See the following articles on the income approach and hotel/motel leasing: James E. Liek, "The Income Approach to Motel Leasing," *The Real Estate Appraiser,* January-February 1970, Society of Real Estate Appraisers, Chicago, Ill., pp. 6-9; Stephen W. Brener, A. Carmi Ganiora, "Problems in Appraising Lodging Facilities," *The Appraisal Journal,* October 1972, American Institute of Real Estate Appraisers, Chicago, Ill., pp. 611-617.

Hospitality Industry

It is also a good idea to become familiar with the general parameters of the hospitality industry. This will give you exposure to gross income estimates, occupancy rates, expenses and potential net profits.[3]

Real EstateAssessment

Finally, information about the *real estate assessment* should be obtained by reviewing real estate tax bills and the assessor's property record cards. These property record cards are sometimes in great technical detail showing precise measurements and calculations. Other times they are not so detailed. In one major northeast metropolitan jurisdiction (not too long ago) a hotel property record card consisted of a 3 × 5 card saying: "$400 × 1,000 hotel rooms = $400,000 in real property taxes." And that was the sole basis for the assessment.

Personal Property Assessment

Pertinent data should also be reviewed regarding your *personal property assessment*. This involves study of the asset ledger of the taxpayer to ascertain date of acquisition and original cost; review of the personal property return (if this is a personal property tax jurisdiction) filed by the taxpayer; and an analysis of the basis for the assessment levied by the assessor. This would include trending and depreciation schedules and useful life determinations.

Having now assembled and reviewed all pertinent data, let us look at some specific examples.

EXAMPLE #1: TYPICAL 100-UNIT MOTEL

Cost

Assume a typical Holiday or Ramada Inn of 100 rooms or units costs new $1,500,000, including land, building and furnishings. This works out to a unit cost new of $15,000.

Income Approach

Assume an income estimate as follows:

1. 100 rooms × 365 days = 36,500 rooms for sale per year.
2. Occupancy rate is 75% = 27,375 rooms actually sold per year.
3. Average daily room rate is $15.00 ($15.00 × 27,375 rooms = $410,625 gross annual room sales).
4. Food and beverage sales are 80% of room sales or $328,500. (Say $164,250 food, $164,250 beverages.)
5. Gross sales are therefore $739,125.

Gross Income Multiplier

If the motel were to sell for approximately cost, the gross income multipler would be 2. (2 × $739,125 = $1,478,250.)

[3]Two good sources are *Trends in the Hotel-Motel Business* published by the national accounting firm of Harris, Kerr & Forster and Company, N.Y., N.Y., and *U.S. Lodging Industry,* Laventhol & Horwath, Philadelphia, Pa.

Capitalization of Rental Income

Developing this mathematical exercise one step further, if we refer to the rental factors mentioned in the preceding section, indicating that national chains lease these operations at 25% of room sales, 10% of beverages sales, and 5% of food sales, we find the following:

Room Sales	= $410,625 @ 25% =	$102,656
Beverage Sales	= $164,250 @ 10% =	$ 16,425
Food Sales	= $164,250 @ 5% =	$ 8,213
	Net Rent	$127,294

If the indicated capitalization rate is 10%, the value of the real estate via the capitalization of rental income is $1,272,940.

A second income approach might look like this:

Gross Income		$739,125
Cost of Goods Sold and Salaries (Say 50%)		369,563
Gross Operating Income		$369,562
Deductions from Income (Admin., Advertising, Management, Heat, Light, Power, Repairs and Maintenance) (Say 20%)		$147,825
Gross Operating Profit		$221,737
Real Estate Taxes (say 3% of $1,500,000)	$45,000	
Allowance for Income to Personal Property (See Example #2)	20,000	$ 65,000
Profit as if Free and Clear		$156,737

Net Income Multiplier

Using a net income multiplier range of from 6 to 10, you would need a 9.5 net income multipler to achieve cost (9.5 × $156,737 = $1,489,000). If a net income multiplier of 8.1 is used, you arrive at a $1,269,570 value, which approximates the $1,272,940 value in our first income approach exercise.

The wide difference in value conclusions when a multiplier is used (6 × $156,737 = $940,422; 10 × $156,737 = $1,567,370) illustrates the weakness of sole reliance on multipliers as a basis for valuation. I have often challenged the assessor's use of a given multiplier, and in just such a case I was successful in achieving a reduction on a Massachusetts Holiday Inn. The assessor argued 8. I argued 6. We settled on 7. It meant a $15,000 tax reduction on a 100-unit motel.

The point of all this is to show that it is a matter of opinion with regard to what income figure will be used and how it will be processed into value. As the next case illustrates, you have the assessor's opinion, the taxpayer's opinion, the Board's opinion and, eventually, the Court's opinion.

This case involved a motel-restaurant-shop. The County Board of Supervisors were presented with cost evidence of $1 to $1.5 million. They were also presented with the assessor's income approach as follows:

1968 Gross Income		$1,971,891
Less		
Cost of goods sold:	$529,398	
Other Expenses:	908,630	
Income from Land:	34,711	
Income from Personal Property:	53,225	1,525,964
Income Attributable to Improvements		$ 445,927
Capitalize @ 12.5% =		$3,569,600 ±

Madonna Inn argued and the Board believed that this income approach included enterprise property and reduced the assessment from $3.5 to $2.5 million. They were of the opinion that the assessor's income approach was inappropriate and misleading.

On appeal to Superior Court, the Judge remanded the case back to the Board for further consideration. He was of the opinion that the Board's reduction was not supported by substantial evidence.[4]

Raise All Issues to Influence Opinion

You must always be sure to present all arguments to influence opinions to the degree possible. This allows the deciding body to hang their hat on whichever of the issues you raise that fits into their pattern of decision. For example, owners of a hotel claimed they were losing money and should be assessed on an income basis. The Ontario Municipal Board (OMB) disagreed and looked to existing mortgage, replacement cost of buildings, and nearby motel land values. However, taxpayer had also introduced facts concerning an inoperative heating system and a condemned swimming pool. The OMB upheld the assessment except for the assessed value of the heating system, which was deleted.[5]

The point here is that the OMB was given the opportunity to grant some relief to taxpayer, albeit token, because taxpayer presented all his problems for the Board's consideration.

Similarly, a taxpayer argued that his Ocean Royal Hotel was not constructed with the most economical use of space contained within its walls, its construction was too expensive for the neighborhood, the season was short, and rents obtainable were comparatively low. The assessor argued a $200,000 reproduction cost. The New Jersey Division of Tax Appeals agreed with the taxpayer and reduced the assessment from $128,700 to $110,000. The Court of Errors and Appeals of New Jersey upheld the Board and confirmed the reduction.[6]

Having addressed ourselves to the standard 100-unit motel, now let us study the larger hotel/motel assessment problems.

EXAMPLE #2: LARGER (488-UNIT) RESORT TYPE MOTOR LODGE WITH BANQUET FACILITIES

In an actual case, I handled an assessment appeal on a two-year-old motor hotel in southern California. The fact situation and the appraisals presented to the County Board were as follows:

[4] *Madonna Inn vs. County of San Louis Obispo,* 39 Cal. App. 3d 57, 113 Cal. Rptr. 916 (1974). This insufficiency of evidence decision is one of the rare instances where a California court will overturn a County Board decision in an ad valorem tax matter.

[5] *Whi-Bol Investments, Limited vs. The Regional Assessment Commissioners, et al.* R. 6640 Ontario Municipal Board (1972). I have appeared before the OMB and, as this case illustrates, there is a reluctance to accord the income approach to value any great weight.

[6] *Borough of Bradley Beach v. State Board of Tax Appeals,* 124 N.J.L. 36, 11 A. 2d 91 (1940).

Basic Facts

Land: 11 acres. Land is leased from the city. This ground lease is for 50 years with one 10-year option. Minimum ground rent: $80,000 per year.[7] Additional percentage rental: an amount equal to the difference between the $80,000 minimum and the total of:

a. 5½% of gross receipts from room rentals.
b. 4% of conference and meeting room rentals.
c. 3% of gross food sales.
d. 10% of all other gross receipts of any nature whatsoever.[8]

The ground lease is triple net to the hotel operator, meaning he pays real estate taxes, utilities, insurance and maintenance in addition to his rent.

Location: Subject motor hotel is located near a major convention center and nationally known amusement park, with good access to major arteries, all utilities and adequate parking.

Improvements: The plot plan in Figure 7-1 shows the general layout of the motor hotel complex. There is a 13-story hotel of 488 units; a lobby/office/shop building which also houses meeting and convention rooms, two restaurants and a lounge; a cabana-sauna building and an outdoor pool complete the complex. There is parking for 800 cars.

The square-foot breakdown is as follows:

Hotel	235,560 square feet
Lobby, etc.	53,311 square feet
Cabana and Sauna	4,200 square feet
Total	293,071 square feet

Construction: Foundation, floors and exterior walls are reinforced concrete. Structural members are steel beams encased in concrete. Roof is concrete with a layered composition covering.

Interior floors are mainly carpeted. There is some ceramic, quarry, vinyl, and asphalt tile; guest room ceilings are sprayed acoustic drywall. There is suspended acoustical tile in most functional areas.

There is one 3,000-lb. capacity exterior glass elevator and four 4,000-lb. capacity elevators in the hotel tower.

The hotel tower has a roof-mounted two-pipe system with a 350-ton Westinghouse centrifugal refrigeration unit and Raypack boilers for heating and cooling. The hotel lobby, banquet facilities and shops are centrally air conditioned. The equipment is a four-pipe Westinghouse system employing two 60-ton recirculating units and a Raypack boiler. A Lennox package unit provides heating and cooling to the two restaurants and lounge.

Water softening treatment operates for the restaurants, laundry, and air conditioning cooling towers. Water heating comes from Raypack central boilers.

Electrical wiring is enclosed in metal conduit with interior lighting in lobby and function areas mainly fluorescent. Good quality plumbing is found throughout, and guest rooms have a sink, water closet, and a bathtub with overhead shower.

---

[7]Under the terms of the lease, the motor hotel operator paid only $1,000 per month during the first year after taking possession of the parcel.

[8]These percentages are different than those we have been referring to. But here we have a ground lease only. The motor hotel operator built and paid for the structure and improvements.

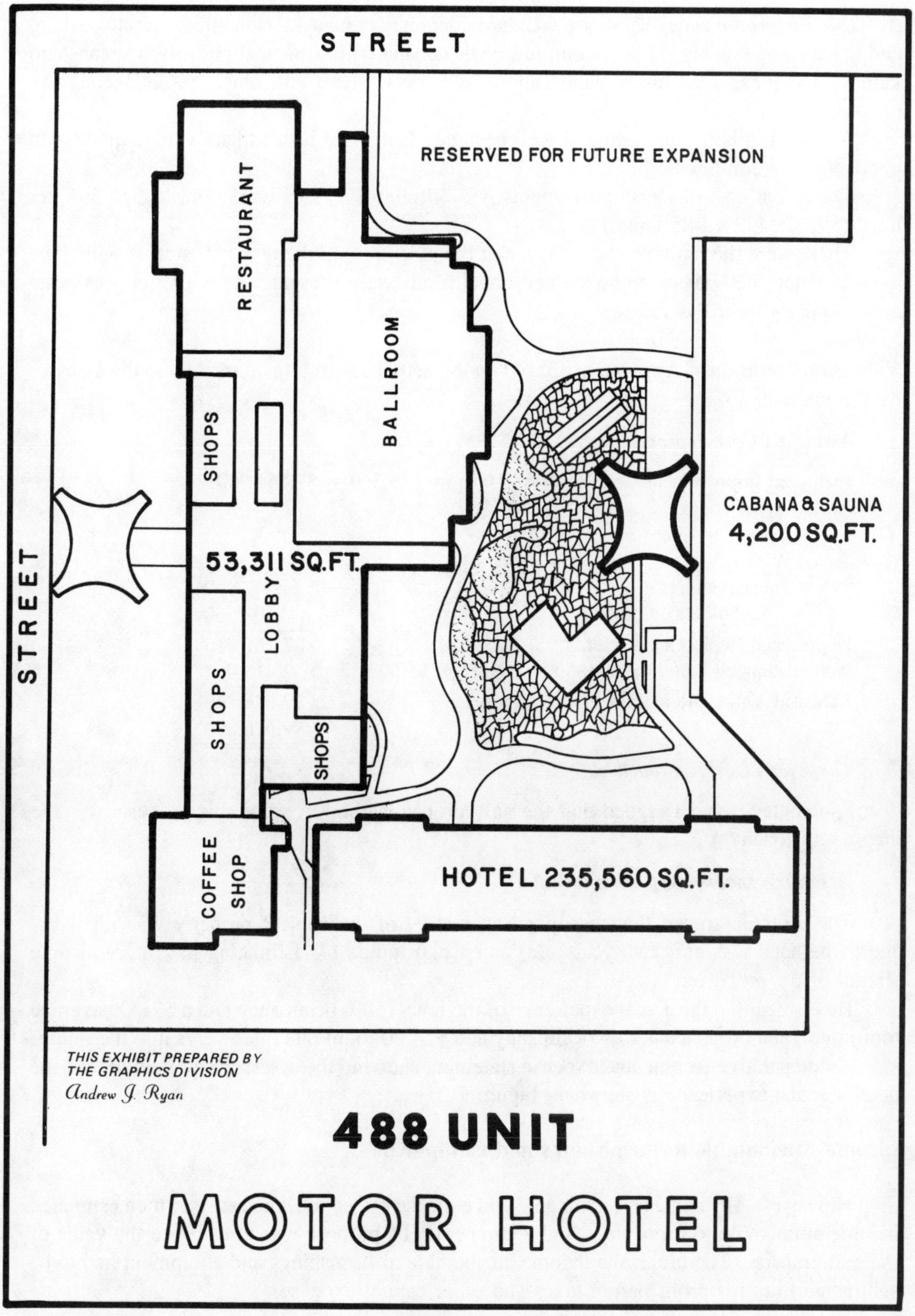
STREET
RESERVED FOR FUTURE EXPANSION
RESTAURANT
BALLROOM
SHOPS
CABANA & SAUNA
4,200 SQ.FT.
53,311 SQ.FT.
LOBBY
STREET
SHOPS
SHOPS
COFFEE SHOP
HOTEL 235,560 SQ.FT.
THIS EXHIBIT PREPARED BY
THE GRAPHICS DIVISION
Andrew J. Ryan
488 UNIT
MOTOR HOTEL

FIGURE 7-1

Other Improvements: These are standard concrete walkways, asphaltic-concrete parking and driveways, fencing, large swimming pool, cabana with a Jacuzzi pool, two saunas and laundry facilities, yard lights, landscaping, a porte cochere and other miscellaneous improvements.

All in all, this is a modern and well-designed facility of better-than-average quality, in good physical condition.

The actual cost of the improvements was $7,608,492. This works out to $15,591 per unit. ($7,608,492 ÷ 488 units.)

These were the basic physical facts that the assessor and the taxpayer started with. The two valuation methods of approach and conclusions were presented to the County Assessment Appeals Board as follows:

Valuation Methods of Approach: Based on the actual cost figures furnished to the assessor by the taxpayer.)

Assessor's Cost Approach

Estimated Improvement Cost New 488 Units @ $15,500		=	$7,564,000
Less: Depreciation			
Economic Life	50 years		
Actual Age	2 years		
Depreciation	4%		
$7,564,000 × .04		=	302,560
Depreciated Replacement Cost			$7,261,440
Add: Estimated Land Value 483,080 sq. ft. @ $5.00			2,415,400
Indicated Value—Replacement Cost Approach			$9,676,840
		Say	$9,676,800

Taxpayer's Cost Approach

I submitted none! I argued that the only proper method to value this property was the income approach.

Assessor's Income Approach to Value

The assessor argued that the operating history of the subject property was relatively short (the hotel was only two years old) and a poor guide for estimating the future income stream of the property.

He disregarded the actual experience of the hotel (50% occupancy and a $21.00 average room rate), and projected a 70% occupancy at a $24.00 room rate three years into the future.

A comparative income and expense statement showing the assessor's projection and the hotel's actual experience is shown in Figure 7-2.

Income Attributable to Furnishings and Equipment

Having established his basic income and expense projection, the assessor then estimated income attributable to furnishings and equipment. His purpose was to estimate the value of the real property. Therefore, the income attributable to furnishings and equipment had to be subtracted from his profit before taxes and other capital expense.

He obtained cost new figures from taxpayer's books and records:

Comparative Income & Expense Statement

Gross Income	Assessor's Projection		Actual
Rooms			
483 units × 365 days × \$24.00 × .70 occupancy (a)	\$2,961,800		\$1,684,423(b)
Food and Beverage ± 85% of room sales	2,519,000		1,926,815
Other	270,300		29,768
Total	\$5,751,100		\$3,641,006
Cost of Goods Sold			
Rooms	\$ 810,900	(c)Cost of Goods Sold	\$ 716,552
Food & Beverage	1,961,100	Wages, etc.	1,210,866
Other	120,800	Supplies	272,684
Total	\$2,892,800		\$2,200,102
Gross Operating Income	\$2,858,300		\$1,440,904
Deductions From Income			
Administrative & General	\$ 460,100		\$ 264,519
Advertising & Sales Promotion	287,600		146,134
Heat, Light, Power	230,000		83,073
Repairs & Maintenance	287,600		64,709
Management	387,600		168,443
Total	\$1,552,900		\$ 726,878
House Profit	\$1,305,400		\$ 714,026
Store Rental	35,600		35,618
Gross Operating Profit	\$1,341,000		\$ 749,644
Fire Insurance & Franchise Taxes	(44,100)		(27,511)
Profit Before Taxes and Other Capital Expenses	\$1,296,900		\$ 722,133(d)

(a) Assessor's Estimates
(b) Actuals from taxpayer's books and records.
(c) No breakdown between rooms and food/beverage.
(d) The difference between the assessor's projection and the actual profit before taxes and other capital expenses is \$574,767. The projection is almost twice the actual figures.

FIGURE 7-2

Hotel Furniture and Fixtures	\$ 531,401
Miscellaneous Equipment	9,565
Linen, Glass and Utensils	62,773
Restaurant Equipment	472,527
Signs	16,936
TV and Music System	46,630
Totals	\$1,139,832

Since these items were one or two years old, he used a cost index to factor them up to a reproduction cost new of $1,197,730. He used an estimated life of ten years, applied depreciation, and arrived at an estimated value of $960,000.[9]

The assessor developed his personal property capitalization rate by using a 14% return on an 8-year remaining economic life (REL).

14%, 8 yr. REL	.215570[10]	
Provision for Property Taxes	.025500	
(± 10.20/100 A. V.; 25% ratio $\frac{\$10.20}{4} =$ $2.55/$100 of M.V. or @ 2.55%)		
Rate of Return on Personal Property	.241070	
Say	.241	
Estimated Value of Personal Property	$960,000	
Income to Personal Property $960,000 × .241 =	$231,360	
Assessor's Stabilized Profit Before Taxes and Other Capital Expenses		$1,296,900
Less Income to Personal Property		231,360
Income to Land and Improvements		$1,065,540

This figure is the assessor's stabilized income figure to be used in his capitalization exercise.

Assessor's Capitalization Rate

Basic Elements:

Maximum institutional loans available @ 8.25% — 8.75%, 20 — 25 years amortization; @ 75% of appraised value. For this property, assessor estimates at 8.5% for 25 years at 75% of appraised value.

Yield on equity return 12% — 20%. This property: 14%.

It was also estimated that this type of property is held by an investor for ten years and that the property will increase in value by 20% over the ten-year holding period.

These considerations developed an overall capitalization rate of 9%.

To this, the assessor added a provision for real estate taxes based on the current tax rate.

Tax Rate = ± 10.20 per $100 of assessed value.

Assessment Ratio is 25% ± .

$\frac{\$10.20}{4}$ = $2.55 per $100 of market value or 2.55%.

Provision for Taxes .0255.

Thus, his capitalization rate is:

Basic Overall Rate	.0900
Provision for Taxes	.0255
Adjusted Overall Rate	.1155
Call	.115

[9]Please see Chapter 11 for detailed handling of personal property valuation estimates.

[10]The level periodic installment which will pay interest and provide full amortization of an investment of one in a given number of periods (8) with interest at a given rate (14%) per period. See *The Appraisal of Real Estate,* 6th Edition, American Institute of Real Estate Appraisers, Chicago, Illinois, 1973, Chapter 21, Annuity Capitalization, pp. 394 and Annual Table, p. 553, Col. 6.

Assessor's Value per the Income Approach

$$\text{Value} = \frac{\text{Income}}{\text{Rate}}$$

Value $\frac{\$1{,}065{,}540}{.115}$	=	$9,265,565
Plus: Excess Land		
Hotel Addition 90′ × 320′ = 28,800 sq. ft.		
@ $5.00/sq. ft.		144,000
Excess Parking		
285 Spaces @ 350 sq. ft. = 99,750 sq. ft.		
@ $5.00/sq. ft.		498,750
		$9,908,315
	Say	$9,908,300

You will recall that the assessor forecasted income during a three-year period in order to develop his income projections. These forecasts were:

1st Year	$ 711,900
2nd Year	973,100
3rd Year	1,296,900

He discounted the income loss as follows:

Yr.	Stabilized Income		Forecast Income		Income Loss		Present[11] Worth of Reversion @ .115		Discounted Income Loss
1st	$1,296,900	—	$ 711,900	=	$585,000	×	.896861	=	$524,664
2nd	1,296,900	—	973,100	=	323,800	×	.804360	×	260,452
3rd	1,296,900	—	1,296,900	=	-0-				-0-
							Total		$785,116
							Say		$785,100

Therefore:

Indicated Value at Stabilized Occupancy:		$9,908,300
Less: Discounted Rent Loss		785,100
Indicated Value		$9,123,200
	Say	$9,100,000

Taxpayer's Income Valuation

In my presentation to the Board on behalf of the taxpayer, I took issue with the basic approach the assessor used. I argued that income projected three years into the future did not take into consideration the actual experience of the hotel on assessment day. It was a two-year-old hotel struggling to establish itself in a very competitive market. Occupancy was at a low 50% and start-up expenses were, of course, high.

I argued that actual income figures should be used to value this hotel:

Room Sales: $1,684,423 @ 25% =	$ 421,106
Food & Beverage Sales: $1,926,815 @ 10% =	192,682
Net Rental	$ 613,788

[11]Present worth tables are predicted on the principle that a payment due at some future time is worth less today and must be discounted. They are frequently referred to as reversionary factors. See Irvin E. Johnson, *Mini-Math for Appraisers*, International Association of Assessing Officers, Chicago, Ill. (1972), p. 23.

Capitalization Rate 11.5%	
Fair Market Value ($613,788 ÷ 11.5%) =	$5,337,287
Say	$5,300,000

The Board's Decision

The Board agreed that actual experience was a factor here and reduced the assessment by $1,000,000, resulting in $25,500 in tax savings to taxpayer.

Additional Example (1,000-Room Major Hotel)

The experience factor in a new hotel was also my argument in a larger 1,000-unit operation just outside a major airport.

Again, the assessor projected income three years into the future and used the actual cost to support his assessment. He also argued the following exotic approaches: a range of 6½ to 8½ gross income multipler; 40 times real estate taxes; development of a room rental rate based on 1/10 of 1% of actual investment as a rule of thumb; argument that a projection of rental increases for rooms was valid because new hotels will rent at lower rates in order to draw customers away from competing hotels.

I presented actual figures from the books and records of the taxpayer. I argued that the assessor's projections were not realistic, especially in view of the fact that a new 1,000-room hotel was being built and would soon be competing with the subject hotel.

The Board felt that the assessor's references were too vague and general and that the best evidence came from the actual experience of taxpayer. The result: the assessment was reduced by $2.4 million, resulting in annual tax savings to the taxpayer of a whopping $100,000.

EXAMPLE #3: DOWNTOWN HOTEL

Tax Relief Possibilities

The best approach to a problem downtown hotel is to pay no property taxes at all. This is what a developer is trying to do with the 60-year-old, 1,800-room, 1.5 million square foot steel and frame Commodore Hotel next to Grand Central Terminal in New York City.

The purchase price for $10 million from the bankrupt Penn Central Transportation Co. is dependent upon a sale and leaseback to the city for 99 years, thereby eliminating about $4 million a year in property taxes when the new hotel is fully assessed. The present assessment is about $14 million with $1.4 million in annual real estate taxes.

The developer is prepared to purchase and modernize at a cost of $100 million or about $70,000 for each of the 1,400 projected rooms. The developer will realize an 11.1% rate of return if financing goals are achieved, room rates are $65, and the occupancy rate is 71%.

Many believe that the city's history in making complex real estate deals has been "sorry" and that this long shot possibility will be mired in red tape for years to come. Nevertheless, tax relief possibilities for major new commercial projects should always be explored. It certainly is better than fighting an unfavorable assessment.

Unfortunately, most downtown hotels are required to pay property taxes. Often assessments are levied based on a bygone era of elegance and occupancy rates which have long since vanished. Businessmen have many new hotels to choose from and they must pass several modern motels on their way from the airport to downtown. All this reduction in traffic takes its toll in the economic and physical decline of the former Grand Hotel.

Downtown Hotel Fact Situation

Again, in this situation I find it best to argue the *actual* experience of the hotel. Consider the following fact situation.

Assume a 384-unit hotel on 2.2 acres of land in serious financial difficulty due to a lack of business activity downtown. The lease is ten years old and calls for 30% of gross room sales, 5% of food sales and 10% of beverage sales.

Ten years ago, net income was in excess of $500,000. Today, the actual income figures at these percentages and less income attributable to personal property worked out to some $360,000. An 11% capitalization rate was used to develop a fair market value of $3,272,727. Substantial market data confirmed this figure. This was a 384-unit operation, and similar hotels were selling at $9,000 per unit. This worked out to a value of (384 × $9,000) $3,456,000.

The assessor relied mainly on the original cost of $5.7 million and carried fair market value on his books at $5,150,000. He is also relying on that $500,000 net income which can never again be attained.

I am presently arguing this case. I am quite confident that the trier of the facts will give greater weight to the actual experience of the subject hotel than to a ten-year-old original cost and a ten-year-old net income figure.

RESTAURANT EXAMPLE

The New England Oyster House, using a 6 times earnings multiplier, challenged its assessment to the Appellate Tax Board of Massachusetts arguing a value of $155,000. The assessor, using a 9 times earnings multiplier, placed the value at $387,000. As in previous examples, both parties used the capitalization of income approach with differences in repairs allowance, treatment of real estate taxes, fair rental value and capitalization rate.

The Board, without specifics, decided that the value was $250,000 and this decision was upheld on appeal to the Supreme Judicial Court of Massachusetts. The Court even went so far as to say that the Board did not err when it considered the assessment presently levied on the Ship Restaurant on the opposite side of Route 1. Both the Ship and subject had about three acres of land and 6,000 square feet of building. Generally, other assessments are not pertinent to a real estate appeal case because only the subject's fair market value is in issue.[12]

Again, a different opinion and a result favorable to the taxpayer.

CHECK LIST

( ) Land.
( ) Location.
( ) Zoning.
( ) Building.
( ) Other improvements.
( ) Cost of furnishings.
( ) Five-year income and expense statement.
( ) Review of lease.
( ) Hospitality industry familiarity.
( ) Real estate assessment data.
( ) Personal property assessment data.

---

[12] *Board of Assessors of Lynfield vs. New England Oyster House, Inc.*, 362 Mass. 696, 290 N.E. 2d 520 (1972).

8
How to Successfully Appeal Assessments Levied Against Office Buildings, Apartment Houses, Condominiums and Cooperatives

8

A Florida office building owner found that the assessor had not considered the income produced by the property in developing the assessed value. The owner brought an action for assessment reduction and the court held that statutes and case law require that income be considered in establishing assessments.[1]

A New Jersey apartment house owner received a substantial increase in assessment. His investigation showed that the assessor was using a rental figure 20% in excess of the actual rents received from the property. The assessor based his decision on the income of a two-building complex several miles from the subject property. The assessment was appealed and the court held that actual rental is a significant probative factor when there is no plurality of comparables. The case was sent back for a new hearing before the Division of Tax Appeals.[2]

These two cases illustrate that an alert taxpayer can challenge an assessment and win if an assessor disregards or incorrectly applies an accepted valuation technique. The technique is the capitalization of net income.

It is a well-settled rule that the capitalization of net income is the best measure of value of commercial rental property. It follows that the focal point in the valuation investigation of office buildings and apartment houses is the income and expense statement. This is not to say that the market data or comparable sale approach is not considered. If comparability can be proven, the market data approach is always an important and sometimes decisive factor. As a matter of fact, sales data will become more important as we get into the valuation and assessment of condominiums and cooperatives. To begin, however, we look at the income and expense statement.

ASSEMBLING PERTINENT DATA

Five-Year Income and Expense

If possible, you should obtain a *five-year history of your property's income and expenses* to review and analyze. This will give you a reasonably clear picture of the trend of economic activity at the property and it will offset any one-year distortions which might not reflect a true economic image of the property. This is important because the assessor is interested in long-term trends in setting his uniform assessments. One-year cyclical aberrations are not generally accepted by assessors as the basis for assessment changes.

---

[1]*Exchange Realty Corporation vs. Hillsborough County, Florida, et al.*, 272 So. 2d 534 (1973).

[2]*Parkview Village Associates vs. Borough of Collingwood,* 62 N.J. 21, 297 A. 2d 842 (1972).

Gross Income

Your income and expense statement tells you what the actual gross income or *contract rent* for the subject property has been for the last five years. You are seeking to establish a market value for the current tax year so *economic rent* data is also important. This means you have to determine what other similar property is renting for in today's market. If you are faced with a situation where economic rent is *less* than your actual rent, you can argue that the property should be valued on the basis of the economic rent. To do otherwise would result in setting assessments based on the negotiating ability of some long-gone rental agent. Unless property is valued for assessment purposes on economic rent, the rule of uniformity of assessments is violated.

You must also review your *rent roll* very carefully. If the lease of one of your key tenants expires at the end of the year and he intends to leave, you will be faced with a serious vacancy at that time and this fact should be allowed for in your projection of income for the tax year in question. I successfully argued this in an office building appeal where the federal government occupied several floors. The lease expired at year end and the government was vacating. No tenant of comparable size was available in this particular market, and large renovation sums would have to be invested to ready the space for smaller tenant use. The assessor agreed to recognize these factors in his valuation considerations. Result: a $75,000 tax reduction ($25,000/year for three years), which helped to offset the rent loss and the renovation expenses.

This is an example of how important the proper treatment of the allowance for vacancy is in the development of adjusted gross income. The gross income was adjusted to recognize the *lack of durability of the current rent roll.* This reserve factor varies with the property and the economic times. You should determine what factor the assessor uses. If it is 5% or 10% for *vacancy and collection loss* and this amount exceeds your actual experience at your property, you can use *his* factor in your income and expenses statement and reduce your gross income figure. An example of this will be set forth under "Example" in the Apartment House Section of this chapter.

Expenses

Operating statement expenses break down generally into four categories:

1. Operating expenses (administration, utilities, payroll, supplies, cleaning) and repairs.
2. Fixed expenses (real estate taxes and insurance).
3. Reserve for replacements (allows for replacement of short-lived items: roof, elevators, parking lot surface, building equipment, and, in apartments, stoves, refrigerators, carpets, furniture).
4. Other charges: not usually proper deductions from effective gross income for the appraiser. Consists of depreciation reserves, debt reduction: mortgage interest and amortization, income tax, etc.

These various expense items will be touched upon again and treated individually in the "examples" sections of this chapter.

Net Income

You must reconstruct the income and expense statement to develop a net income which can be capitalized into value. You value the property as if it were on the market today, free and clear of other than expenditures essential to the operation of the property. You therefore do not consider reserve for depreciation, mortgage interest and amortization, income tax, special corporation costs (franchise taxes) and additions to capital which are not items of annual expenses.

Bottom Line Losses

Throughout this exercise of developing a net income to be presented to an assessor, the accountant's income and expenses statement must be reconstructed to conform with accepted appraisal methods. There are many areas involving judgment and opinion which include reference to the experience of subject property, to the market area surrounding the subject, and to standards in the general experience of the office building and apartment house industry.[3] If the facts permit you to assemble data to support a case for an assessment reduction, then you should do so and pursue that result with vigor.

Most assessors I have dealt with are reasonable and practical. They will listen to your position and if it is their practice to respond to your individual fact situation, they will do so. Therefore, if you have completed your income and expense statement investigation and you find that the facts do not permit you to make a valuation case through the capitalization of income, you are not necessarily without an argument. Assume your difficulty lies in a bad original deal where your debt reduction expense wipes out what would otherwise be a healthy net income situation. Call this to the assessor's attention. Acquaint him with your *losses* and see if he will react to your reduction request on those grounds. There may not be textbook logic to such reductions, but they occur all the time and you should be sure to place any such facts before your assessor for his consideration.

Other Areas of Investigation

Other areas which must be reviewed in your preliminary analysis include tax bills, equalization ratio in effect in the jurisdiction, the property tax cards in the assessor's office, your cost of construction, comparable rental information, and sales of similar type properties on the open market.

The Physical Plant

The *location* of your building is a significant factor in your analysis. Have negative neighborhood and/or racial changes[4] resulted in factors which detract from the value of your property? If so, don't be afraid to call them to the attention of the assessor. Poor upkeep of surrounding properties, a change to a one-way street making access less convenient, noise offsetting the benefits of being located on a major artery, and the construction of another building blocking what once was a beautiful view of the ocean, are all factors that have a bearing on value.

They will be reflected in your income and expense statement in the form of lower gross rentals, a greater vacancy factor, and increased costs for security.

These inharmonious, incongruous, illegal or even immoral *neighborhood changes* should be argued under the broad heading of economic obsolescence.

---

[3]See, for example, the current edition of *Income and Expense Analysis Apartments, Condominiums and Cooperatives,* Institute of Real Estate Management, Chicago, Illinois.

[4]You can talk about this, but don't incite the jury. Better to show it as it negatively affects your income and expense statements. *The City of Chicago in Trust for the Use of Schools vs. Baird,* et al., 288 N.E. 2d 110 (1972).

Land

If you have ever had to search for a *parking* space, then you know how important land size is to an office building or apartment house complex. A very acceptable ratio for office buildings is one parking space for every 250 feet of leasable area. If parking space is not available at your site, then close-by parking facilities are required.

In addition, if the competition dictates, you must also consider the availability of playgrounds within view of the apartment house, park-type open areas, and shopping convenient to offices.

Egress and ingress also play an important role in value, and if you have problems in getting into or out of your property because of one-way or narrow streets, tight turns or heavy traffic, these facts should be duly noted when you are gathering your basic data.

These amenities are necessary to achieve the optimum in rental property. The lack of these enhancements to the property will reflect itself in reduced rentals. The assessor should know about them, and it is up to you to see that he does and that he takes them into consideration in levying his assessment.

Building

Physical deterioration is directly related to age and degree of repairs, maintenance and refurbishment. Once your building begins to show its age, you run the risk of losing tenants and reducing rents. This will also reflect itself in the form of increased expenses in your profit and loss statement.

Office or apartment buildings are generally accorded a 40- to 50-year life for depreciation purposes. This life range for the development of a depreciation schedule is accepted by the IRS and will generally not be challenged by assessors. It allows for the *normal* wear and tear on an office or apartment building.

There are always exceptions to general rules of physical deterioration allowances in buildings and you should be on the lookout for indications of above-average wear and tear in your property. If defects in original construction have resulted in roof leaks or wall cracks, then you may be able to request that the assessor grant additional depreciation to his average depreciation schedule in order to recognize these factors.

Perhaps the ultimate in construction bad luck involves the tallest building in New England, the 60-story John Hancock Tower in Boston. There were aesthetic objections, zoning disputes and lawsuits when ground under the building cracked. The mysterious shattering of thousands of windows in high winds resulted in the replacement of all 10,344 windows with specially tempered panes, at a cost of $7.7 million. In addition, the central core of the tower has had to be strengthened with steel plates and giant shock absorbers or dampers to cushion wind away because the building's designer warned that the structure might not withstand "extreme and rare wind conditions which could possibly occur over the next hundred years." The original cost estimate of $55 million has almost doubled due to these changes and delays. Construction took place in 1969. Occupancy, which was to have taken place in 1971, finally took place in 1976.

How is the property assessed? Alas, similar to all other office buildings in Boston: capitalization of projected net income, broken windows notwithstanding.

This illustration also points up the need for a detailed examination of the basic construction costs of your building. Construction costs can range from $60.00+ per square foot for best metal or stone, solar glass, luminous ceilings with hot and chilled water, to $30.00+ per square foot for minimum fenestration, dry wall interiors with warm and cool air. In either case however, if you can show cost overrides due to strikes, delays and changes in original design, you have an argument that can result in a downward adjustment in your original book cost figure. Again, the assessor is striving for uniformity in his assessments, and industry means via cost manuals are better than individual non-representative cost figures in his achieving his uniform result.

Building Equipment

Building equipment is also an area worthy of careful investigation since it too can add to your store of examples of depreciation in the form of functional obsolescence provable by accepted measurement techniques. For example, sophisticated computer control systems can reduce your energy costs by 15% or 20% by controlling fans and blowers to vary the output of heating and cooling equipment. If you don't have these modern controls, then you should argue functional obsolescence and prove the amount by calculating what the 15% or 20% savings in dollars would be each year. Be prepared, of course, to counter any arguments to the effect that the initial cost of such a system would eliminate itself as a savings factor.

OFFICE BUILDING

While net income is our primary area of inquiry, do not forget the impact of original cost on the valuation of a new office building. The Seagram's building in New York City was the subject of a famous certiorari case finally decided in favor of the assessor.

Cost vs. Income: The Seagram's Case

The practice in New York City is to value office buildings through the capitalization of net income. The case involving the Seagram's 38-story headquarters building at 375 Park Avenue was an exception to this general rule. (See Figure 8-1.)

> *Facts*: The building, with its unique and expensive bronze outer skin, has 618,000 rentable square feet. The structure is set back from Park Avenue to allow for reflecting pools, fountains and a large plaza area. Had maximum advantage been taken of building zoning laws, twice the rentable square footage could have been erected.
>
> It was constructed in 1954 for $36 million.
>
> Its rental income ranged from $6.75/square foot, 29th to 38th floors; $6.00/square foot and less below the 16th floor; to $2.50/square foot in the garage. Gross rental potential: $3.3 million. Seagram's real estate expert valued the building via the income approach at $15 million.
>
> Building assessment: $21 million.
>
> *Seagram's Position*: Capitalization of actual rental income indicates a value of $15 million and that should be the assessment.
>
> *New York City's Position*: Summation appraisal relying on the cost of the structure only as the basis for the $21 million value.[5]
>
> *The Court's Position*: Case tried in 1961 and finally decided in 1964.

---

[5]Lawrence W. Krieger, "Cost vs. Value in a Monumental Office Building," in *Assessment Administration*, International Association of Assessing Officers, Chicago, 1964, pp. 194-202.

FIGURE 8-1

1. Special referee who tried the case: "On the record before this court the total assessments are not excessive. Petitions are dismissed."[6]

2. Appellate Division: Affirmed with two written decisions. "Consequently, in the absence of credible qualifying explanation, for a new building the cost of construction is, *prima facia,* the true value." And, so as not to abandon the capitalization of income

[6]*Seagram's & Sons, Inc. v. Tax Comm.*, N.Y.L.J., April 12, 1962, p. 14.

entirely, "The prestige building has a rental value not based alone on commercially rented space, but on the building's value in promoting the economic interests of an owner. This increment could be added to the estimated rental of the owner-occupied space."[7]

3. The Court of Appeals, New York's highest appellate court, confirmed but it was a 4-3 decision. The dissenting opinion criticized as erroneous in law that cost of construction is *prima facia* evidence of value *and* rejected the idea that "the building is a specially built structure representing more of a real estate investment in its owner-occupant's business than a commercial office building."[8]

This case seems to stand alone because the "magnificent structure" was built "especially for prestige and advertising value." Just three months later, a similar case was sent back by the Appellate Division for a new trial seeking additional information on *rental* value.[9]

The example is set forth here to show the relationship between cost new and income. Further, it emphasizes that all value for ad valorem tax purposes is based on opinion and even the highest court in New York State split 4-3 on this issue. Had one judge's *opinion* been different, the case could have been decided in favor of the taxpayer. It was certainly worth the effort.

EXAMPLE

Office Building Fact Situation

Assume a downtown 100,000 square foot office building. The basic percentage relationships remain the same for 10,000 square foot or 1 million square foot properties, so that by simple arithmetic you can apply this example to your own individual situation.

Land: Purchased 5 years ago for $1 million.
Building: 5 stories @ 20,000 s.f./floor = 100,000 s.f.
Constructed 5 years ago @ $20.00/s.f. = $2 million.
Total Cost: $3,000,000
Assessment Ratio: 100%
Current Assessment:

Land (no issue)	$1,000,000
Building: 100,000 s.f. @ $30/s.f.	3,000,000
Total Assessment	$4,000,000

Cost Approach Exercise

It should be remembered that many assessors still do not completely agree with the "well-settled rule" that capitalization of net income is the best measure of value for commercial rental property. They continue to rely on the cost approach. You must, therefore, be prepared to present a cost approach valuation argument.

Assume that similar type office buildings cost between $30 — $35/square foot to build today. This would tend to confirm the assessor's opinion of fair market value unless you can show that depreciation should be allocated to the property. You can assume that the assessor

---

[7]*Matter of Seagram & Sons v. Tax Comm.*, 18 A.D. 2d 109, 238 N.Y.S 2d 228; affd. 14 N.Y. 2d 314 (1964).
[8]*Matter of Seagram & Sons. v. Tax Comm.*, 14 N.Y. 2d 314 (1964).
[9]*Matter of Pepsi-Cola Co. v. Tax Comm.*, 19 A.D. 2nd 56, 240 N.Y.S. 2d 770 (1963).

will argue that inflation has outrun depreciation and therefore he is correct in not using any depreciation in his cost approach exercise.

Physical Depreciation: A 50-year life is not unreasonable for this office building. You are therefore justified in taking at least 10% (2%/year × 5 years) for physical depreciation. Be sure you are able to argue that your physical depreciation factor is based on your observation of the subject property and that it is not just an automatic mathematical computation. Some assessors will not accept a straight-line depreciation formula and insist on physical depreciation based on the observation of the property. If maintenance and upkeep are outstanding, the assessor will argue that very little or no physical depreciation should be allowed despite the age of the structure.

Functional Obsolescence: This should be investigated here. Assume that due to a deficiency in original design (access area around elevator passageways larger than necessary) you have lost 10% of your rentable area. Obviously, all things being equal, your net would be improved by 10% and you are, therefore, adversely affected by this design shortcoming.

Economic Obsolescence: Assume also that one of your key tenants left you at the termination of his lease and moved five blocks north to a new office building. He advised you that his decision was based on the fact that your area had begun to deteriorate as reflected by the lack of neighborhood upkeep and he wanted to be in a more active business area. He pointed out that several other tenants from your general area had done the same thing. This is a case of economic obsolescence. Adverse environmental factors result in a degree of market rejection. If you find that you have had to reduce your rentals by $1.00/square foot, you have mathematical proof of the economic obsolescence.

The calculation of these three depreciation factors is as follows:

Physical Depreciation:

Total reproduction cost of building:	$3,000,000
Less 10% (50 yr. life, 2%/yr × 5 yrs)	
for physical depreciation:	300,000

Functional Obsolescence: 10,000 sq. ft. ×$5.00/sq. ft. (due to original design deficiency) = $50,000 gross rent loss. Less 50% expenses − $25,000 net loss capitalized @ 10% = $250,000.

Economic Obsolescence: 30,000 square foot tenant paying $7.00/sq. ft. leaves. New tenants will pay only $6.00/sq. ft. resulting in a loss of $1.00/sq. ft. or $100,000 a year. After expenses of 50%, this is a $50,000 net loss capitalized @ 10% = $500,000 loss due to economic obsolescence.

Cost Approach Summary:		
Building reproduction cost:		$3,000,000
Less Physical Depreciation:	$300,000	
Less Functional Obsolescence:	250,000	
Less Economic Obsolescence:	500,000	$1,050,000
Reproduction Cost Less Depreciation and Obsolescence:		$1,950,000
Add Land:		$1,000,000
Value Per Cost Approach		$2,950,000

Income Approach Exercise

You prove your allocation of depreciation and obsolescence through your income approach to value. If your economic gross rent here is $6.00/square foot, and your expenses are 50%, your net rental income is $300,000/year. If a reasonable capitalization rate is 10%, then your fair market value indication is $3,000,000 for the land and building.

Summary

Assessor's Market Value	$4,000,000
Your Market Value	3,000,000
Difference	$1,000,000

Tax Rate − Say 3.5% = Potential tax savings of $35,000 per year.

Comment: Your cost and income approaches result in about the same value conclusion. You have proven your depreciation and obsolescence allocations mathematically to a cost-oriented assessor. You have confirmed your value through the more generally accepted capitalization of net income approach.

APARTMENT HOUSES

Pursuing our original thesis in this chapter that the capitalization of net income is the best measure of value in a commercial rental property, we make the following income estimate for an apartment house.

EXAMPLE

Apartment House Fact Situation

Assume a 100-unit garden apartment complex. The income: $200/unit/month × 100 units = $20,000 × 12 mos. = $240,000 gross income. Expenses are 45% of gross or $108,000, leaving a net income of $132,000. (See Year 1 on following income and expense statement.) A fair capitalization rate at that time was 10%. Thus, $132,000 ÷ 10% = $1,320,000 Fair Market Value. A similar value would also be indicated by a gross rent multiplier of 5.5 (5.5 × $240,000 = $1,320,000). Real estate taxes are $36,000 or 2.7% of market value. This works out to 15% of gross income, which is within reason.

When the assessment was originally levied, this was the fact situation—but due to the fact that the Navy closed down a base (actual experience in Newport, Rhode Island), the income situation has changed drastically as shown in the Year 5 column on the income and expense statement presented in Figure 8-2.

Comparing Year 1 to Year 5, the income and expense statement illustrates that due to the Navy base closing (economic obsolescence), the rental income from the subject apartment house has fallen off during a five-year period by some $58,000 or 24%. This is a drastic decline in gross, but your net income is even further reduced by the fact that some costs have gone up drastically during that same period.

Some cost increases are, of course, offset by reduced use of the property, but others cannot be so easily controlled. Note particularly the increase in heating fuel costs. On the

Five-Year Comparison of Income and Operating Costs—Apartment House and Reconstructed Income and Expense Statement for Presentation to Assessor

	Year 1	Year 5	—For Presentation to Assessor—	
Gross Rental Received	$240,000	$182,000		$182,000
			Less 10% Vacancy Factor	18,200
			Gross Rental After Vacancy Factor	$163,800
EXPENSES				
Operating				
Payroll	$ 35,400	$ 34,000		$ 34,000
Maintenance & Repairs	9,100	5,000		5,000
Painting	500	100		100
Utilities				
Electricity	10,000	12,000		12,000
Water	2,300	2,500		2,500
Heating Fuel	5,000	10,000		10,000
Administration				
Management	5,000	6,000		*9,100
Taxes & Insurance				
Insurance	2,700	3,000		3,000
Real Estate Taxes	36,000	48,000		48,000
Other Taxes	2,000	2,000		2,000
Total All Expenses	$108,000	$122,600		$125,700
Net Operating Income	$120,000	$ 60,000		
				38,100
				**1,000
			Net After All Adjustments	$ 37,100

*Management Fee Factor: 5% of gross income.
**Enter adjustments for anticipated roof repairs *not* included in $5,000 actual amount recorded as Maintenance & Repairs. Replacement of roof cover in 5 years @ $5,000—thus, $1,000 per year for next 5 years is a proper expense.

FIGURE 8-2

other hand, payroll and maintenance and repairs expenses are down due to curtailed services on the part of the owner.

Real estate taxes have continued their upward trend and while in Year 1 they were 15% of gross income, in Year 5 they are 26% of gross, or 29% of the $163,800 gross rental after allowance for vacancy factor set forth in the Presentation to Assessor column. In either of the latter two examples, the real estate taxes exceed the reasonable range of 20% of gross income.

Pursuing the comparison between the Assessor Presentation column and the 1 and 5 Year columns further, you will note certain changes in the figures.

The first is the use of a 10% vacancy factor in the development of a gross income figure to be used to value the subject property. This is valid for two reasons. The first is that it is the assessor's policy to value apartment houses in his jurisdiction with the use of a 10% vacancy factor. This is a practice of which you became aware during your early investigation of the assessor's methods of approach. Second, the downward trend in the rental income has been established for this property and the vacancy factor will help cover the negative transition and turnover problems into the future. Any prudent investor would make this allowance.

The next adjustment factor is the allowance for a 5% management expense. Here again, assume the assessor automatically uses this factor. You should use it too, even if it is in excess of your actual experience. The average experience should prevail in the interest of uniformity of assessments.

Finally, an adjustment was made to recognize that certain items such as roof repairs must be allocated against current income by a prudent investor. This is necessary in order to offset the impact of the roof repair in the year it is actually experienced. This is certainly logical and many assessors will accept this item or some portion thereof to properly reflect this type of expense in a current income and expense statement.

Summary

Over a five-year period, your net income has been cut in half. A property once worth $1,320,000 is now worth, to a prudent investor and for assessment purposes, only $371,000. ($37,100 capitalized at 10%.) If your assessor's fair market value is in excess of that figure, you should challenge his valuation. Taxpayer's challenge in this case resulted in tax savings of some $30,000.

In this example, we used a Navy base closing which resulted in lack of tenants and a severe decline in rental income. Economic obsolescence could have been just as easily argued if neighborhood changes had the same negative effect on the property.

An extreme example involving apartment houses is the now abandoned Pruitt-Igoe Public housing project in the City of St. Louis. This 1955 project, once the premier example of federal government housing program, has deteriorated to the worst example of "how not to do it." An unbelievable 33 12-story apartment houses are standing vacant, stripped of anything of worth inside (all copper piping, etc., is gone) and the negative influence on property values on the near north side of St. Louis is immense. Every urban ill was involved: crime, vandalism, drug traffic and human despair.

I have argued assessment reduction cases on properties in this area before the City of St. Louis Board of Review and the Missouri State Tax Commission. I obtained reductions from both bodies based on this economic obsolescence argument.

CONDOMINIUMS AND COOPERATIVES

In the real estate market, condominiums and cooperatives compete with apartments. The essential differences among these interests for the taxpayer include the following.

The condominium owner, in his quest for home ownership with a minimum of property care burden, buys title to certain air space depicted by a three-dimensional air lot survey. He obtains his own mortgage, pays his own taxes, utilities and maintenance, and pays an additional fee for maintenance of common area such as lobby, hallways, parking lot, pool, etc.

The co-op apartment owner owns stock in a cooperative housing corporation and his number of shares usually corresponds to the value his apartment bears to the total value of the project. He also usually has a lease with the co-op corporation, the true owner of the real estate. The co-op market appears to have dwindled in recent years. HUD estimates that 85% of the nation's 440,000 co-op units were built before 1970.

Assessing a Condominium

This is a relatively new assessing problem dating back to about 1965 when the condominium market began in substantial numbers in the United States. Half of the 1,250,000 condominium units in the United States are in Florida, New York, and California.

As might be expected, current assessment practice is to value land separately and then value the building via the cost approach. Proration of the taxpayer's individual fee interest is based on percentage of ownership as set forth in Declaration of Ownership documents common to all condominiums.

An alternative method also in use is using original sales of units in a new condo and resales as years go by to keep the assessment current from a market data point of view. If resale experience is slight in a given condo, then the assessor goes into the market to develop value from comparable sales.

For example, suppose your condo is divided into four groups: (1) lower floors with and (2) without views and (3) upper floors with and (4) without views. The following analysis of resales could be the basis for your assessment:

			Resales		
Group	Orig. Sale Price	Year 1	Year 2	Year 3	Assessor's Market Value for Group
(1)	$30,000		$33,000	$35,000	$35,000
(2)	25,000	$27,000	29,000		30,000
(3)	40,000			45,000	45,000
(4)	35,000	37,000			40,000

If you've got problems, call them to the assessor's attention. If monthly maintenance fees are in excess of original estimates or there are steep extra charges to lease recreational facilities from developers—this means you would, or should, have paid less for your condo. Some experts believe that for every $10 increase in monthly maintenance charges, the value of the apartment unit decreases by between $500 and $1,000 in value. Thus, a unit worth $50,000 with maintenance of $450 might sell for only $45,000 if maintenance were increased to $500 per month. Make sure the assessor is aware of these facts.

Also, be sure to obtain a 5% or 10% allowance or discount from the sale price if personal property is included in the sale.

Keep in mind one very important thing when discussing your assessment. You are a homeowner for property tax purposes, no matter what technical terms are used. As a homeowner, you are entitled to be treated like any other homeowner even though you live 23 stories up. Be sure to ask if the assessor is treating you—not as other condominium residents—but as general homeowners in the community who are generally assessed below fair market value. Be sure to read Chapter 5 on residential property tax appeals.

Assessing a Cooperative

Much careful consideration must be given to establishing value from the co-oping of a building which typically involves three transfers: (1) owner-promoter; (2) promoter-co-op corporation; (3) co-op corporation-individual co-operators. Sale (1) is a good indication of value; Sale (2) is of little probative force since the market is restricted to one seller and one buyer; Sale (3) is distorted because there is greater liquidity for individual apartments due to larger potential market—increasing prices. There may be items of personal property included.

Be sure to thoroughly examine the above transactions when testing the validity of your assessment. Again, your best argument is to attempt to get the assessor to treat you as individual homeowners. This will result in your gaining the advantages that most residential taxpayers enjoy. See Chapter 5 on residential assessments.

CHECK LIST

( ) 5-year income and expense statement.
( ) Contract rent vs. economic rent.
( ) Durability of rent roll.
( ) Vacancy and collection loss factor.
( ) Reserve for replacement.
( ) Bottom line losses.
( ) Tax bills, ratios, property record cards.
( ) Location.
( ) Economic obsolescence.
( ) Neighborhood changes.
( ) Parking.
( ) Egress and ingress.
( ) Physical deterioration (abnormal).
( ) Building equipment.
( ) Cost vs. income.
( ) Functional obsolescence (design shortcomings).
( ) Comparable sales.

9
Methods and Approaches To Tax Dollar Savings In Industrial Plant Assessment Appeals

Assembling Pertinent Data

- Tax Bills
- Equalization Rate or Ratio
- Assessor's Property Tax Record Cards

How to Use Physical, Functional/Technological, and Economic Obsolescence Arguments to Achieve Assessment Reductions

- The Physical Plant
- Land
- Buildings
- Physical Deterioration
- Functional Obsolescence
- Building Equipment and Yard Improvements
- Industrial Park

How to Present Cost, Income, and Market Data to Support Your Industrial Plant Value Conclusions

- Fact Situation
- Cost Approach with Excess Operating Cost Example
- Income Approach Exercise
- Market Data Approach Exercise
- Preliminary Conclusions
- Correlation and Future Action

Out-of-State Industrial Comparables: Are They Admissible?

When Is an Industrial Plant a ''Specialty?''

Check List

9

A taxpayer recently challenged a property tax assessment levied against one of the oldest primary metal plants in the United States. It was argued that its age and design caused it to be functionally obsolete. A State Tax Commission agreed with the taxpayer and granted an assessment reduction of 25%, resulting in tax savings of $150,000 for a single tax year.[1]

A new 1 million square foot industrial plant was constructed for $15.00 per square foot, but due to change in consumer demand for its product line, the owner/builder never occupied the structure. It was offered for sale and remained on the open market for two years with no serious offers. Finally, it was purchased for $6.00 per square foot and the new owner/taxpayer was successful in reducing the assessment from the structure's original cost to its purchase price. It was argued that the fair market value of the plant was its sale price, not its cost. Taxes were reduced from $500,000 to $200,000 per year.

These "old" and "new" examples show the potential tax savings achievable when "functional obsolescence" and "market data" arguments are properly presented on appeal and through negotiations with assessing officials. The potential is enormous because the vast majority of the industrial plant assessments in the United States are excessive.

Modern industrial facilities (Figure 9-1) *can* be the subject of successful property tax assessment appeals. Do not be misled into thinking that the cost approach is the only proper method of valuing a new plant. Proper use of the income and market data approaches to value can offset the assessor's sole reliance on the cost approach.

Court decisions in state after state have recognized that mass appraisal techniques generally employed by the assessor do not allow for proper treatment of physical, functional, and economic obsolescence in individual plants. Further, the weakness in relying solely on the cost approach to value, again the method generally followed by the assessor, is that the depreciation factor is not proved by any of the following methods: (1) mathematical development of present worth of excessive operating costs; (2) income approach; and (3) market data approach to value. This chapter will examine these factors in detail and, through example, illustrate their use in presenting an assessment appeal valuation argument on a typical industrial plant.

ASSEMBLING PERTINENT DATA

The first order of business in analyzing an industrial plant assessment is to become familiar with the basic data that makes up the assessment.

---

[1]For a case in which the author was directly involved, see *In the Matter of the Appeal of Aluminum Company of America vs. July 1973 Board of Equalization of Clark County,* Docket No. 9026, State of Washington Board of Tax Appeals, September 27, 1975.

FIGURE 9-1

Tax Bills

The tax bill or bills will tell you the name of the taxing jurisdiction you are dealing with; the name of the owner of the subject property as listed on the tax rolls; a brief description of the property or, at least, identification by lot and block number; and the assessment, hopefully showing an individual value for both land and building.

Equalization Rate or Ratio

Since most property in the United States is assessed at a percentage of its true or fair market value, you will have to determine what percentage applies in your case. This is not always an easy task, and sometimes it is necessary to try this issue along with overvaluation if you eventually go to court. However, to start, there are several sources for an equalization figure. They include percentages acknowledged by the assessor; percentages published by State Equalization Boards, private ratio studies; prior court cases where ratios have been established by precedent; and ''common knowledge'' ratio levels that everyone seems to accept as the ''general level'' in that taxing jurisdiction.

Assessor's Property Tax Record Cards

These cards are generally recognized as a public record available for review by an interested party. Some jurisdictions require authorization from the owner of record before permitting a third party to review them. They will tell you what information the assessor has used to develop his value. They will usually contain a brief sketch of the layout of subject property, together with data on date and cost of construction, additions, number of elevators, etc. Most important is the calculation by the assessor of cost less depreciation to arrive at his assessment. This will show his reproduction cost factors for the various structures and what, if any, depreciation allowances he made for physical, functional and economic obsolescence. You will not usually find an income and market data approach to value recorded on the property record card.

HOW TO USE PHYSICAL, FUNCTIONAL/TECHNOLOGICAL, AND ECONOMIC OBSOLESCENCE ARGUMENTS TO ACHIEVE ASSESSMENT REDUCTIONS

The Physical Plant

A necessary ingredient of any successful assessment challenge is complete familiarity on your part with the subject property. You will find that there is no substitute for your first-hand knowledge of all pertinent facts, and this preparation will pay dividends to you in the form of property tax savings.

The *location* of your plant is most important. Are you in a modern industrial area with good access to major arteries, rail and water? Or are you in an out-of-the-way older industrial section that is run-down and where your employees' safety is threatened? I argued *economic obsolescence* at one plant where a mugging murder occurred at the main gate, resulting in female personnel having to be taxied to and from work at the employer's expense. The judge agreed that any prudent investor in this property would have to take this expense item into consideration and he reduced the fair market value of the plant accordingly.

Another successful economic obsolescence argument involved the fact that a plant was serviced by only one railroad line and was, therefore, a captive customer subject to increases in transportation charges. Other arguments are interruptible power supply and lack of availability of services to the plant, such as water, sewerage, police and fire protection.

Thus, changes in the neighborhood or market area surrounding your property which adversely affect its value, the text book definition of economic obsolescence, should be carefully examined during your preparation effort.

Land

Is your plant located on flat land or is there hilly terrain resulting in multi-level construction and material handling difficulties? *Topography* considerations should be referenced in land valuation analysis.

The land itself should be scrutinized. What is the *weight-bearing capacity* of the soil? Is it adequate for your current and future needs or will expensive piling and special foundations be necessary? These factors might tend to alienate a potential purchaser and therefore lessen the value of the land. If you have a problem, the assessor should certainly be asked if he took this into consideration when he valued the land for assessment purposes.

Look for *flooding problems,* too. On several occasions, I have obtained acreage value adjustments for that portion of the land subject to flooding.

Do you have enough land?

Is there *lay-down storage space,* or for example, do you have to keep raw material stored on freight trains, resulting in expensive demurrage charges? Is there adequate *truck turn-around area,* or is there congestion causing costly delay?

The general rule is that you should have about a three-to-one *land-to-building ratio*. That is, your land area square footage should be at least three times your building square footage. If you have adequate land area for present operations, that is fine. But, you must also consider your requirements for expansion. If you have no excess land, then you are limited to the present size of your plant, and that may be a severe drawback to future investment at this site. It would certainly be a crucial factor in any potential investor's analysis into the purchase of this property. The "no-room-for-expansion" factor would tend to limit the marketability of the plant and decrease its value. It is a good assessment reduction argument too, and it should be used.

FIGURE 9-2

Do you have proper *egress and ingress* at your plant? Can your traffic get in and out without problems? Truck access to one waterfront plant was via a small bridge over a railroad track. (See Figure 9-2, and also note the outdated sawtooth roof construction and the lack of available land for expansion.) Negotiating a trailer-tractor through the tight turns leading onto the bridge took fully 30 to 45 minutes, and 75-foot trailers simply could not make it. Rail and sea access was good, but truck traffic was exceptionally poor due to egress and ingress difficulty. Again, an assessment reduction argument.

This problem sometimes extends beyond your plant's gates. Do your drivers have to come through a residential area with narrow streets and community relation problems due to the noise and danger of heavy truck traffic?

Buildings

Now that we have examined your location and land area situation, let us look at your buildings. How many are there? What are their sizes? What is the total square footage of building area? You may be dealing with one structure or several. They may be free standing or connected by common walls or utility passageways. You may have to consider a main plant with support buildings such as maintenance shop, boiler house, gate houses, change houses, truck dispatch and weigh stations, etc.

Age is an extremely important factor here. If the buildings are 50 or more years old, you most certainly would have a strong functional obsolescence argument. Much construction during the 1940-1946 period was haphazard and specific in design for wartime use. This is outdated in the main, with respect to current standards. 1950 to date is generally the modern period in basic construction. However, technological advances in many industries have made many ''modern'' structures obsolete, even though their construction dates back only 10 or 15 years.

Physical Deterioration

When considering the age of your structure, you must, of course, examine *physical deterioration*. This is the wearing out of your building due to the wear and tear of the elements.

Sometimes *corrosive elements* of your manufacturing process can have a severe detrimental affect on your structures and shorten their useful lives dramatically. If present, these matters should be documented with photographs showing the extreme wear and tear on columns, walls, floors, etc.

Figure 9-3 illustrates the effect that corrosive elements in a manufacturing process can have on the metal walls of a typical plant. Note how the walls have been eaten away where the wall meets the ceiling. This type of photo should be included in any presentation to a Board or Judge as support for additional physical depreciation.

What is the basic construction? Is it a first-class building with concrete walls and floors fully fireproof? Is it a second-class building only partially fireproof? Or is it a third-class building of wood construction?

FIGURE 9-3

You should have that portion of a standard cost manual with you to check off those items that apply to subject. This will help later on if you decide to work up a cost approach to submit to the assessor.

Functional Obsolescence

Functional obsolescence or decreased capacity of your plant building to perform the function for which it was designed must be considered here.

Specific problem areas that you should be concentrating on are: (1) *ceiling heights* (if they are too low for your use, you may have serious functional obsolescence); (2) *size of bay areas* between support columns—also extremely important. If your product flow is continually hampered because you have to work around tight spaces between columns, you can argue that the plant would *not* be easily adaptable to general marketability, which, of course, would tend to reduce its value on the open market. Hence, a supportable argument for functional obsolescence; (3) *steel sash* window walls in older industrial buildings. They create expensive glass paning and heat loss problem vs. the modern plastic maintenance-free wall tops where indirect lighting is required; (4) *sawtooth roof* construction (older plants) involving leaks and high maintenance costs; (5) adequacy of *crane capacity*; (6) height of loading and shipping *docks*; and (7) any other *unique aspect* of subject property that may be pertinent to your investigation.

Figure 9-4 shows an excellent comparison between old and new construction at the same plant. The older portion is brick (with cracks), with steel sash windows and sawtooth

FIGURE 9-4

roof construction. The newer addition is aluminum with plastic panels for indirect light and a flat roof. Functional obsolescence in the older portion is clearly illustrated by this visual comparison.

Another example of this type of comparison is illustrated by the "existing" and "modern" plant layouts seen in Figures 9-5 and 9-6.

The existing plant drawing (Figure 9-5) shows that the plant is trisected by two railroad rights of way. This causes substantial delays in material handling among the three operating sections of the plant. Note also that there is no room for expansion. These are functional obsolescence problems.

The modern plant drawing (Figure 9-6) corrects these design shortcomings. The site still has maximum access to rail, but intra-plant material handling is not hindered. There is room for future expansion and central service (maintenance) and spare parts have been centralized for greater efficiency.

Plant layout considerations can be the most important aspect of your physical review. Is it a modern one-story, one-building layout facilitating work flow and material handling? Or is it a World War II facility with two to four miles between the major buildings? I actually worked on one in upstate New York. The layout was designed to avoid vulnerability to sabotage and air raid. The plant operates today, but is severely penalized by this functional detraction inherent in its design.

Go over the work flow with the plant engineer, using an aerial photo or a plant layout drawing. You will be looking for *bottleneck problems*. Ideally, your engineer will have experience at other plants with more modern layouts. His experience will allow you to make comparisons to show where you can highlight functional obsolescence due to plant design shortcomings.

One way to do this is to ask the engineer how he would lay the plant out if he had unlimited funds and he could start from scratch. Be sure to have your drawing of the floor plan handy so you can draw the new plant outline on top of the old. This will give you an overlay perspective of the "ideal plant" vs. the subject. This comparison can be used very effectively later on if an appeal follows.

Be sure to check out *maintenance charges*. This expense will tell you where the problems are. If money is being spent to repair a continually leaking roof—that's an indication of physical wear or faulty original construction. If there is excessive wear on crane wheels due to excessive weight demands—the maintenance charges will show this up. This exercise will enable you to highlight those areas where you can apply physical depreciation in higher amounts than you would ordinarily. Don't forget to photograph these areas if you can.

You should also be very interested in what portions of the plant are *idle* or *not being used to capacity*. A good idea is to get two copies of the floor plan and to take notes right on the drawing. Keep the other drawing clean, because your notes may obscure parts of the drawing that may be referred to later. One very effective method of showing an assessor those parts of your plant that are not in use is to draw red hash marks over the idle portions of the plant. The drawing then becomes your reference point in developing a percentage factor of obsolescence for non-use. Many assessors will automatically grant a reduction for non-use. (See Chapter 14 for an example of the effective use of a floor plan.)

Remember, some portions of a plant that are not in full use will be used for *convenience storage*. Items that would ordinarily be stored outside are simply moved inside because the space is available. This is an area where you can argue non-use and get support from the plant engineer.

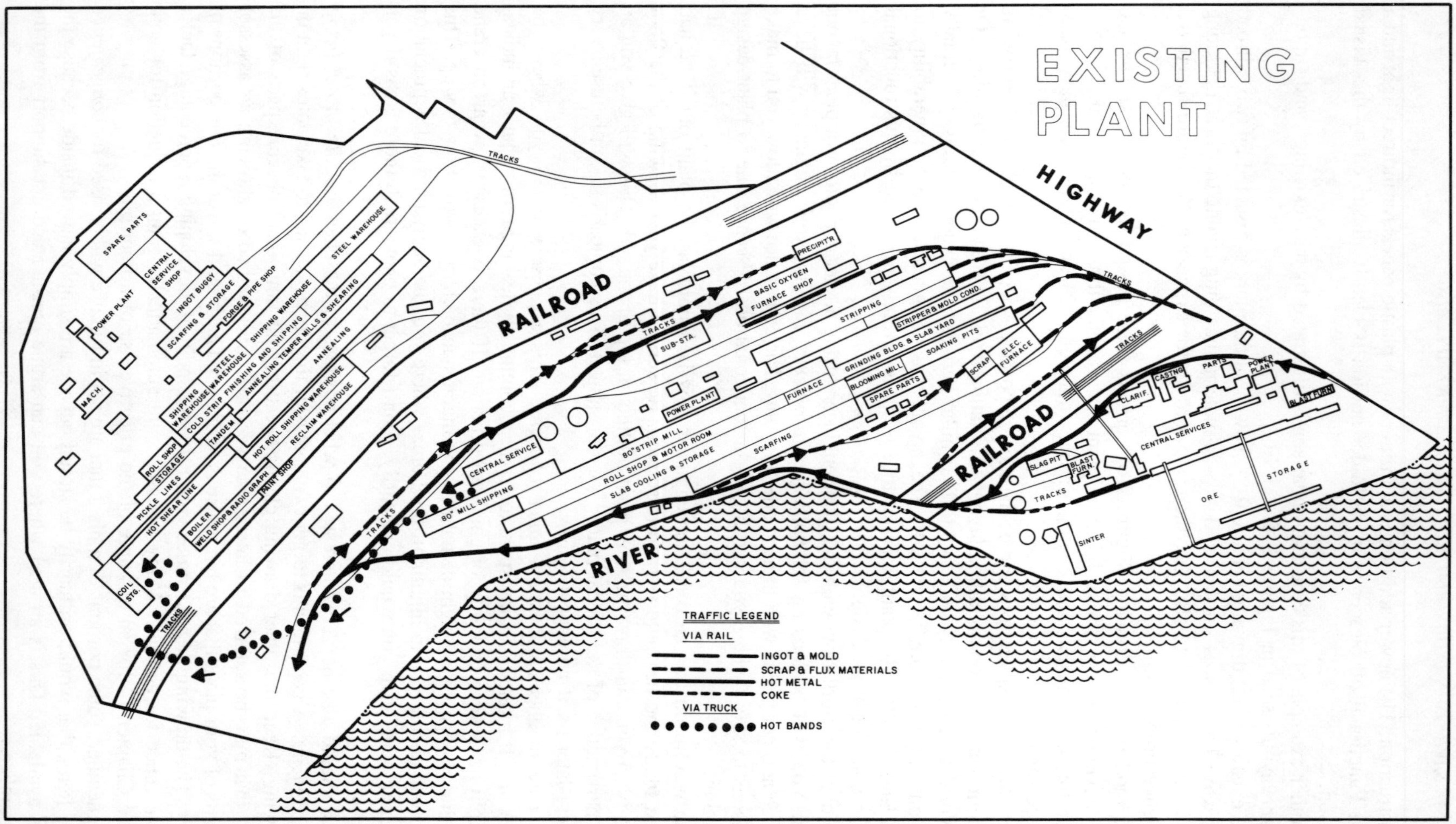
EXISTING
PLANT
HIGHWAY
RAILROAD
RAILROAD
RIVER
TRACKS
SPARE PARTS
CENTRAL SERVICE SHOP
POWER PLANT
INGOT BUGGY
SCARFING & STORAGE
FORGE & PIPE SHOP
MACH
STEEL WAREHOUSE
SHIPPING WAREHOUSE
ANNEALING TEMPER MILLS & SHEARING
ANNEALING
SHIPPING WAREHOUSE
STEEL WAREHOUSE
COLD STRIP FINISHING AND SHIPPING
TANDEM
HOT ROLL SHIPPING WAREHOUSE
RECLAIM WAREHOUSE
ROLL SHOP
STORAGE
PICKLE LINES
HOT SHEAR LINE
BOILER
WELD SHOP & RADIO GRAPH
PAINT SHOP
COIL STG.
CENTRAL SERVICE
80" MILL SHIPPING
80" STRIP MILL
ROLL SHOP & MOTOR ROOM
SLAB COOLING & STORAGE
SCARFING
POWER PLANT
FURNACE
SUB-STA.
BASIC OXYGEN FURNACE SHOP
PRECIPIT'R
STRIPPING
STRIPPER & MOLD COND
GRINDING BLDG. & SLAB YARD
BLOOMING MILL
SOAKING PITS
SPARE PARTS
SCRAP
ELEC. FURNACE
CLARIF.
CASTING
PARTS
POWER PLANT
BLAST FURN
CENTRAL SERVICES
SLAG PIT
BLAST FURN
SINTER
ORE
STORAGE
TRAFFIC LEGEND
VIA RAIL
INGOT & MOLD
SCRAP & FLUX MATERIALS
HOT METAL
COKE
VIA TRUCK
HOT BANDS

FIGURE 9-5

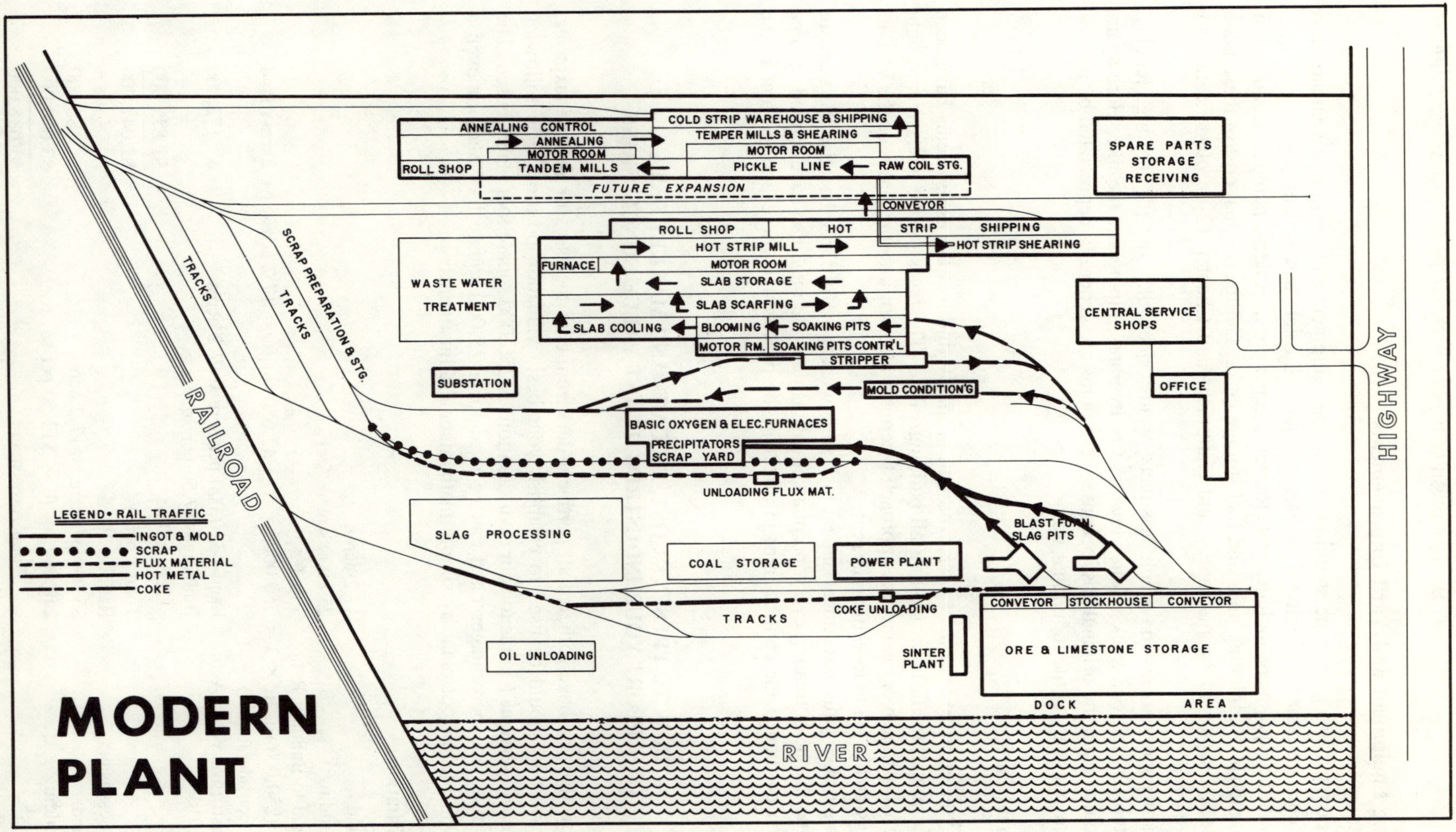
MODERN PLANT
LEGEND• RAIL TRAFFIC
INGOT & MOLD
SCRAP
FLUX MATERIAL
HOT METAL
COKE
RAILROAD
HIGHWAY
RIVER
TRACKS
SCRAP PREPARATION & STG.
TRACKS
ANNEALING CONTROL
ANNEALING
MOTOR ROOM
ROLL SHOP
TANDEM MILLS
COLD STRIP WAREHOUSE & SHIPPING
TEMPER MILLS & SHEARING
MOTOR ROOM
PICKLE LINE
RAW COIL STG.
FUTURE EXPANSION
CONVEYOR
SPARE PARTS STORAGE RECEIVING
ROLL SHOP
HOT STRIP SHIPPING
HOT STRIP MILL
HOT STRIP SHEARING
FURNACE
MOTOR ROOM
SLAB STORAGE
SLAB SCARFING
SLAB COOLING
BLOOMING
SOAKING PITS
MOTOR RM.
SOAKING PITS CONTR'L
STRIPPER
WASTE WATER TREATMENT
CENTRAL SERVICE SHOPS
OFFICE
SUBSTATION
MOLD CONDITION'G
BASIC OXYGEN & ELEC. FURNACES
PRECIPITATORS
SCRAP YARD
UNLOADING FLUX MAT.
BLAST FURN.
SLAG PITS
SLAG PROCESSING
COAL STORAGE
POWER PLANT
CONVEYOR
STOCKHOUSE
CONVEYOR
TRACKS
COKE UNLOADING
ORE & LIMESTONE STORAGE
SINTER PLANT
OIL UNLOADING
DOCK AREA

FIGURE 9-6

Building Equipment and Yard Improvements

You must also give some attention to building equipment and yard improvements since these items are generally included as part of your real estate assessment.

Building equipment includes transformers, generators, boilers, pumps, heating, ventilating and air conditioning units and fuel storage tanks. Get the original cost of these items and check Chapter 11 on machinery and equipment and Chapter 12 on classification for proper handling.

Yard improvements may include streets, roads, sidewalks, outside lighting, fencing, utility tunnels, railroad tracks, water towers, fire hydrants, piping and the like. Here again, you should obtain the original cost because these items are generally depreciated by observing wear and tear on the individual items.

Industrial Park

If you are in an *industrial park,* you will probably find that the assessments have been levied in a uniform fashion, treating all buildings alike. The basis for the assessment might be the cost approach or the income approach where the assessor uses the leases on the various buildings as his guide to economic rent.

This makes your assessment appeal task somewhat more difficult because the assessor can argue that he is treating everyone in an equal fashion. He may also have a good income approach position if the contract rent in effect in the park equals the economic rent in the area.

HOW TO PRESENT COST, INCOME, AND MARKET DATA TO SUPPORT YOUR INDUSTRIAL PLANT VALUE CONCLUSIONS

Now that you have gathered all pertinent data from both the assessor and the taxpayer, the information should be used to establish your basic valuation position. The following example will serve as a guide to your own situation. A 250,000 square foot plant is used. The general rules and percentages cited can be used for a 25,000 square foot plant or even a 2,500,000 square foot plant by simple mathematical adjustments.

Fact Situation

Land:	17.2 acres	
Building:	250,000 square feet	
Land-to-Building Ratio:	3 to 1	
(250,000 sq. ft. × 3 = 750,000 sq. ft. ÷ 43,650 sq. ft. = 17.2 acres. No excess land considerations.)		
Cost: Five Years Ago:	Land—$10,000 per acre x 17.2 acres	= $ 172,000
	Building—$7.50 per sq. ft. × 250,000 sq. ft.	= $1,875,000
	Total Cost	= $2,047,000
Assessment:	Ratio is 100%	
Land:	$5,000 per acre × 17.2 acres	= $ 86,000
Building:	250,000 sq. ft. × $12.50 per sq. ft.	= $3,000,000
	Total Assessment	= $3,086,000
	or $12.34 per square foot for land and building	

Building is assessed above five-year-old cost, but the assessor has used a trending factor to bring that cost to current level. His calculations, using a national cost manual, might look like this:

> Replacement cost of eastern industrial plant built five years ago was $1,875,000. The multiplier for this Class B building, five years old, is 1.580. The monthly comparative cost multiplier to assessment day is 1.017 (1.580 × 1.017 = 1.606, call 1.6). 1.6 × $1,875,000 = $3,000,000, the assessor's building value for the current year.
>
> Taxes: 3% or $92,580 per year ($3,086,000 × 3%).
> Taxes per Square Foot: $92,580 ÷ 250,000 sq. ft. = 37¢ per sq. ft. for land and building.

Cost Approach with Excess Operating Cost Example

Land is now selling for between $12,000 and $15,000 per acre. A new plant would cost between $12.00 and $15.00 per square foot to build today.

250,000 sq. ft. × say $12.00 per sq. ft. = $3,000,000
Less physical depreciation (50 year life = 2% per year)
5-year-old building = 10%

Current Cost		$3,000,000
Less Physical Depreciation		300,000
Cost Less Physical Depreciation		$2,700,000
Less Functional Obsolescence		
Assume that due to poor layout of the plant, you are required to do double-handling of material and incur excess costs per year as follows:		
6 men—labor and benefits	$ 64,000	
Operating Supplies	1,000	
Maintenance of Equipment	36,000	
Depreciation	5,000	
	$106,000	
Additional Annual Costs after Federal taxes @ 50%	$ 53,000	

To determine the effect on a "willing and rational" buyer, the present value of these excess costs must be computed by capitalizing at an appropriate rate.

Using a Present Worth per annum table at 10% (reasonable return for this industry) for 45 years (remaining life of plant) = Factor 9.862808 = Functional Incurable Obsolescence Due to Excess Labor and Operating Costs
= $53,000 × 9.962808 = $522,729

Say	$523,000[2]
Cost Less Physical Depreciation	$2,700,000
Functional Obsolescence	− 523,000
Cost Less Physical and Functional Obsolescence	2,177,000
Less Economic Obsolescence—5% per Appraiser's Opinion	− 109,000
Building Value Per Cost Approach	$2,068,000
Add Land (Use assessor's value)	86,000
Value per Cost Approach	$2,154,000

[2]For actual cases involving this method of approach, see *Reynolds Metals Company v. Department of Revenue*, 258 Ore. 116, 477 P 2d 888 (1971) and *Publishers Paper Co. v. Department of Revenue*, 270 Ore. 737, 530 P. 2d 88 (1974).

Income Approach Exercise

Industrial plants of a comparable nature are leasing for \$.75 to \$1.00 per square foot, net.

A reasonable capitalization rate is 12%.

E.g., Income Approach: 250,000 square feet × \$1.00 p.s.f. net = \$250,000 Capitalized at 12% = \$2,083,333.

Market Data Approach Exercise

Similar type plants are selling on the open market for about \$6.00 per square foot, land and building. Some very old plants have sold for \$1.50 per square foot and some more modern plants, easily adaptable to general industrial use and in good locations, have sold for \$10.00 per square foot, land and building.

E.g., Market Data Approach: 250,000 square feet × \$6.00 p.s.f. = \$2,000,000.

Preliminary Conclusions

Your preliminary conclusions are:

Land is assessed low, but the assessor is probably bound by a land map pattern where all taxpayers are assessed at the same level. You, of course, might risk a land value increase by challenging this assessment.

Taxes are high per square foot. Say your estimate is that taxes should be \$.25 per square foot for land and building vs. \$.37 for subject.

Income and market data information indicates that the assessor's \$3,086,000 value for land and building is extremely high.

Your preliminary conclusion is that your plant is overassessed by at least \$1 million and that you are paying \$30,000 per year in excess property taxes.

Correlation and Future Action

Thus, your analysis and review of the fact situation presented indicates that an appeal of this assessment is warranted. The tax savings potential is substantial and the machinery of appeal should be carefully followed to protect your interests. A fair but aggressive path to an assessment reduction should be pursued with vigor.

OUT-OF-STATE INDUSTRIAL COMPARABLES: ARE THEY ADMISSIBLE?

If the subject is commonly bought and sold in its local environ (office buildings in New York City), the comparable must come from the local area. If some characteristic (size: 300,000 to 500,000 square foot industrial, golf course land) a Board or Judge may look beyond county or even state lines. If subject has a unique regional or nationwide market (food processing plant, 1 million+ square foot industrial), it is within the discretion of the trial judge to look beyond the immediate vicinity of subject. And he may or he may not do it!

The General Rule. As you know, the general rule in the market data approach to value is that a comparable must be in close proximity to the subject property in order to be considered as a value reference point. Close proximity can mean right next door, across the street, or down the block. Taxpayers are never so lucky. They must often look beyond the immediate vicinity of the subject neighborhood. This may take you several miles from the subject. Hopefully, the comparable will be in the same taxing jurisdiction.

The Board said yes to in-State regional—but no to out-of-State. Sometimes, and especially when dealing with larger industrials (say 300,000 to 500,000 square feet), one has to look beyond the jurisdiction. This happened to me recently when I tried to find comparables in San Diego County. There were none to be found, but I introduced several from comparable industrial sections of Los Angeles and San Francisco. The San Diego Board thought this was a good sampling of industrial values in California and allowed the the comparables to be introduced. The value range of these comparables was from $3.83 to $15.56 per square foot, land and building. The Board applied my value per the appraisal to the property, saying they relied on the California comparables.

I also tried to introduce comparables from outside California. This was a cable plant and I did a nationwide survey of cable plant sales. The Board refused to consider these comparables at all. Their position was that out-of-state comparables had no bearing on California real estate values.

The Board said yes. Well, what happens when you are dealing with a one million+ square foot plant in Montana? I recently completed appraisals on two 1 million+ square foot plants there, introduced comparables in that same size range outside Montana, and the comparables were accepted in evidence by the Montana State Tax Appeal Board. They also accepted a sampling of smaller comparables from every major city in Montana as a general indication of industrial market value in that state.

The same was true in Ohio where I appraised an integrated steel mill of 3 million+ square feet. The Ohio Board of Tax Appeals accepted the comparables from outside the State of Ohio, including the recent sale of an integrated steel plant in Illinois.

The good A & P Tea Company[3] faced this very problem because there was no local market for their plant near Elmira in western New York State.

The Court said yes. The subject property is one of the world's largest food processing plants consisting of some 1,544,916 square feet. The assessor valued it at $22.3 million, or $14.13 per square foot, land and building. At the trial, A & P's appraiser valued it at $13.9 million or $9.00 per square foot. The trial court accepted A & P's figure and then adjusted it to $16.7 million, or $10.80 per square foot.

The A & P appraisal expert relied on comparable sales in the eastern United States. Some were 500 to 1,000 miles distant from the subject property. The court said that while it is generally true that comparable sales should not be too remote in location from subject, receiving sales beyond the immediate vicinity of subject rests in the sound discretion of the trial judge.

The court also made the point that although no adjustments were made for differences in the localities where the out-of-state comparables were located, there was testimony that business climate, labor, transportation, and availability of public utilities made the out-of-state properties more desirable than subject.

The Judge said no. Subsequent to the *A & P* decision, I appraised a food processing plant in Virginia and neither I nor the assessor could find any comparables in Virginia. I attempted to introduce a rather extensive comparable sales study of food processing plants in several states other than Virginia (value ranges went from -0- [charitable contribution] to $11.16) in the market data approach. I, of course, relied on the *A & P* case as precedent and the assessor objected.

[3]*A&P Tea Co. v. Kiernan,* 42 N.Y. 2d 236, 397 N.Y.S 2d 718, 366 N.E. 2d 808 (1977).

The Circuit Court Judge read the *A & P* case and promptly disallowed my market approach on the grounds that New York law is not Virginia law. He cited one word in the *A & P* case for his decision. "The trial court, relying on the *unchallenged* testimony of the appellant's appraisers that the market for the subject property was regional in nature, found that there was an active market for the type of building here involved throughout the eastern United States."

The Virginia trial judge felt that the "unchallenged" nature of the testimony gave the New York trial judge greater discretion in the receiving of evidence. I argued that my position was unchallenged too, in that both sides agreed that there were no comparables in Virginia. Nevertheless, the Virginia court relied solely on the cost approach in its decision.

The Federal Court said yes. Finally, there is also federal court precedent for the use of comparables in another state. In a condemnation case,[4] out-of-state sales were accepted by the court as proximate in location to the subject golf course. There is a catch, however. Subject golf course was in Pennsylvania and the comparables were 31, 33, and 51 miles away, all in an *adjoining* county in New York State. The Court accepted them on the grounds that golf course land was not commonly bought and sold. It was, therefore, not an abuse of discretion to permit them to be presented to a jury who would give the data its appropriate weight.

The assessor in *A & P* failed in his argument that the plant was a specialty, and therefore, reproduction cost less depreciation was the proper method of valuation. The court expressed concern over the fact that this method might result in serious overvaluation of the property due to rising construction costs and its failure to adequately account for factors such as functional obsolescence and physical depreciation.

WHEN IS AN INDUSTRIAL PLANT A "SPECIALTY"?

Taxpayer should avoid having property treated as "specialty." Use of only reproduction cost less depreciation puts taxpayer at a disadvantage because depreciation may not be adequately accounted for and favorable market data cannot be introduced.

The General Rule. A specialty is a structure which is uniquely designed and adapted to the business conducted upon it or the use made of it, and it cannot be converted to other uses without the expenditure of substantial sums of money. If an industrial plant is deemed a specialty, it is usually valued at reproduction cost less depreciation and the income and market data approaches to value are not used.

The Taxpayer's Problem. When an industrial property is tailor-made to suit the first occupant and it is assessed as a specialty, it is not usually beneficial to the taxpayer. The assessor applies depreciation merely on subjective judgment. This might result in serious overvaluation of the subject due to rising construction costs. In addition, the assessor may not adequately account for excessive physical deterioration and functional/technological and economic obsolescence.

The *A & P* case. In *A & P Tea. Co. v. Kieran*,[5] the highest court in New York was presented with the specialty issue on one of the world's largest food processing plants.

The question is never an easy one. The trial court held the property *not* a specialty. The Appellate Division said it was a specialty. The Court of Appeals reversed and said it was *not* a specialty.

[4]*United States v. 84.4 Acres of Land in Warren County, Pennsylvania,* 224 F. Supp. 1017, Dist. Ct. Penn. (1963).
[5]*A & P Tea Co. v. Kiernan,* 42 N.Y. 2d 236, 397 N.Y.S 2d 718, 366 N.E. 2d 808 (1977).

This difference in opinion is not surprising. For example, the *Encyclopedia of Real Estate Appraising*[6] carries cold storage plants under the appraisal of "special use" property: "Cold storage plants are primarily single-purpose enterprises having little or no alternative use without a major loss of investment."

Those factors which influenced the *A & P* courts in both directions are as follows:

Yes, it's a specialty!

". . . one of the world's largest (1,544,816 square feet) food processing plants.

". . . designed and constructed for *A & P* to accommodate food processing, warehousing and shipping operations.

". . . built to serve the particular purposes of *A & P*'s business.

". . . 73 truck loading docks.

". . . several interior railroad sidings.

". . . laboratories.

". . . offices.

". . . cold storage and refrigeration facilities.

". . . temperature control systems.

". . . other fixtures utilized in food processing enterprise.

". . . large open areas on main floor.

". . . mezzanine walkways above main floor for employee access to work areas.

". . . tunnels beneath main floor to furnish utility services."

No, it isn't a specialty.

". . . building is easily convertible to other industrial uses without substantial expenditure of funds.

". . . no heavy expenditure to remove present fixtures or install others."

NOTE: With these comments, the Court is recognizing that the bulk of the industrial building square footage at a typical large plant has a number of items in common with other heavy industrial buildings. These items include:

- heavy steel beams, columns and frame;
- wide bays and high ceiling heights;
- heavy crane service;
- heavy duty floor structure;
- all utilities with heavy power station and distribution throughout;
- loading/unloading facilities, rail siding;
- adequate office space and parking;
- generally a land-to-building ratio of three-to-one.

". . . building is constructed and laid out permitting simple alteration.

". . . can be readily subdivided into smaller units."

NOTE: The Court here is recognizing that several large industrial properties have been sold to developers who have converted them to multiple tenant use. For example:

- ALCOA to Schreiber, New Kensington, Pa., 1971 sale, 2,041,624±sq. ft. building, 63 acres at $1.47 per square foot land and building.
- Chrysler to Trammel Crow, Commerce, California, 1972 sale, 1,560,000±sq. ft. building, 86.5 acres at $4.80 per square foot land and building.
- FMC to Park, South Charleston, W. Va., 1972 sale, 2,071,348 sq. ft. building, 75 acres at $2.17 per square foot land and building.
- U.S. Government to Park, Cleveland, Ohio (Cleveland Tank Plant), 1977 sale,

[6] *Encyclopedia of Real Estate Appraising,* Friedman, Ed., Prentice-Hall, P. 824.

2,557,101 sq. ft. building, 175.57±acres at $3.13 per square foot land and building (including basement).

Significance of the issue. In the *A & P* case, the assessor valued the subject as a specialty at $22.3 million or $14.43 per square foot, land and building. Taxpayer's market data approach came in at $13.9 million or $9.00 per square foot, which the trial court accepted. If taxes are levied at a 3% rate, this $8.4 million difference is worth a cool $252,000 in annual property taxes.

If the subject had been deemed to be a specialty by the Court of Appeals, taxpayer could not have introduced his market data comparable sales. He would be at the mercy of assessor's judgment opinion on allocation of depreciation.

Thus, it is to taxpayer's advantage to be able to introduce market data as set forth in the sales for multiple tenant use discussion in the previous section. That $1.47 to $4.81 range suggests that the *A & P* comps were high.

CHECK LIST

Pertinent Data

( ) Tax Bills
( ) Equalization Ratio
( ) Assessor's Records

Physical Plant

( ) Location
( ) Topography
( ) Weight Bearing Capacity of Soil
( ) Is Land Subject to Flooding
( ) Excess Land
( ) Egress and Ingress
( ) Construction Factors
( ) Age
( ) Corrosive Elements
( ) Ceiling Heights
( ) Bay Area Sizes
( ) Plant Layout
( ) Idle or Vacant Areas
( ) Maintenance Costs

Value Estimate Factors

( ) Current Selling Price of Land
( ) Current Cost of Construction
( ) Depreciation: Physical, Functional, Economic
( ) Rental Value of Subject
( ) Capitalization Rate
( ) Current Sale Value of Similar Plants

10
Searching Out Unique Unit-in-Use Measures of Value Can Result In Assessment Reductions On "Special Purpose" Properties

10

There are a number of ''special purpose'' properties that present unique valuation problems for both the assessor and the taxpayer. Each requires individual handling, but there are a few general rules that should be considered:

- All relevant data should be used to value special purpose properties.
- If applicable, the standard three approaches to value—cost, income, and market data—should be used to value the property. Information on income and market data is often difficult to find, but never assume that it does not exist. It may make your case.
- If the property is unique *and* special purpose, then reproduction cost less physical depreciation is generally used to arrive at value. You must examine each of the elements of value used by the assessor. You must present a case which properly takes issue with various cost and depreciation factors employed by him.
- You must search for rules of thumb or unit-in-use measures of value to challenge the assessor's sole reliance on the cost approach. These usually involve the income approach and allow you to, in effect, introduce economic obsolescence.

Some examples are:

- gasoline service stations—gallons of gasoline pumped per year.
- bowling centers—lineage: number of paid lines per lane per day.

Structures such as Skylon Park Tower in Niagara Falls, Ontario (Figure 10-1) or the dam in North Carolina shown in Figure 10-2 are special purpose property and would be appraised via the reproduction cost less depreciation method.

GASOLINE SERVICE STATIONS

Gasoline service stations are specially designed to sell refined petroleum products and to service automobiles.

Site Valuation

Oil companies look for at least 200′ of frontage with good visibility and traffic flow accessibility. Interstate sites are best with substantial residential backup and minimum zoning restrictions.

Cost Approach

Equipment costs may be obtained from the service station section of a cost manual. Both you and the assessor have access to such manuals. You can argue about what figures to use or how much depreciation should apply:

FIGURE 10-1

Land:	
200′ × 200′ or 40,000 square feet valued	
by comparable sales @	$100,000
Land Improvements:	
Pump islands, concrete, asphalt, fence,	
Utilities and landscaping	
Cost new—$15,000	
Depreciated value	$ 10,000
Building:	
Average type station—2,000 sq. ft. @	
$30/sq. ft. = $60,000 less 20% depreciation	$ 48,000
Equipment	
Sign, tanks, lift, compressor, etc.	
Cost new—$25,000	
Depreciated value	$ 20,000
(The oil company generally owns the equipment.)	
Total Depreciated Cost:	$178,000

FIGURE 10-2

Income Approach

Assume an annual net rent of 10% required on the owner's investment:

Land:	$100,000
Buildings and Land Improvements:	75,000
Total Cost New:	$175,000

$175,000 @ 10% = $17,500 net rental per year.

Special Measures for Special Property—Gallonage

Another measure would be an annual rental equal to $0.025 to $0.03 cents per annual gallon pumped. Using 3 cents per gallon, this station would have to pump 583,333 gallons per year to warrant the investment of $175,000.

583,333 gallons × $0.03	= $17,500
Capitalized @ 10%	= $175,000

Thus we see the relationship between cost, net rental as a return on investment, and gallons pumped per year.

If your gallonage pumped per year is lower than anticipated, perhaps you can mount an economic obsolescence argument.

If the gas station in this example pumped only 300,000 gallons per year, your argument would be:

300,000 gallons × $0.03 = $9,000 net rental, capitalized @ 10% = $90,000 rather than the $178,000 or $175,000 carried by the assessor.

It is a good argument, but it does not always work. In one case, gas station land (18,000 square feet) was leased for $15,000 per year to a "triple-A" tenant for 20 years with four 5-year options. The taxpayer argued that the lease rent should not be used to measure the value of the land because the station was pumping only 700,000 gallons per year rather than 900,000 gallons per year as projected at the beginning of the lease.

The court rejected the exclusive application of the "gallonage" approach, saying that gallonage depends on brand name, management efficiency, advertising, price, location, suitable improvements, and goodwill—most of which are foreign to the true value of real estate.

But the court went on to say:

> We do not decide whether, under some circumstances, the gallonage approach might be a satisfactory method of valuing gasoline service station property.[1]

The court, in this case, rejected the gallonage concept because it felt the long-term lease was in line with fair market value. But it left the door open to the use of the theory in other cases.

BOWLING CENTERS

Modern bowling as a major recreational business dates back to the early 1950's, which saw the advent of the automatic pinsetter/pinspotter. Bowling centers generally include cocktail lounge and coffee shop. Many also have pro shops, playrooms, billiards, and banquet rooms.

Site Valuation

Bowling center sites must be within easy road access of major residential areas and have adequate parking. Land value is developed from comparable sales.

Cost Approach

A typical assessor's cost approach may look like this:[2]

Land: 2 acres valued via comparable sales:			$400,000
Land Improvements: Paving, Lighting—Depreciated Value			20,000
Assume a 5-year-old, 40-lane house of 40,000 square feet:			
Bowling Area	30,000 sq. ft. @ $16 =	$480,000	
Bar Area	6,000 sq. ft. @ $32 =	192,000	
Coffee Shop	4,000 sq. ft. @ $26 =	104,000	
		$776,000	
25-year life for structure (5 years old) Less 20%		−155,200	
			620,000

[1] *Humble Oil and Refining Company v. Borough of Englewood Cliffs,* 135 N.J. Super. 26, 342 A. 2d 560, 563 (1975).

[2] See *Assessor's Handbook,* "Appraisal of Bowling Centers," California State Board of Equalization, revised February, 1976.

Lanes (including ball return)		
$8,000 @ 40 lanes	$320,000	
15-year life for lanes	−107,000	
⅓ depreciated		213,000
15-year life for pinsetters		
$9,000 × 40 lanes	$360,000	
	−120,000	
⅓ depreciated		240,000
	Total Depreciated Cost	$1,493,000
	Call	$1,500,000

Note: You can take issue with both the cost and depreciation factors used by the assessor. Specific arguments might include the cost of lanes ($8,000) and pinsetters ($9,000). This total of $17,000 exceeds the average cost of $10,000 to $12,000 for the "old and new" lanes/pinsetters going into the new houses. This is due to an excess of used equipment and lanes available as a result of the closing of bowling centers in the United States and Japan.

Another issue might be raised on the 15-year life used for pinsetters. Perhaps a more realistic life would be ten years.

Income Approach

Perhaps you can counter the assessor's cost approach with an income approach.

In Chapter 7, we recognized that only a portion of the business generated from a hotel/motel operation was attributable to the real estate. The income was also attributable to management, goodwill, brand name, etc. The same is true with regard to bowling centers.

A sampling of typical bowling center leases indicates that investors will lease *land and building* within the framework of the following general formula:

6% — 10% of bowling receipts
5% — 10% of bar receipts
5% — 6% of food sales

Assume the following gross receipts (all numbers are rounded):

Bowling		
40 paid lines per lane per day @ $.75 per line =		
$30.00 × 40 lanes = $1,200 × 365 days =		
$438,000 × .08%	=	$35,000
Billiards		
Say 10% of bowling gross receipts =		
$44,000 = .08%	=	3,500
Bar		
Say 85% of bowling gross receipts =		
$372,000 × .075%	=	30,000
Food		
Say 75% of bowling gross receipts =		
$329,000 × .055%	=	18,000
Total Gross Income		$86,500
Less 5% Vacancy Factor		− 4,325
Effective Gross Income		$82,175

Less Expenses		
Insurance (excluding pinsetters)	$5,000	
Maintenance	3,000	− 8,000
Net Income Before Amortization and Property Taxes		$74,175
Less Income Attributable to Land		
Land Value (estimate from comparable sales) $400,000 × .125 (yield rate 10% + taxes 2.5%) =		−50,000
Income Attributable to Building		$24,175
Building Value: ($24,175 ÷ .165 − Yield Rate 10%, Taxes 2.5%, and Amortization 4% − assume a 25-year remaining economic life.)		
Indicated Building Value:		$146,515

Another method to value the lanes and pinsetters might be as follows:

Lanes:			
$6,000 cost new × 67% good = $4,000 depreciated value per lane × 40 lanes =			$160,000
Pinsetters			
40 lines per day × 365 days = 14,600 lines per lane per year			
Rent per lane per standard industry contract:			
10,000 lines @ 12¢ =		$1,200	
4,600 @ 6¢ =		276	
		$1,476	
Gross Income			
$1,476 × 40		$59,040	
Less − 5% Vacancy		− 2,952	
Effective Gross Income		$56,088	
Expenses			
Insurance	$5,000		
Maintenance	8,000		
		−13,000	
Net Income Attributable to Pinsetters		$43,088	
$43,088 ÷.225 (10% yield, 2.5% taxes, 10% amortization)			$191,500

The summary of these values is:

Land	$400,000
Building	146,515
Lanes	160,000
Pinsetters	191,500
Total Value—Income Approach	$898,015
Call	$900,000

As you can see, there is a substantial difference between the assessor's cost approach of $1,500,000 and your income approach of $900,000. This is income producing property and the assessor should certainly consider the income approach in his valuation considerations.

Special Measures for Special Property—Lineage

Here the special measure is lineage—the number of paid lines per lane per day. This establishes the income stream from which the value of the bowling center, lanes, and pinsetters is derived. If negative economic factors have caused a decline in lineage, you should present an income approach similar to the one set forth above and press for an assessment reduction.

COUNTRY CLUBS/GOLF COURSES

Country clubs (usually consisting of golf course, swimming pool and clubhouse) present a unique assessment problem. They are generally operated as non-profit, and collect dues and fees from members to pay for operation costs.

Site Valuation

The golf course land may be valued by comparable sales of other golf courses.

For example, in a condemnation case[3] the subject property was the 84.4 acre Kinuya Valley Golf Course in Warren County, Pennsylvania. Comparable sales accepted by the court as sufficiently similar and proximate in location to subject were:

a 56-acre tract, 31 miles away
a 51-acre tract, 51 miles away
a 110-acre tract, 33 miles away

All were in an *adjoining* county—but in New York State. The Court accepted them on the grounds that this golf course land was not commonly bought and sold. (By the way, it was not an abuse of discretion to permit these out-of-state sales to be presented to a jury who would give the data its appropriate weight.)

The land value may also be developed by "abstraction." This is the process of evaluating the land as if developed for sale and then making deductions for developing costs, overhead, selling expenses, and profit. This results in a raw land value estimate.[4]

Cost Approach

A country club is a "special use" property and the reproduction cost less depreciation is commonly used.

Building, swimming pool and parking area improvements are easily costed from a standard cost manual.

Golf course costs depend upon size, layout and quality of sprinkler systems. Costs per hole can range from $17,000 (minimal improvements) to $90,000 (built on marshland). Typical private club: $38,000. Championship course: $46,000.[5]

Thus, the typical private country club golf course of 18 holes, 150 acres, 6,500 yards

---

[3]*United States v. 84.4 Acres of Land in Warren County, Pennsylvania,* 224 F. Supp. 1017, Dist. Ct. Penn. (1963).

[4]M.R. Carb and A. Helbing, Jr., "Appraisal of a Country Club," *Encyclopedia of Real Estate Appraising* (1968), Prentice-Hall, Inc., Englewood Cliffs, N.J., pages 837-842.

[5]*Marshall Valuation Service,* Recreational Facilities Section.

long with average greens and tees, would cost $684,000 (18 × $38,000) plus clubhouse, pool, parking, etc.

Income and Market Data Approaches

The typical country club is a non-profit operation, and the income approach is not applicable. If comparable sales of other country clubs (golf courses) are available, they are certainly admissible as valuation reference points. Do not simply introduce comparable assessments with no evidence of market value. A Pennsylvania taxpayer did this and received an assessment increase![6]

Special Measures for Special Property

One of the difficulties in appraising a country club/golf course special purpose property is how to measure the effect of a higher use for the property. For example, if the golf course land is surrounded by expensive residential land, would the assessor be within his rights to attribute the residential land value to the golf course acreage?

The tax practitioner must convince the assessor or the Board of Review that the full value of the golf course related improvements should not be added to the land value because this would result in an inflated value.

For example:

A)	Value of golf course land developed from sales of comparable land that has sold for golf course use:	$ 500,000
B)	Value of land for alternative use (say residential):	2,000,000
C)	Value of land improvements to golf course:	1,000,000
D)	Buildings related to golf course:	500,000

Don't let the assessor do this—

B + C + D = $3,500,000

This value is inflated. Value should be

A + C + D = $2,000,000

or

B + ⅓ of C & D = $2,000,000 + $500,000 = $2,500,000[7]

You must be sure that the assessor takes into consideration *all* factors[8] relevant to a determination of market value. The B + C + D approach results in the highest possible value, and disregards a key factor: the price at which comparable golf course land is selling on the open market.

In these special purpose valuation matters, you must always press the assessor to look at *all* relevant factors in his valuation analysis.

In a Missouri case, the assessor took the direct approach and assessed a tennis/swim club via the cost approach. The improved value of the land was added to the reproduction cost of the improvements. No depreciation on the improvements was granted because it was

---

[6] *Valley Forge Golf Club, Inc. v. Board for the Assessment and Revision of Taxes of Montgomery County,* 285 A. 2d 213 (1971).

[7] Stanley T. Ooka and Herbert R. Welder, Jr., "Valuation of a Golf Course for Assessment Purposes," *Assessors Journal,* Vol. 4, No. 1, April 1969, pages 3-12.

[8] *State Board of Tax Commissioners v. Valparaiso Golf Club, Inc.,* 330 N.E. 2d 394 (1975).

new construction. The total cost of the land and improvements was $657,176 for a clubhouse, 5 indoor and 9 outdoor tennis courts, a swimming pool and parking area. The assessor's value was $614,918.

The court required the assessor to take *all* factors relevant to market value into consideration. The court listed the following factors: The tennis/swim club's special permit limited its income producing capacity; the special permit also limited the field of potential buyers of the property because the property could only be used as a tennis/swim club; there were limited rental payments (ten-year lease at $41,400 per year); depreciation contemplates *any* reduction in or lessening of value and depreciation should have been considered even though the improvements were new.[9]

MOTION PICTURE THEATERS

There are several problems that challenge the continued existence of the ''movie house'' as we know it. Attendance has been cut in half since 1946. This has to do primarily with TV and other leisure time competition.

Pay TV will make further inroads. Many believe 50% of the present theaters will close due to insufficient patronage and insufficient product.

Others believe that there will always be a market for large screen movies. But there is a great demand for high quality product which is the responsibility of the producer and beyond the control of the exhibitor.

Site Valuation

The typical ''movie house'' assessment problem might involve a downtown (central business district—CBD) theater. Land value is usually set on a front foot value basis. This method of value may seriously penalize the movie theater land, not unlike the downtown retail store example set forth in Chapter 6.

Cost Approach

Theater costs, including stage, booths and light lofts, can reach $50 per square foot. This price contemplates a good steel frame, fireproofed structure. Seating ($75 per seat), booth equipment, curtains and screens would be additional. The entire cost might be $500 per seat not including land. Thus, the assessor might value a ten-year old, 800-seat theater (10,000 square feet) at $400,000 less 25% for physical depreciation (40-year life), which equals $300,000.

Income Approach

Sales of comparable property are generally hard to find. Therefore, the best valuation approach for the taxpayer is capitalization of net income. This method would allow you the advantage of recognition of economic obsolescence if income has fallen off in recent years.

Special Measures for Special Property

Assume receipts have fallen off from $500,000 ten years ago to $250,000 today. The following comparison illustrates the effect of this economic decline.

[9] *Stephen and Stephen Properties, Inc. v. State Tax Commission of Missouri,* 499 S.W. 2d 798 (1973).

Cost New		Best Year's Income	Current Year Income
Land:	$100,000	$500,000	$250,000
Bldg. &		Rent @ 10% = $50,000	Rent @ 10% = $25,000
Equip.	400,000	Capitalize @ 10% =	Capitalize @ 12% =
Total	$500,000	Market Value of $500,000	Economic Rent Market Value of $208,333

Clearly the income approach should dictate market value. Because of economic decline in the CBD, the property is now worth only about one-half of the assessor's cost approach to value. Note that the capitalization rate changed from 10% to 12% between the good and bad years. This properly reflects the fact that a potential investor would want a greater return on his investment due to the additional risk involved in the movie theater business today.

DRIVE-IN THEATERS

A drive-in theater is unique in structural character and produces income from the movie exhibition business carried on in its structures. It is, therefore, a specialty.[10]

Site Valuation

A drive-in theater location must be within easy access of major arteries. Land preparation includes clearing, grading, and paving. Comparable land sales are the best evidence of value.

Cost Approach

Drive-in theater cost per car space can range from low ($550) to excellent ($1,000). In the *Westbury Drive-In* case referred to above, the court held that reproduction cost less depreciation plus land value (comparable sales) was the proper valuation approach.

Income Approach

In *Westbury Drive-In,* the taxpayer attempted to value the property by capitalizing the ground rent of a 12-year-old ground lease. The lease rent was $30,000 for 42 years and $35,000 for the last 21 years of the 64-year lease.

The Court rejected this approach because the taxpayer paid no attention to sales of vacant or improved land in the vicinity of subject property. Judicial notice was taken of the fact that land values had increased since 1954, when the lease was made, and 1966-71, the tax status dates under appeal.

The Court relied on a previous case where it was held: ''In arriving at the true value for tax assessment purposes of real property subject to a lease, an appraisal is to be made of the property as a whole regardless of the effect of the lease upon the value of the owner's interest.''[11]

[10] *Westbury Drive-In v. the Board of Assessors of the County of Nassau,* 335, N.Y.S. 2d 361, 70 Misc. 2d 1077 (1972).

[11] *People ex rel. Gale v. Tax Comm.,* 17 A.D. 2d 225, 229, 233 N.Y.S 2d 501, 506 (1961).

Special Measures for Special Property

In the Westbury case, the taxpayer was unsuccessful in convincing the Court to recognize the burden of the lease which encumbered the property. The Court preferred to look at current, comparable land sales as a a better indication of value. Thus, a special measure was not used and the assessor's market value of some $830,000 was sustained.

RACETRACKS

Racetracks are big business. Major cities like New York, Miami, Toronto, and Los Angeles have as many as three thoroughbred tracks.

Cost Approach

One general rule is to value racetracks as a specialty. Income is derived from the business conducted on the property and not from the occupancy of tenants who pay for rental of space therein, as in an office building or apartment house. Therefore, the proper valuation is reproduction cost less depreciation plus land.

This was the rule set forth in *Delaware Racing Association v. McMahon.*[12] Delaware Park, a thoroughbred racetrack, had been losing money as a result of competition from other area racetracks. The taxpayer argued that for economic reasons the racetrack operation does not constitute a highest and best use for the property. The expert appraiser argued that the highest and best use for the property was a Diversified Planned Unit Development including residential, light industry, office and commercial uses.

The issue presented to the Court was to determine the proper valuation for property tax purposes of racetrack facilities worth several millions of dollars as a racetrack, and less than one million dollars as a residential site.

The Court cited the *Fitzsimmons* case[13] holding that market value assumes the highest, best and most valuable use for which property is reasonably adaptable and available. The Court interpreted this to mean the most valuable use for which the property was *then* reasonably adaptable and available (a racetrack)—not some speculative use in the imagination of the owner (a diversified development).

The Court also rejected taxpayer's argument that the fair market value of the racetrack stock was worth only $2.3 million which further demonstrated the absurdity of the $9.5 million assessment. The Court held that it was common knowledge that corporate stock has little relation to the value of the corporate assets.

Finally, the Court held that it was improper to value racetrack property based on the income generated.[14] The assessment was upheld based on the reproduction cost less depreciation plus land concept set forth in *Westbury Drive-In,* supra.

Here we see that the Court applied several of the general rules that we have been discussing throughout this chapter. However, it failed to apply the basic general rule that *all*

---

[12]320 A. 2d 758 (1974).

[13]*Fitzsimmons v. McCorkle,* 59 Del. 94, 214 A. 2d 334 (1965).

[14]The Court cited *People ex. rel. Metropolitan Jockey Club v. Mills,* 190 Misc. 277, 72 N.Y.S. 2d 757 (1947), aff'd. 273 App. Div. 971, 79 N.Y.S. 2d 304 (1948); *Metropolitan Dade County v. Tropical Park Inc.,* 231 So. 2d 243 (1970); *Homer v. Hialeah Race Course Inc.,* 249 So. 2d 491 (1970).

relevant data must be taken into consideration in valuing these special purpose properties for tax assessment purposes.

In a later appeal it was held that economic obsolescence should have been taken into consideration in valuing the racetrack.[15]

Income Approach

Despite the holding in the first *Delaware Racing Association* case, the income approach is not necessarily excluded from the valuation of a "horse racing plant." In 1950, the Detroit Fair Grounds track was offered for lease by the Michigan Agricultural Commission. Bids ranged from $365,000 to $550,000. The Michigan Racing Association was awarded the lease at $450,000.

The mutual handle was $44,441,943 and the track's share, under Michigan law, was 11% or $4,480,000. Thus, the rental paid was about 10% of the track's gross.

Perhaps not a fixed rule, but certainly a reference point.[16]

In Pennsylvania, where the cost approach is not permitted as evidence of value in court,[17] the income approach was used to value a racetrack. The basis was strongly secured leases.

Capitalization rates used ranged from 12% to 15%.

The actual average net operating income (1969-1971) was $606,700. The taxpayer used a $538,000 net and capitalized at 15% based on taxpayer's alleged insecurity of their racing license to arrive at a value of $3,600,000. The assessor used $676,358 net capitalized at 12.9% to arrive at a value of $5,947,162 (plus land). The lower court used a net of $550,000 and a capitalization rate of 12% to arrive at $5,253,333 (plus land) which the appeal court upheld as fair.[18]

Special Measures for Special Property

The simple point again is that *all* relevant data must be considered in valuing these special purpose properties. The taxpayer does not always have to accept the reproduction cost less depreciation plus land concept with no adjustments.

Thus, Aqueduct Racetrack which opened in 1959 at a cost of $34.5 million might argue that its assessment should be reduced because its receipts are off, due to competition from Off Track Betting and other racetracks; and that its stable area is small and there is no room for expansion.[19] These arguments might put a substantial dent in Aqueduct's 5 million annual property tax bill. It is *all* relevant data which should be considered.

PROPERTY USED FOR A SPECIAL PURPOSE IS NOT ALWAYS VALUED AS SPECIAL PURPOSE PROPERTY

A property used for a special purpose such as a roller rink may not be of such unique design as to preclude it from other uses. This is important because it allows the taxpayer to

[15]*Delaware Racing Association v. McMahon,* 340 A. 2d 837 (1975).

[16]Jack N. Oppenheim, "Racing Plant Appraisal," *Technical Valuation* (now *Valuation*), July 1950, pages 11-14.

[17]Reproduction costs less depreciation held improper. *Buhl Foundation v. Board of Assmt.*, 407 Pa. 567, 180 A. 2d 900 (1962); *Pennsylvania Northern Lights Shoppers City Appeal,* 419 Pa. 31, 213 A. 2d 268 (1965).

[18]*Pocono Downs, Inc. v. Board,* 312 A. 2d 268 (1965).

[19]*New York Times,* December 27, 1977 at Page 49, Column 1.

introduce income and market data information from the general real estate market that may be helpful to establish a lower value.

In one case the taxpayer was operating a roller rink but was able to show that the property could be used as a warehouse, dance hall or supermarket.[20]

[20] *Servstation Realty Co. v. Board of Assessors,* 392 N.Y.S. 2d 674 (1977).

11
Techniques for Establishing More Equitable Personal Property Assessments

11

The equitable assessment and taxation of personal property is a particularly vexing problem to both the assessor and the taxpayer. In those jurisdictions where items of personal property are taxed, the taxpayer must acquaint himself with the pertinent statutes, case law, assessors' guides and handbooks and, most important, local practice.

The personal property taxpayer must also address himself to the definition of personal property, its situs, exemptions, rendition or return compliance practice, audit, and appeal efforts.

As in real estate, a personal property assessment is presumed to be correct and the taxpayer has the burden to show specific instances of error or discrimination in order to recover personal property taxes paid under protest.[1]

The taxpayer must therefore adequately prepare himself to overcome this burden of proof.

DEFINITIONS

What Is Personal Property?

Personal property is defined in general as everything that is the subject of ownership that is not realty and not permanently affixed to realty. It has to do with property of a movable nature such as goods, chattels and money.

In the United States, the ad valorem tax levied against goods, chattels and money translates into an inventory, machinery/equipment and an intangibles tax.

Inventory can consist of goods, wares and merchandise including raw materials, work-in-process and finished goods; supplies (including fuel); and agricultural products (including livestock, grain, tobacco and bee hives).

Machinery/equipment can consist of furniture and fixtures; manufacturing machinery, tools, dies, jigs and patterns; signs; storage tanks; automotive equipment (from heavy construction equipment to snowmobiles); leasehold improvements (portable partitions, counters and shelving); leased or rented items; household furniture; books and periodicals; dams and railroad side tracks privately owned; and other assets.

Intangibles (property having no intrinsic and marketable value, merely representative of value) that are assessed in the United States are: stocks, bonds, notes, mortgages, royalties, checking and savings accounts, cash on hand or in safe deposit boxes, accounts receivable, judgments, goodwill, patents and franchises.

[1]*Leach Corporation v. County of Los Angeles*, 228 Cal. App. 2d 634, 39 Cal. Rptr. 654 (1964).

HOW TO DETERMINE SITUS

Permanently Fixed or Movable Distinctions

When personal property acquires a more or less permanent or fixed situs (not a transient or temporary one), that jurisdiction and no other may impose a tax.[2]

Situs is sometimes difficult to ascertain when dealing with movables. The general rule is that personal property is assessed where it is permamently located or regularly used.[3] When property is not permanently located (a movable bituminous plant) the rule of *mobilia sequuntur personam* (movables follow the person) is recognized and the property is assessed at the owner's residence[4] unless justice demands otherwise.

Justice demanded otherwise in a Texas case where it was held that movable construction equipment was taxable at the *principal office* of the company rather than at the residence of the company officers. Job contracts were handled at the office, employees lived there, the city and schools gave the company and employees services there, and should tax the equipment.[5]

Situs in Connecticut is defined by statue as being permanently located for a minimum of seven months. Taxpayer leased computer equipment and placed it in Connecticut only six months prior to assessment date. The City of Hartford levied an assessment and argued that it should be able to levy because otherwise the taxpayer could move the equipment every six months and avoid the tax. The court disagreed because the assessor's approach could result in double taxation.[6]

In a similar case, colonies of honeybees were in California after January 1st and brought into Nebraska before July 1st of the same year. The court held that the taxpayer who reported the colonies to the assessor in California and paid the taxes, cannot be discriminated against and taxed again in Nebraska.[7]

On the other hand, the taxpayer cannot avoid taxation by simply moving goods out of a jurisdiction on assessment day.

Property temporarily removed from a taxing jurisdiction is still subject to tax at its place of permanent situs. In a California case, a taxpayer removed jewelry from Los Angeles to Hawaii in order to display the jewelry for purposes of sale and to avoid the California personal property tax. The court held that "temporary absence from home . . . was ineffective to defeat the imposition of the tax at the place of permanent situs."[8]

When Personal Property Is Traveling in Interstate Commerce, It May Not Be Subject to a Local Property Tax

Since situs is the basis for the levy of a state personal property tax, the taxpayer must first determine if his personal property has acquired the necessary situs in a given state which would subject those goods to a tax.

If the taxpayer's *goods are in transit* among the several states, they are in *interstate commerce* and they are immune from state and local taxes because only the U.S. Congress

---

[2] *Union Refrigerator Transit Co. v. Kentucky,* 199 U.S. 194, 50 L.Ed. 150, 26 S Ct 36 (1905).
[3] Calif. Cons. Art XIII, Sec. 10.
[4] *Kennedy & Son, Inc. v. Town of Albany,* 66 Wis. 2d 447, 225 N.W. 2d 624 (1975).
[5] *Nacagdoches Independent School District v. McKinney,* 504 S.W. 2d 832 (1974).
[6] *Levin-Townsend Computer Corporation v. City of Hartford,* 349 A. 2d 853 (1974).
[7] *Knoefler Honey Farms v. County of Sherman,* 243 N.W. 2d 760 (1976).
[8] *Brock & Co. v. Board of Supervisors,* 8 Cal. 2d 286, 292, 65 P2d 791, 795. 110 A.L.R. 700, 705.

has the right to regulate interstate commerce. No state may impose a burden on interstate commerce.[9]

Movement begins when the goods are legally committed to a carrier by bill of lading, for transportation to a given place in due course. The immunity will not attach if the goods have merely been laid down at a depot or packing house.[10]

Continuity of transit is not necessarily broken if the goods physically come to rest,[11] but if the stop is for some local advantage independent of interstate commerce, the immunity may be lost.[12] And, the immunity ceases when the interstate movement ends.

Several states have extended this ''situs'' rule and have created an exemption designed to meet unique state requirements of an economic nature. This exemption is generally referred to as the ''freeport law.'' The hope is that the economic activity generated by exempting the personal property would be more beneficial to the state than would the levying of a tax.

Nevada is a good example of a state with a very liberal freeport law. It is, of course, aimed at bringing warehousing storage business into Nevada and it has been very effective due to its close proximity to the lucrative California and West Coast market.

Property is deemed not to have acquired situs in Nevada if goods are consigned to a warehouse in Nevada from outside Nevada for storage in transit to a final destination outside Nevada. This is the OUT-IN-OUT rule and it is very liberally construed. The goods may be assembled, manufactured, processed, relabeled or repacked as long as the items are to be resold outside the state of Nevada. Many major firms do much of their West Coast distribution from Nevada and thereby pay no personal property tax.

Caution: In order to take advantage of the freeport exemption, the taxpayer must file Claim of No Situs Status and keep appropriate books and records. Failure to do this will result in the property losing its no situs status and it will be subject to the Nevada personal property tax.[13]

The transient character of *carriers in interstate and foreign commerce* also creates situs issues. Two general theories have been developed by the United States Supreme Court.

The ''home-port'' doctrine permitted only the home port to impose a tax. The ''apportionment'' rule permits more than one jurisdiction to levy a tax based on some reasonable method such as length of time spent or number of miles traveled in a jurisdiction.

The apportionment doctrine has been recognized with regard to aircraft,[14] railroad rolling stock,[15] and vessels traveling in interstate commerce.

There Are Still Some Gray Areas in the Ad Valorem Taxation of Imports and Exports

The validity of the imposition of a local property tax had long depended on whether or not the item is considered to be an import or export.

---

[9]U.S. Const. Art. S, *Case of the State Freight Tax,* 15 Wall. 232 (1872).

[10]*Heisler v. Thomas Colliery Co.*, 260 U.S. 245, 43 S.Ct. 83, 67 L.Ed. 237 (1922); *Coe v. Errol,* 116 U.S. 517, 6 S.Ct. 475, 29 L.Ed. 715 (1886).

[11]*Minnesota v. Blasius,* 290 U.S., 54 S.Ct. 34, 78 L.Ed. 131 (1933).

[12]*Kelley v. Rhoads,* 188 U.S. 1, 23 S.Ct. 259, 47 L.Ed. 359 (1903).

[13]Nevada Revised Statutes 361.160 to 361.185.

[14]*Braniff Airways v. Nebraska State Board of Equalization and Assessment,* 347 U.S. 590, 74 S.Ct. 757, 98 L.Ed. 967 (1954).

[15]*Central Railroad Co. of Pennsylvania v. Commonwealth of Pennsylvania,* 370 U.S. 607, 82 S.Ct. 1297, 8 L.Ed. 2d 720 (1962).

The U.S. Constitution prohibits states from levying imposts or duties on imports or exports.[16] Early U.S. Supreme Court cases upheld this general rule as long as the goods remained the property of the importer in their original form or package.[17] This concept was expanded to include goods imported through brokers and awaiting entry into the manufacturing process.[18] Ohio's arguments that the goods were not imports because they were not for sale was disregarded by the Court.

In 1959, the court held that iron ore from foreign countries essential to current manufacturing requirement ceased to be an import. The immunity was lost if the importer broke the original package; if the goods were sold or consumed in the manufacturing process; or if the goods were put to the use for which they were imported.[19]

In the recent Michelin case, this doctrine was severely altered when it was held that a *non-discriminatory* ad valorem property tax was *not* prohibited by the import-export clause[20] as long as the *goods were no longer in transit*.

In this case, Michelin imported tires and tubes from France and stored them in warehouses for distribution. The tubes were in packages; the tires were not. Georgia levied a property tax, Michelin appealed, the trial court held both tires and tubes immune from the property tax as imports. Georgia appealed.

On appeal, the Supreme Court of Georgia held that only the packaged tubes were immune. The tires were held to be taxable because they were not in original packages and were comingled with tires from prior shipments.

Michelin appealed once too often. The U.S. Supreme Court did not address itself to the original package doctrine. It held that a non-discriminatory ad valorem property tax levied on these imported goods (in packages or not) was not prohibited by the Import-Export Clause of the Constitution because the tax did not interfere with the flow of goods among the states. The framers of the Constitution wanted to permit inland states to get imported goods without paying duties to seaboard states and this tax was not directed at imports.

Technically, only the "unpackaged tires" were appealed by Michelin. Therefore, it can be argued that the court did not pass on the question of the "packaged tubes."

Nevertheless, some states reacted immediately to this decision and began to tax these previously immune inventories. At least two counties in California even went so far as to pursue escaped assessments for four back years because the immunity had been erroneously granted in previous years. Applying this decision retroactively and levying escaped assessments appears to be a little too aggressive, even for California.

With regard to exports, the general rule is that the goods must enter the export stream to be immune.

In a California case, the taxpayer was shipping cement plant assets overseas. On assessment day, the property tax was levied on the still unexported remainder of the plant. The court held that the entrance of the articles into the export stream was necessary. There had to be a certainty that goods are headed for foreign destination such as delivery to common carrier.[21]

In a Michigan case, oil was held 15 months in storage because taxpayer was unable to

---

[16]U.S. Const. Art. 1, Sec. 10.

[17]*Brown v. Maryland,* 12 Wheat 419 (1827).

[18]*Hooven & Allison Co. v. Evatt,* 324 U.S. 652, 65 S.Ct. 870, 89 L.Ed. 1252 (1945).

[19]*Youngstown Sheet & Tube Co. v. Bowers* (Ohio. *United States Plywood Corp. v. City of Algonia* (Wis.) 358 U.S. 534, 79 S.Ct. 383, 3 L.Ed. 2d 490 (1959).

[20]*Wages v. Michelin Tire Corp.,* 214 S.E. 2d 349 (1975). *Michelin Tires v. Wages,* 423 U.S. 276, 96 S.Ct. 535, 46 L.Ed. 2d 495 (1976). See Annotation: 46 L.Ed. 2d 955.

[21]*Empresa Siderurgica, S.A. v. County of Merced* (Calif.) 337 U.S. 154, 69 S.Ct. 996, 93 L.Ed. 1276 (1949).

obtain shipping space. The court held the oil taxable. The clause confers immunity from location taxation on property being exported—but is not intended to relieve property eventually to be exported from its share of the local tax burden.[22]

EXEMPTIONS: WHAT THEY ARE AND HOW THEY CAN BE APPLIED TO YOUR ASSETS

Your investigation should include whether or not you are subject to a personal property tax at all. Some states do not assess personal property. Others permit various types of exemptions to the levy.

Examples of exemptions are:

Manufacturing Exemptions

A statute in Minnesota (M.S.A. S272.02(11)(6)) allowed for a manufacturing exemption that included tools and machinery used in manufacture, processing, production, sale or distribution of marketable products. The Minnesota Supreme Court held that a computer used for order writing and invoicing (Honeywell Series 1800) and laboratory equipment for quality control and R & D came within the statutory exemption.[23]

Pollution Control Exemptions

Where the equipment in question removed pollutants and other impurities from the used industrial oil, the court granted a *pollution control* exemption. The purpose of the statute was to encourage the building and using of such equipment.[24]

Caution: But, as in all these exemption situations, be sure to comply with the pertinent statutes. These may require you to obtain prior approval and to comply with start-up deadline dates. This decision was reversed on appeal due to these circumstances.[25]

Please see Chapter 13 for additional comments on exemptions.

METHODS FOR MINIMIZING TAX LIABILITY IN PERSONAL PROPERTY TAX COMPLIANCE PRACTICE

Preliminary Considerations: Detecting the Major Weakness in Personal Property Assessment Practice

Having first determined that your personal property has situs in a given jurisdiction and that it is not immune or exempt from the personal property tax, you must now address yourself to compliance practice dictated by the pertinent statutes, assessors' handbooks and local custom.

One of the distinctions between assessing real estate and personal property is that the assessor is working with figures supplied to him by the taxpayer via a rendition or personal property return. The basic information enables the assessor to pursue an "audit appraisal"

---

[22] *Joy Oil Co., Ltd. v. State Tax Commission* (Mich.) 337 U.S. 286, 69 S.Ct. 1975, 93 L.Ed. 1366 (1949).

[23] *General Mills, Inc. v. Comm. of Taxation,* 294 Minn. 175, 199 N.W. 2d 636 (1972). Statute has since been amended to exempt all tools and machinery.

[24] *Wallover Oil Company v. Ohio Water Pollution Control Board, Department of Health,* 279 N.E. 2d 648 (1971).

[25] 291 N.E. 2d 469 (1972).

relying on the books and records of the taxpayer. A "physical appraisal" is seldom conducted because it is expensive and time consuming.

The taxpayer should be aware of the fact that the "audit-appraisal" technique results in the same shortcomings experienced with regard to the mass appraisal of real estate. There is simply no substitute for a detailed physical appraisal of the subject property. The broad guideline measures used by assessors do not consider the individual asset being appraised. These generally applied reporting requirements and schedules do not adequately allow for inventory valuation variations, abnormal physical depreciation, functional/technological and economic obsolescence and intangible valuation problems unique to a specific item of personal property.

The taxpayer should be aware of these factors and he must convincingly supply them to the assessor so that they may be properly weighed. The assessor, in his audit/mass appraisal approach, cannot be expected to become familiar with every detail pertaining to the property. It is therefore the taxpayer's responsibility to prepare and present his valuation arguments if he expects them to be considered in the assessor's valuation exercise.

A typical fact situation will be presented at the conclusion of this chapter to illustrate what a taxpayer must do on a property valuation issue: audit through appeal.

Assembling Pertinent Data

Your data gathering effort should include a review of the last three returns filed by the taxpayer. This will acquaint you with the format of reporting practice followed to date.

If inventory levels are stable and additions to machinery and equipment accounts are similar for each year, you will have an immediate picture of the personal property investment in the subject jurisdiction.

After reviewing the returns in detail and investigating any fluctuations, you must also study the worksheets that taxpayer used to develop the figures rendered to the assessor. In most instances this will involve the review of primary ledgers and computer print-outs indicating investment at a particular location. These should be the same primary data used for federal income tax reporting and annual report publication. In the event of audit you are always faced with the assessor's requirement that reported figures be certified by an independent CPA firm. Therefore, you should be sure that the worksheets reflect the "actual" figures from the taxpayer's official books and records.

Finally, you should determine how the assessor treated the figures after they were reported to him. This involves a review of the tax bills and, if available, the taxpayer's personal property record card on file at the assessor's office, which is the basis for the assessment.

This exercise enables you to see what the taxpayer reported, how he developed his numbers, and what the assessor did with those numbers to develop the assessment.

Mastering the Mechanics of Personal Property Tax Compliance Practice Assures You of Rendering Your Data in the Most Advantageous Light

In General

In general, the statutes require the taxpayer to: . . . file a personal property return listing his assets . . . on a form furnished by the assessor . . . to be submitted by a certain date . . . signed and sworn to by the taxpayer.

The assessor has the right to propound questions about the return, to examine books, records and documents and to ascertain other pertinent information.

Incomplete entries are subject to penalties; failure to report assets in some jurisdictions can result in their taxation at double or ten times value; and willful intent to evade is a misdemeanor in some jurisdictions subject to fine and imprisonment.

The Return

Although personal property returns differ in each jurisdiction, the California Business Property Statement (Figure 11-1) is a typical example of the type of information the assessor is interested in to enable him to levy an assessment.

The form calls for identification of the taxpayers and then requires entries for inventory, supplies, M&E, furniture and equipment, buildings and construction in progress. It also calls for reporting property belonging to others but in the possession of the reporting taxpayer.

There are three additional pages with over 100 entry spaces for details.

Upon completion, the return is mailed to the assessor, and subsequently, the taxpayer receives a tax bill with an assessment based on the reported figures which are subject to audit.

Inventory

The typical personal property return calls for the 100% value of the *inventory.* This usually means raw materials, work-in-progress and finished goods. This could include the cost of the goods plus carrying charges such as receiving, shelving, and insuring of the goods. Assessors will usually accept the taxpayer's value per his books if:

(1) the inventory is physically complete.
(2) the proper trade level is reflected (valued according to its stage of production).
(3) present day pricing is reflected.
(4) values are adjusted for realistic obsolescence.

The taxpayer's general ledger will be the assessor's primary source of inventory data. He is looking for market value which in most accounting systems is either cost or market, whichever is lower. If the accounting method of approach is FIFO, moving average or retail method and the books tend to reflect current cost, the assessor will generally use taxpayer's figures. However, LIFO may be rejected by the assessor on the grounds that current costs are not reflected.

The basic inventory cost reference for a retailer is generally:

(1) invoice price
plus
(2) freight and handling
less
(3) trade, quantity and cash discounts, allowances for damaged, shopworn and out-of-style stock.

For a manufacturer, the inventory cost reference is usually:

(1) raw materials cost
plus
(2) freight and handling
plus

FORM **571**

BUSINESS PROPERTY STATEMENT
To Dwight L. Mathiesen
Assessor of Santa Clara County
70 W. Hedding St., San Jose, Calif. 95110 - Phone 299-3821

1978

FILE RETURN BY APRIL 1, 1978
DECLARATION OF COSTS AND OTHER RELATED PROPERTY INFORMATION
AS OF 12:01 A.M., MARCH 1, 1978

ASSESSMENT NO.

DATE

NAME
DBA
MAILING ADDRESS
CITY AND STATE
BUS. TYPE
LOC ADDRESS
CITY AND STATE

ECN EX.
AUD.
A.P.N.
SEC. CODE
A.N.
CLASS CODE

PROCESSING DATA		
OPER	BY	DATE
REC		
ANAL.		
COMP.		
REV.		
F.B.		
E.D.P.		

Part I GENERAL INFORMATION

COMPLETE (a) THRU (h) AS REQUESTED

a. Make necessary corrections of the printed name and mailing address.

b. Enter type of business: ____________

c. Enter local telephone no. (____) ____________

d. ☐ (✓) Check if ownership of land at LOCATION OF THE PROPERTY is in your name

e. When did you start business at this location? DATE: ____________

f. Check (✓) description of operation at this location.

☐ Retail ☐ Manufacturer
☐ Wholesale ☐ Professional
☐ Distributor ☐ Service

g. Enter location of general ledger and all related accounting records (include ZIP)

h. Enter name and telephone no. of person to contact at location of accounting records.

TAXPAYER'S COPY

Part II DECLARATION OF PROPERTY BELONGING TO YOU

Attach Schedule For Any Adjustment To Cost	COST (Omit Cents) (See Instructions)	ASSESSOR'S USE ONLY — FULL CASH VALUE	TOTAL F.C.V.	LINE NO
1. Inventory, March 1 (From Line 43)			INVENTORY EXEMPTION	1
2. Supplies				2
3. Equipment (From Line 91)			PERSONAL PROPERTY	3
4. Equipment Out on, or Held For, Lease or Rent to Others — Attach Schedule				4
5. Bldgs., Bldg. Impr., and/or Leasehold Impr., Land Impr., Land (From Line 67)				5
6. Construction in Progress — Attach Schedule				6
7.			IMPROVEMENTS	7
8.				8

Part III DECLARATION OF PROPERTY BELONGING TO OTHERS

Name and Mailing Address of Owner (Attach Continuation Sheet If Necessary)	(SPECIFY TYPE BY CODE NUMBER) 1. Consignments 2. Leased Equipment 3. Vending Equipment 4. Other businesses 5. Lease-Purchase Option Equipment	Cost to Purchase New (If Available)	Annual Rent (If Applicable)	LINE NO
9.				9
10.				10
11.				11
12.				12
13.				13

OWNERSHIP TYPE (✓)
Proprietorship ☐
Partnership ☐
Corporation ☐
Other ☐

ATTACHMENTS (✓)
Supplemental Schds. ☐
Computer Printouts ☐
Other ☐

SIGNATURE:

Under penalty of perjury, I declare that I have examined this return, including accompanying schedules and statements, and to the best of my knowledge and belief it is true, correct, and complete and covers all property required to be reported which is owned, claimed, possessed, controlled, or managed by the person named in the statement at 12:01 a.m. on March 1, 1978. If prepared by a person other than the taxpayer, his declaration is based on all information of which he has knowledge.

Full Legal Name if Incorporated

Signature of Owner, Partner, Officer, or Authorized Agent — Title — Date 1978

Signature and Address of Preparer Other Than Taxpayer — Date 1978

ASSESSOR'S USE ONLY

SBE-ASD AH 571-L 7-15-77 6988

FIGURE 11-1

SCHEDULE A - INVENTORY SCHEDULE

LINE NO	WHEN USING PHYSICAL OR PERPETUAL INVENTORY, START AT LINE 15	AMOUNT (Omit Cents)		ASSESSOR'S USE ONLY	
	COMPUTE MARCH 1ST INVENTORY (if book figure not current)				
14	a. Inventory, beginning of fiscal year starting ________ 19 ___	$			
	b. Add purchases and freight from above date to March 1				
	c. Add direct and indirect labor cost from above date to March 1				
	d. Add mfg. expense (burden) from above date to March 1				
	e. Total of Lines a through d				
	f. Net sales from above date to March 1 $________				
	g. Less gross profit @ ____% $________				
	h. Cost of goods sold (Line f minus Line g)				
15	MARCH 1ST INV. (Line e minus Line h, or physical ☐; or perpetual ☐)		$		
	ANY ADJUSTMENTS MUST BE SHOWN BELOW				
16	ADD unrecorded inventory not included in Line 15.				
17	" freight-in not included in inventory				
18	" direct and indirect labor cost not included in inventory				
19	" mfg. expense (burden) not included in inventory				
20	" unrecorded trade level not included in inventory				
21	" other inventory supplies not included in inventory				
22	" adjustment from L.I.F.O. to current replacement cost				
23	" adjustment from standard cost to actual cost				
24	" applicable research and development cost				
25	" other (specify)				
26					
27					
28					
29	TOTAL (Lines 15 through 28)		$		
30	DEDUCT interstate or foreign shipments recorded but not on hand *	$			
31	" goods held for transshipment (file exemption claim)				
32	" case, trade, and purchase discounts				
33	" inventory consigned to others				
34	" inventory out on, or held for, lease or rent to others				
35	" other (specify)				
36					
37					
38					
39					
40					
41					
42	TOTAL Deductions (Lines 30 through 41)		$		
43	**NET INVENTORY** (Line 29 minus Line 42; enter here and on Line 1, PART I)		$		

REMARKS

ASSESSOR'S USE ONLY

Description	Amount
TOTAL ADJUSTED INVENTORY	

*** CLAIM FORM MUST BE FILED, SEE INSTRUCTIONS**

SBE-ASD AH 571-L 7-15-77 6988

- 2 -

FIGURE 11-1 (continued)

SCHEDULE B - COST DETAIL: **BUILDINGS, BUILDING IMPROVEMENTS, AND/OR LEASEHOLD IMPROVEMENTS, LAND IMPROVEMENTS, LAND AND LAND DEVELOPMENT**

LINE NO.	Calendar Year of Acquis.	**BUILDINGS, BUILDING IMPROVEMENTS, AND/OR LEASEHOLD IMPROVEMENTS** 1. STRUCTURE ITEMS ONLY (See Instructions)		2. FIXTURE ITEMS ONLY (See Instructions)		3. **LAND IMPROVEMENTS** (e.g., blacktop, curbs, fences)		4. **LAND AND LAND DEVELOPMENT** (e.g., fill, grading)		LINE NO.
		COST	**ASSESSOR'S USE ONLY**	COST	**ASSESSOR'S USE ONLY**	COST	**ASSESSOR'S USE ONLY**	COST	**ASSESSOR'S USE ONLY**	
44	1978									44
45	1977									45
46	1976									46
47	1975									47
48	1974									48
49	1973									49
50	1972									50
51	1971									51
	1970									52
53	1969									53
54	1968									54
55	1967									55
56	1966									56
57	1965									57
58	1964									58
59	1963									59
60	1962									60
61	1961									61
62	1960									62
	1959									63
64	1958									64
65	PRIOR									65
66	TOTAL									66
67	Add Totals on Line 66 and any supplemental schedules.					ENTER HERE AND ON LINE 5, PART II				67

TO AVOID DUPLICATE AND OVER ASSESSMENT, explain in detail additions and retirements (see instructions): ______

SBE-ASD AH 571-L 7-15-77 6988 -3-

FIGURE 11-1 (continued)

SCHEDULE C - COST DETAIL EQUIPMENT

Include equipment expensed and fully depreciated items. Include sales or use tax, freight and installation costs. Attach schedules as needed.

LINE NO.	Calendar Year of Acquis.	1. MACHINERY AND EQUIPMENT FOR INDUSTRY, PROFESSION OR TRADE		2. OFFICE FURNITURE AND EQUIPMENT		3. TOOLS, MOLDS, DIES, JIGS		4. OTHER EQUIPMENT Describe		LINE NO.
		COST	ASSESSOR'S USE ONLY	COST	ASSESSOR'S USE ONLY	COST	ASSESSOR'S USE ONLY	COST	ASSESSOR'S USE ONLY	
68	1978									68
69	1977									69
70	1976									70
71	1975									71
72	1974									72
73	1973									73
74	1972									74
75	1971									75
76	1970									76
77	1969									
78	1968									78
79	1967									79
80	1966									80
81	1965									81
82	1964									82
83	1963									83
84	1962									84
85	1961									85
86	1960									86
87	1959									87
88	1958									
89	PRIOR									89
90	TOTAL									90
91	Add Totals on Line 90 and any supplemental schedules					ENTER HERE AND ON LINE 3, PART II				91

ASSESSOR'S USE ONLY

ADJUSTMENT								
NET FULL VALUE								
FIXTURE %			%		%		%	
PERSONAL PROPERTY								

SBE-ASD AH 571-L 7-15-77 6988 - 4 -

FIGURE 11-1 (continued)

(3) goods in process (including direct labor and manufacturing overhead)
plus
(4) finished goods (including direct labor and manufacturing overhead)

In order to properly reflect value of inventory for ad valorem purposes, the taxpayer must be prepared to present arguments which include:

(1) goods in transit which do not have situs in the jurisdiction; even though books and records may prematurely record them as being located there;
(2) adjustments for transactions between inventory and lien date which may reduce inventory levels;
(3) proper recognition of damaged or distress merchandise, unsalable goods and odd or broken lots;
(4) exclusion of certain general administrative expenses from inventory costs such as central office overhead, selling and research and development.

Machinery and Equipment

There are two general classes of machinery and equipment (M&E) that form the basis of the ad valorem personal property tax levy in the United States. The first are those items that are frequently exchanged in the open market such as automobiles, trucks, tractors, boats and planes. These assets can usually be valued by reference to a published price schedule with adjustment for condition, wear and tear, etc. These schedules are easily obtainable for reference purposes. Some examples are:

Truck Blue Book and Identification Book, Official Used Truck Valuations, National Market Reports, Inc., Chicago, Ill.

Green Guide, The Handbook of New and Used Construction Equipment Values, Equipment Guide Book Company, Palo Alto, Calif.

Blue Book of Current Market Prices of Used Heavy Construction Equipment, Forke Brothers, Lincoln, Neb.

BUC, an authenticated record of the value of used boats and marine engines from 1929 to date. Another volume prices new boats. BUC International Corp., Fort Lauderdale, Fla.

Trade a Plane, Crossville, Tennessee.

A second category of M&E are those operating groups of equipment for which a price schedule is not available. Since there is no organized market for this type of M&E, the valuation exercise usually involves obtaining historical or original cost, factoring that figure via an index or trending schedule to current cost and subtracting depreciation from all sources: physical, functional/technological and economic.

In arriving at original cost, the assessor is interested in that cost which the taxpayer carries on his books as his capitalized cost for federal income tax purposes. This figure includes the basic invoice price (including general administrative and in-house labor), freight charges, installation charges and the sales tax.

A typical personal property return calls for the taxpayer to list his M&E's original cost by year of acquisition. The assessor then applies his trending and depreciation schedules to these figures to arrive at the "true" value of the M&E.

A condensed version of the exercise is as follows:

Schedule 1

	Year of Acquisition	Original Cost (O.C.)	×	Index or Trending Factor	=	Trended Original Cost (TOC)	−	Normal Depreciation (ND) Factor	=	TOC − ND
	Current	1,000		1.00		1,000		-0-		1,000
Age −	1 yr. old	1,000		1.13		1,130		95%*		1,074
	2	1,000		1.32		1,320		85%		1,122
	3	1,000		1.36		1,360		75%		1,020
	4	1,000		1.40		1,400		65%		910
	5	1,000		1.48		1,480		55%		814
	6	1,000		1.57		1,570		45%		707
	7	1,000		1.63		1,630		35%		571
	8	1,000		1.67		1,670		25%		418
	9	1,000		1.74		1,740		15%		261
	10 & prior	5,000		1.80		9,000		15%**		1,350
		$15,000				$23,300				$9,247

*Half the normal depreciation factor applied in first year.
**15% residual figure recognizes value in use.

These factors may also be combined and applied as a single factor as follows:

Schedule 2

TABLE	1	2	3	4	5
TITLE	Gas Distribution	Electric T&D & Pipelines	Long-Lived	Average-Lived	Short-Lived
SERVICE LIFE	30½ Years & Over	20½ to 30 Years	15½ to 20 Years	7½ to 15 Years	7½ Years or Less
AGE	Multiplier	Multiplier	Multiplier	Multiplier	Multiplier
1	99	98	94	93	89
2	97	94	83	79	69
3	94	90	74	67	53
4	93	88	68	60	45
5	92	86	63	54	38
6	90	84	59	49	32
7	90	83	56	46	30 min.
8	89	82	54	44	
9	88	81	52	42	
10	88	80	50	40	
11	87	79	48	38	
12	86	78	46	36	
13	86	77	44	34	
14	85	76	42	32	
15 & over	84 min.	75 min.	40 min.	30 min.	

A comparison of these two schedules to the subject assets reveals the following when using a 10-year life and an averaged-lived 7½ to 15 years:

Schedule 3

	Original Cost	Multipler	Depreciated Value
Current	1,000	-0-	1,000
Age 1 yr. old	1,000	93%	930
2	1,000	79%	790
3	1,000	67%	670
4	1,000	60%	600
5	1,000	54%	540
6	1,000	49%	490
7	1,000	46%	460
8	1,000	44%	440
9	1,000	42%	420
10 & prior	5,000	40%	2,000
	$15,000		$8,340

The difference between the $9,247 and the $8,340 depreciated values results in substantial personal property tax levy differences in the United States. These can range from below 1% to over 6% of the market value of the M&E.

The foregoing examples show the wide disparity of results that can occur if the mathematical computations involved in the replacement cost less depreciation method of valuation are simply applied without tempering with appraisal judgment. Courts have looked elsewhere for guidance.

The Supreme Court of Ohio has held that an arm's-length sale of the subject property, after two years on the market, was the best reference in determining value.[26]

In Illinois, personal property is assessed at its fair cash value (Illinois Revised Statutes, 1969, Chapter 120, Section 502). Fair cash value has been interpreted to mean "fair market value" or the price an item would sell for between a willing buyer and seller, cognizant of all pertinent facts and under no duress.[27]

Illinois courts have further developed and refined this basic definition. It has been held that where market value is not truly reflective of the worth of an item, reproduction cost less depreciation, capitalization of income, functional obsolescence, changes in technology, age, life expectancy, condition, location, and resale value are all factors to be considered in valuing property for tax purposes.

The court rejected the assessor's valuation formula, not explained, and not shown to have any relation to actual cash value.[28]

Thus, we see the courts looking to an arm's-length sales transaction if one actually took place. We also see the courts tempering the replacement cost less depreciation schedules with appraisal judgment in the form of obsolescence. The following examples are cases in which I provided expert testimony and which set precedent in both Washington and Montana.

The Washington Board of Tax Appeals held "*In the Matter of the Appeal of Aluminum Company of America vs. July, 1973 Board of Equalization of Clark County,*" Docket No. 9026 State of Washington Board of Tax Appeals, September 27, 1975, as follows:

[26]*The Grabler Manufacturing Company vs. Kosydar,* 330 N.E. 2d 924 (1975).

[27]*People ex rel. Rhodes v. Turk,* 391 Ill. 424, 63 N.E. 2d 344 (1945), *Springfield Marine Bank v. Property Tax Appeal Board,* 44 Ill. 2d 428, 430, 256 N.E. 2d 334 (1970).

[28]*Consolidation Coal Company v. Property Tax Appeal Board,* 29 Ill. App. 3d 465, 331 N.E. 2d 122 (1975).

> When functional obsolescence is evident in a plant, an allowance should be made. . . . Economic obsolescence should be treated in a like manner. . . .

The Board did not "recognize the use of [the State's] 28-year-old trended investment schedule as being justifiable." The Board applied a shorter life to value the plant and equipment saying, "The schedule does not allow for functional and economic obsolescence."

The decision is well founded in Washington law.[29] True and fair value in money means fair market value; fair market value means the willing buyer-willing seller concept; original cost, estimated cost of reproduction, rental income, the uses to which the property is adaptable and the sale price of other properties are all factors to be taken into consideration when assessing property. Economic and functional obsolescence was also recognized as a result of a sawmill not operating at optimum efficiency.[30]

Similarly, the Montana State Tax Appeal Board found that, based on the evidence presented, an allowance of 10% for functional obsolescence and 10% for economic obsolescence should have been made when assessing machinery and equipment.[31]

But, how does an appraiser support his allocation of obsolescence?

One method of checking the accuracy of this allocation is to conduct an excess cost inquiry to determine the effect obsolescence would have on an informed prospective buyer of the subject assets. (The method involves the computation of the present value of an annual excess cost and capitalizing the after-tax difference at the appropriate rate.) The excess cost comparison is made between current state-of-the-art and obsolescent assets. Examples of these methods were accepted by the Supreme Court of Oregon.[32]

Differences in value due to excess operating costs are a direct, objective measure of the degree of obsolescence which must be periodically evaluated. Such obsolescence may be attributable to additional manpower or higher repair and maintenance charges necessary to operate obsolescent equipment.

Thus, if excess operating costs are $2 million per year and a fair and reasonable return on investment is 10%, the appraiser could develop his allocation of obsolescence as follows:

Excess Operating Costs	$2,000,000
$2,000,000 @ 50% = Allowance for Federal Income Taxes	−1,000,000
Excess Costs After Taxes	$1,000,000
$1,000,000 × 5.33493 (Present Worth of 1 per Period Table @ 10% for 8 years*	$5,334,930
Additional Obsolescence Call	$5,335,000

*Average Life of M&E

Leased Equipment

There are any number of methods in use in the United States to assess leased equipment. These methods range from replacement cost less depreciation through arm's-length sales to variations of the income approach to value.

---

[29] *Northwest Chem. Sec. Co. vs. Chelan Co.*, 38 Wn. 2d 86, 228 P.2d 129 (1951).

[30] *Weyerhaeuser Co. vs. July 1969 Bd. of Eq. of Pacific County*, Washington Bd. of Tax Appeals, Dockets Nos. 68-22 and 68-23.

[31] *The Anaconda Company vs. The Department of Revenue of the State of Montana*, Doc. No. PT-1965-268 (1975).

[32] *Reynolds Metals Company v. Department of Revenue*, 258 Ore. 116, 447 P. 2d 888 (1971); *Publishers Paper Company v. Department of Revenue*, 270 Ore. 737, 530 P. 2d 88 (1974).

The basic income or capitalization method involves arriving at the annual net income (before amortization of investment, expenses and property taxes are deducted) to the lessor over the life of the property, times a present worth factor plus a discounted salvage value for the equipment at the end of the lease term. This figure should equal market value.

There are many variations on this approach:

- In a Missouri case, the State Tax Commission used a formula of 40 times the average monthly rental divided by three to value Xerox equipment. This method was upheld by the Missouri Supreme Court. It was mentioned that this was a fast method with some drawbacks and inequities.[33]
- In a Michigan case, the assessor attempted to use only list prices and not alternative measures to value the subject electronic data processing equipment. Evidence showed that less than 10% of the machines were sold and only a small number were sold at the list price. The court found that the use of the list price to value the items was unrealistic and at variance with financial realities.[34]
- But the Supreme Court of Mississippi upheld the use of catalog selling prices of Xerox machines by the assessor, even though only one machine was sold in the City of Jackson, while 647 were leased. The Xerox income capitalization formula was rejected. However, the jury did apply a more realistic depreciation schedule.[35]

A PROPERLY PREPARED AND PRESENTED VALUATION POSITION CAN RESULT IN SUBSTANTIAL TAX SAVINGS AT THE AUDIT, LOCAL AND STATE APPEAL LEVELS

Actual Case Example of a Personal Property Appeal—Audit Through State Board Hearing

The preceding sections of this chapter have reviewed definitions, situs and exemption issues and compliance practice. To emphasize the practical application of these matters, the following example is presented. It is drawn from my actual experience.

Fact Situation:

Notice of audit is received by taxpayer. The assessor has requested that he be given the opportunity to review the books and records of taxpayer. The assessor, by statute, has the authority to review five years of past assessments including books and records and renditions.

It has been taxpayer's practice *not* to file a personal property return in the past. Historical precedent resulted in taxpayer simply accepting an arbitrary levy by the assessor. This practice seemed to satisfy all parties until audits began to be conducted at the state level to assist local assessors.

The audit has been completed by the assessor's fieldmen and the results indicate that taxpayer owes $630,000 in back taxes as a result of this five-year audit.

An exit audit conference has been arranged between the field auditor (AUD), the supervising auditor (SUPV. AUD) and the taxpayer. The purpose of having the supervising auditor present is to resolve as many issues as possible at this level to avoid having to appeal minor issues.

---

[33] *Xerox Corporation v. State Tax Commission,* 529 S.W. 2d 413 (1975).

[34] *Mohawk Data Sciences Corporation vs. City of Detroit,* 234 N.W. 2d 420 (1975). See also *Xerox Corporation vs. City of Detroit,* Circuit Court, County of Wayne (1974) where less than 1% of Xerox machines were sold at list prices. Xerox received refunds of the taxes it had paid under protest.

[35] *Xerox Corporation vs. City of Jackson,* Supreme Court of Mississippi, No. 48, 819 (1976).

Exit Audit and Negotiations:

TAXPAYER: Hello, Gentlemen. I appreciate your taking the time to sit in on this exit audit.

SUPV.AUD: I'm glad to take the time. I think we should resolve all the issues we can and, of course, if you're not happy, you can present your arguments to the State Board. I also want to thank you for the cooperation you have given to us now that we have finally gotten in here to conduct our audit. I went over the work papers this morning and I must say you gave our auditors a nice office to work in. I was called out on an audit last week and our boys were working in a closet with a 60-watt light bulb. You'd be surprised how disagreeable that makes us, and it doesn't hurry up the audit one bit.

TAXPAYER: Well, your people have been very thorough and we have tried to give them everything they asked for. We've gotten along very well during the audit. To expedite things, I have prepared an outline of our basic differences on the main issues in this audit. If you will refer to Attachment #1, you will find the preliminary audit worksheet figures presented to me by your auditors. Column 1 shows the years in issue. Column 2 shows we are dealing with inventory (INV) and machinery and equipment (M&E). Column 3 shows the audit figures, Column 4 the arbitrary assessment figures, Column 5 the differences which are the same except for 1977

PRELIMINARY AUD WORKSHEET (All Figures Rounded)
INVENTORY & MACHINERY & EQUIPMENT (M&E)

Ratio—100%
Tax Rate—$3.00/100

(1)	(2)	(3) Figures Per Audit	(4) Arbitrary Assessment	(5) Difference	(6) Taxes Due	
Fifth Year	Inv.	$3 Million	$1 Million	$2 Million	$ 60,000	
	M&E	2 Million	1 Million	1 Million	30,000	
Fourth Year	Inv.	3 Million	1 Million	2 Million	60,000	
	M&E	2 Million	1 Million	1 Million	30,000	
Third Year	Inv.	3 Million	1 Million	2 Million	60,000	
	M&E	2 Million	1 Million	1 Million	30,000	
Second Year	Inv.	3 Million	1 Million	2 Million	60,000	
	M&E	2 Million	1 Million	1 Million	30,000	
Current or First Year	Inv.	4 Million*	1 Million	3 Million	90,000	
	M&E	2 Million	1 Million	1 Million	30,000	
				$16 million	$480,000	
					120,000	Penalty & 12%
					30,000	Interest @ 6%
					$630,000	

INVENTORY BREAKDOWN

Raw Materials — $1 Million
Work-In-Process — 1 Million
*Finished Goods — 1 Million

*$2 million in first year

ATTACHMENT 1

when our finished goods inventory increased by $1 million, and Column 6 shows the taxes due together with penalty and interest computations.

SUPV.AUD: The figures per audit are your actual book figures?

TAXPAYER: Yes, you take book inventory figures and eliminate shipping supplies, obsolete goods, slow moving goods, and inventory reserves to arrive at inventory values per the Federal Tax Return.

AUD: We've gone over these figures in great detail and I agree that these are inventory figures properly adjusted by taxpayer's outside accounting firm to reflect the value of their inventory for federal income tax purposes and for reporting their financials in their annual report.

NOTE: The point made here is that the basic ''Figures per Audit'' have been gone over in great detail during the course of the working audit. All the accounting talent of taxpayer's organization was combined to present the best arguments regarding inventory valuation. Having done this, taxpayer is now faced with requesting adjustments which go beyond ''book value'' figures.

TAXPAYER: First, certain of our inventory is located outside of this plant, held by outside vendors. I have here shipping documents which prove that.

SUPV.AUD: Some of these items are in this state and some are not. You know we assess all the items to you if they are in the state.

TAXPAYER: But some of these firms holding our finished products for use in their manufacturing have agreed to pay the personal property taxes on those items.

SUPV.AUD: We have found that most of this inventory held by other vendors goes unreported. Therefore, we assess you and let you chase your vendor. Can you show me that taxes have, in fact, been paid on this inventory at outside vendors within the state?

TAXPAYER: No, but will you eliminate the out-of-state inventory?

SUPV.AUD: Yes. May I suggest we draw up a little horse-trading sheet at this point. I'll call it Attachment #2 and I'll start out with the $16 million difference figure and see where we go from there. [See the end of this section for Attachment #2.]

AUD: The out-of-state inventory at outside vendors amounts to $100,000 per year for each of the five years under audit, or a total of $500,000. We'll enter this under A.

NOTE: Location of inventory is most important and detailed documentation is a must.

TAXPAYER: I would like to also raise the issue of export exemptions. You know, some of our finished product is ordered by foreign countries and foreign corporations and we set that finished product aside in our shipping warehouse area and it is destined for overseas shipment.

AUD: We checked this out, and the goods are destined for overseas shipment, but it is our position that items retained in plant after customer acceptance do not constitute the judicial test of what process of exportation means. It is the position of the State Audit Department that the item must make physical entry into the stream of exportation, such as delivery on shipboard or to a common carrier in a continuous route or journey overseas.

TAXPAYER: I feel this is a gray area and the basic rules are primarily governed by provisions of the United States Constitution which restrict such taxation by states.

SUPV.AUD: We have pretty good case law in this state which makes this type of item taxable. Perhaps your better argument would be who owns the property on lien date. If the foreign country or corporation owns it, then perhaps it is not taxable to you.

TAXPAYER: Well, I've got about $100,000 a year in these types of shipment, and I would certainly like to add this to our horse-trading sheet for further consideration.

SUPV.AUD: We'll add it under B.

NOTE: Immune property arguments should be extensively researched. Many states have freeport exemptions for inventory in interstate commerce. Exemptions are dependent on where the goods come from, what happens to them in the state, and where they go. These ''situs'' rules are written, unwritten, governed by local custom, sometimes even depending on which warehouse they are in. It is a research requirement in every audit.

TAXPAYER: Now, I would like to have an adjustment made to eliminate work-in-process (WIP) since your statute references only raw materials and finished goods as taxable items. The statute reads, and I quote: ''1. Every manufacturer shall be taxed on all raw materials and finished products.''

SUPV.AUD: Pardon me if I laugh—I hope you are not going to waste too much time with this. We certainly cannot allow that adjustment. The attorney general of this state has stated in an opinion letter that WIP was contemplated by the legislature as being included in any inventory measure, and this is well settled in this state.

TAXPAYER: Well, I wish you would add it to our horse-trading sheet. There is a case pending before the State Tax Commissioner, and it is worth $1 million per year to me or one-third of my inventory for each of the five years, per the inventory breakdown on Attachment #1.

SUPV.AUD: I'll add it, but I'll tell you right now I won't adjust it. I'll list it under C.

NOTE: The point made here is a thorough review of applicable statutes must be made by the taxpayer in order to be sure he tests each and every possibility. This particular point may be called a long shot. But sometimes long shots pay off and you may be interested to know that on April 16, 1975, the State Tax Commission of Missouri held that Work-in-Process was *not* taxable under the wording of the statute quoted above.

TAXPAYER: My next point, I guess we'll call it D on our horse-trading sheet, is that, as you know, we allowed for normal excess and obsolete stock in our normal accounting procedures. However, these are abnormal economic times and our inventory backlog has increased immensely over the past year. We believe this should be reflected in an allowance over and above our normal allowance and that the value should be at only 10% of cost, which would reflect approximate salvage value of the inventory.

AUD: That means you want us to make an adjustment beyond what your outside accounting firm has done in order to reflect a kind of economic obsolescence due to current market conditions. In other words, tax your current year's additional finished goods inventory of $1 million at 10% or $100,000.

TAXPAYER: Exactly. I think that would properly reflect current conditions for ad valorem tax purposes.

SUPV.AUD: I don't think we can do that. Can you imagine our task involving all our taxpayers! And in addition, we would be doing something that your own auditors have not done. Nevertheless, I'll add the $900,000 request to our horse-trading sheet just to be consistent.

NOTE: Again, you must test all areas. Perhaps the jurisdiction involved is taking some lenient positions on inventory buildup problems in these hard times. This type of argument is sometimes categorized as the ''mercy factor.''

TAXPAYER: I wanted to talk to you about the interest and penalty charges you have made as outlined on Attachment #1.

AUD: Yes. As a matter of course, we levied 6% interest rate and a 25% penalty per our statutes.

TAXPAYER: I know. But your statutes contemplate willful and fraudulent omissions by taxpayer. There was no deliberate misleading act on our part. And, I believe that the levy of these arbitrary assessments established, more or less, the level of assessment in the community.

SUPV.AUD: With regard to the penalty, if we are satisfied that no fraud or evasion is involved, we can adjust the penalty.

TAXPAPER: And haven't interest charges been a rather individually treated subject with no set pattern?

SUPV.AUD: True. In fairness to you, I must say we do not have a set procedure.

TAXPAYER: Well, how about striking them from the computations?

SUPV.AUD: I can't do that, but I will make some adjustment. I'll add it to our horse-trading sheet and I will be fair with you. I'll enter these items as E and F.

TAXPAYER: Do you think we can get together at all with regard to the issues concerning M&E useful lives and depreciation schedules or the classification issues as to what is personal property and what is real estate?

SUPV.AUD: I think you are going to have to take these issues up on appeal. We have applied our standard life/depreciation schedules and we have made the basic classification decisions in accordance with our state directives. Any questions you have on that will have to be appealed.

TAXPAYER: Do you intend to add in the sales tax on each item as part of its original cost?

AUD: That's right.

TAXPAYER: What is the theory behind that?

AUD: Obviously the sales tax is part of the purchase price of the item, and therefore it must be considered part of the value for ad valorem tax levies.

TAXPAYER: But this is a tax levied separate and apart from the purchase price. It would change from jurisdiction to jurisdiction, depending on the rate.

AUD: Right.

TAXPAYER: I was wondering if it then wouldn't be logical for me to argue that I should have my purchases adjusted downward for the investment tax credit that I am receiving.

AUD: But that is the Federal Government.

TAXPAYER: So what; a tax is a tax. If you adjust by adding a sales tax, you should also adjust by subtracting the investment tax credit.

SUPV.AUD: We'll have to take that one under consideration, too. How much is involved?

TAXPAYER: With adjustments, the two just about cancel each other out.

SUPV.AUD: We'll add this consideration to our horse-trading sheet, and I'll tell you what I'll do. I'll allow the $500,000 on (A) out-of-state inventory. With regard to the exported property problem (B), I believe case law supports my position that the goods have not entered the export stream and are subject to the property tax. I cannot allow the Work-in-Process issue (C), and I cannot allow for any mercy factor allowance (D). With regard to interest and penalty charges (E & F), I'll agree to split these down the middle if you'll agree to drop this as an issue. I feel we do have gray areas in this regard, but I must exact some kind of payment from you under the circumstances.

TAXPAYER: I'll agree to that.

SUPV.AUD: I will recommend that the sales tax be included in the M&E valuation (G). I believe we've done all we can here today.

TAXPAYER: Yes. I'll take the Work-in-Process, the mercy factor and the sales tax/investment tax credit issues to the State capital to talk with the State staff in the hopes of negotiating further prior to any formal appeal to the State Board. Further, I believe I'll be taking the machinery and equipment issue and the classification issue to the State Board, but I would like to get the inventory matter out of the way.

SUPV.AUD: Good luck. I've enjoyed meeting with you.

TAXPAYER: It's been very fine working with you, too. Thank you very much.

AUD: You will be receiving a letter from us with our final findings, and you will then have time to appeal further, if you so desire.

TAXPAYER: Right.

NOTE: The taxpayer subsequently received a letter from the auditors confirming the trading decisions made on the horse-trading sheet. He proceeded to file a letter with the state staff auditors at the Capital, which held the matter open until he was able to meet and negotiate with them. This gave him a second level to attempt settlements. By this time, the State Tax Commission's decision on Work-in-Process had been handed down, and he was able to prevail there. He further found that certain adjustments were being made with regard to the economy in valuing excess inventory on a statewide level, and he was able to achieve another $100,000 valuation reduction on his mercy factor. In addition, the state recognized the wash between sales taxes and investment tax credit and did *not* add sales taxes to the valuation of the M&E.

Thus, taxpayer's negotiation effort succeeded in reducing his audit deficit by some $5,600,000. In addition, he cut interest and penalties in half. A total tax savings of $245,000.

HORSE-TRADING SHEET

Ratio: 100%
Tax Rate: $3.00/100

				Tax Liability
	Inventory & M&E Difference	$16,000,000		
A	Out of State Inventory		$500,000	$ 15,000
B	Exported Property		500,000	15,000
C	WIP not included in Statute		5,000,000	150,000
D	Mercy Factor—carry excess inventory @ 10%		900,000	27,000
E	Interest			30,000
F	Penalty			120,000
G	Sales Tax/Investment Tax Credit on M&E Valuation			-W A S H-

ATTACHMENT 2

He had to recognize that the lack of filing renditions resulting in arbitrary assessments left outstanding amounts on under-reported inventory. The taxes on these amounts were due and payable. He received the final audit findings letter from the state and decided that he would appeal the machinery and equipment valuation issue to the state.

We now turn to the issue of Machinery and Equipment valuation at the State Board.

State Board of Equalization Hearing—Machinery and Equipment (M&E) Valuation Issue

B1, B2, B3 = Board Members
ATTY. T = Taxpayer's Attorney
ATTY. S = State's Attorney
AT = Appraiser for Taxpayer
AS = Appraiser for State

B1: This meeting will come to order. Let the record show that the State Board of Equalization is meeting at the appointed time. All members are present.

B2: The case before us involves taxpayer appealing certain machinery and equipment (M&E) valuation conclusions reached by state auditors.

B3: Taxpayer and the state are represented by counsel. Mr. Taxpayer's Attorney, will you begin for taxpayer.

ATTY. T: Yes, sir. The valuation issue concerns the valuation of taxpayer's M&E and schedules, as listed on Attachment #3. The state has a copy of this sheet and we have agreed to use it as a reference.

ATTY. S: We have agreed, Mr. Chairman.

ATTY. T: The first three columns on this sheet show the replacement cost factors used by both taxpayer and the state.

ATTY. S: There were slight differences and we felt it would simplify things to so stipulate.

B2: This replacement cost factor table means that a piece of machinery purchased twenty years ago would cost approximately twice as much as today?

ATTY. T: That is correct—a factor of 2.06. Columns 4 and 5 show that the state used a 28-year life for this equipment.

ATTY. S: This is our standard table used for all similar taxpayers.

B3: By similar, you mean all manufacturers of primary metal?

ATTY. S: Yes.

ATTY. T: Columns 7 and 8 show the 14-year life used by taxpayer's appraiser and Columns 9 and 10 show taxpayer's actual sales experience in selling these items of M&E.

ATTY. S: During the audit, we satisfied ourselves that the items sold were, in fact, similar to the items used by taxpayer and presently assessed as M&E.

B1: In other words, if you are assessing standard three-phase integral horsepower induction motors, you found that taxpayer, in fact, sold a similar type item.

ATTY. S: Yes. We found similar items. Taxpayer has gone into a general cutback in production and many items were put on the market to be converted to cash.

ATTY. T: Returning now to our M&E Valuation Worksheet—Attachment #3, you can see that the state's 28-year life confirms their audited $2 million value and the taxpayer's 14-year life and actual sales experience confirms his $1 million value. We therefore request no change in the M&E valuation—that the assessment remain at $1 million.

M&E VALUATION WORKSHEET

For Use with the Trended Investment Technique

$100 Reduced Annually at Varying Fixed Rates Applied to Declining Balances to 20% Residuum (Reduction for First Year—½ of Annual Fixed Rates)

REPLACEMENT COST FACTORS									TAXPAYER'S SALES EXPERIENCE	
(1)	(2)	(3)	(4)	(5)	(6)	(7)	(8)		(9)	(10)
		Machinery & Equipment Factors	No. of Years	28 Year Life		No. of Years	14 Year Life		Year	% of Original Cost
				5.5%			11%			
Year	1	1.00	1	97.25	FINAL VALUE CONCLUSION	1	94.50	FINAL VALUE CONCLUSION		
									1	80
	2	1.23	2	91.90	$2 million	2	84.11	$1,200,000	2	43
	3	1.25	3	86.85		3	74.86		3	32
	4	1.30	4	82.07	No Additional	4	66.63	Less Functional	4	38
	5	1.34	5	77.56	Allowance for	5	59.30	Obsolescence	5	31
	6	1.42	6	73.29	Functional and	6	52.78	10%	6	34
	7	1.51	7	69.26	Economic	7	46.97	(−$120,000)	7	36
	8	1.58	8	65.45	Obsolescence	8	41.80		8	19
	9	1.64	9	61.85		9	37.20	Less Economic	9	23
	10	1.71	10	58.45	FMV*	10	33.11	Obsolescence	10	35
	11	1.76	11	55.24		11	29.47	6% — 7%	11	25
	12	1.78	12	52.20	$2,000,000	12	26.33	(−$80,000)	12	14
	13	1.80	13	49.33		13	23.43		13	15
	14	1.81	14	46.62		14	20.00	FMV	14	10
	15	1.82	15	44.06						
	16	1.81	16	41.64				$1,000,000		
	17	1.83	17	39.35					FMV	
	18	1.87	18	37.19						
	19	1.91	19	35.14					$1,000,000	
	20	2.06	20	33.21						
	21	2.26	21	31.38						
	22	2.33	22	29.65						
	23	2.36	23	28.02						
	24	2.39	24	26.48						
	25	2.39	25	25.02						
	26	2.57	26	23.64						
	27	2.67	27	22.34						
	28	2.65	28	20.00						
	29	2.86								
	30	3.50								
	31	4.17								
	32	4.21								
	33	4.29								
	34	4.33								
	35	4.65								
	36	5.01								

*FMV = Fair Market Value

ATTACHMENT 3

ATTY. S: Mr. Chairman, members of the Board, the State Audit Department, in carrying out its function, did review the books and records of taxpayer and found dates and costs of acquisition. We applied our standard formula to these items to determine true value for property tax purposes. This is in accordance with our normal procedure for all taxpayers in primary metals, and we believe taxpayer has been fairly and equitably assessed.

ATTY. T: I would like to introduce Mr. Appraiser T (AT), the appraiser for the taxpayer, who has completed an appraisal of this M&E.

NOTE: At this point, the witness is sworn and his expertise and experience is set before the Board.

ATTY. T: Mr. Appraiser T, have you completed an appraisal report to determine the fair market value of the subject M&E?

AT: I have.

ATTY. T: And what is your valuation conclusion?

AT: $1,000,000.

ATTY. T: Is this a copy of your appraisal report?

AT: It is.

ATTY. T: Mr. Chairman, if it is all right with the state, I would like to pass this report out because there are several numbers to be referenced and it will be less confusing.

ATTY. S: I have no objection, Mr. Chairman, as long as I get a copy. I also reserve the right to object to this going in as evidence at this point.

ATTY. T: I had intended to make it part of the record, but that can wait until we complete our testimony.

ATTY. T: Mr. Appraiser T, would you briefly describe the type of M&E we are dealing with at taxpayer's plant.

AT: Yes. The M&E consists of turbines, pumps, compressors, precipitators, motors, presses, grinders, drills, conveyors, mills.

NOTE: Here, of course, the expert would describe the equipment, its age, its use. He would reference his photographs and his M&E layout drawing to show the Board his complete familiarity with the M&E.

ATTY. T: Now, Mr. Appraiser T, would you describe in general your method of approach in completing this appraisal.

AT: I reviewed the books and records of taxpayer. I physically inspected and photographed the M&E. Using original cost of acquisition, I trended to current replacement cost.

B1: Was freight and installation included?

AT: Yes.

B2: You used the trending schedule on Attachment #3?

AT: Yes. I then considered the useful life of the subject and decided to use a 14-year life per Attachment #3.

B3: Where did the 14 years come from?

AT: My own experience, primarily. I referenced several sources.

B1: Name a few for us, please.

AT: The experience with the M&E itself. How many years has it been used in useful production, what are repair and maintenance schedules like, does it run 24 hours a day, are there corrosive elements at work eating it away? I also discussed useful life with plant engineers, manufacturers of the equipment, and I referenced Asset Depreciation Range Guidelines used by the IRS and cost manuals used nationally in the appraisal profession.

ATTY. T: And after reviewing all these sources, you felt that the best measure of useful life for this M&E is 14 years?

AT: In my opinion, 14 years. If you will refer to Attachment #4, you will find a typical page from my appraisal. It shows a description of the item of M&E, acquisition date, original cost, trended installed cost, the percentage of physical depreciation applied, and the Value in Place of the item of M&E.

DESCRIPTION	DPT	ASSET #	ACC.	COST	TR.INST COST	%	V. I. P.
CLASS 713							
ADD COST	088	7130007	8/72	465	605	27.0	442
ADD COST	088	7130007	11/72	4,992	6,490	27.0	4,738
CONVEYOR	088	7130008	3/69	27,988	42,262	54.0	19,441
ADD COST	088	7130008	5/71	631	846	36.0	541
ADD COST	088	7130008	8/72	265	345	27.0	252
CONVEYOR	088	7130009	3/69	437,828	661,120	54.0	304,115
ADD COST	088	7130009	3/72	4,653	6,049	27.0	4,416
ADD COST	088	7130009	5/72	452	588	27.0	429
ADD COST	061	7130009	8/72	2,414	3,138	27.0	2,291
ADD COST	088	7130009	1/73	14,882	18,328	18.0	15,029
ADD COST	088	7130009	3/73	542	678	18.0	556
CONVEYOR	088	7130010	3/69	50,013	75,520	54.0	34,739
ADD COST	088	7130010	7/71	2,576	3,452	36.0	2,209
ADD COST	088	7130010	3/72	745	969	27.0	707
GATE	092	7130011	3/69	479	723	54.0	333
HANDLING	088	7130013	4/69	214,431	323,791	54.0	148,944
ADD COST	088	7130013	3/72	4,112	5,346	27.0	3,903
ADD COST	088	7130013	1/73	14,662	18,328	18.0	15,029
ADD COST	088	7130013	3/73	542	678	18.0	556
CHUTE	092	7130017	6/69	2,988	4,512	54.0	2,076
FEEDER	092	7130020	12/69	2,656	4,011	54.0	1,845
TRIPPER	092	7130029	6/71	9,957	13,342	36.0	8,539
ELEVATOR	092	7130030	6/71	16,282	21,818	36.0	13,964
ADD COST	092	7130030	3/72	259	337	27.0	246
UNLOAD SYS	067	7130033	11/71	347,643	465,842	36.0	298,139
ADD COST	067	7130033	6/72	9,130	11,869	27.0	8,664
HANDLING SY	067	7130035	1/72	112,696	146,505	27.0	106,949
ADD COST	067	7130035	6/72	29,608	38,490	27.0	28,098
CONVEYOR	092	7130036	3/72	10,027	13,035	27.0	9,516
HANDLING SY	088	7130038	10/72	204,663	266,062	27.0	194,225
ADD COST	088	7130038	2/73	21,630	27,038	18.0	22,171
ADD COST	088	7130038	3/73	2,550	3,188	18.0	2,614
ADD COST	088	7130038	4/73	2,652	3,315	18.0	2,718
ADD COST	088	7130038	4/73	900	1,125	18.0	923
ADD COST	088	7130038	4/74	2,432	2,772	9.0	2,523
ADD COST	088	7130038	7/74	729	831	9.0	756
CONVEYORS	088	7130040	10/72	66,300	86,190	27.0	62,919
ADD COST	088	7130040	2/73	3,728	4,660	18.0	3,821
CARRIERS	092	7130050	3/67	3,040	4,986	70.0	1,496
LOAD BAR	096	7130051	11/73	17,002	21,253	18.0	17,427
CARRIERS	092	7130052	11/73	5,218	6,523	18.0	5,349
CONVEYOR	067	7130054	5/74	22,881	26,084	9.0	23,736
CONVEYOR	067	7130055	5/74	19,389	22,103	9.0	20,114
CLASS 741							
TRUCKSTER	075	0740630	11/67	2,454	4,025	70.0	1,208
ELEC CART	075	7410080	5/70	1,245	1,768	45.0	972

ATTACHMENT 4

ATTY. T: What was your next step?

AT: I felt that the 14-year life adequately covered my physical depreciation under normal conditions. But, certain of this basic M&E warrants consideration of functional and economic obsolescence.

ATTY. T: Could you pursue that further?

AT: Yes. Please refer to Column 9 on Attachment #3. You will see I allocated 10% for functional obsolescence and about 6.5% for economic obsolescence.

B3: What is your basis for that allocation?

AT: I found that taxpayer had recently purchased a more modern production system to produce the same product as this plant, and installed that system in another plant which now out-performs this one by a two-to-one basis. In other words, twice as much finished product is produced with the same man-hour effort. The new machines are numerically controlled, meaning, for example, a computer tells what size holes to drill, minimizing human error which the subject hand-operated machines are subject to. The new machines are faster and larger. They are able to handle wider items. The market today demands 68″ panels as opposed to the 42″ panels previously in demand.

ATTY. T: Did you also observe factors involving maintenance and lubrication of the new machines?

AT: Yes. The new machines are raised up above the ground to facilitate ease of maintenance and lubrication, whereas the older machines are below ground involving severe difficulty in maintenance and lubrication.

ATTY. T: And what did these observations cause you to conclude?

AT: That this particular system was 50% obsolete from a functional point of view.

B1: In other words, technological advances have created a system twice as efficient as the one you are appraising.

AT: Exactly.

B2: But you only applied 10% functional obsolescence.

AT: Correct. There are five basic systems in this plant. I found three to be reasonably modern and applied only a percent or two functional. Two were similar to the obsolete system I just described. I applied a specific percentage to each system and its peripheral support equipment, depending on that system's obsolescence, and it worked out to 10%.

B3: And the functional obsolescence is a negative valuation factor inherent in a system's design due to technological advances which have passed it by.

AT: I couldn't have said it better myself.

B1: What about your economic obsolescence? Influences outside the M&E?

AT: Yes. I allowed 6.5% for general lack of demand in this economy (growth should be 6% a year; it will be much less for this year); transportation costs in this area have increased tremendously in the last year, and pollution and noise abatement restrictions have also increased costs of M&E. All of these factors would cause a prudent purchaser of this M&E to discount its value by at least 6.5%.

ATTY. T: Mr. Appraiser T, were you able to confirm your findings through any other means?

AT: Yes.

ATTY. T: Would you explain what that other measure was.

AT: Yes. Please refer to Attachment #3, and note Column 10. I extracted these figures from the actual experience of taxpayer in selling the equipment on the open market. The sales came about as a result of the turn in the economy requiring taxpayer to curtail much of his manufacturing operation. The company policy was to sell as much of the equipment as they could on the open market, in order to convert idle equipment into cash to be used for other purposes.

ATTY. T: And how does this experience factor chart compare with your own measure of depreciation?

AT: Column 8 on Attachment #3 shows the depreciation schedule that I used, and as you can see, it ties in pretty closely insofar as the total depreciated figure is concerned. There are some variables involved in that taxpayer's experience is somewhat sporadic due to individual years sales experience.

ATTY. T: Nevertheless, you feel that the experience on the part of the taxpayer is a reasonable valuation factor to be used in evaluation exercise of this type?

AT: Yes, I do. It is the market data approach in machinery and equipment appraisals. It is a particularly good measure because it involves the same type of machinery that we are valuing for ad valorem tax purposes here, and it is a valid schedule, indeed.

ATTY. T: Is this exercise then a way of proving your functional and economic obsolescence allocation from the marketplace?

AT: Precisely, it is.

ATTY. T: I have no further questions.

BI: Mr. Atty. S, would you like to ask questions?

ATTY. S: Now, Mr. Appraiser T, you say you used a trending schedule to establish replacement cost of the M&E.

AT: Yes.

ATTY. S: And is there anything startling about the trending schedule these days?

AT: Yes.

ATTY. S: And what is that?

AT: That M&E costs have gone up some 25% in the last year.

ATTY. S: As compared to an average over the last five years of what?

AT: About 5% per year.

ATTY. S: Would you say this is extraordinary?

AT: Yes.

ATTY. S: Then how can you argue a figure so much lower than the state's figure in a market where prices have skyrocketed? We're thinking of revising our entire state schedule upward, and you're proving our case!

ATTY. T: Mr. Chairman, I'm going to object to that as entirely out of order. Mr. Appraiser T has answered the question. If Mr. Atty. S. needs a grandstand to give evidence, let him go out in front of the Capitol building.

BI: Objection sustained. Mr. Atty. S, stick to the case. We're not here to revise the state schedule, we're here to pass on the validity of the assessment in question.

ATTY. S: You say you compared this old system with the new system at the other plant and that the new mill was just purchased and it does everything twice as well as the old mill.

AT: That is correct.

ATTY. S: What was the cost of the old mill?

AT: $100,000.

ATTY. S: And you trended it up to current value of $257,000.

AT: Yes. It was purchased in 1950. Per Column 3 on Attachment #3, a 2.57 factor.

ATTY. S: What, Mr. Appraiser T, is the cost of the new system?

AT: $400,000.

ATTY. S: Do you expect the Board to use this as a fair comparison when the new system is so much more expensive than the old system?

AT: The comparison I make is not between the cost of the new and old system. I say the old system would cost $257,000 to reproduce. I argue that a prudent investor would only pay $43,253 for it, because it is technologically obsolete. My figures come from Column 8 on Attachment #3. I use a 20% depreciation factor because the system is over 14 years old and I recognized that it has some residual value because it is in use. I then subtract 10% functional and 6.5% economic. The arithmetic is replacement cost of $257,000 @ 20% = $51,400 after physical depreciation; − 10% functional = $46,260 − 6.5% economic = $43,253. The $43,253, therefore, is its fair market value and that is what it should be assessed at. It should not be assessed at some ridiculous figure conjured up by an outdated mysterious state schedule.

ATTY. S: Now, now, Mr. Appraiser T, just answer the questions. Could you show us how you proved your $43,253 from the market?

AT: Yes. Column 10 on Attachment #3 shows that items sold by taxpayer returned 10% of original cost. 10% of the original cost is $10,000, so I am conservative in my $43,253 figure.

ATTY. S: No further questions.

B1: Mr. Atty. S, are you ready to put your case on?

ATTY. S: Yes, I would like to call Mr. Appraiser S, the appraiser for the state (AS).

NOTE: Appraiser S is sworn, and his credentials are placed before the Board.

ATTY. S: Did you appraise the M&E at taxpayer's plant?

AS: Yes, I did. I visited the plant and inspected the M&E.

ATTY. S: Did you follow normal procedures during the course of this appraisal?

AS: Yes. I saw no reason to do other than the normal application of our statewide depreciation schedule to this M&E.

ATTY. S: And you used the schedule under Column 5 on attachment #3.

AS: Yes. You will note that it is a 28-year life depreciated over that period to a 20% residual, also recognizing that M&E in use has value.

ATTY. S: And this is the same method that you apply systematically to all such taxpayers?

AS: Yes.

ATTY. S: I have no further questions.

ATTY. T: Now, Mr. Appraiser S, who made up this table of depreciation?

AS: It was formulated some years back by a state appraiser.

ATTY. T: And where is that appraiser now?

AS: He retired some years ago.

ATTY. T: Was it made for this industry alone or was it worked up for several industries with several different tables?

AS: There are several different tables in effect for various industries.

ATTY. T: And are they changed or updated from time to time?

AS: Yes.

ATTY. T: Has this one been updated lately?

AS: Not within the past few years.

ATTY. T: But some schedules for some industries have been updated.

AS: When the facts warrant it, yes.

ATTY. T: You did not see anything at the subject plant that would lead you to believe that this table should be updated in view of technological or other type obsolescence?

AS: I did not.

ATTY. T: Why is a 28-year life an accurate one for this type of M&E?

AS: The state appraisers and engineers believe it to be the most accurate available.

ATTY. T: And you use it as a matter of course.

AS: Correct.

ATTY. T: You do not consider individual M&E?

AS: On the contrary, we do consider individual M&E. I looked at all the M&E at subject and I did not think it was necessary to deviate from the table.

ATTY. T: Thank you, I have no further questions.

B1: The Board will take this matter under consideration.

NOTE: In this actual case, the Board decided in favor of the taxpayer and granted a 26% assessment reduction, resulting in $320,000 in tax savings to the taxpayer.

Of utmost significance to the taxpayer is the fact that state promulgated depreciation schedules can successfully be challenged. They do not generally allow for functional and economic obsolescence and, if the evidence warrants, state boards will recognize these additional depreciation factors.

12

Using Gray Area Subtleties To Your Tax Advantage When Distinguishing Between Real and Personal Property

12

The distinction between real property and personal property can be very difficult to determine. Basic definitions and long accepted traditional or common law concepts can be completely altered by statutes that declare certain items to be real or personal property.

The issue is of extreme importance to the property taxpayer. This is especially true in those jurisdictions which do not tax personal property. Obviously if a questionable item is classified as personal property, it is not subject to any property tax at all.

In jurisdictions where both real property and personal property assessments are levied, the distinction can also be important. It may, for example, be to the taxpayer's advantage to have a process tank classified as personal property rather than real property. This can be due to the fact that a lower assessment is achieved after application of personal property depreciation rates. The same item could be assessed higher if real estate depreciation rates were applied.

Another variable which must be considered is the difference, if any, in the real estate or personal property tax rate to be applied to the assessment.

In order to take full advantage of proper classification, the taxpayer must:

(1) Be completely familiar with the assets subject to the classification issue. This includes:

- a detailed physical description
- method of annexation to real estate
- function and use of the item and the real estate
- intent of party making the annexation.

(2) Thoroughly examine the appropriate statutes in the jurisdiction which set forth the basic definitions of real and personal property.

(3) Review and analyze court decisions.

(4) Become familiar with local assessment practice including directives and guides set forth in the assessor's manual or handbook.

HOW TO PROPERLY DEFINE REAL OR PERSONAL PROPERTY AS A FIRST STEP IN PROPER CLASSIFICATION

Basic Definitions

In the previous chapter, we defined *personal property* as everything that is the subject of ownership that is not realty and not permanently affixed to realty. This included inventory, machinery and equipment, furniture and "fixtures," and intangibles.

We have also defined *real property* as follows:

Land and whatever is erected or growing upon or "affixed" to land.

Fixtures could be included in both definitions. They are generally realty because of the particular manner or nature of their attachment to realty.

Fixtures are sometimes referred to as ". . . a species of property which lies along the dividing line between real and personal property, and to decide on which side of the line certain items of property belong, is often a difficult question."[1]

Thus, it is up to the taxpayer to take his position on that side of the dividing line that is to his advantage.

Statutory Definitions

As stated, these basic definitions can be completely altered by statute. In general, taxes cannot be assessed except by authority of the legislature. And, the legislature ". . . by proper classification has the power to make any kind of property personalty for the purpose of taxation, though it is real estate by the common law and for all other purposes, and vice versa."[2]

Thus, a New York statute declares that ". . . Real Property . . . mean(s) and includes(s): . . . Telephone and telegraph lines, wires, poles and appurtenances; . . ."[3]

In New York, by common definition, realty includes land, buildings and improvements affixed to the land. Here we see the legislature expanding on that definition with respect to utility property because substantial taxpayer assets consist of distribution lines and supporting apparatus or "appurtenances." This expansion has resulted in central office equipment (computerized message processing and switching equipment—easily detachable and movable) being subject to a real property tax in New York.[4]

Under the New York statute cited above, if the bank of movable units shown in Figure 12-1 were computerized message processing and switching equipment, it would be taxed as real estate.

The New York courts have not, however, extended the statute to include subscriber-owned telephones which the assessor of Syracuse tried to assess as real property. The court made a distinction between "appurtenances" as a part of the "system as an integrated whole" and items involved solely because telephone facilities are used to transmit the data produced.[5]

Summary Comment

The above examples show that the statute and court interpretations of that statute are paramount considerations in the classification issue as to what is real property and what is personal property.

In the remainder of this chapter, we will consider these statutes in certain key states. We will also consider how the assessor classifies the property under these statutes. We will review how the courts have interpreted these statutes by examining general guidelines and their application to the facts in specific cases.

---

[1]22 Am. Jur. 713, *Fixtures* §2.

[2]*Kolodney v. Laconia,* 96 N.H. 337, 338, 76 A.2d 507, 508 (1950).

[3]New York Real Property Tax Law §102-12(d).

[4]*Matter of New York Telephone Co. v. Ferris,* 257 App. Div. 415, 13 N.Y. S.2d 359, affd. 282 N.Y. 667, 26 N.E. 2d 805.

[5]*Crystal v. Syracuse,* 47 A.D. 2d 29, 364 N.Y.S. 2d 618 (1975).

FIGURE 12-1

GENERAL GUIDELINES USED BY THE COURTS

In order to examine the thinking of the courts, one must look beyond ad valorem tax law. Many of the cases deciding issues of classification involve condemnation, lessor/lessee, and mortgagor/mortgagee relationships. The courts have used these areas of the law as reference in dealing with the issue in ad valorem tax cases.

The general guidelines as to when a former chattel becomes realty for property tax purposes include the following:

Annexation to the Realty

Annexation to the realty, either actual or constructive, generally involves the old common law principle sometimes called the institutional theory. The question is: "Because of the manner of annexation (nuts, bolts, concrete foundations), will removal of the item result in extensive damage to the item or to the realty?" The basic issue of movability is considered here. If "damage results," the "fixture" is considered part of the realty.

Intention of the Parties

This is sometimes referred to as the intentional theory. Did the owner of the "former chattel" intend to make the article a permanent accession to the freehold? If the owner did *not* intend to make the article a permanent accession, the article retains its personal property character. ''Intent'' is a question of fact for a jury to decide.

Appropriation of the Annexed Article to the Use to Which the Realty Is Applied.

We saw for example, in Chapter 2, that a court held a ski lift taxable as real estate because it was ''intimately intertwined'' with the primary use of the land. The court did not feel that in this instance the machinery exemption in New Hampshire extended beyond factory machinery. Therefore, ''cables, engines, gear boxes, towers, motive sources, sheave wheels, chairs, t-bars, cable grips and all other peripheral property comprising ski lifts'' were taxable as real estate.[6]

Is the Item Used in the Manufacturing Process?

And, where statutes dictate, the courts have looked to whether the equipment is used to service the structure or if it is *used in the manufacturing process* going on in the structure. If the equipment is ''used'' in ''manufacturing'' it is classified as personal property.

EXAMPLES OF STATUTORY ''USED IN BUSINESS'' CONCEPT

The Ohio Rule

In Ohio, ''. . . all personal property . . . used in business . . . are subject to taxation. . . .'' ''Used in business'' means instruments used or capable of being used to carry on a business operation.[7]

Thus, manufacturing machinery and equipment and even a lawyer's reference library are subject to the Ohio personal property tax.

In order to assist assessors and taxpayers in making classification distinctions, Ohio has promulgated Tax Commissioner's Rules and Bulletins interpreting the Rules.

For example, Rule TX-1-01 classifies the following as real property:

> Land and land improvements; buildings, heating, air-conditioning, lighting, plumbing, elevators and generating equipment.

The rule states further, ''All other items of property including their foundations and all things accessory thereto which are devoted primarily to the business conducted on the premises, are to be considered as personal property.

This rule has been refined by bulletins and Ohio Tax Commissioner position letters as follows:

- air conditioning ''systems'' improving the building are real property; window and cabinet type air conditioners are personal property—except in the rare instance when part of an overall plan to improve the building.
- equipment and enclosure of florist's cold room serves the business and is personal property; ''the fact that a portion of the enclosure is common to the building does not prevent the *remaining* portion from being classified as personal property.'' (Emphasis added.)
- underground fuel storage tanks primarily serve the business and are personal property.[8]

---

[6]*King Ridge, Inc. v. Sutton,* 115 N.H. 294, 340 A.2d 106 (1975).

[7]Ohio Rev. Code §§5709.01 and 5701.8.

[8]Ohio State Tax Reporter, Vol. 1, Parag. 23-944, CCH.

FIGURE 12-2

The statutes have led the Ohio courts to find that basic oxygen furnaces, blast furnaces, oil refinery cracking plants, and open overhead crane runways not attached to a building are personal property.[9] An example of this is the steel plant basic oxygen furnace (BOF) shown in Figure 12-2.

The Indiana Rule

The basic definition of personal property in Indiana is ". . . all other tangible property (other than real property) which is being: . . . (ii) held, used, or consumed in connection with the production of income. . . ."[10]

This definition is amplified in Indiana's Appraisal Manual[11] as shown in Figure 12-3. I have set forth this real and personal property guide in toto because it presents a good cross-section of real property/personal property distinctions in a statutory "used in business' type state. The reader should be aware that this list is only a guide and gray area issues must be treated on an individual basis depending on the facts in each case.

EXAMPLES OF THE TRADITIONAL OR "COMMON LAW" CONCEPT

The Illinois Rule

In the preceding section, we reviewed the statutory "used in business" concept. The statutes referred to changed "common law" or custom and made items used in business taxable. Now we will look at examples where statutes have not changed custom.

---

[9]*Wheeling Pittsburgh Steel Corp. v. Jefferson County Board of Revision,* 270 O.S. 2d 45 Aff'g. Ohio BTA, July 24, 1970 (1971). *In the Matter of National Tube Co.* Ohio BTA, December 26, 1950. *Standard Oil Co. v. Glander,* Ohio BTA, November 19, 1949. *Atlas Steel & Supply Co. v. Cuyahoga County Board of Revision,* Ohio BTA, March 5, 1956.

[10]Indiana Code, Art. 1.1 Property Taxes, §11.(6).

[11]*Indiana Real Property Appraisal Manual,* State Board of Tax Commissioners of Indiana, Indianapolis, pages G-01 to G-03.

GENERAL
REAL AND PERSONAL PROPERTY GUIDE

STATE OF INDIANA
REAL AND PERSONAL PROPERTY GUIDE

The use of a questionable unit of machinery, equipment or structure will determine its classification as Real or Personal Property. If the unit is directly used for manufacture or a process of manufacture, it is to be considered as Personal Property. If the unit is a land or building improvement, it is to be considered as Real Estate.

Land Improvement — Real

Retaining walls, piling and mats for general improvement of site, private roads, walks, paved areas, culverts, bridges, viaducts, subways and tunnels, fencing, reservoirs, dikes, dams, ditches, canals and drainage.

Fixed river, lake or tidewater wharves and docks.

Permanent standard gauge railroad trackage, bridges and trestles.

Walls forming storage yards and fire protection dikes.

Note-on-site utility piping—i.e., sanitary and storm sewers, potable water and fire-prevention lines, gas lines, etc.—are considered as on-site improvement costs and are to be valued with the land.

Buildings — Real

Structural and other improvement to buildings, including their foundations, walls, floors, roof, insulation, stairways, partitions, loading and unloading platforms and canopies, areaways, systems for heating, central AC, ventilating, sanitation, fixed fire protection, lighting, plumbing, and drinking water, building elevators and escalators.

Miscellaneous —

Air Conditioning—building air conditioning, including refrigeration equipment, for comfort of occupants—Real

Air Conditioning—Window units and Package units—Personal

Air Conditioning—for special process to maintain controlled temperature and humidity—Personal

Aluminum pot lines—Personal

Anhydrous Ammonia Tanks and Equipment —Personal

Ash handling system, pit and superstructure (see boilers)

Asphalt mixing plant and equipment (movable)—Personal

Auto-Call and telephone system—Personal

Bar and equipment—Personal

Bins—permanently affixed for storage—Real

Boilers—for service of building and manufacture with primary use for manufacture —Personal

Boilers—for service of building—Real

Booths for welding—Personal

Bowling Alley Lanes—Personal

Bucket Elevators—Open or enclosed (including casing)—Personal

Building—special constructed storage, poultry, livestock processing buildings—(not including machinery or equipment)—Real

Bulkheads—making additional land area to be assessed with and as part of the improved land.

Carpeting, Commercial—(Real or Personal)—The real property assessment includes a finished floor. If carpet is installed over an existing finished floor, then carpeting becomes personal property. If, as in the case of many newer buildings, carpeting has been specified and is the only finished floor, then carpeting is assessed as real property.

Cistern—Real

Coal-handling system (see Boilers)

Cold storage—build-in cold storage rooms —Real

Cold storage refrigeration equipment—Personal

Control booth—Personal

Conveyor housing, structure or tunnels—Real

Conveyor unit including belt and drives—Personal

Cooling towers—primary use for manufacture—Personal

FIGURE 12-3

Cooling towers—primary use for building —Real

Crane—moving crane—Personal

Crane runways including supporting columns or structure and foundation inside or outside of buildings—Real

Crane runways—bolted to or hung on trusses—Personal

Dock levelers—Personal

Drapes—Personal

Drying rooms structure—Real

Drying rooms heating system—Personal

Dust catchers—Personal

Fence—security—Real

Fire alarm system—Personal

Fire walls—masonry—Real

Floors, Computer room—Real

Foundations for machinery and equipment —Personal

Gas lines for equipment or processing—Personal

Gasoline tanks—(see Tanks)

Grain bins—Portable—Personal

Grain Drying Equipment—Personal

Grain elevators (Commercial, Industrial), storage, silos, tanks, cupolas, workinghouse, headhouse, milling space—Real (see Schedule)

Grain elevator machinery and equipment (Commercial, Industrial) including but not limited to legs (inside or outside), conveyors, spouting, hopper scales, man lifts, aeration systems, grain cleaners, grain dryers, mechanical grain dumping equipment, loading unloading systems, truck scales, all processing machinery and equipment—Personal

Gravel Plant—machinery and equipment —Personal

Greenhouses—Real

Greenhouses—benches and heating system—Personal

Hoist pits—(see Pits)

Irrigation equipment—Personal

Kilns—lumber-drying kiln structure—Real

Kilns—concrete block-drying kiln structure —Real

Kilns—Circular down draft (Beehive)—Real

Kilns—heating or drying system—Personal

Laundry steam-generating equipment—Personal

Lighting—yard lighting—Personal

Lighting—special purpose—inside—Personal

Lighting—service stations (except building) —Personal

Mixers and mixing houses—Personal

Monorail Crane runways—Personal

Ore bridge foundation—Real

Ovens—processing—Personal

Piping—process piping above or below ground—Personal

Pits for equipment or processing—Personal

Pools, Swimming (not portable)—Real

Power lines and auxiliary equipment—Personal

Pumps and Motors—Personal

Pump house (including sub-structure)—Real

Racks and shelving (portable or removable)—Personal

Railroad siding (except belonging to Railroad)—Real

Ready-mix concrete batch plant and equipment—Personal

Refrigeration equipment (see Air Conditioning)—Personal

Sanitary system—Real

Scale houses—Real

Septic system (priced with land)—Real

Scales—truck or railroad scales including pit—Personal

Scales—dormant scales—Personal

Sheds or buildings, portable or on skids—Personal

Signs—Personal

Silos—Farm storage silos—Real

Silo equipment—Personal

Silos—containing a manufacturing process —Personal

Silos—all storage—Real

Spray ponds—masonry reservoir—Real

Spray pond piping and equipment—Primary use classification

Sprinkler system—Real

Stacks—mounted on boilers (see Boilers)

FIGURE 12-3 (continued)

Stacks, supported individually and servicing heating boilers—Real

Stacks, servicing personal property units or a process—Personal

Steam electric generating plant and equipment—Personal

Stone crushing plant—equipment—Personal

Storage bins, portable—Personal

Storage facilities, permanent, of masonry or wood—Real

Storage vaults and doors, including bank vaults and doors—Real

Substation building—Real

Substation—equipment—Personal

Tanks—Storage only (except as indicated below) above or below ground—Real

Tanks—used as part of a manufacturing process—Personal

Tanks—underground gasoline tanks at service station—Personal

Towers—TV or radio broadcasting—Personal

Transformers—Personal

Tunnels—Real

Tunnels—Waste heat or processing—Personal

Unit heaters—non-portable—Real

Unit heaters—Portable—Personal

Unloader runway—Real

Ventilating—Real

Ventilating system for manufacturing equipment—Personal

Walls—Partitions, portable—Personal

Water lines—for process above or below ground—Personal

Water pumping station—building and structure—Real

Water pumps and motors—Personal

Water treating and softening plant building and structure—Real

Water treating and softening equipment—Personal

Wells, pumps, motors and equipment—Personal

Wiring—Power wiring—Personal

FIGURE 12-3 (continued)

In Illinois, for example, land, building and fixtures are included in the basic statutory definition of real estate.[12] The Illinois Real Property Manual[13] says this has resulted in the general rule: "Whatever is not declared to be real estate is personal property for the purpose of taxation."

Note that there is no statute which says the item is personal property if it is "used in business." The Illinois courts have, therefore, applied common law principles in these cases.

Fixtures in a building that cannot be removed without physical injury either to the building or the fixture are real estate (annexation guideline).[14]

Fixtures that can be removed without substantial injury, but are attached to the building by screws, nails, etc., are real estate if owned by the owner of the building (intention guideline).[15]

Fixtures in a building that can be removed without substantial injury, but are attached by nails, screws, etc., are real estate even if owned by tenant—if the lease provides that such fixtures shall remain in the building (intention guideline).[16] And the Illinois Real Property Appraisal Manual goes on to say: "Sometimes cases may arise when none of the above rules

[12]Ill. Rev. Act of 1939, §1(13) as amended.

[13]Dept. of Local Govt. Affairs, Springfield, Ill. (1976), pp. M13-M15.

[14]*Cross v. Weare Commission Co.*, 153 Ill. 499.

[15]*Fifield v. Farmers Nat. Bank,* 148 Ill. 163.

[16]*Baker v. McClurg,* 198 Ill. 28.

seem to apply.'' In that situation, the Illinois Supreme Court has held that the intent of the owner of the property controls. If he intends to make the property a permanent part of the real estate to which it is attached, it must be considered real estate and assessed as a part of such real estate. Such intent must be determined (1) from the nature of the property (i.e., whether easily removable), (2) whether the owner of the property also owns the building, (3) the way the property ''fits in'' with the real estate (for example, whether a fixture could be used as well in another type of building), and (4) from any lease or agreements concerning the property.[17]

If the machinery is intended for permanent use in carrying on the business for which the building was erected or is used, and as a permanent accession to the realty, it becomes a part of the realty on being installed thereon, and if such was the intention, it is immaterial that the machines may be removed and used elsewhere, and that they may be removed without injury to the building. This rule has special application to heavy machinery intended for the building and not intended to be moved from place to place, though resting in position by its own weight, and to machinery which is a constituent part of a factory or shop and indispensable thereto, though not actually fastened.[18]

At this writing, there is a movement in Illinois to do away with the personal property tax altogether, provided a substitute source of revenue can be found. This problem has resulted in efforts on the assessor's part to move as much property as possible into the ''real property'' category so that it remains taxable.

I recently appeared in Illinois on a number of assessment appeals and I have found that everything except the plant manager and employees is being classified as real estate. If the proposal eliminating the personal property tax goes through, there will be much litigation in this classification area in the future.

The Maine Rule

In Maine, real estate is defined by statute[19] as all lands, buildings and other things affixed to same. Personal property is defined by statute[20] as including all tangible goods and chattels.

The Maine Municipal Association's Assessors Manual[21] advises assessors on how to handle fixtures. It sets forth the following:

> . . . When articles of personal property which are specially adapted and designed to be used in connection with realty and essential to the convenient and profitable enjoyment of the estate are affixed to it with an intention to make them a permanent accession to the land, they become a part of the realty though not so fastened as to be incapable of removal without serious injury to themselves or the freehold.[22]

The case involved machinery in a mill subject to a conditional sales agreement. The mortgagee of the mill foreclosed and an action was brought to recover the machinery. It was held that the conditional seller *could* recover the unpaid balance due on the machinery

---

[17] *Sword v. Low,* 122 Ill. 487; *Fifield v. Farmers' National Bank,* 148 Ill. 163; *Cross v. Weare Commission Co.,* 153 Ill. 499; *Fehr Construction Co. v. Postal System,* 288 Ill. 634; *Bradley Supply Co. v. Ames,* 359 Ill. 162, at p. 169.

[18] *Planter's Bank v. Lummus Cotton Gin Co.,* 132 S.C. 16, 128 S.E. 876; *Fifield v. Farmers' Nat. Bank,* 148 Ill. 163; *Owings v. Estes,* 256 Ill. 553; *Otis v. May,* 30 Ill. App. 581; *Calumet Iron & Steel Co. v. Lathrop,* 36 Ill. App. 249.

[19] 36 M.R.S.A. Sec. 551.

[20] 36 M.R.S.A. Sec. 601.

[21] Third Edition 1973, Augusta, Maine, pp. 25-28.

[22] *Hawkins v. Hersey,* 86 Me. 394.

because there was no intent to make such machinery a fixture until paid for (intention guideline).

The Maine Assessor's Manual also cites the Hayford case[23] where the court said:

> . . . that to constitute a fixture there must be, (1) an actual physical annexation, at least juxtaposition to the realty or some appurtenance thereof, (2) it is so annexed with intention on the part of the person making the annexation, to make it a permanent accession to the realty.

In this case "intent" was a question of fact left to the jury—not a matter of law left to the judge (intention guideline).

A subsequent case[24] reaffirmed the Hayford rule. Again, a conditional vendor was successful in not having refrigerators classified as fixtures and part of the real estate. The conditional sales contract showed a lack of intent to make the refrigerators fixtures until they were paid for (intention guideline).

Of course, when a fixture becomes permament, it will be taxed as realty. Construction within a building of a six-story cold storage unit which, if removed, would have left the building without floors, is a permament fixture. It is taxable as realty to the landlord and not as personalty to the tenant even though the tenant installed the unit (appropriation to the use of the realty guideline).[25]

In Maine, as in Illinois, we find no statute directing the courts to look to "used in business" in classifying real and personal property. Thus, common law principles involving annexation, intent and appropriation of the annexed article to the realty's use are applied.

Let us now look at a case in which judges at different levels in the same jurisdiction attempted to apply both the "used in business" and common law principles.

TRADITIONAL "COMMON LAW" CONCEPTS ARE NOT EASILY CHANGED UNLESS THE LEGISLATURE IS SPECIFIC IN ITS "USED IN BUSINESS" STATUTORY LANGUAGE

The New Jersey Rule

The following New Jersey case touches upon the issues examined in the previous two sections of this chapter. It is basically a case concerning the construction of a statute. It brings the loose ends of "used in business" and "common law" together, but never quite ties a knot.

Background

In New Jersey, real estate is assessed at the local level and personal property is assessed by the state.

The taxpayer contended that his machinery and equipment (large, heavy 80-ton ore and ball mills) were not assessable locally as real estate. He relied on N.J.S.A. 54:11A-1. The pertinent sections of the statute are:

> . . . (b) Personal property used in business shall mean tangible goods and chattels used or held for use in any business, transaction, activity or occupation conducted for profit, but

---

[23] *Hayford v. Wentworth*, 97 Me. 347.

[24] *Cumberland Power and Light Co. v. Hotel Ambassador*, 134 Me. 153.

[25] *John P. Squire & Co. v. City of Portland*, 106 Me. 234, 76 Atl. 679 (1909).

shall not include: . . . (2) goods and chattels so affixed to real property as to become a part thereof and not to be severable or removable without material injury thereto; . . .

Lower Court Decision

Judge Mott of the Division of Tax Appeals found as follows:

- machinery and equipment essentially attributable to the maintenance of real estate—and *not* an integral part of the manufacturing process—is *deemed* real property.
- all immovable machinery and equipment that is affixed to the realty, which is used for purposes other than actual manufacturing process such as a storage tank—is *deemed* to be real property.
- all equipment in structures, no matter how large, that is movable and directly related to the manufacturing process is *deemed* to be personal property.
- machinery and equipment, even through not movable and permanently affixed to the realty—if it is an integral part of the work process, shall be *deemed* to be personal property.

As you can see, he interpreted the statutes as creating a ''used in business'' rule in New Jersey. He seemed to have completely disregarded N.J.S.A. 54:11A-1(b)(2) set forth above.

Lower Court's Reasoning

Judge Mott said case decisions indicated that the institutional theory (annexation) had been modified by intent of the parties. The intentional theory might be equitable in determining title issues between mortgagor and mortgagee, vendor and vendee, and landlord and tenant.

However, intent was not even remotely connected to issues between the taxpayer and local assessor. The intent of the taxpayer must be to avoid additional tax wherever legally permissible. The intent of the assessor would be to construe the original placing of all items in a building as intending to create real property.

Judge Mott got very little help from the intentional theory. He interpreted the statute in a black and white manner. In his mind, the ''used in business'' rule would be reasonably easy to apply. It would relieve assessors of insurmountable tasks in making gray area determinations as to what was locally taxable as real property.

Superior Court Decision[26]

Judge Mott's decision was reversed on appeal to the Appellate Division of the Superior Court as contrary to both New Jersey's decisional law on fixtures and the legislative intent expressed in the Business Personal Property Tax Act.

Superior Court's Reasoning

The court reviewed various statutes pertinent to this issue together because they formed a part of a comprehensive plan of taxation of real and personal property in New Jersey. From the wording of the various statutes, the court did not believe that it was the legislative intent

[26]*National Lead Co. v. Sayerville,* 132 N.J. Super. 30, 331 A.2nd 633 (1975) Reversing Decision of Tax Appeals, November 7, 1973.

to exclude machinery and equipment used in a manufacturing process from *ever* being considered as part of the real estate.

This was the court's thinking despite the fact that N.J.S.A. 54:30A-50(b) defines real estate to include land and buildings and "*to eliminate items of personal property such as machinery, apparatus and equipment which by reason of their attachment to the lands or buildings might otherwise be regarded as real property under the common law doctrine of fixtures.*"

The court looked to the common law doctrine of fixtures concerning goods and chattels "so affixed to real property as to become part thereof and not to be separable or removable without material injury thereto." It also reviewed the classic determinants by which a movable chattel loses its character as personalty and becomes part of the realty. These include "(1) actally affixed to the realty or something appurtenant thereto, (2) appropriated to the use or purpose of that part of the realty with which it is annxed, and (3) intended by the party making the annexation to be a permanent accession to the freehold." The court referred to material injury as that which "will prevent the structure from being used for the purpose for which it was erected or for which it has been adapted."

The court "perceived no sound reason for fashioning different principles to be applied to machinery and equipment used in a manufacturing process." The matter was remanded back to Judge Mott, and his holding that machinery and equipment used in the work process was personal property regardless of its affixation to the realty was reversed. He was told to describe fully the machinery and equipment in controversy with particular reference to the manner of attachment to the realty. He was told it was important to discuss the interrelationship between such machinery and equipment and the buildings in which it is housed and that he must make a determination of whether the machinery and equipment is so affixed as to become part of the realty and whether it is severable or removable without material injury thereto.

Thus, in New Jersey, machinery or equipment owned by a manufacturer which is used in the manufacturing process can be real property and taxed locally if: (1) it is permanently attached to a building, (2) it carries out the purpose for which the building is designed or adapted, and (3) its removal would cause material damage to the building.

The court refused to make New Jersey a "used in business" state. It said in passing that it did not believe this issue presents an insurmountable problem for the assessor, and he would simply have to solve this problem along with many others.

Insurmountable Problems?

Thus, New Jersey's gray areas in the classification of real and personal property were left nicely undisturbed. Each case stands on its own facts. Each of these sets of facts is distinguishable from every other set of facts.

Consider a New Jersey case involving four radio broadcasting towers, approximately 200 feet high, made of steel angle irons and fastened together with nuts and bolts and bolted to four concrete pier foundations, each topped with a steel plate.

This case is funny because it shows that no one is really sure of how to classify these gray area items. In this case, the local assessor levied a real property tax on the towers and the taxpayer appealed, saying the towers were personal property. While the appeal was in progress, the state levied a personal property tax on the same towers. Taxpayer filed a claim to preserve its rights if, contrary to its original contention, the towers were subject to a real estate tax.

The claim for refund was denied when the Director of the State Division of Taxation concluded that the towers were personal property.

On appeal to the Division of Taxation, the towers were held to be real estate, a slight reduction was granted, and everybody, including the Director, appealed to the Superior Court.

The Superior Court held the towers to be real estate, emphasizing that the items were fixed with the *intention* that they should remain permanently and their presence adapted the land to a functional use.[27]

Summary Comment

The courts' decisions on these matters lead us to the following conclusions:

- New Jersey continues to apply traditional or "common law" principles in these classification cases.
- Somewhere in Lyndhurst, New Jersey, there are four radio towers that are real property even though the Director of the State Division of Taxation thinks they are personal property.

OTHER RULES—THE TRADITIONAL TEST AND THEN SOME!

The California Rule

California has long applied traditional or common law principles to determine whether a chattel has become part of the real property. These principles are familiar and include:

- method of annexation
- the adaptability of the item to the use and purpose for which the realty is used.
- The intention in making the annexation.

But, the assessor may guide on outward appearance and is *not* bound by hidden intent of parties to a lease. Thus, bank vault doors, removable at the termination of the lease, have been held taxable as real estate.[28]

It should be noted that banks are exempt from personal property taxes in California and the vault door, if classified as personalty, would not have been subject to any tax.

The assessor, having successfully levied on the vault door, despite the intent of the parties, also tried to tax the safety deposit boxes. The court held, however, that since boxes were easily removable despite their sturdy outward appearance, they were personalty and not subject to property taxation.[29]

The assessors in California never say die, and so they also levied on a bank's electronic computer system as improvements to real property.

The bank argued that the computers retained their character of personal property because the items could be and were moved from place to place.

The court rejected this idea and held the computers to be taxable fixtures (part of the real property) because:

---

[27]*Westinghouse Broadcasting Company v. The Director of Division of Taxation,* 141 N.J. Super. 301 (1976).

[28]Kenneth A. Ehrman and Sean Flavin, *Taxing California Property,* Bancroft-Whitney Company, San Francisco, 1967, §47.48.

[29]*Pajaro Valley Bank v. Santa Cruz County,* 207 Cal. App. 2d 621, 24 Cal. Rptr. 639 (1962).

(1) buildings were special purpose with fewer windows
(2) floors of the building were raised at great expense
(3) air conditioning and humidity control were installed for efficiency
(4) components of systems were interconnected by hundreds of signal and power cables and could be relocated only at great expense
(5) size and weight—11 tons of computers are difficult to move.[30]

I did not quite follow the court's reasoning in this case. I believe it can be referred to as the traditional test and then some!

The New York Rule

This "and then some" rule has also been applied in ad valorem tax cases in New York where it has been held that historic tests and common law rules defining fixtures are not determinative of what is properly taxable as real property.[31]

In this case, barges on which were mounted gas turbine plants designed to generate electrical power, fuel oil barges which supplied fuel oil to power-plant barges, and accessory equipment mounted on barges, all of which were an integral part of power distribution system, were subject to the real property tax.

This case involved a utility but it followed the general statutory test in New York in determining what property is real property for taxation purposes.

The measure is physical movability and not intent of owner as in the typical common law fixture problem. Economic factors are also considered and where they negate movement, the property is taxable as real property.

Thus blast furnaces, coke ovens, soaking pits, piping and pumps, are taxable real estate in New York.[32]

Under the New York Rule, the steel plant blast furnace shown in Figure 12-4 is taxable as real estate. This *same* blast furance would be classified as personal property in Ohio and other "used in business" states. This is quite significant. If the blast furnace were classified as personal property in New York, it would not be subject to a property tax *at all* because New York does not levy a tax on personal property.

Summary Comment

These "and then some" rules serve to alert the taxpayer to the fact that courts may ignore what seem to be perfectly reasonable traditional tests in any given case.

The taxpayer can only identify his asset and its function; review statutes, guidelines and court decisions; analyze annexation, intention, use of realty and "used in business" issues; and hope that the court will see it his way with a given set of facts on a particular day.

CHECK LIST

Is It Real Property or Personal Property?

( ) Identify and describe item.
( ) What is its function and use?

---

[30]*Bank of America National Trust and Savings Association v. County of Los Angeles,* 224 Cal. App. 2d 108, 36 Cal. Rptr. 413 (1964), 6 ALR 3d 491.

[31]*Consolidated Edison Co. of New York, Inc. v. City of New York,* 80 Misc. 2d 1065, 365 N.Y.S. 2d 377 (1975).

[32]*City of Lackawanna v. State Board of Equalization and Assessment,* 21 A.D.2d 318, 250 N.Y.S. 2d 369 (1964), 16 N.Y. 2d 222, 264, N.Y.S. 2d 528, 212 N.E. 2d 42 (1965).

FIGURE 12-4

( ) How is it annexed to the real estate?
( ) How is it joined to the land's function and use?
( ) What is the intent of the parties in making the annexation?
( ) Review statutes.
( ) "Used in business" rule.
( ) Traditional or common law rule.
( ) Traditional "and then some" rule.
( ) Review court decisions.
( ) Local assessment practices.
( ) Assessor's guidelines.
( ) Real property and personal property tax rates.

13
Exempt Property: How to Qualify for Exempt Status And Pay No Property Tax at All

A Thorough Knowledge of the Source of Your Exemption Is a Necessary Ingredient in Establishing and Protecting Your Exempt Status

If You Can Fit into One of the Following Categories You Can Eliminate Your Property Tax Burden

Federal Government Exemptions
State and Local Government Exemptions (Public Property)
Possessory Interests
Airport Exemptions
Foreign Government Exemptions
Religious Exemptions
Educational Exemptions
Charitable, Non-Profit, and Welfare Exemptions
Preferential Exemptions
Homeowner's Exemptions

How Lessees and Lessors Can Gain Exempt Status When Involved in a Lease with an Exempt Entity

''Unwritten'' Exemptions in ''Common'' Places Are Often Overlooked at Great Expense to the Taxpayer

A Taxpayer with Some Imagination Can Sometimes Create His Own Exemption

An Assessor with Some Imagination Can Sometimes Get a Taxpayer to Make ''In Lieu of Tax Payments Despite an Existing Exemption

Check List

13

This chapter will acquaint the taxpayer with the many exemptions to the property tax that exist in the United States today. Each type of exemption described will be followed by comments and summaries of court decisions showing how the exemption statutes were interpreted.

Several facts are clear at the outset. Most state constitutions exempt religious, educational and charitable organizations from the property tax. The idea is that a better need is served. For example, a charitable hospital is exempt from the property tax to keep patient care low. Additional exemptions are legislatively enacted to meet additional better needs. Plant expansion might be exempt in the hope of increasing employment levels in a given state.

The taxpayer who qualifies for exempt status seeks to maintain and expand his exemption. He pursues a liberal interpretation of the statutes. The assessor seeks to halt the ever-increasing erosion of his tax base, and he challenges exemptions where doubt exists.

The courts, faced with arguments from both sides, attempt to arrive at a fair and reasonable interpretation of the statutes. The general rule is that exemption statutes are strictly construed against the taxpayer. But, an interpretation so literal and narrow as to defeat the purpose of the exemption is also to be avoided. Words in a statute such as "exclusive use" become very important. They usually connote a "principal" or "primary" use of the property for exempt purposes. Other phrases upon which exemption cases are decided include: "governmental or public purpose," "relieving the burden of government," "worthy social value," the "purpose of the organization," and the "actual use" of the property.

Thus, the issues are drawn. Each case stands on its own and, similar to the value issue, there are many and varied opinions. It is up to the taxpayer to (a) seek out exempt status if he is entitled to it; (b) establish his exemption through presentation of supporting facts and the timely filing of the appropriate exemption application form; and (c) protect and maintain his exempt status once he achieves it.

A THOROUGH KNOWLEDGE OF THE SOURCE OF YOUR EXEMPTIONS IS A NECESSARY INGREDIENT IN ESTABLISHING AND PROTECTING YOUR EXEMPT STATUS

The introduction section indicated that the source of your exemption is most important. In general, property tax exemptions find their origins in state constitutions. Power to grant exemptions is given to the legislature, who can revise and revoke unless the property is used exclusively for religious, educational or charitable purposes.

The power of the legislature is such that it may giveth or taketh away. And the legislature may delegate that right to the local municipalities!

In New Hampshire it was constitutional for the legislature to delegate to cities and towns the right to grant certain exemptions to the elderly. The local municipalities could decide for themselves whether or not to grant the exemptions. No equal protection rights would be violated even if other municipalities decided not to adopt the exemptions, resulting in an uneven system of taxation among the elderly citizens. There was no unconstitutional delegation of authority because the legislature established the general terms of the act but left the determination as to whether it had the force of law to the localities.[1]

The source of this exemption flowed from the constitution to the legislature and filtered down to the local municipalities in what appears to be a rather unwieldy tax scheme. Nevertheless, the taxpayer should be familiar with all aspects of his source of exemption in order to protect his interest.

Sources of exemptions can dry up! In New York City, the Bar Association and the Explorer's Club enjoyed real estate exempt status since 1927 and 1964, respectively. In 1972, the legislature decided to stem the erosion of the property tax base of New York City which was at 33% and projected to go to 50% by 1985. The properties were placed on the tax rolls and this action was upheld by the highest court in the state.[2]

Sources of exemption can change! The Massachusetts legislature was given the right to change the enabling act of the Massachusetts Port Authority and tax hitherto exempt leased property used for other than public purposes. In the opinion of the justices, bondholders were not justified in relying on the irrevocability of the property tax exemption and the lessees could not rely on the continuing tax exempt status.[3]

And sometimes the source of the exemption was never there at all! The City of Daytona Beach had agreed by contract that no taxes would be levied on the Daytona International Speedway. The court held that the property was taxable because it was operated for profit and it was not performing a governmental function. The agreement not to tax the Speedway was beyond the authority of the city, and invalid.[4]

These cases make it very clear that property tax exemptions are a matter of legislative grace and the taxpayer must study the legislative sources of his exemption to test the strength of his exempt status.

IF YOU CAN FIT INTO ONE OF THE FOLLOWING CATEGORIES YOU CAN ELIMINATE YOUR PROPERTY TAX BURDEN

Federal Government Exemptions

The Federal Government is the largest owner of property exempt from the property tax in the United States. It owns 761 million acres of land, including 96% of Alaska and 25% of the area of twelve western states.

State and local governments cannot, however, levy a tax on the Federal Government under what is commonly referred to as the "supremacy clause" of the U.S. Constitution. In 1819 the U.S. Supreme Court said that since ". . . the power to tax involves the power to

[1] *Opinion of the Justices,* 338 A.2d 553 (1975).

[2] *In the Matter of the Bar of the City of New York v. Lewisohn, In the Matter of the Explorers Club v. Lewisohn,* 34 N.Y. 2d 143, 313 N.E.2d 30 (1974).

[3] *Opinion of the Justices,* 365 Mass. 665, 313 N.E.2d 882 (1974). Opinions of the justices are advisory in nature and if this matter were litigated, the issues would be considered anew. If a lessee could show that this change went to the essence of the bond contract, materially reducing the attractiveness of the revenue security, he could possibly prevail.

[4] *Volusia County v. Daytona Beach Racing and Recreational Facilities District,* 341 So. 2d 498 (1977).

destroy . . . the states have no power, by taxation or otherwise, to retard, impede, burden or in any manner control, the operations of the constitutional laws enacted by congress to carry into execution the powers vested in the general government.''[5]

Thus, the tax imposed by Maryland on a bank of the United States was unconstitutional and void and this remains the law today. As recently as 1968, the court invalidated a sales and use tax imposed by Massachusetts on a National Bank.[6]

This immunity, however, is limited to taxes with a direct incidence on the United States. The use of federal property by a contractor for profit, for example, is a separate and distinct taxable activity.[7] The constitutional immunity does not extend to cost-plus-fee contractors even though the U.S. ultimately pays the tax.

The courts have upheld this type of levy on government contractors by recognizing the legislative attempt to close gaps in the state tax structure by placing a tax upon the privilege of possessing and using any property, otherwise exempt, in a business for profit.[8]

Therefore, when the Nye County assessor in Nevada levied an assessment on the real and personal property of the U.S. Government (Atomic Energy Commission) used by contractors in their for-profit business, the tax was upheld.[9]

State and Local Government Exemptions (Public Property)

State and local government is generally exempt from the property tax via state constitutional immunity. There is no revenue gain to a taxing authority taxing itself. If the cost of collection and administration is considered, there would actually be a loss of revenue.

Nevertheless, the State of New Jersey is considering legislation that involves the state making an ''in lieu of'' payment of taxes of up to 25% of the level of taxation on local property. The idea is to reimburse the municipal governments for cost of police and fire protection, street construction, and maintenance and refuse collection relating to state property located in the local municipality.[10]

As in the case of the Federal Government, the immunity does not necessarily extend to third parties who lease *public property* for profit.

Based on this assumption, the assessor of Pittsburgh levied assessments on parking lots owned by the Public Parking Authority of Pittsburgh, because the properties were leased by private parties who were deriving profits therefrom.

The court held that the Parking Authority Law exempted the parking lots as public property and their for-profit use by lessees did not destroy the exemption. In this case, the for-profit lessees were protected by the specific wording of a statute and $1,250,000 in property taxes was refunded.[11]

In another case, the Douglas County Assessor relied on a statute which said: ''All improvements put on leased public lands shall be assessed to the owner of such improvements as personal property, together with the value of the lease, . . .'' He sought to assess all improvements of the for-profit barge line lessee which were owned by the City of Omaha.

The court held that the land and improvements were not solely used for the profit of the

---

[5]*McCulloch v. Maryland,* 17 U.S. (4 Wheat.) 316, 4L.Ed. 579 (1819).
[6]*Agricultural Bank v. Tax Commission,* 392 U.S. 339, 88 S. Ct. 2173, 20 L.Ed. 1138 (1968).
[7]*United States v. Boyd,* 378 U.S. 39, 84 S. Ct. 1518, 12 L.Ed. 713 (1964). This case involved a sales and use tax.
[8]*Thiokof Chemical Corporation v. Peterson,* 15 Utah 2d 355, 393 P. 2d 391 (1964). This case involved a use tax.
[9]*United States of America et al. v. the State of Nevada ex rel. Beko,* 493 P. 2d 1324 (1972).
[10]*New York Times,* April 7, 1977, p. B2.
[11]*City of Pittsburgh v. Public Parking Authority of Pittsburgh, et al.,* 11 Pa. Cmwlth. 442, 314 A.2d 887 (1974).

barge line. All facilities were open to the public and promotion of their use was in furtherance of the statutory obligations placed on the Dock Board. Thus, the assessment was not valid.[12]

In this case, the public purpose use of the property apparently influenced the court.

It also should be noted that the Dock Board had warranted that any ad valorem tax that might have to be paid by the for-profit lessee would be credited back via an offset or a deduction in rent. This is similar to the cost plus contracts where the Federal Government ultimately pays the tax.

Thus, it would seem wise practice to be sure to arrange for the exempt entity to be ultimately responsible for the tax if there is the slightest possibility that an assessment could eventually be levied.

Possessory Interests

In the case just cited, the assessor relied on a statute permitting him to levy on improvements placed on leased public land. Many states tax the leasehold estate in lands leased from the U.S., state or local government or other exempt body (e.g., Port or Harbor Authority) and it is not considered a tax on the governmental body.

The Leasehold Taxing Act of New Jersey was the basis for taxing the interest of a lessee who occupied a dwelling within the confines of the Delaware Water Gap National Recreation Area. The lessee had agreed to repair, restore and maintain the dwelling in return for the right of occupancy under a lease.

The value assessed in this case was the leasehold interest, not the fee.[13]

Essentially, a possessory interest is the possession of, claim or right to the possession of land or improvements except when coupled with ownership of the land or improvements in the same person.

This is an important property tax revenue source to California because fifty percent of all the land is publicly owned. The taxation of possessory interests dates back to the gold rush days when miners were extracting millions of dollars from the tax exempt public domain.[14]

Back in the 1930's, possessory interests in tax exempt lands were assessed on the "bonus value" of the lease. This is the fair rental value over the lease rents paid to the lessor similar to the measure of a leasehold interest. In practice, this method resulted in few or no taxes imposed on possessory interests in California.[15] This rule changed in 1955 when *DeLuz Homes, Inc. v. San Diego County,*[16] held that there should be no deduction for rent or amortization of improvements. This resulted in valuing the leasehold or possessory interest at the approximate value of the fee where long-term leases were involved.

The California Assessor's Handbook calls for three techniques in valuing possessory interests:

(1) the present worth of the benefits of the use of the property for the probable period of possession;

---

[12] *Sioux City and New Orleans Barge Lines, Inc. v. Board of Equalization of Douglas County,* 185 N.W. 2d 866 (1971).

[13] *Township of Sandyston v. Angerman,* 134 Super. 448, 341 A.2d 682 (1975).

[14] Kenneth A. Ehrman and Sean Flavin, *Taxing California Property,* Bancroft-Whitney Company, San Francisco, 1967, p. 60.

[15] *Hammond Lbr. Co. v. Los Angeles County,* 104 CA.235, 285 P 896 (1930) and *Blinn (L.W.) Lbr. Co. v. Los Angeles County,* 216, C474, 14 P2d 512, 84 ALR 1304 overruled 45 C2d 570, 290 P2d 559 (1932).

[16] 45 C2d 546, 290 P2d 544 (1955). Legislation was subsequently passed to alleviate hardship on lessees who had negotiated possessory interest leases prior to DeLuz and who were now suddenly faced with large property taxes and no way to renegotiate their lease.

(2) the present full fee value, less the present worth of the reversion to the public agency at the end of the term of the lease;
(3) sales data of comparable possessory interests, to which must be added the present worth of the future rents payable.[17]

An example of one of these exercises is set forth in Chapter 7, Example 2. The entire property is valued and the result tends to be valuation of the leasehold interest at approximately the value of the fee.

As so often is the case, the practical result of this type of effort cannot always be measured in the form of increased property tax revenue.

The *DeLuz* decision has tended to depress rentals that government agencies secure for leases of public property, and competition between government and the private sector is more keen.

Premium rentals obtained on airport leases formerly used to help improve airports are no longer available and airport districts must look to increased tax rates to replace lost revenue.[18]

Airport Exemptions

Possessory interest cases often involve airport property where the importance of the use of the property is clearly illustrated.

Several cases have been litigated throughout the country under this broad category of public property exemptions when a third party leases land or buildings for profit from the governmental unit that owns the airport.

The general test of exemption is: is the property used for governmental or public purposes?

As a first step, the taxpayer must review the enabling statute. A special statute will overcome "exclusive municipal use" requirements and allow the exemption even if the buildings are leased to a third party for profit.[19]

If the basic statute is not so special, then "governmental purpose" becomes the test. Thus, the entire landing area of an airport is exempt.[20] Buildings used to fuel and service planes are exempt.[21] Those items necessary and essential to the efficient operation of the airport and available to the general public[22] are exempt.

However, where a third party lessee is the true beneficial owner of the improvements, the assessment can be upheld.[23] The question of governmental purpose can often become clouded and the exemption will depend upon the jurisdiction in which your property is located.

For example, in Florida, property leased by PAN AM from the Miami International Airport was exempt because it was used predominantly for public purpose and only incidentally for private purpose.[24] Similarly, a Hertz car rental facility, connected to and leased from the Tampa International Airport, was exempt as an important service to air travelers.[25]

---

[17]*Assessor's Handbook* AH 517-10, Assessment Standards Division, Property Tax Department, California State Board of Equalization.

[18]Ehrman, *op cit.*, p. 304.

[19]*Bd. of Park Comm., City of Wichita v. Bd. of Cty. Comm. of Sedgwick Cty.*, 480 P.2d 81 (1971).

[20]*William J. Ballor, et al., v. City of Fraser*, 207 N.W. 2d 408 (1973).

[21]*City of Cheyenne v. Bd. of Cty. Comm. of the Cty. of Laramie*, 484 P.2d 706 (1971).

[22]*State Bd. of Equalization and Assessment*, 5 Op. Counsel SBEA No. 20 (1975).

[23]*State ex rel. Mitchell Aero, Inc. v. Bd. of Rev.*, 246 N.W. 2d 521 (1976). 5G5 339 A.2d (1975).

[24]*Dade Cty. et al. v. Pan American World Airways, Inc.*, 275 So. 2d 505 (1973).

[25]*Hertz Corporation v. Walden*, 299 So. 2d 121 (1974).

But the Hertz remote car storage facility was held to be predominantly private and subject to taxes on the leasehold interest.

In Washington, the Board of Tax Appeals held that the lease agreements of all car rental companies at the SEA-TAC International Airport created taxable estates and no "governmental purpose" exemption applied.[26]

CAUTION: Finally, make sure that you always protect your interests by timely filing an application for exemption if you think you are entitled to exempt status. Failure to do so cost TAN Airlines their exempt status in Dade County for 1972 even though the Florida Supreme Court found these leasehold interests exempt from tax under the PAN AM case, supra.[27]

Foreign Government Exemptions

Real property owned by the United Nations and foreign governments is exempt in New York.[28] The exemption generally extends to the residence of the principal representative of the country and the property may be subject to certain special ad valorem levies.

This same general rule applies to foreign government property in Washington, D.C. where special treaties also exempt property.

Assessors in both jurisdictions have sought legislation that would pass this burden of exemption from the city onto the Federal Government—but to no avail.

Religious Exemptions

The U.S. Constitution prohibits the making of laws which infringe upon religion and the free exercise thereof. This applies to federal and state legislatures.[29] This declares a policy that churches are more important than local taxes and it is in the furtherance of the general welfare to exclude such institutions from taxation.[30] The theory is that the maintenance and encouragement of religion is a benefit to society.

In general, the definition of "religion" in religious exemption statutes has been very broad and the truth or error of theological beliefs is not within the purview of the assessor.[31] Worship of, or belief in, a diety is not essential to the status of a religious society. The basic question is: does the group conduct itself the way conceded-to-be-religious groups conduct themselves?[32]

This broad definition, however, does not mean the courts will automatically grant religious exemptions. New York appears to be particularly tough in granting these exemptions.

For example, it has been held that a religious exemption will *not* be granted to persons interested in metaphysics who have ". . . no tenets, ritual, dogma, or other characteristics of a religious organization except, possibly, the solicitation and receipt of funds."[33]

And, the New York City Tax Commission, in a 4-3 decision, formally denied exemp-

---

[26] *Appeal of Jerry's U-Drive, Inc., Bd. of Tax Appeals,* Docket No. 13732, 13734 (1976).

[27] *Dade County v. Transportes Aereos Nacionales, S.A.,* 298 So.2d 570 (1974).

[28] New York Real Property Tax Law, §§ 416 and 481.

[29] U.S. Const. Amend. I and Amend. XIV, §1. See "Tax Exemption of Church Property," Arvo Van Alstyne, 20 *Ohio State L.J.* 461 (Summer 1959) for a detailed breakdown of statutes and cases from the various states.

[30] *Diocese of Rochester v. Planning Board of Town of Brighton,* 1 N.Y. 2d 508, 154 N.Y.S 2d 849 (1956).

[31] *Saint Germain Foundation v. Siskiyou County,* 212 CA 2d 911, 28 Cal Rptr. 393 (1963).

[32] *Fellowship of Humanity v. County of Alameda,* 153 Cal. App. 2d 673, 315 P.2d 394 (1957); *Washington Ethical Society v. District of Columbia,* 249 F. 2d 127 (D.C. Cir. 1975).

[33] *In re Peace Haven,* 175 Misc. 753, 755, 25 N.Y.S.2d 974, 977 (Sup. Ct. 1941).

tions on the real property of Rev. Sun Myung Moon's Unification Church. The majority felt that politics were "so interwoven with religion" that the church could not be considered exclusively religious. The dissenting opinion "argued that all the world's religions were politically motivated, some more than others."[34]

Finally, New York has also held that a corporation organized exclusively for the purpose of publishing and distributing the Holy Bible and not affiliated with a religious denomination, is *not* entitled to a religious exemption.[35]

Having addressed ourselves to the issue of whether or not a religious organization qualifies for exemption, let us now determine to what the exemption applies.

The "house of religious worship" exemption usually extends to the land on which the building stands and the land around it for ingress, egress, light and air.

The question of the exemption of the rectory is handled differently in the various states.

In Virginia, the exemption applies not only to the minister's residence but also to the Bishop's residence because he is Bishop over all his churches who enjoy the exemption.[36]

This is *not* the case in California where the rectory or other areas are not used "solely and exclusively" for religious worship, and therefore, they are subject to taxation.[37]

A similar situation exists with regard to church parking lots.

Pennsylvania has held that "parking lots" contiguous to a church were "an adjunctive use of the property not part of regular stated worship and thus *not* exempt as an actual place of religious worship."

California, on the other hand, recognized that the streets were badly congested in Los Angeles and the parking lot was exempt by statute as "required for the convenient use and occupation of said building."

And, in New Jersey, the church's land exemption could not be extended across a highway to land purchased for future expansion where a few people parked while attending services.[38]

Other uses of church-related property and its use have come before the courts on the exemption issue.

In Idaho, where the code stated "used exclusively" for religious purposes, an exemption was not allowed on a summer camp owned by a religious corporation. This was because the camp was also used for recreational activities.[39] Exactly the opposite conclusion was reached in a New York case where the entire summer camp was held to be exempt.[40]

Similarly, tax exemption of cemetery grounds prevails in every jurisdiction. As in all of the above examples, statutory language results in substantial differences in the application of exemptions reflecting the diversities of local policy.

Educational Exemptions

Educational institutions enjoy treatment similar to religious institutions insofar as exemption from the property tax is concerned. For example, a State University is usually considered to have a standard exemption from the property tax applying to all buildings,

[34]*The New York Times*, April 14, 1977.

[35]*American Bible Society v. Lewisohn*, 40 N.Y. 2d 78, 351 N.E.2d 697 (1976).

[36]*William Cudlipp, Jr. et al. v. City of Richmond*, 180 S.E. 2d 525.

[37]*Sierra Retreat v. Los Angeles County*, 35 C2d 755, 221 P. 2d 59 (1950).

[38]*See First and Second Church of Christ Scientists of Philadelphia v. City of Philadelphia*, 398 Pa. 65, 157 A2d 54, 75 ALR 2d 1103 (1960).

[39]*Upper Columbia Mission Society of Seventh Day Adventists v. Kootenai County*, 477 P.2d 503 (1970).

[40]*Gospel Volunteers, Inc. v. Village of Speculator*, 324 N.Y.S. 2d 412 (1971).

faculty housing and dormitories. The exemption was even held to include a hotel, a motel, an apartment house and gas station owned by the University and leased to commercial enterprises.

The Shelby County Assessor argued that the "modern concept of taxation" was that "all properties irrespective of ownership should bear their share of the tax burden when they are used or leased for commercial enterprises which are in like business who are subject to taxation."

The Court did not agree because the income derived from the commercial enterprises was used for public purposes.[41]

Not all educational exemption statutes are so liberal. The Supreme Court of Kansas denied exemption for a fraternity house at the University of Kansas. The court stressed the social activities carried on and that the house was not "used exclusively" for educational purposes.[42] Those who claimed did not show themselves clearly within the terms of the statute and the fraternity house was not a property used exclusively for educational purposes.

And don't forget to timely file your exemption application! A fraternity house is exempt under Florida law, but failure to file timely application resulted in a loss of the exemption which was denied for untimeliness.[43]

The range of these exemptions for educational purposes varies widely from state to state. The test is how the general public is benefited and this often depends on location.

For example, a school to train apprentice electricians in Alaska was exempt because it was an "increased opportunity for Alaskans to obtain vocational training.[44]

A similar effort was made to obtain an exemption for the California College of Mortuary Service offering a one-year course in embalming. The court held that the community as a whole must benefit—and this college primarily benefits the funeral service industry.[45] The effort expired.

Charitable, Non-Profit and Welfare Exemptions

Several entities enjoy exemption from the property tax under this broad heading. The general rule in most jurisdictions is that an organization must be substantially engaged in charitable works and that must be the *primary use* of the property. If you derive considerable monies from hall rentals, dinners and liquor and you spend more time on bingo than charitable pursuits, you may not be allowed an exemption.[46]

The burden is on the taxpayer to show that the property is used exclusively for non-profit purposes. When property is used by non-exempt parties for private business, no exemption will apply. Thus, a non-profit professional building erected next to a charitable hospital but rented to doctors as private offices was *not* exempt.[47]

However, an apartment building occupied by hospital staff and foreign exchange nurses was held to be exempt as reasonably necessary to the charitable purposes of the hospital. The close proximity of the apartment to the hospital served as an inducement in recruiting nurses as well as in aiding the hospital in emergencies.[48]

---

[41] *Lamanna, Shelby County Assessor v. University of Tennessee,* 462 S.W.2d 877 (1971).

[42] *Sigma Alpha Epsilon Fraternal Association v. Board of County Commissioners of Douglas County,* 485 P.2d 1297 (1971). See also 66 A.L.R.2d 904 annotation.

[43] *Gamma Phi Chapter of Sigma Chi Bldg. Fund Corp. v. Dade County,* 199 So.2d 717 (1967).

[44] *Glen M. McKee and Greater Anchorage Area Borough v. Gerald M. Evans et al.,* 490 P.2d 1226 (1971).

[45] *California College of Mortuary Science v. County of Los Angeles,* 100 Cal. Rptr. 588 (1972).

[46] *United Veterans Organization et al., v. New Mexico Property Appraisal Department,* 500 P.2d 199 (1972).

[47] *Greater Anchorage Area Borough v. Sisters of Charity of the House of Providence,* Supreme Court of Alaska, No. 1299 (August 6, 1976).

[48] *Presbyterian-University of Pennsylvania Medical Center v. Board of Revision of Taxes,* 357 A.2d 696 (1976).

Senior citizens or "welfare" exemptions are available in all the states and involve age and income requirements. It is necessary to complete and file eligibility forms to qualify for the exemption.

The burden of the property tax on senior citizens with fixed income is a necessary concern to the assessor and to the rest of the taxpaying public. Senior citizens living in their own homes of course support homestead exemptions and "circuit breaker" type legislation limits property taxes to a specified percentage of their income.

Surprisingly, senior citizens living in their own homes do not always support exemptions for "old age homes." They argue that since their homes are subject to the property tax, the government should not subsidize old age homes where, in fact, richer senior citizens may be living.

When the senior citizen moves into an old age home, a new set of issues is presented. Generally, an exemption will be granted where any "profits" are used to pay for patient care and institutional costs.[49]

But not always! The Nebraska Supreme Court held that the primary purpose of the OEA old age home was to furnish housing to a selected group at cost and this was not enough to qualify for an exemption.[50] The exemption will probably be upheld if the benefit is to the general public without restriction.

Similarly, the courts in Tennessee will not grant an exemption if the owners receive pecuniary profit.[51]

Some jurisdictions look to the financial ability of the individuals who will benefit from the exemption.

In Florida, where the income and "predominantly charitable use" tests are applied, a luxury condominium type home for the aged did *not* qualify for exempt status.[52]

However the test in California is *not* the financial ability of the recipient, but what his needs are, "alleviation of which constitutes a worthy social value."[52]

These cases highlight the different approaches taken by the courts in the various states. But approaches can differ in the *same* state and among the judges on the *same* court.

Again, all interpretations are a matter of opinion. In Michigan, a home for the aged limited to healthy and wealthy (average net worth $74,274) was *not* exempt. The dissent in that case argued that non-profit and beneficial interest to society tests were met and the home should be exempt.[54]

Opinions can also differ between courts in the same state. For example, the Oregon Tax Court held that YMCA property leased for tailor and barbershops, offices, food service area, and offices used by the armed services and Job Corps was taxable.

The Supreme Court of Oregon agreed as to the shops and offices, but held that the food service area and armed forces and Job Corps offices were exempt. It was stated that "a charitable enterprise does not lose its exemption merely because it engages in competition with businesses which are subject to taxation." The exemption was granted because the food service area and armed forces and Job Corps offices activity substantially contributed to the furtherance of the charity's goals.[55]

---

[49] *City of Winter Park v. Presbyterian Homes for the Synod of Florida,* 242 So. 733 (1970).

[50] *OEA Senior Citizens, Inc. v. County of Douglas,* 185 N.W.2d 464 (1971).

[51] *Rosewood, Inc. v. Riley Garner, et al.,* 476 S.W.2d 273 (1972).

[52] *Mikos v. Plymouth Harbor, Inc.,* 316 So. 2d 627.

[53] *Fifield Manor v. Los Angeles County,* 188 CA2d 1, 17, 10 Cal. Rptr. 242 (1961).

[54] *Michigan Baptist Homes and Development Company v. City of Ann Arbor,* 242 N.W. 2d 749 (1976).

[55] *Young Men's Christian Association v. Department of Revenue,* 5 Oregon Tax Court 281 (1973), and 522 P.2nd 464 (1974).

Finally, it should be noted that when a *charitable fraternal organization* accepts an exempt status, it is not without obligation to the state.

An Oregon court held that the denial of membership to blacks by the Elks violated the equal protection clause of the 14th Amendment to the U.S. Constitution. It was also held that by accepting the exempt status, the Elks were obliged to comply with the 14th Amendment.[56]

Preferential Exemptions

Preferential exemptions exist in some form or another in every state. They are generally woven into the state's scheme of taxation in order to accomplish economic and other goals. Personal property may be exempt in order to keep a state in a competitive tax structure with sister states. Legislation allowing exemption of business expansion investment is designed to increase employment levels. And, in the 1960's, much legislation exempting pollution control facilities was passed as an incentive to protect the environment.

For example, Delaware, Hawaii, Minnesota, New Hampshire, New York, North Dakota and Pennsylvania levy no personal property tax at all. Many states exempt merchants' and manufacturers' inventories either in whole or in part. In still other states, tax credits are granted on certain personal property.

These exemptions are statutory and are generally set forth on the personal property rendition forms filed by the taxpayer. These instructions should be followed carefully in order to take full advantage of the exemptions.

Property tax exemptions as inducements to industry to locate or expand in a given state or jurisdiction are frowned upon for several reasons. It is argued that these exemptions violate uniformity requirements in the treatment of taxpayers.[57] Or as one judge wrote, as far back as 1887:

> An exemption to one person is but an additional burden to another. To take from one, and give to another, under the guise of taxation, is, indeed, but robbery under a legalized form, and counter to the spirit and genius of our system of government.[58]

It is also argued that these exemptions serve no real purpose as an inducement to industry to locate in a given area because property taxes are not a major concern when compared to labor force and marketing requirements.

Nevertheless, these exemptions are available and, as always, the taxpayer seeking to use the exemption must be aware of its source in the Constitution or statutes of the state in order to avoid any unpleasant surprises later on.

For example, an amendment to the 1877 Georgia Constitution, ratified in 1924, permitted a five-year exemption for all ad valorem taxes for any resident building or enlarging a manufacturing plant. Unfortunately for the taxpayer, this exemption was abolished by Georgia's 1945 Constitution. A subsequent grant of the exemption to the industrial taxpayer was invalid since no authority existed on the part of the local jurisdiction to do so.

Thus, the taxpayer erroneously relied on a non-existent exemption when he constructed and expanded his plant.

This case is also interesting because it permitted Wasden, as a citizen and taxpayer of Jenkins County, to attack the original judgment upholding the exemption. The court said that

---

[56] *Michael Falkenstein and Clifford V. McGlotten v. the Department of Revenue,* U.S. District Court of Oregon, Civil No. 71-816 (1972).

[57] *Village of Moyie Springs, Idaho v. Aurora Manufacturing Co.,* 82 Idaho 337, 353 P.2d 767 (1960).

[58] *Lancaster v. Clayton,* 86 Ky. 373, 5 S.W. 864 (1887) at p. 865.

each taxpayer has an interest in seeing that no other taxpayer is illegally exempt because that would place a greater burden on those taxpayers who have to pay.[59]

Even valid statutes must be read very carefully. In South Carolina, the statute contained words exempting the plant and expansion from ''all county and township taxes,'' and ''all county and township taxes, except taxes for school purposes.''

The Supreme Court held that any refund should *not* have included school taxes since it was not the legislative intent to include school taxes within the exemption. The legislature had, in fact, made an unmistakable distinction between county, township, and school district taxes.

Since the school tax made up the largest part of the total tax (56½ mills of 60½ mills), the incentive was greatly diminished and taxpayer should not have relied on the school tax exemption in his decision to construct and expand.[60]

Our concern for protecting the environment has resulted in the enactment of pollution control exemptions as an incentive to industry to control emissions and waste.

Common statutory language refers to pollution control equipment or facilities used ''*primarily for the purpose of*'' treating, isolating, reducing, controlling or stabilizing waste.

Courts will construe ''primarily for the purpose of'' according to the common meaning of the language. This can mean only those items ''basic or fundamental to such control'' of pollution will be granted an exemption. The issues are: (1) Did the legislature intend to extend the exemption beyond ''primary usage?'' (2) Does the dual purpose of an item of equipment—production and pollution control—indicate primary and secondary usage? (3) Should, therefore, only a portion of the investment be exempt?

If you pursue a pollution control exemption, you must review the pertinent statutes to define these issues. Your request for exemption may have to go through a Board of Environmental Protection rather than the assessor. You must show clearly that the items you seek to have exempted fit within the language of the statute.

Sometimes there can be a very thin line between whether the facilities are used primarily for pollution control or for manufacturing. Your presentation to an Environmental Board should involve all necessary detail, and expert engineering testimony is recommended to resolve these issues in your favor.[61]

Homeowner's Exemptions

The homeowner's exemption principally functions to promote public interests in preserving owner-occupied residential property.

The source of this exemption is the State Constitution or statutes and it should be noted very carefully that the taxpayer homeowner does *not* have an absolute right to the homestead exemption.

A Florida case held that the exemption applied only ''upon establishment of a right thereto in the manner prescribed by law.'' Thus, when the homeowner failed to file his homestead exemption application form by the April 1st deadline, he was not entitled to the exemption.[62] Quite simply, the legislature has the power to establish the manner in which to provide for the exemption and the taxpayer must comply.

Legislative intent concerning homeowner's exemption was the catalyst in Florida changing its assessment level from about 50% to 100% of just value in 1964.

---

[59] *Wasden v. Rusco Industries,* Inc., 233 Ga. 439, 211 S.E.2d 733 (1975).

[60] *Bowaters Carolina Corporation v. Cody W. Smith,* 186 S.E.2d 761 (1972).

[61] *Statler Industries, Inc. v. Board of Environmental Protection,* 333 A. 2d 703 (1975).

[62] *Horne v. Markham,* 288 So. 2d 196 (1974).

The homestead exemption in Florida was $5,000. Prior to going to the 100% level of assessment, the homeowner received a double benefit. If his home was worth $10,000 and the equalization ratio was 50%, the assessment would be $5,000. Applying the $5,000 homestead exemption to the assessed value would result in no tax payable. After going to 100%, the taxpayer would have to pay taxes on a $5,000 assessment.

	Equalization Rate @ 50%	Equalization Rate @ 100%
Just or Fair Market Value	$10,000	$10,000
Assessed Value	5,000	10,000
Homestead Exemption	−5,000	−5,000
Taxable Base	-0-	$5,000

In the McNayr case in Florida, commercial property taxpayers sued for mandamus demanding that all Dade County assessments be doubled to bring them to a one-hundred percent just value. The assessor appeared and admitted that he was assessing at about one-half of just value.

The commercial taxpayer's argument was that the one-half of just value assessment level discriminated in favor of homestead exempt property by inflating the value of the constitutional exemption.

The court held that after the assessor arrived at just value he did not have the discretion to adopt 50% of it for his assessment roll value. He was ordered to complete his 1964 tax roll at 100% of just valuation.

The entire state followed suit, illustrating the importance of legislative intent in these statutes.[63]

HOW LESSEES AND LESSORS CAN GAIN EXEMPT STATUS WHEN INVOLVED IN A LEASE WITH AN EXEMPT ENTITY

When a lessee leases from, or a lessor leases to, an exempt entity, this relationship does not automatically extend the exemption to the leased property. Issues concerning taxability revolve around constitutional or statutory language involving ownership, use, or both, liberal or strict interpretations by the courts, and the facts of each case.[64]

In a typical case, a for-profit corporation leased X-ray equipment for use in a non-profit exempt hospital. In accordance with the terms of the lease, the exempt hospital had to pay any taxes. The assessor levied a tax and the hospital protested.

The issue turned on the language of the statute which exempted property *owned* by certain specific entities and property *used* for certain specific purposes. Ownership, therefore, was not the criterion of exemption. The court noted the legislative purpose of lower costs for patients and held that the exemption applied to the X-ray equipment.[65]

It should be noted that if the statute demanded ownership or, perhaps, if the for-profit corporation had to pay the tax under the terms of the lease, the result might have been different.

Notice can also play an important part in these lessee/lessor/exempt entity situations.

[63]*McNayr v. State of Florida,* 166 So. 2d 142 (1964) and Ernest E. Means, "Assessment Standards and Property Tax Equity in Florida," *University of Florida Law Review* (1964-1965), Vol. 17, pp. 83-108.

[64]55 ALR 3d 430.

[65]*Montana Deaconess Hospital v. Cascade County,* 521 P.2d 203 (1974).

In an Illinois case, it was held improper practice where the lessee taxpayer's first notice was the tax bill on property listing the city as owner and heretofore exempt. The taxpayer was entitled to an opportunity for hearing of the assessment increase.[66]

"UNWRITTEN" EXEMPTIONS IN "COMMON" PLACES ARE OFTEN OVERLOOKED AT GREAT EXPENSE TO THE TAXPAYER

The taxpayer should be aware that there are many instances where an exemption exists because property has been totally assessed and no separate additional assessment can be levied. The proper assessment is -0- and the property is, in fact, exempt or at least not subject to taxation.

For example, the Supreme Court of Washington held that where restrictions concerning the right of homeowners to use a golf course in a planned development rendered its continuous use unprofitable, ownership is of no benefit or value and there is no fair market value to assess. The assessor's $660,000 value via the cost approach failed.[67]

Similarly, assessors have been told by the courts not to separately assess common areas of a condominium. The court held eight acres of open space used for recreation should be reflected and absorbed by the value of surrounding property.[68]

The same decision was reached with regard to a beach area reserved exclusively to nearby lot owners with easements to the beach. Again, the value should have been reflected in the assessed value of the surrounding lots. The beach itself had no fair market value.[69]

Finally, over 19 acres of private roads were assessed even though they had been dedicated in the plot and were owned by all the lot owners. The Board held that the roads were equivalent to a grant of easement and the value should be reflected in each lot. The assessment was reduced to -0-.[70]

The point made by this series of cases is a significant one. Do not be misled by the fact that the holdings say the common areas should be absorbed into the value of the surrounding parcels. This does *not* mean these assessments will be increased. In most instances, the assessor will have valued the surrounding lots at the market value. He will therefore be hard-pressed to increase this value further since the common area values will already be reflected in the assessed value.

Result: The common area items receive a -0- assessment and are, for all intents and purposes, exempt.

A TAXPAYER WITH SOME IMAGINATION CAN SOMETIMES CREATE HIS OWN EXEMPTION

It is possible to create your own exemption where none existed before. Mahoney did this—or thought he did—in Watertown, Mass., when he granted an easement to the town to be used for public off-street parking. The easement was subject to the land being exempt from property taxes and the selectmen agreed but, unfortunately, the assessors did not.

---

[66]*Marty v. Brown,* 338 N.E.2d 920 (1975).

[67]*Twin Lakes Golf and Country Club v. King County,* 548 P.2d 538 (1976).

[68]*Supervisor of Assessments v. Middlebrook Home Owners Assn., Inc.,* Maryland Tax Court, Nos. 58 & 59 (June 9, 1976).

[69]*Supervisor of Assessments of Anne Arundel Coutny v. Bay Ridge Properties, Inc.,* 270 Md. 216, 310 A.2d 773 (1973).

[70]*Four Seasons Maintenance Commission v. Clallam County Board of Equalization,* Washington Board of Tax Appeals, Docket 13637 (1976).

The exemption failed here, but had the town legally agreed to the terms of the easement, the exemption would have been valid.[71]

AN ASSESSOR WITH SOME IMAGINATION CAN SOMETIMES GET A TAXPAYER TO MAKE "IN LIEU OF" TAX PAYMENTS DESPITE AN EXISTING EXEMPTION

As a result of the assessor's continuous effort to stem the erosion of his tax base because of exemptions, an organized effort is being made to collect "in lieu of" property tax payments.

Simply stated, the assessor approaches the taxpayer who enjoys an exemption and requests a payment in lieu of property taxes. The idea is to help offset the cost of services (police and fire protection, street lights, etc.) enjoyed by the exempt party.

There is a very practical aspect to these "in lieu of" payments that may come about very subtly. After having located an industrial facility in a particular state and having enjoyed exempt status for a year, I was approached by the assessor with the following problem.

As a result of the industry locating there, employment increased, families moved in, school costs have increased—and would the corporation consider making an "in lieu of" payment?

The "good citizen" image of the corporate conscience was tweaked and the "in lieu of"payment was made at about one-half of what the corporation would have paid without the exemption in the first place.

The assessor confided in me later that he did not think his request for "in lieu of" payment had a prayer. Nevertheless, his jurisdiction was the beneficiary of this substantial tax payment.

CHECK LIST

( ) U.S. Constitution.
( ) State Constitution.
( ) Local statutes.
( ) Enabling acts.
( ) Ownership of property.
( ) Use of property (exclusive use?)
( ) Court interpretations (strict or liberal).
( ) Facts of the case.
( ) Who ultimately pays the tax?
( ) "Unwritten" exemptions.
( ) Can you create your own exemptions?
( ) What is your exposure to "in lieu of" tax payments?

[71]*Frederick J. Mahoney v. Bd. of Assessors of Watertown, et al.*, 362 Mass. 210, 285 N.E. 2d 403 (1972).

Part III

Techniques and Methods In Successful Property Tax Appeal Practice

14

How to Plan an Effective Appeal: Initial Negotiations Set the Stage For Subsequent Tax Savings Results

14

In the preceding sections of this manual, we considered the investigation necessary to assemble pertinent data regarding the assessed property. We also considered the procedures necessary to analyze this data in order to draw valuation conclusions on various types of property. We now come to that portion of the property tax control effort which could be described generally as presentation.

PRELIMINARY CONSIDERATIONS FOR THE TAXPAYER

How Much to Invest

The taxpayer who believes his property is overassessed must decide on a course of action to correct that situation. He must consider what alternative methods are available to him to attempt to adjust his assessment. He must decide how much he will *invest* in his effort to save tax dollars. In this regard, it should be remembered that assessment reductions achieved in a given year usually repeat themselves annually. Accrued tax savings over a period of years, therefore, may be the correct dollar amount against which to measure any investment required to reduce the current assessments.

When to Seek Professional Help

Having decided to appeal, the primary judgmental decision facing the taxpayer is when to seek *professional help*. In the case of the homeowner appealing his residence assessment, any investment in professional help might offset the benefits of any tax savings. The opposite is true in the case of the owner of property of substantial size. Problems are more technical in nature and demand the input of professional techniques and advice.

The decision as to how to proceed is, of course, the taxpayer's. It has been my experience that the best method of approach is to retain professional help at the point when you seriously decide to pursue a formal appeal. The important elements of continuity of action and direction become fixed at the outset. The resultant organized and systematic approach based on experience provides the surest route to a successful appeal effort.

GROUNDS FOR APPEAL

There are two basic grounds for assessment appeal (other than illegality) and they are overvaluation and equalization.

Overvaluation

When you claim overvaluation, you must prove that the assessment is in excess of the fair market value of the subject property.

Equalization

When you claim equalization or inequality, you must prove that your property is assessed at a greater percentage of value than other similar property on the same tax roll.

These two basic issues form the technically and legally correct measures of a fair market value assessment: Is the property equitably valued and is the proper equalization rate applied?

"Local" Grounds for Appeal

But, we are now dealing with initial negotiations with the local assessor and fair market value concepts just may be the last thing the assessor wants to talk about. He may be concerned about uniformity of assessments and he might argue that he cannot give you special treatment; he may be worried about the jurisdiction's budget, the elderly citizens on his tax roll, new ratables being added to the roll or old ratables being removed from the roll; he may be worried about the next election or the local school board's criticism of his office.

This is the "local" in local property taxes. This is the strength and the weakness of this very important revenue source. This is why you have to "be there" to discuss these local matters in person. This is why property tax control does not lend itself to the same control effort in Federal or state level franchise, income, or sales and use taxes.

Your job is to determine what the "grounds for appeal" are in this jurisdiction. You already know what the textbooks say, but you want to find out what will get you a reduction from *this* assessor on *your* valuation issue.

If he is strong on cost then you had better be strong on cost. If he insists on knowing if you make a profit you can argue all day that it is not relevant—but, if you want a negotiated settlement, you had better talk profits. It might not be in your best interest to talk profits and you must then avoid it. But I say, if it supports my valuation position and the assessor wants to know about it, I present it in detail. An actual case example involving this issue is set forth later in this chapter.

My point is that "grounds for appeal" might not always turn on strict fair market value concepts and you must seek out what the "grounds" are locally in order to effect your assessment reduction through initial negotiations with the assessor.

TIMELINESS OF INITIAL MEETING WITH THE ASSESSOR

Ideally, you should request a meeting with the assessor to present your data so that it can be considered in the setting of the current assessment. This should be long enough in advance of assessment date to allow him to absorb your input. He can either accept or reject it prior to levying the assessed value that you, in turn, will accept or reject.

This procedure will eliminate the possibility of the assessor's claiming that he was surprised by the appeal and that he did not have enough time prior to fixing the assessment to review and analyze your data.

The assessor may need time to call in experts from the state, a revaluation firm, or an outside consultant to assist him if the problem demands it. Data will have to be reviewed and a tour or inspection of the facility might be in order. All this requires reasonable lead time.

The tour of the subject property is very important and you should be prepared to make the offer of such an inspection opportunity early in your negotiation tactics. This gives you the chance to highlight physical, functional and economic obsolescence factors firsthand to the assessor or his representative.

A phone call to the assessor's office will generally enable you to determine the "right time" to drop by and present your "preliminary" data. However, it should be kept in mind that, if the assessment is inequitable, any time is the right time to appeal. It is paramount to protect your interests and the sooner you begin the appeal machinery, the better.

A hurried appeal filed in a rush because of a surprise deadline may be troublesome. But, at worst, you may file an appeal which you might later withdraw upon detailed examination of all the facts.

More importantly, however, you have protected your interests for the current year. I have often used this first year appeal as leverage in negotiations on the second year under appeal. The assessor knows you are serious in that you previously have filed a formal appeal. In the heat of negotiations on the second year appeal, offering to withdraw the first year (which you were lucky to hurriedly get in the previous year) can work wonders in getting a current reduction. The idea is that the assessor can eliminate an appeal year with no refunds. He looks good and you have a current reduction.

You must also be aware that you cannot file careless appeals with no idea of the consequences. You might upset a very good assessment or you might get a whopping assessment increase as a result. But, if all the facts seem to bear out your preliminary valuation position, then by all means protect your rights in the current year.

You also risk the possibility of upsetting the assessor, especially in smaller jurisdictions. But waiting another year to give the assessor the opportunity to review data presupposes that you will achieve an assessment reduction by this method of approach. Unfortunately, this is not always the case and you may simply have to file a formal appeal in the following year. All you succeeded in doing in this situation is to give up an appeal year to receive a "no" from the assessor.

Hence the absolute necessity for an awareness of all pertinent appeal dates.

A WORD ON APPEAL DATE PROCEDURES

In the simplest situation, an appeal date is fixed by statute, it remains the same each year, and a prescribed form must be filed on or before that date.

Other procedures involve a thirty-day period from date of notification of a changed assessment or thirty days from the date of payment of a tax bill. This is most important! Be sure you know exactly when you have to file. There are many catches. In some jurisdictions you can be negotiating with the assessor or the Board of Review but you must file your appeal to court within a certain number of days from the payment of the first quarter tax bill. This can cause you to have to file formal court papers while you are awaiting the Board's decision. And to top it all off, to properly perfect the later appeal, you had to file an accounting early in the year indicating the value of your property!

Whatever the procedure, you should be sure to file all papers on a timely basis and plan on meeting with the assessor at least two to four months prior to his finalizing of the assessment figure. This should give him more than enough time to weigh your data as it impacts upon the assessment. You have then at least attempted to be cooperative and to enable the assessor to consider your valuation position.

MEETING WITH THE ASSESSOR

In General

There is, of course, no specific guide to successful negotiations in property tax appeal matters. Some general rules, perhaps, do apply. *Be prepared.* You have to do your homework. This does not mean you must go in with a full-blown appraisal report. But you should know all there is to know about your property. You must have ''assembled all your pertinent data.'' And you must be able to show that you have good grounds for challenging the present assessment.

As in all negotiations, it is probably best to open light. Weather or football (hockey in Canada) is always a good way to break the ice. Stay away from politics and religion.

The middle of your presentation is where your preparation pays off. This is where you have to make your valuation points.

Having raised the basic issues, it is probably best to close on a light note. The meeting should end on an ''everybody doing his job with no hard feelings'' level and should leave the door open to future dialogue and input of information for review by the assessor.

Defining Subject Matter

As the first point in my basic presentation, I make it a practice to be sure that all facts are generally agreed on before I get into valuation specifics. The exact acreage and building square footage; dates of construction, descriptions on tax bills; applicable jurisdictions: is it the city, county and village who are involved, or is the property only in the city but not the village; does the property record card tie into the tax bills exactly so that you are sure you are dealing with all your parcels and that you are not forgetting the parking lot across the street; examine exactly how your personal property is assessed by referring to your personal property renditions as filed and the mathematical computations done by the assessor to establish your personal property assessment.

Negotiation Goal

Having established the basic facts surrounding the property to be appealed, it is time to pursue your negotiation goal. You are, of course, convinced of the fact that you are entitled to an assessment reduction for a few specific reasons. Let us assume that basically the assessor has used a cost approach to establish value and has given little weight to functional and economic obsolescence. In addition, he has, in your opinion, not given sufficient weight to the income and market data approaches to value.

Your goal is to have him consider these items in his valuation exercise and to make a downward adjustment in the assessment.

Should Your Presentation Be Oral or Written?

This is a difficult question at this point in your early appeal effort. The problem is just how much you want to disclose at this stage. If you do not disclose enough, you will probably not be complying with the assessor's requests for information. If you disclose too much, you may later regret giving your entire case away at the start.

The method that I have found to be most productive is *not* to submit any information in writing to the assessor at this meeting. However, I do present a follow-up taxpayer's position letter telling exactly where I stand on value and why.

This gives you the opportunity to highlight those items which the assessor appeared most sensitive to. It also gives you the opportunity to do a little further detailed homework to bolster your arguments in those areas where the assessor's arguments showed strength.

This formal letter summarizing your meeting serves many purposes. It initiates the significant dialogue in the case by beginning to draw the issues into focus; it is a ready reference of the highlights of the matter; and it serves to establish the direction and tone of your appeal effort.

It gives you the opportunity to do some homework for the assessor. If he is leaning toward granting you an assessment reduction, then you should present him with the logical and documented backup for such a decision. The assessor is busy with many other matters and you have to do his digging for him so that, if he is so disposed, he can grant you a reduction on good, supportable grounds.

An example of a typical taxpayer's position letter is set forth later in this chapter.

How Much of a Reduction Do You Want?

Be sure to specifically request the amount of reduction you are seeking in this taxpayer's position letter. Here again, a difficult question. Should you take a conservative point of view and ask for an amount limited to what the property is worth if you recognize the merits of the assessor's position? Or should you assume that later a Board of Review or a judge may simply cut any difference between you and the assessor in half? This would dictate that you decide all gray areas in your favor and go in with a lower end-of-the-spectrum figure.

Another problem here is that if you ask for too much off the assessment, the assessor may think you are not willing to consider a smaller reduction offer. I personally am always willing to discuss settlement offers with assessors, regardless of size. You can always say "no thanks." The important thing is movement in your direction.

If an assessor offers a 10% reduction for the current year, perhaps you can get him to agree to an additional 10% in each of the next two years. This gives you a 30% reduction over three years. It takes some patience but so does an appeal to court. You might wind up with the same reduction in three years. Crowded court calendars might hold up your result for that period and a 30% reduction in assessment on an appeal to court is not a bad result.

In addition, if you go to court and win, you may be faced with collecting three years of refunds from a taxing jurisdiction that cannot afford to pay. So you will probably end up by taking the refund as a credit against current tax payments for another three years.

My philosophy in initial negotiation strategy is to try to cut away any of the fat that is in the assessment. I try not to be too greedy if the assessor shows a willingness to move in my direction with regard to concepts of valuation.

You can always formally appeal next year. By that time, the fat you cut away this year has been reflected in the new reduced assessment and you have a second year's tax savings accruing to you.

Thus, the importance of setting your negotiation achievement goals vis-a-vis formal appeal.

The Assessor May Not Be Your Last Stop in Your Negotiating Effort

When the assessor says, "NO!," that does *not* mean you have to pick up your marbles and go home. In one major midwest city, I ran into the following set of facts.

An industrial plant of 800,000 square feet sold arm's-length for $4,000,000 or $5.00 per square foot of land and building. The assessment on the plant on the date of sale was $4,000,000 but the equalization rate in the jurisdiction was 50%, so that, in effect, the assessor's fair market value was $8,000,000. I opened my negotiations on behalf of the new owner by simply requesting that the assessor set the fair market value of the plant at its sale price of $4,000,000, and that he apply the 50% equalization rate and assess it at $2,000,000.

The assessor advised me that he did not consider the sale to be arm's-length. It was rather a "dump" sale and did not indicate fair market value. The fact that the property had been on the market for two years with no serious offers did not interest the assessor.

I simply refused to accept this arbitary position and walked across the hall where I was able to talk some common sense to the mayor. The new owner was about to hire 2,000 people to work in the city and all we wanted was a fair assessment that would reflect our purchase price.

The mayor was more receptive to my arguments. He overruled the general rule in the jurisdiction of not recognizing sales of older industrial properties as valid indications of market value and the assessment was immediately reduced to $2,000,000, one-half of its former level.

There was one catch, however. All news releases about the plant and the new jobs had to be handled through the mayor's office with suitable fanfare publicity. This was no problem and the ribbon-cutting ceremony at the plant opening was fun. Paying the new tax bill at $50,000 less than the previous year was more fun.

Another source of negotiated reductions, other than the assessor, is the corporation counsel. He is the attorney responsible for eventually trying the case. If you can convince him of the merits of your position, he can, perhaps, prevail on the assessor to take a more reasonable position as to value. The corporation counsel, like all attorneys, doesn't like to lose cases. Additionally, he has the responsibility of advising the assessor concerning the prudent investment of the jurisdiction's monies. If you lay your facts before him and he agrees (and sometimes he does), you may find that the assessor will change his position and offer you some sort of a reduction.

Doublecheck Appeal Procedures

Be sure to casually doublecheck on the appeal dates that are in effect for the current tax year. They sometimes surprise you and change from year to year and there is no better source for the current information than the assessor himself. This should confirm what you already know as far as the specific date to file papers is concerned. If there is a conflict of information, then you will have to check further to make sure you are following the correct procedures to protect your interests for this year.

I used the phrase "casually doublecheck" in the paragraph above. You certainly do not want to threaten the good assessor with the fact that if he does not give you what you want you will appeal. He realizes that you have the responsibility to examine and challenge, if warranted, this property assessment, and part of that exercise is to confirm the accuracy of your information regarding appeal dates. As a matter of fact, many assessors will advise you to appeal to protect your interests.

Obtain Appeal Forms

As long as you are both talking about it, you might as well pick up a copy of the necessary appeal form. This can save you a lot of trouble later on when you're pressed by a fast-approaching filing deadline and you find that you do not have the appropriate form on hand.

FOLLOW-UP TO THE MEETING WITH THE ASSESSOR

I believe the follow-up to your initial negotiation session with the assessor is most important. The meetings and the matters discussed are often forgotten immediately after you leave the assessor's office. The press of other business does not necessarily make your property the most serious problem that the assessor is battling with. Therefore, a friendly reminder that you mean business and were serious about your valuation position can be set forth in the form of a taxpayer's position letter.

The outline of the letter should run somewhat parallel to your presentation during your negotiation session. As a matter of fact, if you take careful notes during the meeting you can quickly dictate your position letter from them.

A typical taxpayer's position letter is set forth in the following actual case history.

ACTUAL CASE HISTORY

Background Information

The subject property is a nonferrous metal castings and forgings plant in northern Ohio. It is made up of 1,850,000 square feet of buildings on 200 acres of land. Construction dates back to the 1940's.

A significant change in production orientation occurred here with the decline of aircraft production in the United States. Fifty percent of the plant buildings were no longer occupied.

This situation reflected itself in the general industrial real estate market in northern Ohio. Excess industrial square footage was available and potential purchasers of a 1,850,000 square foot plant were few. Market indications reflected a fair market value range of from $4.00 to $5.00 per square foot, land and building.

Nevertheless, the assessor valued the complex at $14,800,000 or $8.00 per square foot, land and building.

Preliminary Considerations for the Taxpayer

Taxpayer was aware of these facts and decided to appeal. Because of the complexity of the valuation problem, professional assistance was engaged at the outset.

Grounds for Appeal

Taxpayer knew that the grounds for appeal in Ohio were overvaluation and equalization based on fair market value concepts. However, an initial meeting with the assessor (auditor in Ohio) was arranged in order to seek out what factors would have impact on this assessment from a ''local'' point of view.

Initial Meeting with Assessor

An initial meeting was held with the assessor two months in advance of assessment day. General valuation points were raised and he requested that we meet with the revaluation firm experts who actually established the assessment and who were responsible for defending their figures if the matter went to the Board of Review. During the course of the conversation, we were advised that, due to the very serious economic problems facing the area, consideration was being given to economic factors impacting on industrial real estate values. These factors included decline in profit, decline in production, idle space and decline in number of employees. The assessor realized that these were not strictly real estate valuation factors but he was seeking a level of assessment which would reflect the health of the local economy.

Here, of course, was taxpayer's "local grounds for appeal." If we could show profit, production and employment level problems and idle space, the assessor would consider these as having a bearing on the current real estate assessment.

The revaluation people were contacted and they requested a tour of the plant to refamiliarize themselves with the facility.

Defining Subject Matter

At a brief meeting prior to the tour we made sure that we were talking about the same parcels, assessments, tax bills, acreage and building square footage. I also made sure that they were aware of the assessor's position with regard to the economic conditions prevelant in the area that would have a bearing on the development of this assessment. They stated that they knew this to be the case and if we could provide them with factual data to support economic obsolescence, they would certainly consider it in light of the assessor's overall position.

Here, of course, was my opportunity to do some homework for the revaluation people representing the assessor. They would certainly not have time to do this type of digging on every property, so it was up to me to provide them with the necessary data to assist them in reaching supportable conclusions of industry reorientation economic obsolescence factors. This will become a significant part of my follow-up taxpayer's position letter.

Having basically agreed on all pertinent issues, we proceeded to the tour of the facility.

Tour of Facility

Here I was dealing with two professional appraisers who were rechecking their original cost approach to determine if our claim for additional functional and economic obsolescence was founded in fact. They were aware of the general market conditions on which I based my \$4.00 to \$5.00 per square foot value and I had to prove to them that additional physical, functional and economic depreciation conditions existed, warranting a downward adjustment in their previous value conclusion.

The tour included the entire plant. Individual examples of severe physical depreciation and functional obsolescence were highlighted in detail. Specific areas of idle plant space were walked through and pinpointed on a plot plan. Throughout the tour, the revaluation team was accompanied by a plant engineer who was familiar with the problems and who could answer any technical questions that might come up.

At the conclusion of the tour, certain requests for information were made, and we agreed to furnish the revaluation people with that data in a taxpayer's position letter which would address itself to all matters discussed to date regarding this assessment. We were asked to send the letter directly to the assessor.

The following letter in this actual case history was worth $120,000 in tax savings.

Taxpayer's Position Letter

Mr. Assessor
City Hall
City, State Zip

Re: Subject Property
Address
Parcel Number(s) Identification
Current Assessment Period

Dear Mr. Assessor:

Thank you for the courtesy you extended to us during our recent visit to your office. Pursuant to our conversation, we contacted the ABC Company revaluation firm and Messrs. Jones and Smith visited with us and toured the plant on Tuesday of this week. They requested certain specific data pertinent to their investigation and I agreed to furnish it to them in the format of this taxpayer's position letter. They asked that I address the letter directly to you. It is hoped that this information will assist you in arriving at an assessment equitable to all concerned.

Comment: This is a simple opening paragraph. But it is important to establish the circumstances under which you are submitting the data, and what you hope to accomplish by doing so.

1. This letter should not in any way be interpreted as limiting our valuation arguments with regard to any future appeals that may or may not be filed. It is merely furnished to you to assist in the establishment of the current fair market value assessment. It is my understanding that all information will be kept in strict confidence and will be used only in connection with the current assessment negotiations.

Comment: This is a ''limitations'' paragraph which indicates your desire for flexibility with regard to possible future action. In addition, it is always a good idea to reemphasize the confidential nature of the data you are dealing in. Note that the paragraph is numbered. This is a good idea because easy reference can be made in subsequent phone calls, correspondence, etc.

2. Identification of Subject Property: As you know, the subject property is known as the XYZ Nonferrous Metal Castings Plant located at 100 Castings Road. It consists of 200 acres of land and 1,850,000 square feet of buildings constructed in the 1940's. The parcel numbers which identify this property on the City tax rolls are:

Parcel 100
Parcel 100-1
Parcel 101
Parcel 101-1-1

It should be noted that the Parcel known as 102 is not included in this letter. It is part of the plant operation but it is owned by the Federal Government.

Comment: Again, a simple reference paragraph to be sure you have identified all the parcels that make up the assessment you are concerned about. It is important for example to flag the fact that a contiguous parcel owned by the Federal Government and used for specialty U.S. Government work is not a part of the appeal. Note also that the paragraph has given an underlined heading to its subject matter. This is most important. It enables you to stick to the subject of that paragraph and prevents rambling. After all, your whole purpose here is to be sure that the assessor understands you. Thus, your position letter should be as clear as possible.

3. Current Assessment: The current assessments as listed on the tax rolls are:

Parcel 100	Land 100 ac.	$ 1,500,000
Parcel 100-1	Bldgs.	5,900,000
Parcel 101	Land 100 ac.	1,500,000
Parcel 101-1-1	Bldgs.	5,900,000
	Total	$14,800,000

(To the reader: To simplify this presentation, it is assumed that the assessment is levied at 100% of market value.)

These assessment figures indicate that the land is assessed at $15,000 per acre and the buildings are assessed at $6.38 per square foot ($11,800,000 ÷ 1,850,000 square feet). Assuming no excess land (5:1 ratio) the overall assessment is levied at $8.00 per square foot ($14,800,000 ÷ 1,850,000 square feet).

4. Economic Obsolescence Factors: Pursuant to your general comments at our recent meeting, and in accordance with the specific request for detailed information by Messrs. Jones and Smith, we are submitting the following economic obsolescence data which we believe should have a significant bearing on the establishment of the current year's tax assessment.

You have requested a detailed breakdown as to production rates, profit levels and employment levels at the five operating units of this plant. We believe, as you do, that these facts will illustrate severe economic obsolescence due to industry reorientation.

The plot plan in Attachment 1 shows the five operating units and their relationship to each other. They are (1) Specialty Metals; (2) Research and Development (R&D); (3) Sand; (4) Ingot; and (5) Forgings.

Note particularly that three of the five units have ceased to operate as productive units in this plant. R&D, Sand, and Ingot are indicated on the plot plan by hash marks. These areas are vacant except for some convenience storage. These vacant areas make up approximately 50% of the entire square footage of the plant. These vacancies were present on this assessment day and a similar situation has existed for the past three to five years. Projections do not indicate any changes. This then is a permanent condition rather than a cyclical one.

Attachment 2, also requested by you, is a schedule showing basic data regarding volume of business in pounds, income and employment levels for the five operating units over the past five years.

This schedule illustrates the severe impact that the decline in the aerospace industry had on this plant's production, income and employment level. Commercial airline travel and, therefore, aircraft orders reached its height in the early 1960's with annual growth rates in excess of 20%. Growth rates began to falter in the mid-1960's, resulting in a complete aerospace industry reorientation by 1970. This situation carried over to the

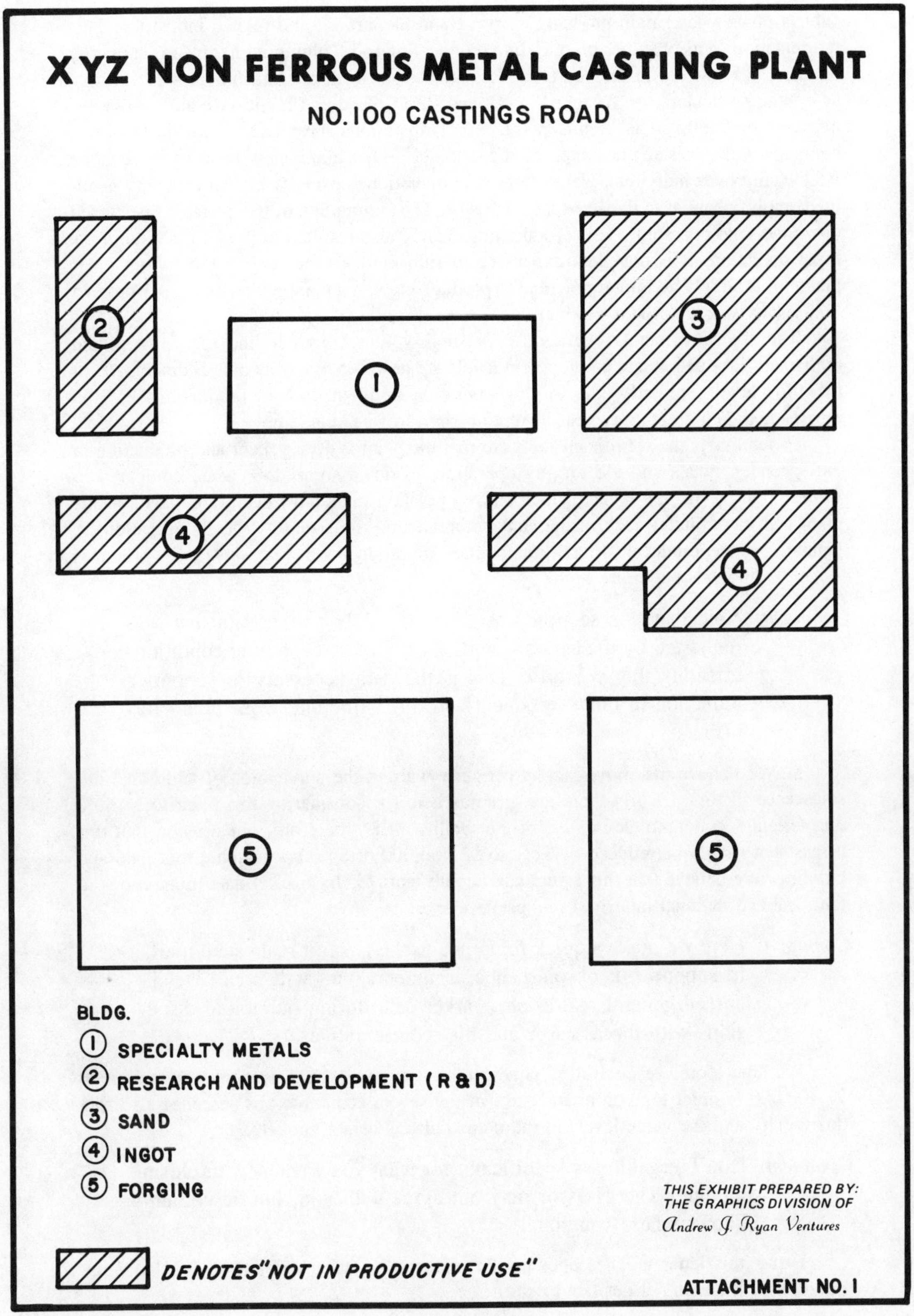

ATTACHMENT 1

subject plant whose main products were used in the aircraft and related industries. This reorientation to a consumer product line (connecting rods, plumbing hardware, spraygun handles) has resulted in the comparative statistics set forth on Attachment #2.

Note particularly on Attachment #2 that R&D, Sand and Ingot have all been terminated as operating units at this plant. R&D operations have been consolidated on a company-wide basis and this expense reduction effort has eliminated the need for separate R&D facilities at individual plants. The sand operation was necessary for specialty handmade molds peculiar to the aerospace industry. The elimination of this product line closed down the sand operation. This product line change also resulted in the termination of the ingot operation. It is now less expensive to ship ingot to the subject plant from other plants. It is simply no longer practical to produce ingot at a plant with a consumer product line vis-a-vis an aerospace product line.

The specialty metals operation is a small-volume product line requiring skilled craftsmen. Production and employment levels are down 45% and income is down 38% of the 1969 level. Similarly, the forging operation is down 44% in production, 25% in income and 37% in employment level compared to five years ago.

In summary, the significant facts are that the plant is 50% vacant and production in the specialty metals and the forging operations is down some 45% when compared to former high production levels. Three entire operating units have been eliminated at this plant and a continuing lack of demand is threatening the specialty metals operation. A plant that once produced 16 million pounds of product per year now only produces 3,250,000 pounds per year.

Comment: Note that this section was devoted solely to the data that was requested by the assessor with regard to the economic conditions affecting this property. This is the data necessary to support a reduction in this assessment and this is the data you should furnish.

5. We believe the above factors certainly warrant the application of additional obsolescence factors. Clearly there are grounds here for considering this plant to be 50% obsolete due to nonproductive use of the facility. It is, therefore, our opinion that this assessment should be reduced by 50% to $7,400,000 or $4.00 per square foot land and building. We believe that this figure can be substantiated by market data transactions in the local and national industrial real estate market.

Comment: Here we make a quick reference to the general real estate market to support our obsolescence argument. You will recall we discussed general real estate market data during our initial discussions with the assessor and his representatives.

We, therefore, respectfully request that you reduce the present assessment to $7,400,000 in order to appropriately reflect the severe economic obsolescence affecting this facility and the value levels in the industrial real estate market.

Comment: Don't forget to ask specifically for what you want as your closing thought. The assessor may not agree with you, but he certainly knows where you stand.

I trust this letter touches upon all the matters we discussed and if you have any questions, please do not hesitate to call.

Very truly yours,

ECONOMIC DATA BY UNIT OF OPERATION
XYZ NONFERROUS METALS CASTINGS PLANT

Volume of Business	1971	1970	1969	1968	1967
Specialty Metals	1,000	1,330	1,833	1,500	1,333
R & D	-0-	-0-	-0-	-0-	-0-
Sand	-0-	-0-	167	250	250
Ingot	-0-	133	8,917	9,340	10,371
Forge	2,250	2,334	3,340	3,750	4,040
TOTALS	3,250	3,797	14,257	14,840	15,994
					(000 pounds)
Income					
Specialty Metals	830	1,081	1,332	1,167	1,083
R & D	-0-	-0-	-0-	-0-	-0-
Sand	-0-	-0-	334	500	417
Ingot	-0-	53	3,567	3,829	4,356
Forge	3,625	3,666	3,432	4,083	4,830
TOTALS	4,455	4,800	8,665	9,579	10,686
					(000 dollars)
Employees					
Specialty Metals	361	492	675	570	557
R& D	-0-	-0-	15	38	40
Sand	-0-	-0-	200	361	370
Ingot	-0-	12	141	153	180
Forge	1,393	1,646	1,494	1,554	2,223
TOTALS	1,754	2,150	2,525	2,676	3,370
					(number of employees)

ATTACHMENT 2

You have now done all you can in the initial negotiations stage of your appeal. You met with the assessor and his representatives and furnished them with all the data they requested. All this was done prior to the establishment of your current assessment. Now you must wait for the assessment to be published to see if your efforts to date have been rewarded.

If you are not satisfied with the assessment, you must carry your appeal to the next level: The Board of Review.

CHECK LIST

( ) Potential tax savings.
( ) Investment.
( ) Professional help.
( ) Local grounds for appeal.
( ) Timetable of appeal.
( ) Tour of facility.
( ) Protect your appeal rights in current year.
( ) Appeal date procedures.

( ) Define subject matter.
( ) Negotiation goal.
( ) How much of a reduction do you want?
( ) Assessor-mayor-corporation counsel.
( ) Doublecheck appeal procedures with the assessor.
( ) Copy of appeal form.
( ) Taxpayer's position letter.

15

How to Present Appeals To a Board of Assessment Review: Key Techniques and Procedures

Administrative Review or Court Proceedings?

The Application for Assessment Review

- In General
- Timeliness
- Mailing of Assessment Notice
- Proper Completion of the Application for Assessment Reduction Form—the Stanjim Case
- The Form
- Appeal Year
- Jursidiction

Part One–General Information

- Proper or Aggrieved Party
- Agent's Authorization
- Identification of Property
- Present Assessment

Part Two–Grounds for Complaint on Assessment

- Overvaluation
- Taxpayer's (Complainant's) Opinion of Fair Market Value
- Extent of Overvaluation
- Inequality
- Illegality

Part Three–Information to Support Complainant

Part Four–Verification

- Transcript Requests
- Service of Papers

The Board of Assessment Review

Examples of Informal Board of Assessment Review Hearings

Example of a Formal Board of Assessment Review Hearing

Check List

15

This chapter deals with that portion of your property tax appeal effort that involves the filing of an application for an assessment reduction and an appearance before and presentation to a Board of Assessment review. This is an administrative procedure which follows your initial negotiation session with the assessor. The Board hearing comes prior to your formal court action. In most cases, exhausting this administrative remedy is a necessary first step to an appeal to the courts.

ADMINISTRATIVE REVIEW OR COURT PROCEEDINGS?

It is not always necessary for you to pursue this administrative remedy as a prerequisite to court appeal. To avoid this administrative step, however, it is necessary that a legal question be involved. For example, in a Michigan case the taxpayer imported steel from outside the state and warehoused it in its original package. The local assessor levied a property tax and taxpayer paid under protest. Taxpayer did not file an appeal with the local board and he did not appear before the local board. He appealed directly to court on the U.S. constitutional question of immunity from taxation. The court heard the case, agreeing that this was a legal question and no administrative appeal steps were necessary.[1]

In the standard property tax appeal case, however, you will probably be confronted with overvaluation and inequality issues. These issues generally require you to exhaust your administrative remedy by appeal to the local Board of Review prior to court action.

THE APPLICATION FOR ASSESSMENT REDUCTION

In General

In the preceding chapter we discussed the necessity for accurate knowledge of appeal dates, proper completion of application for assessment reduction forms, and compliance with filing procedures.

In addition to statutes and written procedures review, it was suggested that a doublecheck with the assessor be made during your informal negotiations. It was also recommended that a copy of the appropriate Application for Assessment Reduction form be obtained from the assessor so that you would have one immediately available for completion and timely filing.

It should be noted at the outset that getting your papers properly before the board can be one-half the battle in a successful Board of Review appeal.

It cannot be emphasized too strongly that filing procedures may be tricky and can cause

[1] *Interstate Steel Corp. vs. City of Detroit,* 59 Mich. App. 438, 229 N.W. 2d 491 (1975).

you great embarrassment if you should file late because you are not aware of all the time elements involved. It should also be emphasized that your appeal can fail if your application form is incomplete, incorrectly filled out, or improperly filed. Therefore, three primary considerations are timeliness, correct completion of the form, and proper service.

It should also be remembered that your Application for Assessment Reduction form is the first legal paper in your case. It is a prerequisite to, and incorporated into, any petition you subsequently file with the courts. Hence, the requirement for consideration of obtaining professional help at this crucial first step in your appeal effort.

Timeliness

In many jurisdictions there is a specific date or period of time for filing: for example, October 1st; the third Tuesday in July; between the first and 20th of June. Some jurisdictions make appeal dates contingent upon the happening of another event: 20 days from notice of a change in assessment; within ten days from payment of the first half tax bill. These contingent events may change from year to year, and therefore you cannot always rely on the date the appeal was filed in the previous year.

You should, of course, read the pertinent statutes governing the time requirements for filing your application. Often the assessor publishes filing instructions on the form itself and these can generally be relied on. But you must be careful because you can easily be misled.

The importance of being aware of the statutory requirements with regard to filing appeals with a Board of Assessors is illustrated by the following case. In a Georgia case, nonresidents were permitted 20 days to appeal after notice of assessment was mailed. The taxpayer asked for a ten-day extension to file and the Board granted the extension. The Supreme Court of Georgia held that the Board had *no* authority to extend the statutory time for appeal and the extension was void and the Board could not hear the case. Thus, you cannot rely on even the Board's willingness to hear your case if you are not timely in your filing.[2]

Mailing of Assessment Notice

Beware if notice from the assessor starts your appeal time running. In the preceding case, the taxpayer had 20 days from the date the assessment notice was mailed to appeal.

It is no excuse for you to claim that you never received notice of assessment and therefore you did not file an appeal. You may be in a jurisdiction where there is a rebuttable presumption that the notice was mailed. In such a jurisdiction, the assessor does not have to show that he mailed your notice to you. He need only show his custom as to preparation and mailing of notices and it will be presumed that assessors discharged their public duties. The taxpayer then has the burden to prove that the notice was not mailed.

If you are in such a jurisdiction, you cannot afford to sit back and wait for a notice of assessment. You actually have to check the assessment rolls each year to see if there have been any increases, revaluations, etc., and you have to do it early enough so that you will have time to appeal.[3]

Keep in mind that the pertinent statute is the key reference point for a timely appeal. If formal notice starts the appeal period running, then revaluation firm appointments do not

---

[2] *Tift vs. Tift County Board of Tax Assessors,* 234 Ga. 155, 215 S.E. 2nd 3 (1975).

[3] *Canyon Crest Villas South vs. the Board of County Commissioners,* 542 P. 2d 395 (1975) Colo.

extend the time for filing your papers.[4] You must file in accordance with statutory requirements.

Proper Completion of the Application for Assessment Reduction—the Stanjim Case

The preceding section illustrated the pitfalls in failure to comply with time requirements. This section highlights the pitfalls you face with regard to the proper completion of your appeal form.

In 1972, for example, taxpayer Stanjim filed a written application for assessment reduction with the Mahoning County Auditor in Ohio, Stephen R. Olenick, complaining that the 1971 real property assessment was too high. The auditor (assessor) not only would not reduce the assessments, but also he rejected the appeals saying that the forms were essentially blank. Taxpayer had typewritten under PERTINENT FACTS: "All other pertinent data substantiating this complaint of overvaluation will be presented at requested hearing."

This taxpayer, and most other appealing taxpayers in Ohio, had followed this same procedure for years. In general, no pertinent information had ever been included on the appeal forms and these forms had always been accepted in the past by the various County Boards.

Taxpayer brought a mandamus action to the Court of Common Pleas asking the judge to compel the auditor to accept the complaint forms as filed. The judge agreed with the auditor and dismissed the Petition for Mandamus! Stanjim appealed to the Ohio Court of Appeals and that court held that under Ohio law, the auditor has a mandatory duty to present all complaints as to the valuation of assessment of real property to the County Board of Revision. The question of whether or not these complaints were defective was not properly before the County Auditor and was not an issue in this case.

This was, of course, a good decision for the taxpayer, but only a temporary one because the auditor in Ohio is also a member of the Board of Revision. Thus, when Stanjim presented his Application for Decrease in Valuation together with supplemental information, Assessor Olenick and the Board again rejected the complaints saying that filing requirements were not originally met and supplemental information will not correct this defect. Again, taxpayer appealed and this time the Ohio Board of Tax Appeals agreed with the Board!

Stanjim was forced to appeal to the Supreme Court of Ohio. That decision held that the Ohio Board of Tax Appeals (BTA) has the authority by statute to prescribe and furnish blank appeal forms. This presented two issues:

(1) Is full compliance with Ohio statutes necessary to confer jurisdiction upon a County Board of Revision to consider a real property overassessment claim?
(2) Is BTA Form 1 a reasonable and lawful reflection of the data requirements of these statutes?

To both questions the Ohio Supreme Court answered "Yes!" The pertinent statutes say: "The County Board of Review shall not decrease any valuation complained of unless the party affected thereby or his agent makes and files with the Board a written application therefor, verified by oath, showing the facts upon which it is claimed such decrease should be made." The Court read this language to mean that a complaining party must state the valuation complained, and must aver facts under oath to support the requested decrease. And

[4]*Peagler vs. Georgetown Associates,* 209 S.E. 2d 186 (1974).

full compliance with the pertinent statutes is necessary before a County Board of Review is empowered to act on the merits of the claim.

Further, the court found that the questions asked on BTA Form 1 were wholly reasonable, non-oppressive, and clearly designed to elicit information required by statute. The form is brief to expedite orderly administrative process, and represents a lawful interpretation of the minimal data requirements of the statutes.

Stanjim, of course, argued that it had long been the practice of the Board to accept partially complete forms and that any change in this procedure should have been preceded by notice. The court expressed sympathy for the taxpayer but pointed out that there are cautionary statements on the reverse side of BTA Form 1, which should have alerted the taxpayer on the hazards of relying on such dubious, albeit locally sanctioned, practice.

Stanjim also tried to argue that his constitutional and statutory rights were violated because he was not assessed at a uniform percentage of market value. The court said Stanjim's failure to comply with reasonable procedural prerequisities lost him the opportunity to have the claim heard on the merits.

This decision was handed down in 1974 and the U.S. Supreme Court denied certiorari on January 13, 1975. As a result, some 5,000 appeals were dismissed throughout the State of Ohio. The impact of these dismissals was no more keenly felt than in a case I was involved in before the Cuyahoga County Board of Revision on a Cleveland real estate assessment appeal. We had just completed some ten days of testimony (two appraisers on each side) and the Board had taken its final evidence. Coincidentally, the Ohio Supreme Court decision on Stanjim had just been published. At 5:00 P.M. on a Friday, after our ten days of testimony was on the record, the Cuyahoga County Attorney appeared at the hearing, conferred with the Board Chairman, and it was announced that on advice from counsel, the Board was without jurisdiction in the matter and the case was dismissed! Indeed a dramatic moment in the annals of property tax appeals.

This type of situation was the basis, however, for sister appeals related to the Stanjim matter. The board actually heard the case—was that not enough information before the board to allow it to render a decision? After all, they had four appraisals and ten days of expert testimony to draw on. Certainly the taxpayer's complaint should not be dismissed on a technicality at this late stage. This decision was appealed.

Sister appeals were also based on the fact that in some instances some information was recorded on BTA 1. For example, the Board accepted one of my applications in another case because I had recorded a few unimportant details such as the number of floors in the building on the appeal form.

Taxpayers are a hardy bunch, and the Stanjim setbacks did not deter for an instant the basic aggressiveness of a wronged taxpayer. Sister appeals are being resolved favorably to this extent. At least one Common Pleas judge has held that Stanjim does not apply to all fact situations. Therefore, it is conceivable that the above-mentioned Cayahoga County case will be resolved in favor of the taxpayer and the Board will eventually have to render a decision on that valuation issue. *The Stanjim Co. v. Board of Revision of Mahoning County,* 380 S. 2d 233 (1974), certiorari denied by U.S. Supreme Court, January 13, 1975.

Unfortunately, the ultimate success of the taxpayer in this type of situation can come only after several frustrating years of delay and substantial legal fees. All could have been avoided by the proper completion of the application for reduction form. Although this case is extreme in that Ohio, almost overnight, went from requiring almost no information on an appeal form to requiring extremely detailed information, it certainly illustrates most emphatically the requirement for the proper completion of your Application for Assessment Reduction form.

The Form

A typical Application for Assessment Reduction form is set forth in Figure 15-1 and is followed by a step-by-step review of the various sections of that application with explanation.

COMPLAINT ON REAL PROPERTY ASSESSMENT FOR 19____

Before the Board of Assessment Review for ____________________
(County, City, Town or Village)

PART ONE: GENERAL INFORMATION

1. Name of Owner or Owners of Property — Post Office Address
2. Name and address of agent or representative of owner, if agent or representative is filing application.
3. Description of property or tax map number as it appears on the Assessment Roll.
4. Location of property (street, road, highway number, and city, town or village)
5. Type of Property:
   ____Residence ____Farm ____Resort ____Apartment ____Industrial
   ____Business (indicate type) __________
   ____Vacant Land ____Other (specify) __________
6. Assessed valuation appearing on the Assessment Roll.
   Land $________ Building $________ Total $________

PART TWO: GROUNDS FOR COMPLAINT ON ASSESSMENT

A. ____OVERVALUATION
Taxpayer's (Complainant's) Opinion of Fair Market Value $________
The assessment is erroneous by reason of overvaluation: the assessment exceeds the fair market value of the property.
Fair Market Value of Property: $________ Assessed Valuation of Property: $________
Amount of Overvaluation claimed: $________
Complaint believes the assessment should be reduced to $________

B. ____INEQUALITY
The assessment is erroneous by reason of inequality: the property is assessed at a higher percentage of full (market) value than the average of all other property on the assessment roll.
Full (market) value of property: $________
Percentage of full value at which complainant believes his property should be assessed is ________%, based on one or more of the following:

1. ____The latest equalization rate for the city, town or village in which the property is located (enter latest equalization rate: ______%).
2. ____A sample of other parcels on which complainant relies for objection (list parcels on a separate sheet and attach).
3. ____Statements of the assessor or other local official that property has been placed on the roll at ______%.

Complainant believes the assessment should be reduced to $________

FIGURE 15-1

C. ____ILLEGALITY
The assessment is illegal for the following reasons:
1. ____Property is totally or partially exempt.
2. ____Property is totally outside the boundaries of the city, town or village.
3. ____Property cannot be identified from description or tax map number on the assessment roll.
4. ____Other (explain).

PART THREE: INFORMATION TO SUPPORT COMPLAINT

A. Information to support the full (market) value claimed:
1. ____Purchase price of property $________
a. Date of purchase________
b. Terms: ____Cash ____Contract ____Other (explain)
c. Amount of mortgage, if any $________Year mortgage______
Rate of interest______%
d. Relationship between seller and purchaser ________________
e. Personal Property, if any, included in purchase price (furniture, livestock, etc.)

2. ____If property is insured, state amount: $________
3. ____If property has been recently offered for sale:
When and for how long: ________________
How offered: ________________
Asking price: $________
4. ____If property has been recently appraised:
When: ________ By whom:________________
Purpose of appraisal: ________________
Appraised value: $________
5. ____Describe any buildings or improvements located on the property and present condition: ________________

Year of construction: ________
6. ____If buildings have been recently remodeled or constructed, state:
Year remodeled or constructed________ Date commenced: ________
Date completed:________ Cost: $________
Complainant is prepared to submit construction cost details where available. Such information may be attached and submitted with complaint, if desired.
5. ____If property is leased or rented, complainant is prepared to submit rent schedules and other pertinent information. Such information may be attached and submitted with complaint, if desired.
____If property is income producing, commercial or industrial property, the complainant is prepared to present detailed information about the property, including rental income, operating expenses, sales volume and income statements. Such information may be attached and submitted with the complaint, if desired.
____If property is specialized property (i.e. utility property) complainant is prepared to submit detailed facts concerning the property. Such information may be attached and submitted with the complaint, if desired.
____Explain briefly any additional facts relied on. (Use attachments, if necessary.)

PART FOUR: VERIFICATION

City
Town of ________________ ss:
Village

FIGURE 15-1 (continued)

County of ________________

________________, being duly sworn, says that he is
(owner)
the ________________, (agent of the owner) of the real property described above; that the statements contained in his complaint are true to the best of his knowledge; that he claims to be aggrieved by the assessment; and that he hereby makes application to the Board of Assessment Review to have same reviewed and revised as indicated in this complaint.

Sworn to before me this __________
day of __________ 19______

____
Signature or owner or agent

____
Commissioner of Deeds or Notary Public
(or other officer authorized by law
to administer oaths)

FIGURE 15-1 (continued)

Appeal Year

The first entry called for on this form is a reference to a tax year. (COMPLAINT ON REAL PROPERTY ASSESSMENT FOR 19____) This can sometimes lead to complications depending on whether you are dealing with an assessment levied in one year but with taxes payable in the following year. Just be sure to correctly indicate the year you are dealing with so that there can be no question later on as to what year you have appealed. Sometimes it is the practice of the jurisdiction to carry a dual year reference when working with an assessment appeal covering a fiscal year from July 1st to June 30th. You should also be sure to be consistent throughout your application form so that the appeal year is continually referenced in the same manner.

Jurisdiction

The second entry (Before the Board of Assessment Review for ________________) requires identification of the jurisdiction you are petitioning
(County, City, Town or Village)
for an assessment reduction. While this appears to be a simple entry, you should be sure to properly determine where your property is located. Are there some portions in two jurisdictions? Different parcels or portions thereof in two different towns? The same parcel in both the town and the village?

Remember, they might have to be appealed at different times in the year.

Detailed reference has to be made to *all* the property tax bills paid by the taxpayer during the course of the year to establish exactly what parcels are involved and in exactly what jurisdictions they are located.

PART ONE: GENERAL INFORMATION

Proper or Aggrieved Party

The general information Section 1 on this typical complaint form calls for name of owner or owners of property, and post office address.

In general, if the owner of record whose name appears on the tax roll is filing, there is no problem. However, if a person other than the owner of record is filing, you may encounter proper or aggrieved party difficulties. The basic question is: Has the complainant the legal right to appeal?

For example, a lessee under a net lease who was obligated to pay *all* taxes is an aggrieved party in New York and can appeal in his own name.[5]

In Massachusetts a tenant must show he is under obligation to pay more than one-half the tax assessment on the entire parcel. And the tax due must be paid before he can appeal.[6]

In other states there may be a serious question as to whether or not a tenant on a net lease has the right to appeal in his own name. This should be determined in advance in order to avoid delays, costly procedural arguments, and, possibly, dismissal of your case.

Other proper party issues include an owner who buys property and fails to record the deed. He may not be a proper party to bring the action.[7]

The better rule of course is to overlook technicalities as to status and to permit anyone whose pecuniary interests are or may be adversely affected to appeal. This would include a net lessee, mortgagee, owner of property even though the property is not assessed to him, or a vendor who sold the property subject to taxes a few days after instituting an appeal.[8]

Agent's Authorization

Section 2 calls for the name and address of the agent or representative of the owner, if one is involved. Be careful here because some jurisdictions require an agent's authorization to be filed with the application form or it will not be accepted. In addition, they specify that the mere fact that you are represented by an agent does not release you from being present at the hearing. I have appeared before some Boards of Review in California where the Board insisted on having an employee of the corporation present at the hearing. This, of course, resulted in delay and time lost because an employee had to be produced on short notice. If possible, try to ascertain the Board's procedure beforehand to avoid unpleasant surprises.

A typical example of a California Agent's Authorization form is set forth in Figure 15-2.

Identification of Property

Sections 3-5 reference description, location and types of property. It is most important to accurately identify the subject property by recording here *all* the information that appears on the assessment roll pertaining to this property. Most of this data should also appear on your tax bill.

If you are filing on more than one parcel, be very careful. Some jurisdictions require *separate forms to be filed for each parcel* and it is not enough that the parcels are contiguous. If they are separately identified on the tax roll, you must consider the possibility of a requirement that separate forms must be filed for each parcel. This could, conceivably, involve the filing of many appeal forms and, unfortunately, if it is required, you must comply.

---

[5] *Matter of McLeans Stores v. Comm. of Asst.*, 2 App. Div. 2nd 98, 153 NYS 2nd 342 (1956).
[6] *Newhall, Trustee v. Board of the Assessors of the City of Cambridge*, 1935 A.T.B. Adv. Sh. 113.
[7] *Canron, Inc. vs. Board of Assessors of Everett*, 322 N.E. 2d 83 (1975).
[8] *Peo. ex rel. Luxemberg Realty Corp. v. Miller*, 289 N.Y. 710, 45 N.E. 2d 920 (1942).

Janata

Page 18
July 30, 1976

COUNTY OF ALAMEDA

ASSESSMENT APPEALS BOARD

AGENT'S AUTHORIZATION

Date ....

I, ... , the person af-
(NAME OF APPLICANT – PLEASE PRINT)

fected by the assessment described in my application for reduction of assessments before the Assessment Appeals Board of the County of Alameda do hereby appoint

....
(NAME OF AGENT – PLEASE PRINT) (ADDRESS)

.... , as my agent to act in connection with said application.
(PHONE NUMBER)

I know that this does not relieve me of my obligation to be present at the time and place my application is considered by the Assessment Appeals Board.

(Signed) ....

....
(ADDRESS)

....
(TELEPHONE NUMBER)

NOTE: If Applicant is a corporation, this authorization must be signed by an officer of the Corporation as designated in its articles of incorporation.

FIGURE 15-2

Present Assessment

Section 6 calls for the "assessed valuation appearing on the assessment roll." This should be entered exactly as it appears on the current roll. If possible, a breakdown between land and building should be obtained.

PART TWO: GROUNDS FOR COMPLAINT ON ASSESSMENT

There are three basic grounds for complaint on assessment: overvaluation; inequality; and illegality.

Overvaluation

Your complaint here is that the assessment is erroneous because the assessment exceeds the fair market value of the property.

Taxpayer's (Complainant's) Opinion of Fair Market Value

This entry sometimes presents a problem because you may not know what your property is worth at this early stage of the appeal. It should be remembered that in most jurisdictions you cannot get more than you ask for, meaning that if you record too high a figure in your opinion of value entry, it may come back to haunt you later on if a subsequent appraisal obtained by you indicates a lower value.

For example, in his application for abatement, taxpayer alleged a fair cash value of $50,000. At the hearing he argued a much lower figure. The Massachusetts Appellate Tax Board held that taxpayer was bound by the figure in his petition.[9] Therefore, I recommend that a safe value be used in this entry. If certain market parameters are apparent to you, then the lower end of the value spectrum should be used for this entry. Nothing is worse than to have a $2,000,000 figure entered here when your appraiser comes in with a $1,000,000 figure later on and you are bound by the $2,000,000 figure as originally entered on your application form.

In the event that questions are raised later on as to where your fair market value figure came from, you can argue that it was merely an entry for the completion of the application on your best judgment of value and was not meant to be an appraised value. This usually resolves the issue nicely and enables you to file an appeal figure that you will not have trouble with later on.

Of course, if you have a recent appraisal indicating fair market value or a recent arm's-length sale of the property, that value can be used for this entry.

Extent of Overvaluation

Your basic contention within the overvaluation issue is that your property is assessed in excess of its fair market value and you should allege the extent of that overvaluation. The form should be completed as follows:

Taxpayer's Opinion of fair Market Value:	$100,000
Assessed Value of Property (Assume 100% Equalization Rate)	$200,000

[9] *E. Sohier Welch & Another, Trustees v. Board of Assessors of the City of Boston,* 1934 A.T.B. Adv. St. 1, January 19, 1934.

Amount of Overvaluation Claimed $100,000
Taxpayer believes the assessment should be reduced to: $100,000

Inequality

You should also raise the issue of inequality in your complaint form by alleging that your property is assessed at a higher percentage of fair market value than the average of all other property on the same assessment roll. You may not always be able to prove this with the information available to you at the time of filing the complaint form, but you should raise the issue in order to protect your interests. To my mind, it is common knowledge to most who deal with assessments that the inequality issue exists in every jurisdiction to some degree and that the complaining taxpayer has a right to raise this issue in his initial papers.

This portion of your complaint form should allege what you believe the equalization rate to be, your source of that information, and the assessment that should be levied based on the application of the property equalization rate to your fair market value opinion:

Taxpayer's Estimate of Fair Market Value of Property: $ 100,000

Percentage of full value at which complainant believes his property should be assessed is 50 %, based on one or more of the following:

1. X The latest equalization rate for the city, town or village in which the property is located (enter latest equalization rate: 50 %).
2. ___ A sample of other parcels on which complainant relies for objection (list parcels on a separate sheet and attach).
3. X Statements of the assessor or other local official that property has been placed on the roll at 75 %.

Taxpayer believes the assessment should be reduced to $ 50,000 .

In the above example, the taxpayer relied on an equalization rate published by the State Board of Equalization for this jurisdiction. The assessor in this example does not agree with the state study and alleges a different ratio. Thus, the inequality issue is drawn.

Note that entry 2 in the inequality section of the form allowed for the presentation by taxpayer of sample parcels to show inequality. This is generally a matter that is pursued at the Court level of appeal. This overall issue is presented in greater detail in the inequality section of Chapter 2.

Illegality

Most appeal forms allow for illegality to be raised, involving such issues as exempt property (see Chapter 13); property outside the boundaries of the jurisdiction; property that cannot be identified from the description on the assessment roll; and any other legal issues.

PART THREE: INFORMATION TO SUPPORT COMPLAINANT

This is the section that got Stanjim in all that trouble. So whatever you do, don't just enter "All other pertinent data substantiating this complaint of overvaluation will be presented at requested hearing."

You again have to walk the tightrope here with regard to how much you want to divulge without giving your case away at this early stage of the proceedings. You must reasonably comply with this request for data, but you do not have to make the assessor's case for him. Nor do you have to make public personal financial or other data unrelated to the issues which may hurt you from a competitive point of view. If you are serious about your appeal, you will eventually have to disclose this data, but common-sense strategy dictates that you do not play your entire hand this early in the game.

As a general rule, I would attempt to answer all questions even with "not applicable" entries.

I have no quarrel with answering general questions regarding year and type of construction but cost of construction needs a great deal of study and perhaps expert testimony at the hearing.

With regard to leased or income producing properties, some jurisdictions insist that a copy of the pertinent lease or income and expense statement be attached to the appeal form. This is statutory and, since the appeal will fail without the attachment, you must comply with this request.

I cannot, however, furnish any data that I do not have access to. If I am a net lessee required to pay real estate taxes and I am not privy to my landlord's mortgage arrangements, I cannot produce any such data.

In addition, I simply refuse to furnish any data on insurable value since this has no bearing on the market value of the property. Since most insurance policies are blanket in nature covering more than just the property which is the subject of the appeal, "Blanket Policy" will usually avoid arguments.

I am also reluctant to submit my appraisal, if I have one, with the application. The appraisal should be exchanged only when you can have the same opportunity to review the other side's appraisal for the same period of time prior to the hearing.

I have gone the "exchange of information" route several times in California prior to Board hearings. There are several advantages. The matter may be settled. The issues are more keenly defined. Evidence at the Board hearing is limited to that which you exchange. You get a feel for the weakness or strength of your adversary prior to the hearing.

Always keep alert for last-minute problems. New Jersey, for example, requires that you attach a photograph of subject property to the County appeal form. Yes, I have been seen racing through the New Jersey countryside with my Polaroid camera on the last day to appeal.

You will recall that we went to great pains in the last chapter to prepare our taxpayer's position letter. I will generally use this as my guide to prepare my Application for Assessment Reduction forms. The introduction of any additional information will depend on local practice and availability of data.

PART FOUR: VERIFICATION

This section calls for verification of the facts alleged in your complaint form by signature under oath. This is in accordance with the pertinent statute in this jurisdiction.

Nothing could be easier than to simply sign the form, have it notarized, and file it. Well, consider the following actual case that I was directly involved in:

Taxpayer's senior in-house appraiser and local comptroller appeared before the Board on Grievance Day and presented a written complaint signed by the taxpayer's manager, but not sworn to, and appraisal reports. The hearing was conducted and later the request for assessment reduction was denied.

During the hearing, the assessor gave taxpayer a complaint form and informed taxpayer that it was not necessary to complete the form during the meeting but that it could be completed and filed within a few days. The form was completed, executed, sworn to and delivered to the assessor the following day, one day after Grievance Day deadline for filing.

Later, the assessor moved to dismiss the complaint on the grounds that failure to file a sworn statement on the protest day as required by statute was fatal to taxpayer's proceeding.

I argued that the Board waived strict compliance with the statute by accepting the unsworn letter of protest and appraisal reports, hearing the complaint on the hearing date, permitting the filing of the sworn complaint on the following day and, thereafter, having considered and passed on the merits of the complaint.

The judge agreed with my arguments and the assessor's motion to dismiss the petition was denied. This was, of course, a good victory but one that never should have been necessary if proper filing procedures had been followed in the first place.[10]

Transcript Request

You may encounter obstacles to an appeal from a Board decision even though you timely filed a properly completed complaint form. Consider the Massachusetts taxpayers who appealed a Board decision to court claiming that discriminatory assessments had been levied by the assessor. The court agreed that full fair cash value was the proper standard but no stenographic record of the Board proceedings and oral testimony was made or requested. Since the court could only rule on questions of law, the court could not consider whether, as a matter of law, the evidence before the Board warranted a denial or abatement.[11]

Be sure to check your appeal form to see if you have to request that a stenographer be present. Here again, there is need for professional guidance as to procedure since this is the first step in what may become a court action.

Service of Papers

Assume now that you are absolutely sure of your deadline filing date and that you have properly completed your Application for Assessment Reduction. Be sure that you serve the papers on the proper party. This may be the assessor, the town clerk, the clerk of the board, or some other individual designated to receive such service.

Check the appropriate statutes or directives to determine who the right party is and if service can be made by mail or must be made in person.

If you use the mails, be sure to check if it is the postmark or the received date that counts. In many jurisdictions your application will not be accepted if it is received by the Board after the deadline even though you mailed it a week before the closing date to appeal.

Take nothing for granted. Always get a receipt. Use some form of Return Receipt Requested if you file by mail. If you file in person, it is always careful practice to have your file copy receipted.

THE BOARD OF ASSESSMENT REVIEW

A Board of Assessment Review is a creature of statute and has only such powers as are given it by statute.[12] It is generally not an assessing body, but a quasi-judicial body with a duty to examine assessment rolls, correct errors and hear evidence. The board weighs the

---

[10]*Facet Enterprises, Inc. v. the Board of Assessors of the Town of Horseheads,* Docket No. 76-225, Supreme Court Chemung County, Special Term, April 12, 1976.

For related cases see: *Matter of Romas v. Huffcut,* 39 Misc. 2d 872, 242 N.Y.S. 2d 113 (1963). *People ex rel. the Western Railroad Corporation v. the Board of Assessors of the City of Albany,* 40 N.Y. 154, 157-158 (1869).

[11]*Coomey vs. Board of Assessors of Sandwich,* 329 N.E. 2d 117 (1975).

Board of Assessors of Kingston vs. Sgarzi, 329 N.E. 2d 121 (1975).

[12]*Brown v. Oneida County,* 103 Wis. 149, 79 N.W. 622 (1899).

evidence to decide whether or not the assessor's valuation, deemed presumptively correct, is actually correct. In many states, the courts will not disturb a board decision unless the taxpayer can show that the board acted arbitrarily or dishonestly. In other states, the court hears the case de novo.[13]

Board of Assessment Review members come in all shapes and sizes—male and female, open minded and prejudiced, nasty and pleasant—and range from laymen who don't know the difference between land and buildings to the most sophisticated property appraisal specialists in the country.

The following examples are some of my actual experiences with appeals before Boards of Assessment Review.

EXAMPLES OF INFORMAL BOARD OF ASSESSMENT REVIEW HEARINGS

In a small or remote jurisdiction, the Board of Review hearing might be conducted right at the assessor's desk. It can be little more than a negotiation session or light roundtable discussion. The assessor will sometimes guide and speak for the board as their valuation consultant. Many times this type of board member will frankly admit his lack of familiarity with a complex valuation issue and advise the complaining taxpayer to take his case to the next higher level of appeal.

This is understandable due to the limited exposure a layman board member would have to in-depth appraisal matters. However, this is no excuse for not being prepared. Often, board members are chosen for their appraisal experience and you can never tell when you will encounter a board member who is also the senior real estate appraiser in the community.

Informal board hearings can be hostile. At an evening session in a New England state, the hearing opened and I presented a brief and, I thought, polite case for the corporate taxpayer. After a short discussion, one of the members stood up and yelled that he thought it was ridiculous for a profit-making corporation to dare to appeal a real estate assessment. He refused to listen to any more and stormed out of the room. The other board members apologized for his actions, but granted no reduction.

These board hearings can be funny. At a West Virginia hearing I began my presentation but my timing was thrown off when the clerk of the board twanged a chaw of tobacco juice into the board room spittoon. After three or four of these twangs, my concentration was completely broken. I interrupted my dissertation and asked the learned clerk if he would be so kind as to time his expectorations to coincide with my making of my important points. He readily agreed and, with the musical accompaniment of the clerk and his cuspidor, the remainder of the hearing went quite well.

In general, most of these informal board hearings are conducted in a pleasant and businesslike atmosphere. The evidence that you present is weighed and considered within the scope of the board's capacity and demeanor. You can never predict what such a board will do concerning your appeal, and you should therefore make every effort to document your evidence so that the board can find in your favor.

EXAMPLE OF A FORMAL BOARD OF ASSESSMENT REVIEW HEARING

A formal board hearing usually has all the trappings of a court case. It is generally held in a formal courtroom setting with board members at a raised desk, microphones, recording

---

[13] Jerome R. Hellerstein, "Judicial Review of Property Tax Assessments," *Tax Law Review* (March, 1959) Vol. 14, No. 3, pp. 327-352.

devices, a stenographer, clerks, and counsel to the board. Procedure is orderly but strict rules of evidence are relaxed to permit all participants to have their say.

A typical formal Board of Review Hearing I recently participated in took place before the San Diego Board of Assessment Appeals. It involved an industrial property on county land, portions of which property were special purpose involving trans-Atlantic cable facilities.

The hearing opened with the Board Chairman leading the group in a pledge of allegiance to the flag. The actual all-day hearing is as follows, as near as I can reconstruct it and shorten it for this chapter.

BD. CH: = Board Chairman
ASSR: = Assessor
PET. ATTY: = Petitioner's Attorney
PET. APP: = Petitioner's Appraiser
BD. MBR: = Board Member
ASSR. APP: = Assessor's Appraiser

BD. CH: The Board of Assessment Review for San Diego County is now in session. The first case on the calendar this morning involves XYZ Corporation vs. the Assessor. Mr. Assessor, would you please describe the property and state the assessment for the record.

ASSR: The property is an industrial plant located on Waterfront Way on county owned land. The facility is used for the production of marine communication cable for the transmission of messages. The current assessment is: Land—$1,250,000; Building—$6,650,000; for a total of $7,900,000.

BD. CH: Mr. Petitioner, you have timely filed your application for assessment reduction with the Board and this is your opportunity to challenge the assessment just stated by the assessor, which we presume to be correct. If you present evidence which supports your value conclusion, we will consider same and then give the opportunity to the assessor to present his case. Would you please proceed with your case?

(This case was complicated by the fact that after petitioner filed an assessment appeal against a $6,700,000 assessment, it was increased by $1,200,000 to $7,900,000.)

BD. CH: Mr. Petitioner's attorney, are you ready to begin?

PET. ATTY: Yes, I am, Mr. Chairman. However, I would like to start with a reference to the fact that when taxpayer appealed this particular assessment, it was levied at $6,700,000, and subsequent to the appeal, the assessor increased it to $7,900,000. At this point, I would like to make a motion that the increase by the assessor be dismissed because it is not based on any factual grounds. It was simply introduced to punish the petitioner for appealing the assessment.

BD. CH: Mr. Petitioner's Attorney, we sympathize with your plight and we have taken due note of the fact that the increase has been made subsequent to your filing an appeal. However, since the assessor has every right to do this upon reviewing the facts in a particular case, we must therefore overrule your motion.

(As you can well imagine, this situation created many a sleepless night because petitioner would not have been faced with this increase if he had not filed the appeal.)

PET. ATTY: Thank you for your sympathy, Mr. Chairman. I would like to call as my first witness, Mr. Appraiser, who has completed an appraisal on the subject property.

(At this point, the appraiser is sworn and his credentials are presented in detail to the

Board. The assessor is given an opportunity to accept or reject this expert witness' credentials and the appraiser, having been accepted as an expert, proceeds with his testimony.

The primary issue in the case before the Board is that the assessor considered the subject property to be special purpose in nature and, therefore, used only the cost approach to value. The petitioner's appraiser felt that the property was a relatively standard industrial property with certain portions thereof which might be considered to be special purpose. But in the main, the property would sell as any other industrial would, and therefore the income and market data approaches were used by the petitioner's appraiser, resulting in a value much lower than the original assessment.

The appraiser proceeded to go through all of his testimony involving the three approaches to value and showed in great detail that he had sampled the industrial markets, not only in the San Diego area which was a limited market, but also in the Los Angeles and San Francisco areas which, he argued, were comparable.

The appraiser also attempted to introduce comparable sales of general industrial properties from major industrial centers from around the country.)

BD. MBR: Just a minute, Mr. Appraiser. This Board is not in the habit of considering sales from outside the State of California. Limit your testimony to California sales!

PET. ATTY: And, Mr. Appraiser, did you personally inspect these comparable properties in these various industrial areas in California?

PET. APP: Yes, sir, I did.

PET. ATTY: And in what respect were they comparable to the subject property?

PET. APP: They were comparable with regard to floor load capacity, ceiling heights, egress and ingress, general age and type of construction.

PET. ATTY: And you would say that the subject property consisting of 20 acres and 320,000 square feet would be subject to the same type of market?

PET. APP: Yes, I would. The market is not local to the San Diego area for this type of property, but rather more general in the Greater California area and on the national market at large.

BD. MBR: Mr. Appraiser, I caution you again. We will not consider national sales!

PET. APP: Excuse me, Mr. Board Member.

PET. ATTY: And once again, Mr. Appraiser, your final value conclusion.

PET. APP: $5,200,000.

PET. ATTY: Thank you.

(On cross examination, the assessor attempted to get Petitioner's Appraiser to admit that the property was special purpose.)

ASSR: Mr. Petitioner's Appraiser, did you not testify on direct examination that portions of the subject property are special purpose?

PET. APP: Yes, sir, I did.

ASSR: And would you describe that portion of the subject property which is special purpose?

PET. APP: Due to the fact that a rather unique product is manufactured here, namely marine communication cable, there are portions of the structure which are designed to enable the large cableholder drums to be off loaded from the plant directly into the cable-laying ocean-going vessels. This involves special purpose construction insofar as crane strength and supporting column strength and floor load bearing capacities are concerned. As I stated on my direct examination, I estimate these special purpose aspects to involve approximately 10% of the entire structure. Further, I state that the remaining 90% of the building is in the general industrial category and would lend itself nicely to sale on the open market, and therefore, I used the income and market data approaches in my valuation exercise.

ASSR: I have no further questions.

BD. CH: Mr. Petitioner, is that your case?

PET. ATTY: Yes, it is, Mr. Chairman.

BD. CH: Mr. Assessor, are you ready to present your case?

ASSR: Yes, Mr. Chairman, and for my first witness, I would like to call the valuation specialist for San Diego County, the Assessor's Appraiser.

(The assessor's appraiser is duly sworn and his qualifications are set before the Board. During the presentation of the qualifications, the following dialogue took place.)

ASSR: Mr. Assessor's Appraiser, you, of course, have had real estate appraisal experience in the County of San Diego?

ASSR. APP: That is correct.

ASSR: And would you acquaint the Board with the types of properties that you have appraised and over what period of time.

ASSR. APP: I have been Senior Appraiser for the County of San Diego for the past twelve years and during that period of time I have appraised numerous properties which include hotels, motels, office buildings, residential properties, raw land, etc.

ASSR: And did you complete an appraisal on the subject property?

PET. ATTY: Excuse me, Mr. Chairman, but may I please ask the Assessor's Appraiser a few questions with regard to his qualifications?

BD. CH: You may certainly do so.

PET. ATTY: Thank you. Mr. Assessor's Appraiser, you stated in your qualifications that you had long experience in appraising various types of properties in San Diego County and these included motels and office buildings and residentials, but you neglected to mention that you had any experience in appraising industrial properties. I'm sure you have, and would you please tell us what your exposure and experience has been in that regard.

ASSR. APP: Yes, certainly. I have appraised numerous substantial industrial-type properties throughout the County of San Diego and I should have included that comment in my earlier testimony.

PET. ATTY: Thank you. Now with regard to the industrial properties that you have appraised, were they similar to the subject property in size, age and type of construction?

ASSR. APP: Yes, they were, in the general sense that they are industrial properties.

PET. ATTY: Fine. And did you call on this experience in the appraisal of the subject property?

ASSR. APP: Yes, I did.

PET. ATTY: And of course, you did a professional job on this appraisal, calling on past experience you have had with other similar general industrial real estate.

ASSR. APP: That is correct.

PET. ATTY: Thank you, Mr. Assessor's Appraiser, and thank you, Mr. Chairman. Petitioner accepts the qualifications of the Assessor's Appraiser as an expert witness.

(The point here is a significant one. The assessor's appraiser admits that he has called upon his experience and background in assessing *general* industrial real estate with regard to the assessment of the subject property. As stated earlier, one of the main issues involved in this matter was the assessor's use of the cost approach only, because he claimed this to be a special purpose property. The fact that the appraiser called upon his general experience in industrial real estate valuations would offset his claim that the subject property was special purpose and, as we will see later, the Board pursued this line of thinking in their questioning of the assessor's appraiser.)

ASSR: Mr. Assessor's Appraiser, would you describe your method of approach with regard to the valuation of the subject property.

ASSR. APP: I appraised the property from a cost approach only because I felt that the property was special purpose in nature and would not lend itself to the general industrial real estate market. I am of this opinion because of the special purpose product which is manufactured in this plant and since this plant was specifically designed for this purpose, it is a special purpose property.

ASSR: And your final value conclusion from the cost approach?

ASSR. APP: $7,900,000.

ASSR: Thank you very much.

BD. CH: Mr. Petitioner's Attorney, do you have any questions for the Assessor's Appraiser?

PET. ATTY: Yes, I do, Mr. Chairman. Mr. Assessor's Appraiser, you state that you are of the considered opinion that this property is special purpose in nature and for that reason you applied only the cost approach.

ASSR. APP: That is correct.

PET. ATTY: Fine. Now if we look at the subject property, would you tell me exactly why you have classified this as a special purpose property?

ASSR. APP: I classified it as a special purpose property due to the fact that special purpose transoceanic cable is manufactured there and the plant was specifically designed for that purpose, making it special purpose.

PET. ATTY: Yes, I realize that, but would you describe for me specifically what makes it special purpose insofar as its construction is concerned?

ASSR. APP: It is special purpose because it was designed especially for the production of the cable.

PET. ATTY: I understand that, but would you tell me how it was specially designed that makes it a special purpose property and takes it out of the realm of general industrial usage which does not warrant consideration on your part by the income and market data approaches to value.

ASSR. APP: Because it is special purpose in that it was specially designed.

PET. ATTY: Now, Mr. Assessor's Appraiser, I have been very patient and Mr. Chairman and Members of the Board, I would like you to listen very carefully to my question to the Assessor's Appraiser. I have asked him several times what is special purpose about construction of the subject property and all he tells me is that it is special purpose because it was designed especially for the construction of underwater cable. Now, Mr. Assessor's Appraiser, I am going to ask you specifically: Are you aware of the ceiling height in the subject plant?

ASSR. APP: Yes, I am.

PET. ATTY: And what are those ceiling heights?

ASSR. APP: Approximately 25 to 35 feet in height.

PET. ATTY: And is that the general height of industrial property that you have had exposure to in your experience in appraising industrial properties in the greater San Diego area?

ASSR. APP: Yes, it is.

PET. ATTY: Then there is nothing special purpose about the ceiling heights of the subject property.

ASSR. APP: I guess not.

PET. ATTY: Now, Mr. Assessor's Appraiser, would you describe for me the size of the subject property.

ASSR. APP: The square footage of the subject property is approximately 320,000 square feet.

PET. ATTY: And would this fall into the general category of size of other industrial properties that you have appraised?

ASSR. APP: Yes, it would.

PET. ATTY: Then there is nothing special purpose about the size of the subject plant.

ASSR. APP: I guess not.

PET. ATTY: Would you describe for me the type of construction that we have here?

ASSR. APP: This is a steel skeleton with concrete footings and concrete floor. It is a one-story structure and it has a corrugated metal siding with some insulation.

PET. ATTY: And in your experience is this the general category of construction of a general industrial property of this age and vintage?

ASSR. APP: Yes, it is.

PET. ATTY: Then there is nothing special purpose about the construction of the subject property.

ASSR. APP: Well, I must say there is, in that there is one very large bay which is necessary in order to allow for the very large cable drums to be loaded onto ships.

PET. ATTY: Yes, I understand that to be the case here. And how much of the total square footage of the plant is that section?

ASSR. APP: I believe it is approximately 10%.

PET. ATTY: Then would it be fair to say, Mr. Assessor's Appraiser, that only approximately 10% of the subject plant could be categorized as special purpose?

ASSR. APP: No, I believe the entire structure to be special purpose because it was designed in that fashion for the specific purpose of producing cable.

PET. ATTY: But you found nothing special purpose about its ceiling height, its square footage, and its type of construction.

ASSR. APP: That is correct.

PET. ATTY: And you categorically reject the Petitioner's Appraiser's point of view with regard to the exhaustive study he did concerning the income and market data information from the San Diego-Los Angeles-San Francisco industrial areas?

ASSR. APP: That is correct.

PET. ATTY: I have no further questions.

BD. CH: Well, I have a couple of questions. I am interested in this point raised with regard to the special purpose aspect of the subject property and my colleagues here on the Board have also raised some questions with regard to the foundation for categorizing this particular property as special purpose. Mr. Assessor's Appraiser, I am going to ask you to repeat what the Petitioner's Attorney asked, in that you've got to tell me something more definite about what actually is special purpose about this property. If the ceiling height, square footage and type of construction are not special purpose, what is special purpose?

ASSR. APP: The point is that the plant was specifically designed to produce underwater cable and this is a special purpose product, and therefore it is my opinion that the plant is special purpose in design.

BD. MBR: I'm sorry. That's not enough for me. You're saying one thing but you're not proving it when you compare other industrials to square footage, type of construction and ceiling heights.

BD. MBR: Well, if that's all the evidence, I suggest we take a short recess and render our decision.

BD. CH: All concur? Fine. We'll have a ten-minute break.

(While it would seem difficult to render any kind of in-depth decision in the period of time allotted, the nature of the Board of Assessment Review hearing demands that quick action be taken. This is quite a different procedure from the deliberative aspect of a court trial.)

BD. CH: The Board of Assessment Review for San Diego County is back in session, and after due deliberation and review of all the facts presented, we find that the subject property is not special purpose and it should be valued on the basis of the income and market data approaches to value as well as the cost approach to value. We find that the data submitted by the taxpayer is well-documented and we find that the value of the subject property is $5,200,000. This meeting is adjourned.

This was, of course, a smashing victory for the taxpayer, resulting in tax savings of $105,000. The unfounded assessment increase was avoided and the original assessment was substantially reduced.

But the significant point is that the Board actually listened to the evidence and rendered an objective opinion. The assessor should have considered all three approaches to value. His restricted view was fatal to his case because the Board agreed that the property was not special purpose.

If the Board of Assessment Review does not so respond, you have the makings of a court case—and that is the subject of our next chapter.

CHECK LIST

( ) Are you required to file an appeal to a Board of Review or do you have a legal question permitting you to go directly to court?
( ) Be certain of local appeal dates.
( ) Do you have the appropriate appeal form?
( ) Is your Application for Assessment Reduction form properly completed?
( ) Appeal year?
( ) Jurisdiction?
( ) Proper party?
( ) Agent's authorization?
( ) Identify the subject property and assessment.
( ) Separate forms for separate parcels?

( ) Allege overvaluation.
( ) Allege inequality.
( ) Have you set forth enough pertinent facts to avoid the Stanjim problems?
  ( ) Signature-notarization?
  ( ) Request transcript?
( ) Have you made proper service?
( ) Are you properly prepared for an appearance before a Board of Assessment Review?

16

Appeal to Court—the Culmination Of the Effort Toward Equitable Assessments

Correct Procedures Preliminary to Trial Must Be Carefully Followed to Avoid Fatal Defects

An Example of a Typical Notice and Petition to Bring a Property Tax Assessment Appeal to Court

- Introduction
- Identify Parties
- Identify Property and Set Forth Assessment
- Incorporate Protest Previously Filed with Board
- Overvaluation and Inequality Issue, Degree of Overassessment
- Petitioner Is Aggrieved
- Relief Requested
- Execution
- Service of Papers

Pretrial Meetings and Exchange of Information Provide an Excellent Opportunity for Settlement

- Preliminary Stipulations
- Exchange of Appraisals
- View of the Property
- Prior Adjudications

How to Achieve Maximum Results When You Present Your Case to the Court

- Preparation
- Courtroom Procedure: a Typical Trial
- Jury Trial
- The Law Is NOT the Same in Each Jurisdiction

Appeal to the Higher Courts

Action After Favorable Decision

- Collection of Refund and Interest
- Credit Against Future Taxes
- Freeze

Be Sure to Watch the Appeal Calendar During Trial

16

You have now exhausted your administrative remedy. You have appealed to both the assessor and a Board of Review. You believe that equity has not been done with regard to your assessment. It is time to formally appeal to the courts.

I have long heard it argued in property tax circles that one should never go to court. It is said that no one ever makes any money in the courtroom and it should be avoided at all costs. This is bunk! There comes a time when a property tax appeal should be taken into the courts. Hopefully, through the application of the formal rules of evidence, the wheat will be separated from the chaff and your facts will properly be heard by an objective and impartial weigher of the evidence. Only then will the ardent taxpayer/petitioner know he has done all he could to achieve equity.

A judgment to take a matter to court can be right whether you win or lose. You cannot always be sure of winning. However, you can take satisfaction from the fact that you have tested your case to the limit. If the assessment stands, so be it! If an assessment reduction is granted, enjoy the fruits of your labor, at least until the next assessment is struck. Then, you may have to start all over again!

CORRECT PROCEDURES PRELIMINARY TO TRIAL MUST BE CAREFULLY FOLLOWED TO AVOID FATAL DEFECTS

Preliminary procedural steps are crucial in bringing a property tax appeal into court. This is why it is so important to retain legal counsel early so that all steps necessary to perfect an appeal to court are followed.

You must establish that you exhausted your administrative remedy by timely filing a protest with the assessor and/or Board of Review. You must allege that an appearance was made before the local Board and no relief was granted.

All this and more must be set forth by your counsel in a petition to the court with a verified complaint.

Of course, procedures differ from jurisdiction to jurisdiction, but the essential elements of exhausting your administrative remedy must always be considered.

AN EXAMPLE OF A TYPICAL NOTICE AND PETITION TO BRING A PROPERTY TAX ASSESSMENT APPEAL TO COURT

Introduction

The basic procedure for commencing an action for a reduction of assessment is set forth in appropriate statutes. The action is often referred to as ''certiorari,'' which is simply a writ issuing from a superior court to a tribunal, commanding the latter to send up the record of a particular case.

It is an extraordinary remedy offering a limited form of review to keep inferior tribunals within their jurisdiction. The writ will not issue unless there is substantial injury or injustice to the petitioner.

Thus, the burden is on the taxpayer, requiring him to allege and prove that he is substantially injured by the overassessment of his property.

Figures 16-1 and 16-2 are examples of a notice and petition which are in use in New York State in assessment appeal matters.

I have set them forth in detail and will comment on each of the various sections.

SUPREME COURT OF THE STATE OF NEW YORK,
COUNTY OF

In The Matter of CORPORATION, Petitioner, -against- THE BOARD OF ASSESSORS AND THE BOARD OF ASSESSMENT REVIEW OF THE CITY OF COUNTY, NEW YORK, Respondents	Index No. NOTICE Year: 19 (19 Taxes)

NOTICE OF APPLICATION FOR REVIEW OF ASSESSMENT

SIRS:

PLEASE TAKE NOTICE, that upon the annexed petition an application will be made at a Special Term of the Supreme Court to be held at the County Court House, New York, on the day of , 19 at the opening of Court on that day, or as soon thereafter as Counsel can be heard, for the review under Article 7 of the Real Property Tax Law of the State of New York, of the tax assessment on certain real property of the petitioner, situate in the said Municipality and said County and State of New York, appearing upon the assessment rolls made for the current fiscal year, being the real property particularly described in said petition, and for an order canceling, revising or correcting said assessment, and granting such other, further and different relief as to this Court may seem just and proper, together with the costs of this proceeding.

DATED:

Yours, etc.

Attorney for Petitioner
Office and P.O. Address

TO: Said Board of Assessors and
Board of Assessment Review

FIGURE 16-1

SUPREME COURT OF THE STATE OF NEW YORK
COUNTY OF

In The Matter Of CORPORATION, Petitioner, -against- THE BOARD OF ASSESSORS AND THE BOARD OF ASSESSMENT REVIEW OF THE COUNTY OF Respondents	:	Index No. PETITION Year: 19 (19 Taxes)

TO THE SUPREME COURT OF THE STATE OF NEW YORK:

The petitioner above named respectfully shows to this Court, on information and belief, as follows:

FIRST: That petitioner is a corporation duly authorized to do business in New York by the Secretary of State, State of New York, and was and still is the owner or net lessee responsible for payment of all real estate taxes of certain real property in the said Municipality described and assessed on the current annual assessment rolls of the said Municipality as set forth in Column 1, Schedule A, hereto annexed and made part hereof.

SECOND: That the said Municipality is a municipal corporation existing under the laws of the State of New York and that at all times hereinafter mentioned, there was a Board of Assessors and a Board of Assessment Review of said Municipality whose duties included the preparation and filing of its real property assessment roll for the current year.

THIRD: That the said Board proceeded to prepare and complete the assessment rolls of the said Municipality for the current fiscal year, and deposited them in their office and thereupon caused notice to be published in the official newspaper of said County containing a statement that the said rolls might be seen and examined by the public within the time prescribed by law.

FOURTH: That at the specified time, petitioner duly protested and filed with said Board a statement of protest under oath specifying the respects in which said assessment was erroneous and should be corrected, revised and reduced. Said statement of protest is hereby incorporated in this petition by reference thereto with the same force and effect as though set forth herein at length. Said Board refused, and still refuses to correct, revise, or reduce said assessment. The said Board thereafter finally completed the assessment rolls, duly made and subscribed their oath thereto, filed same and caused notice to be published in the official newspaper of said County.

FIFTH: Upon information and belief, the valuation and assessment of petitioner's said real property, made as aforesaid, is erroneous, illegal, unjust and unequal for the following reasons, to wit:

(a) While the total value as found by the Board is as shown in Column 2 of Schedule A, the said real property is actually of a full and true value not exceeding the amount as shown in Column 3 of Schedule A, so that the extent of such overvaluation is at least as shown in Column 4 of Schedule A;

(b) According to statements made by the Assessor, local officials, and/or the New York State Equalization Board published figures, real property in the said Municipality is generally assessed at a percentage of full value as shown in Column 5, Schedule A;

FIGURE 16-2

(c) Petitioner's said real property is assessed at approximately the percentage of value as shown in Column 6, Schedule A;

(d) Said assessment is unequal in that it has been made at a higher proportionate valuation than the assessment of other property made on the same rolls by the same assessing officers and such inequality exists not only in specific instances, but generally throughout the assessment rolls of said Municipality, and petitioner specifies, as instances of such inequality, all the other real properties assessed upon the same assessment rolls;

(e) Said assessment is illegal and erroneous in that petitioner's said real property is not assessed on one common and general principle of valuation applied by the assessing officers in assessing generally the real property appearing upon the same assessment rolls;

(f) Said assessment of petitioner's real property is illegal and erroneous, in that the valuation of the improvements thereon is made upon the basis of cost of reproduction less depreciation, or upon some other unlawful and unjust method of valuation, and the valuation of the building and improvements, as well as the valuation of the land thereof, is not made at the actual market or full value thereof, as required by the Statutes in such case made and provided;

(g) That said Board failed and refused to hear petitioner's grievance, complaint and protest against the same assessment before the final completion and filing of the assessment rolls, as aforesaid.

SIXTH: By reason of the foregoing, the petitioner is aggrieved and will be injured thereby and suffer loss, and will be required to pay taxes in a greater amount, than if said assessment had been lawfully, correctly and properly made as set forth in Column 7, Schedule A.

SEVENTH: Thirty days have not elapsed since the final completion and filing of the said assessment rolls for the current fiscal year.

EIGHTH: No previous or other application has been made to this or any other Court for the relief herein sought.

WHEREFORE, petitioner prays that this Court review the assessment of petitioner's real property, made as aforesaid, the assessment rolls of the said Municipality, and that the said assessment be canceled, reviewed or corrected, and that petitioner have such other, further and different relief in the premises, as to the Court may seem just and proper, together with the costs of this proceeding.

DATED:

CORPORATION

By______________________________

FIGURE 16-2 (continued)

Comment on Petition and Notice

The *notice* identifies the Court, County, Petitioner, Respondents, Index Number, and Tax Year.

It is a *notice of application for review of assessment,* advising the Court and the municipality that an action is being brought to revise the assessment. A return date is indicated to show when the matter will be presented to the Court.

The *petition* accompanies the *notice*.

Comment

The attorney must review the pertinent statutes to determine the essentials of the petition. He should then use a standard and accepted form to avoid the possibility of omitting any required item that might cause the action to fail.

In general, technical or minor defects in a petition may be amended. But if you fail to allege overvaluation (a jurisdictional defect), the petition may be quashed.[1]

The petition identifies the court, county, petitioner, respondents, index number and the tax year involved.

Identify Parties

Paragraph FIRST identifies the petitioner as owner or net lessee responsible for payment of all real estate taxes on the subject property. As owner or net lessee, the petitioner is an ''aggrieved'' party and may rightfully bring the action.

Identify Property and Set Forth Assessment

The subject property is also described on ''Schedule A'' (Figure 16-3) by lot, block, street number, and assessment exactly as it appears on the assessment rolls. Be sure to properly (and in detail) identify the subject to avoid any chance of error.

Note that a separate schedule is used to show the assessed value and related figures. Many attorneys prefer this method. All the data can be seen in quick review, rather than searching through many paragraphs on different pages for the numbers.

Paragraphs SECOND and THIRD describe the Board and its actions in publishing the current tax roll.

Incorporate Protest Previously Filed with Board

Paragraph FOURTH states the petitioner duly filed a protest of the assessment which is incorporated into the petition. (See Chapter 15 for a copy of a typical application for assessment review protest form.) It further alleges that the Board has refused to revise the assessment.

Overvaluation and Inequality Issue, Degree of Overassessment

Paragraph FIFTH declares that the assessment ''is erroneous, illegal, unjust, and unequal.''

(a) It references in Column 2, Schedule A, the total value (assessed value ÷ equaliza-

---

[1]*Peo. ex rel. O'Neil v. Purdy,* 188 App. Div. 485, 177 N.Y.S. 48 (1919).

Year - 19

SCHEDULE A

1	2	3	4	5	6	7
Assessment and Parcel Description	Total Value Found By Board	Actual Full & True Value Does Not Exceed	Extent of Overvaluation Is At Least	Property Is Generally Assessed At the Following Percentage of Full Value	Petitioner's Property Is Assessed At Approximately The Following Percentage of Full Value	Lawful, Correct & Proper Assessment Should Be
Block: 66 Lot(s) 10A, 10B, 11A, 11B, 11D						
Land $ 471,000 Total $1,779,600	$5,266,650	$4,330,000	$936,650	33.79%	41.1%	$1,463,100
Block: 86 & 87 Lot(s) 14 thru 19 1 thru 10, 14A 15 thru 30, 43, 44, 46, 47						
Land $ 28,000 Total $ 28,000	$ 82,860	$ 61,200	$ 21,660	33.79%	45.75%	$ 20,700

FIGURE 16-3

tion rate) as found by the Board. It gives the petitioner's opinion of actual or market value in Column 3. In Column 4, it sets forth the difference between these two figures to show the amount of overvaluation.

(b) It sets forth the equalization rate in Column 5 and references the various sources of that percentage.

(c) It shows what percentage the subject property is actually assessed at (total assessed value in Column 1 ÷ Column 3).

(d) through (g) allege basic inequality and overvaluation issues.

Petitioner Is Aggrieved

Paragraph SIXTH states that petitioner is aggrieved and injured because he has to pay higher taxes than he would have to pay if his assessment were properly levied as set forth in Column 7, Schedule A (Column 5 × Column 3).

Paragraph SEVENTH alleges that 30 days have not elapsed since the final completion of the assessment roll. This is the statutory period within which these actions must be brought.

Paragraph EIGHTH alleges no previous or other application made to this or any other court for relief.

Relief Requested

In the WHEREFORE clause, the petitioner asks the Court to review his assessment and correct the assessment roll.

Execution

The petition requires a signature of the owner of the property or some other authorized individual.

I have also included a typical cover (Figure 16-4) showing the various forms of verification necessary to properly execute the petition.

Service of Papers

Note that the outside of the cover contains an affidavit of personal service. Strict compliance with statutory requirements is necessary to properly serve the notice and petition.

Be sure that you do not forget to serve all parties. Statutes may require that you serve the school district within which your property is located. This can be very important because the school tax may be the largest part of your tax bill and improper service might be fatal to your refund request after you win a reduction.

PRETRIAL MEETINGS AND EXCHANGES OF INFORMATION PROVIDE AN EXCELLENT OPPORTUNITY FOR SETTLEMENT

Preliminary Stipulations

Negotiations preliminary to trial are often the best forum for settlement and big tax dollar savings.

Procedures in most jurisdictions afford the adversaries the opportunity to meet prior to

STATE OF NEW YORK, COUNTY OF ss.:

The undersigned, an attorney admitted to practice in the courts of New York State,

Check Applicable Box

☐ Certification By Attorney — certifies that the within has been compared by the undersigned with the original and found to be a true and complete copy.

☐ Attorney's Affirmation — shows: deponent is the attorney(s) of record for in the within action; deponent has read the foregoing and knows the contents thereof; the same is true to deponent's own knowledge, except as to the matters therein stated to be alleged on information and belief, and that as to those matters deponent believes it to be true. This verification is made by deponent and not by

The grounds of deponent's belief as to all matters not stated upon deponent's knowledge are as follows:

The undersigned affirms that the foregoing statments are true, under the penalties of perjury.

Dated:

The name signed must be printed beneath

STATE OF NEW YORK, COUNTY OF ss.:

being duly sworn, deposes and says: deponent is

Check Applicable Box

☐ Individual Verification — the in the within action; deponent has read the foregoing and knows the contents thereof; the same is true to deponent's own knowledge, except as to the matters therin stated to be alleged on information and belief, and as to those matters deponent believes it to be true.

☐ Corporate Verification — the of a corporation, in the within action; deponent has read the foregoing and knows the contents thereof; and the same is true to deponent's own knowledge, except as to the matters therein stated to be alleged upon information and belief, and as to those matters deponent believes it to be true. This verification is made by deponent because is a corporation and deponent is an officer thereof.

The grounds of deponent's belief as to all matters not stated upon deponent's knowledge are as follows:

Sworn to before me on 19

The name signed must be printed beneath

STATE OF NEW YORK, COUNTY OF ss.:

being duly sworn, deposes and says: deponent is not a party to the action, is over 18 years of age and resides at

Check Applicable Box

☐ Affidavit of Service By Mail — On 19 deponent served the within upon attorney(s) for in this action, at the address designated by said attorney(s) for that purpose by depositing a true copy of same enclosed in a post-paid properly addressed wrapper, in — a post office — official depository under the exclusive care and custody of the United States Postal Service within the State of New York.

☐ Affidavit of Personal Service — On 19 at deponent served the within upon the herein, by delivering a true copy thereof to h personally. Deponent knew the person so served to be the person mentioned and described in said papers as the therein.

Sworn to before me on 19

The name signed must be printed beneath

FIGURE 16-4

NOTICE OF ENTRY

Sir:-Please take notice that the within is a (*certified*) true copy of a duly entered in the office of the clerk of the within named court on 19

Dated, Yours, etc.,

Attorneys for

Office and Post Office Address, Telephone

To

Attorney for

NOTICE OF SETTLEMENT

Sir:-Please take notice that an order of which the within is a true copy will be presented for settlement to the Hon. one of the judges of the within named Court, at on the day of 19 at M.

Dated, Yours, etc.,

Attorneys for

Office and Post Office Address, Telephone

To

Attorney for

INDEX NO. .... YEAR 19 .....

STATE OF NEW YORK

SUPREME .... COURT

County of ....

In the Matter of the Application of

CORPORATION,

Petitioner

-against-

THE BOARD OF ASSESSORS AND THE BOARD OF ASSESSMENT REVIEW OF THE CITY OF COUNTY, NEW YORK,

Respondents.

ORIGINAL

NOTICE AND PETITION TO REVIEW ASSESSMENTS

Attorneys for

Office and Post Office Address, Telephone

To

Attorney for

Service of a copy of the within Notice & Petition is hereby admitted.

Dated, ...

Attorney for

STATE OF NEW YORK, COUNTY OF ss.: AFFIDAVIT OF PERSONAL SERVICE

being duly sworn, deposes and says, that deponent is not a party to the action, is over 18 years of age and resides at

That on the day of 19 at approx. ________ A.M./P.M. at No. deponent served the within upon

the herein, by delivering a true copy thereof to h personally. Deponent knew the person so served to be the person mentioned and described as follows: therein.

☐ Male	☐ White Skin	☐ Black Hair		☐ 14-20 Yrs.	☐ Under 5′	☐ Under 100 Lbs.
☐ Female	☐ Black Skin	☐ Brown Hair	☐ White Hair	☐ 21-35 Yrs.	☐ 5′0″-5′3″	☐ 100-130 Lbs.
	☐ Yellow Skin	☐ Blond Hair	☐ Balding	☐ 36-50 Yrs.	☐ 5′4″-5′8″	☐ 131-160 Lbs.
	☐ Brown	☐ Gray Hair		☐ 51-65 Yrs.	☐ 5′9″-6′0″	☐ 161-200 Lbs.
	☐ Red Skin	☐ Red Hair		☐ Over 65 Yrs.	☐ Over 6′	☐ Over 200 Lbs.

Other identifying features:

Sworn to before me, this day of 19 ....

Signature of Server

FIGURE 16-4 (continued)

trial in order to establish areas of agreement and, perhaps, to explore the possibility of settlement.

The petitioner may, through the use of interrogatories, determine who the assessor's witnesses will be and generally what evidence will be presented. The assessor may make similar inquiry to the petitioner.

It is also a great timesaver if the parties will agree to stipulate to certain factual items such as the land area involved, or the square footage of the building, or dates of construction, and the like. The trial court is then not bogged down in arguments concerning technical matters not particularly relevant to the valuation issue.

These preliminary hearings can also be used to test the strength of the other side and to determine the thrust of their case. You can then counter their moves during your preparation for trial.

Exchange of Appraisals

In most sophisticated jurisdictions, procedure requires the exchange of appraisals prior to trial. This gives the court and both sides the opportunity to review the appraisals in detail.

There is no better test of an expert witness than probing questions from a judge and in-depth cross-examination by an opposing counsel. If the appraiser is able to support his value judgment through this interrogation, then much weight should be given to his opinion.

View of the Property

The judge may decide that an inspection of the property is necessary in order to better understand the testimony. He may do this on his own or with the consent of both parties. The appropriate statutes must be referred to because the judge is not generally permitted to rely on his judgment and disregard the evidence submitted.

Prior Adjudications

You should be familiar with the past assessment history of the subject property. It may be beneficial to present this data for the record. Results of trials, stipulations, or settlements may be helpful.

For example, in New York, Section 722 Subdivision 2 of the Real Property Tax Law provides for additional allowances to the petitioner if, after a prior adjudication, an assessment increase was made without cause or the amount was grossly discriminatory. This may be shown by reference to prior adjudications concerning the value of the subject property.

HOW TO ACHIEVE MAXIMUM RESULTS WHEN YOU PRESENT YOUR CASE TO THE COURT

Preparation

You are now ready to enter the courtroom ring. Put your gloves on and come out prepared and concentrating.

Make no mistake about it! Our type of trial is an adversary procedure based on a "fight theory'' which has been called the greatest legal engine ever invented for the discovery of truth.[2]

You have a right to prove every element that has a bearing on market value through the development of all favorable facts.[3]

As always, preparation is of paramount importance. The successful outcome of the case is, of course, in the hands of the attorney and the expert witness.

In the preparation of his case, the attorney should become completely familiar with the appraisal report. He should prepare questions beforehand in writing in order to rehearse the direct testimony by the appraiser. The purpose is to appear before the trial court thinking as one person or a well-coordinated team. The sincerity of the expert witness must, of course, come through but all of the questions presented to the appraiser should have been gone over in great detail so that he is not surprised, and he knows exactly what is expected of him in his answer. This does not mean that the attorney should put words in the mouth of the appraiser. It means that the attorney should examine how to best present his client's case within the factual circumstances. He must elicit the most professional and persuasive testimony from his appraisal expert in order to convince the judge that the taxpayer's value conclusion is the most accurate.

You should ask to be present at these pretrial meetings. You should observe for yourself the degree of preparedness of your attorney and expert witness. Your attorney should play the role of ''devil's advocate'' and cross-examine your expert. This will give the appraiser a chance to anticipate possible lines of inquiry by the other side and permit proper preparation of in-depth responses.

Finally, if you have the other side's appraisal, a critique should be prepared to assist in cross-examination of the assessor's appraisal witness.

Only when you have done all this homework are you ready to enter the courtroom.

Courtroom Procedure: A Typical Trial

The trial in an assessment appeal case generally opens with the fact that all the basic papers are before the court, indicating that the administrative remedy of the taxpayer has been duly exhausted and the court has jurisdiction by way of the petition filed by the taxpayer.

The assessor begins by reading the assessment into the record. In most jurisdictions there is a rebuttable presumption of the correctness of the assessment. The taxpayer must present evidence to make a prima facie case for his value. The burden of proof then shifts to the assessors who must prove his value.

The petitioner's counsel presents his appraisal expert's direct testimony. Courts in general permit hearsay evidence by appraisers with regard to terms and condition of comparables.

The appraiser is then subject to cross-examination by the assessor's counsel. The purpose of cross-examination is to dilute, neutralize, or completely destroy the effect of the witness' direct testimony. The attorney will try to show inconsistencies, ignorance, or lack

---

[2]Wiginore on Evidence, Vol. V., Sec. 1367, Third Ed. (1940).

[3]See Sidney Z. Searles, ''Examination and Cross-Examination of Appraiser in Eminent Domain,'' *New York State Bar Journal,* (April 1976) Vol. 48, No. 3.

of independent judgment on the part of the appraiser. He will attempt to obtain favorable concessions from the appaiser.

After the petitioner rests, the assessor's expert witness comes forward and presents his version of the facts and his fair market value conclusion. He is then subject to cross-examination by petitioner's attorney. Witnesses may be recalled to rebut the testimony of the other side.[4]

After submission of appraisal reports and other evidence and closing remarks by each of the attorneys, the court must make its decision.

The judge may ask for briefs from the attorneys, directing their attention to various issues that came up during the trial and on which the judge wants greater clarification. The importance of these briefs cannot be emphasized too strongly.

After a reasonable time to review and deliberate, the judge reaches his conclusion and presents his findings in a written decision.

Jury Trial

Most ad valorem trials are heard by trial court judges or referees specially appointed. Occasionally, the trial will take place before a jury. We went through one recently in Texas where our local counsel felt that we would receive more objective treatment by a jury.

During preliminary questioning, it was learned that one of the potential jurors was the wife of the school board superintendent—a defendant in the case. She insisted that she could be impartial in the matter and was very upset when we objected to her being considered as a juror.

The trial was similar in all respects to a trial before a judge. The jury listened attentively with only minor dozing during the cost approach testimony. They deliberated for two and a half hours and came in with a verdict favorable to the taxpayer. I have no quarrel with ad valorem tax jury trials.

The Law Is NOT the Same in Each Jurisdiction

This can be a vexing problem if you are working with property tax issues in several states. I recently encountered such a situation involving the admissibility of out-of-state comparables.

You will recall that in Chapter 15, the San Diego Board of Assessment Review did not allow industrial comparables from outside California to be admitted. A recent New York case, *A & P Tea Co. v. Kiernan,*[5] held just the opposite. The highest court in New York said that the general rule was that comparable sales should not be too remote from subject. However, since there was no local market for a large food processing plant, the trial court properly relied on out-of-state comparables showing a broad regional market.

I appraised a food processing plant in Virginia and neither I nor the assessor could find any comparables in Virginia. I attempted to introduce a rather extensive comparable sales study of food processing plants in several states other than Virginia in my market data approach. I, of course, relied on the A & P case as my precedent. The assessor objected.

The Circuit Court Judge read the A & P case and promptly disallowed my market

---

[4]For a detailed example of testimony based on an actual trial, see Jerrold F. Janata, "Mock Trial Depicting Ad Valorem Property Tax Assessment Appeal," *Proceedings of the 65th Annual Conference of the National Tax Association* (Washington, D.C. 1972), pp. 142-173.

[5]42 N.Y. 2d 236, 397 N.Y.S. 2d 718, 366 N.E. 2d 808 (1977).

approach on the grounds the New York law is not Virginia law. He cited one word in the A & P case for his decision. "The trial court, relying on the *unchallenged* testimony of the appellant's appraisers that the market for the subject property was regional in nature, found that there was an active market for the type of building here involved throughout the eastern United States."[6]

The Virginia trial judge felt that the "unchallenged" nature of the testimony gave the New York trial judge greater discretion in the receiving of evidence. We believed our position to be unchallenged too, in that both sides agreed there were no comparables in Virginia. Nevertheless, the Virginia Court relied solely on the cost approach in its decision.

APPEAL TO THE HIGHER COURTS

It may be in the best interest for the petitioner to further appeal if a negative decision is reached by the trial judge. Many of the cases cited throughout this manual indicate that trial court decisions were reversed on appeal and the petitioner should not be hesitant to proceed with the appeal if he feels he is justified in doing so.

After a favorable decision, your adversary may appeal or threaten to appeal. This may tie your refund money up for years. This could lead to another whole round of negotiations. It often boils down to this: How much *less* will you take in order to avoid an appeal delay? It takes some of the fun out of a big win, but it is an unfortunate part of dealing with the aftermath of large multi-year assessment reductions.

ACTION AFTER FAVORABLE DECISION

Collection of Refund and Interest

Whatever you do, don't forget to collect your money. After a favorable decision is rendered reducing your assessment, some jurisdictions might require an immediate demand on the assessor or tax collector to refund your overpayment with interest. Interest may only begin to run after you make your demand. Any delay in doing so will result in your having made an interest-free loan to the taxing jurisdiction.

Statutes and case law must be reviewed to determine your right to receive interest on taxes improperly paid on excessive assessments. The Supreme Court of Minnesota, for example, has allowed 6% interest on illegally collected taxes from the date a petition is filed (personal property) or from the date of payment of the tax, whichever is later, to the date the refund is received.[7]

Interest is not a penalty but rather a payment of a reasonable sum for the loss of use of money. When a state consents to a suit, it should not be given arbitrary advantage beyond what is given to private litigants, unless a statute so requires.

Credit Against Future Taxes

More and more taxing jurisdictions have run out of money and refunds are simply not available. This may require you to negotiate a credit against your future payment of taxes.

---

[6]*Ibid.* at pg. 239. Emphasis added.

[7]*General Mills, Inc. v. State, Minn.,* 303 Minn. 66, 226 N.W. 2d 296 (1975). *Hedberg & Sons Co. v. County of Hennepin,* 305 Minn. 80, 232 N.W. 2d 743 (1975).

This is certainly not as good as a refund, but it may be the only practical way for you to resolve the matter.

Freeze

Check statutes and local practice regarding just how long your reduction will remain in effect. There is sometimes a freeze act that will freeze the assessment subject to any additions or deletions to the property.[8]

BE SURE TO WATCH THE APPEAL CALENDAR DURING TRIAL

Don't forget your appeal calendar requirements during the trial. These trials are often held years after your initial papers are filed. If you are required to file various forms each year, be sure you continue to do so while the matter is pending and while the trial is going on.

Your attorney should be fully aware of the practice and procedures, but a double-check is always a good thing. It shows that you are participating in an active way in the appeal procedure rather than merely as an interested bystander.

[8]See, for example, *N.J.R.S. 54:2-43,* where a final judgment of the Division of Tax Appeals is binding upon the municipality for the assessment year and the next two succeeding assessment years.

Assessors' Manuals

Alabama Appraisal Manual, Department of Revenue.

Alaska Taxable 1976 Municipal Property Assessments and Equalized Full Value Determinations, Department of Community & Regional Affairs, Division of Local Govt. Assistance.

Arkansas Real Estate Assessor's Manual, Act 153 of 1955, Assessment Coordination Division, Arkansas Public Service Commission, Department of Commerce.

Arkansas Personal Property Assessment Manual, Assessment Coordination Division, Executive Building, 2020 W. 3rd, Little Rock, Arkansas 72205.

California Assessor's Handbook, AH 517-10, Assessments Standard Division, Property Tax Department, California State Tax Board of Equalization.

Colorado, AH300 Appraisal Procedures and Instructions for 1977, Division of Property Taxation, Dept. of Local Affairs, Denver, Colo.

Florida Manual of Instructions for Ad Valorem Tax Administration, Department of Revenue.

Idaho. Main articles re assessment of real and personal property obtainable from Dept. of Rev. and Taxation, Boise, Idaho 83722.

Illinois Real Property Manual, Dept. of Local Govt. Affairs, Springfield, Ill. (1976).

Indiana Real Property Appraisal Manual, State Board of Tax Commissioners of Indiana, Indianapolis.

Iowa Real Property Appraisal Manual, Department of Revenue.

Kansas Assessment Guide, Division of Property Valuation, Department of Revenue.

Kentucky Real Property Appraisal Manual, Department of Revenue, Commonwealth of Kentucky.

Maine Municipal Association's Assessor's Manual, Third Edition 1973, Augusta, Maine.

Massachusetts Assessment Administration Manual, The Commonwealth of Massachusetts, Department of Corporations and Taxation.

Michigan Assessor's Manual, Act 122, P.A., Michigan State Tax Commission.

Minnesota Assessor's Manual, Department of Taxation, Department of Revenue, Documents Section, Department of Administration, 140 Centennial Office Building, St. Paul, Minnesota 55155.

Missouri State Tax Commission, Thirtieth Annual Report of the Proceedings and Decisions.

New Hampshire Property Appraisal Manual, Department of Revenue Administration, Property Appraisal Division, Concord, NH 03301, Form No. 74-1.

New Mexico County Assessor's Commercial Manual, Property Appraisal Department.

North Dakota Assessment Manual for Assessors and Boards of Equalization, issued by Office of Tax Commissioner, State Capitol, Bismarck, North Dakota 58505.

Oklahoma Ad Valorem Tax Laws, County Assessors and County Boards of Equalization, Oklahoma Tax Commission, 2501 Lincoln Blvd., Oklahoma City, Oklahoma 73194.

Oregon Property Tax Relief, Department of Revenue, Salem, Oregon, Research and Special Services Division.

Pennsylvania Assessor's Handbook, Third Edition, Harrisburg, August 1976.

Rhode Island Assessor's Handbook, Research Series, No. 17, University of Rhode Island, Bureau of Government Research, Kingston, R.I.

South Dakota Property Appraisal Manual, Division of Property Tax, Dept. of Rev.

Texas Tax Assessor Collector Instruction Manual, Comptroller of Public Accounts, Austin, Tex. 78774.

Utah State Tax Commission, Local Valuation Division, Field Inspection Procedures.

Vermont Appraisal Manual, State of Vermont, Department of Taxes, Montpelier, Vt. 05602.

West Virginia Assessor's Manual, Charleston, West Virginia.

Wisconsin Property Assessment Manual, Department of Revenue, State-Local Finance Division, Bureau of Property and Utility Tax.

Table of Cases

Brown v. Maryland, 12 Wheat 419 (1827), 204.
Brown v. Oneida County, 103 Wis. 149, 79 N.W. 622 (1899), 297.
Buhl Foundation v. Board of Assessment, 407 Pa. 567, 180 A. 2d 900 (1962), 196.
California College of Mortuary Science v. County of Los Angeles, 100 Cal. Rptr. 588 (1972), 258.
Calumet Iron & Steel Co. v. Lathrop, 36 Ill. App. 249, 241.
Campion v. County of Hennepin, 301 Minn. 89, 221 N.W. 2d 549 (1974), 96.
Canron, Inc. vs. Board of Assessors of Everett, 322 N.E. 2d 83 (1975), 292.
Canyon Crest Villas South vs. The Board of County Commissioners, 542 P. 2d 395 (1975), Colo., 286.
Cardinal Federal Savings & Loan Assn. vs. Cuyahoga County Board of Revision, 44 Ohio 2d 513, 336 N.E. 2d 433 (1975), 93.
Central Railroad Co. of Pennsylvania v. Commonwealth of Pennsylvania, 370 U.S. 607, 82 S. Ct. 1297, 8 L.Ed. 2d 720 (1962), 203.
City of Atalnta v. Harriet L. McLucas, et al., 125 Ga. 349, 187 S.E. 2d 560 (1972), 95.
City of Cheyenne v. Bd. of Cty. Comm. of the Cty. of Laramie, 484 P. 2d 706 (1971), 255.
City of Chicago in Trust For The Use of Schools vs. Baird, et al., 288 N.E. 2d 110 (1972), 153.
City of Harrisonburg vs. Grace Taubman, et al., 181 S.E. 2d 654 (1971), 126.
City of Lackawanna v. State Board of Equalization and Assessment, 21 A.D. 2d 318, 250 N.Y.S. 2d 369 (1964), 16 N.Y. 2d 222, 264, N.Y.S. 2d 528, 212 N.E. 2d 42 (1965), 246.
City of New York v. Archie Schwartz, et al., Assessors of Town of Fallsburg, 320 N.Y.S. 2d 983, 36 App. Div. 2d 402 (1971), 100.
City of Pittsburgh v. Public Parking Authority of Pittsburgh, et al., 11 Pa. Cmwlth. 442, 314 A. 2d 887 (1974), 253.
City of Winter Park v. Presbyterian Homes for the Synod of Florida, 242 So. 733 (1970), 259.
Coe v. Errol, 116 U.S. 517, 6 S.Ct. 475, 29 L.Ed. 715 (1886), 259.
Consolidated Edison Co. of New York, Inc. v. City of New York, 80 Misc. 2d 1065, 365 N.Y.S. 2d 377 (1975), 246.
Consolidation Coal Company v. Property Tax Appeal Board, 29 Ill. App. 3d 465, *331* N.E. *2d 122* (1975), 214.
Container Corporation of America et al., v. Rutherford, Etc., et al., 293 So. 2d 379 (1974), 101.
Coomey vs. Board of Assessors of Sandwich, 329 N.E. 2d 117 (1975), 297.
County Executive for Montgomery County v. Supervisor of Assessments, 275 Md. 64, 337 A. 2d 682 (1975), 89.
Crogs v. Weare Commission Co., 153 Ill. 499, 240 & 241.
Crystal v. Syracuse, 47 A.D. 2d 29, 364 N.Y.S. 2d 618 (1975), 234.
Cumberland Power and Light Co. v. Hotel Ambassador, 134 Me. 153, 242.
Dade Cty. et al. v. Pan American World Airways, Inc., 275 So. 2d 505 (1973), 255.
Dade County v. Dupont Plaza, Fla. 117 So. 2d 849, 44.
Dade County v. Transportes Aereos Nacionales, S.A., 298 So. 2d 570 (1974), 256.
Deitch Co. v. Bd. of Prop. Assess., 417 Pa. 213, 209 A. 2d 397 (1965), 44.
Delaware Racing Association v. McMahon, 320 A. 2d 758 (1974) & 340 A. 2d 837 (1975), 195 & 196.
DeLuz Homes, Inc. v. San Diego County, 45 Cal. 2d 546, 290 P. 2d 544 (1955), 254.
Department of Assessments of Baltimore City v. Macht, Maryland Tax Court No. 637 (1971), 100.
Diocese of Rochester v. Planning Board of Town of Brighton, 1 N.Y. 2d 508, 154 N.Y.S. 2d 849 (1956), 256.
Dolphin v. Board of Review, 70 Wis. 2d 403, 234 N.W. 2d 277 (1975), 114.
Donavan G. Houghton et al. v. Department of Revenue, 4 Oregon Tax Court 451 (1971), aff'd. Ore. Sup. Ct. 495 P. 2d 715 (1972), 94.
Dulton Realty, Inc. v. Minn., 270 Minn. 1, 132 N.W. 2d 394 (1964), 44.
Easter v. Dept. of Assessments, 288 Md. 547, 180 A. 2d 700 (1962), 94.
Ed Guth Realty, Inc. v. Gingold, 34 N.Y. 2d 440, 358 N.Y.S. 2d 367, 315 N.E. 2d 441 (1974), 44.

Hooven Allison Co. v. Evatt, 324 U.S. 652, 65 S.Ct. 870, 89 L.Ed. 1252 (1945), 204.
Humble Oil and Refining Company v. Borough of Englewood Cliffs, 135 N.J. Super. 26, 342 A. 2d 560, 563 (1975), 188.
In re Peace Haven, 175 Misc. 753, 25 N.Y.S. 2d 974, 977 (Sup. Ct. 1941), 256.
In re Petition of Hamm v. State, 255 Minn. 64, 95 N.W. 2d 649 (1959), 44.
In re Property in Forsyth County, 191 S.E. 2d 692 (1972), 122.
Interlachen Lakes Estates, Inc., v. Snyder, 304 So. 2d 433 (1974), 97.
Interstate Steel Corp. vs. City of Detroit, 59 Mich. App. 438, 229 N.W. 2d 491 (1975), 285.
In the matter of Kents, 34 N.J. 21, 166 A. 2d 763 (1961), 43.
In the Matter of National Tube Co., Ohio BTA, December 26, 1950, 237.
In the Matter of the Appeal of the Aluminum Company of America vs. July 1973 Board of Equalization of Clark County, Docket No. 9026, State of Washington Board of Tax Appeals, September 27, 1975, 167.
In the Matter of the Bar of the City of New York v. Lewisohn, 34 N.Y. 2d 143, 313 N.E. 2d 30 (1974), 252.
In the Matter of the Explorers Club v. Lewisohn, 34 N.Y. 2d 143, 313 N.E. 2d 30 (1974), 252.
John P. Squire & Co. v. City of Portland, 106 Me. 234, 76 Atl. 679 (1909), 242.
John W. Merrithew, et al. v. State of New York, 329 NYS 2d 476, 38 A.D. 2d 996 (1972), 93.
Jordan Marsh Company v. Board of Assessors of Quincy, 331 N.E. 2d 61 (1975), 44.
Joy Oil Co., Ltd. v. State Tax Commission, 337 U.S. 286, 69 S.Ct. 1975, 93 L.Ed. 1366 (1949), 205.
Kaiser Steel Corporation v. Property Appraisal Department, 83 N.M. 251, 490 P. 2d 968 (1971), 99.
Kelley v. Rhoads, 188 U.S. 1, 23 S.Ct. 259, 47 L.Ed. 359 (1903), 203.
Kennedy & Son, Inc. v. Town of Albany, 66 Wis 2d 447, 225 N.W. 2d 624 (1975), 202.
King Ridge, Inc. vs. Town of Sutton, 115 N.H. 294, 340 A. 2d 106 (1975), 99 & 236.
Knoefler Honey Farms v. County of Sherman, 243 N.W. 2d 760 (1976), 202.
Kolodney v. Laconia, 96 N.H. 337, 338, 76 A. 2d 507, 508 (1950), 234.
Lake County Board of Equalization vs. Dept. of Revenue and Ranch, Inc., 257 Ore. 244, 478 P. 2d 377 (1970), 95.
Lamanna, Shelby County Assessor v. University of Tennessee, 462 S.W. 2d 877 (1971), 258.
Lancaster v. Clayton, 86 Ky. 373, 5 S.W. 864, 865 (1887), (260).
Leach Corporation v. County of Los Angeles, 228 Cal. App. 2d 634, 39 Cal. Rptr. 654 (1964), 201.
Lerner Shops of Connecticut, Inc. v. Town of Waterbury, 151 Conn. 79, 193 A. 2d 472 (1964), 44.
Levin-Townsend Computer Corporation v. City of Hartford, 349 A. 2d 853 (1974), 202.
Lilja v. County of Wright, 307 Minn. 276, 239 N.W. 2d 465 (1976), 106.
Louisville and Nashville Railroad Company v. Public Service Commission of Tennessee, 249 F. Supp. 894 (M.D. Tenn. 1966), aff'd., 389 F. 2d 240 (6th Cir. 1968), 47.
Louisville and Nashville Railway Company v. State Board of Equalization, 249 F. Supp. 894 (1966), 44.
Macht v. Department of Assessments of Baltimore City, Court of Appeals of Maryland, No. 16, September Term (1972), 100.
Madonna Inn vs. County of San Luis Obispo, 39 Cal. App. 3d 57, 113 Cal. Rptr. 916 (1974), 139.
Marty v. Brown, 338 N.E. 2d 920 (1975), 263.
Masters v. Department of Revenue, 5 Oregon Tax Court 134 (1972), 97.
Matheson v. Elcook, 173 So. 2d 164 (1965), 97.
Matter of McLeans Stores v. Comm. of Asst., 2 App. Div. 2nd 98, 153 N.Y.S. 2nd 342 (1956), 292.
Matter of New York Telephone Co. v. Ferris, 257 App. Div. 415, 13 N.Y.S. 2d 359, aff'd. 282 N.Y. 667, 26 N.E. 2d 805, 234.
Matter of Pepsi Cola Co. v. Tax Comm., 19 A.D. 2nd 56, 240 N.Y.S. 2d 770 (1963), 157.
Matter of Romas v. Huffcut, 242 N.Y.S. 2d 113, 39 Misc. 2d 872 (1963), 297.
Matter of Seagram & Sons v. Tax Comm., 18 A.D. 2d 109, 238 N.Y.S. 2d 228; affd 14 N.Y. 2d 314 (1964), 157.
McCulloch v. Maryland, 17 U.S. (4 Wheat.) 316, 4 L.Ed. 579 (1819), 253.
McKnight S. Cen. v. Bd. of Property Assess., 417 Pa. 234 209 A. 2d 389 (1965), 44.

Presbyterian-University of Pennsylvania Medical Center v. Board of Revision of Taxes, 357 A. 2d 696 (1976), 258.
Price v. Department of Revenue, 7 Oregon Tax Court 18 (1977), 115.
Publishers Paper Co. v. Department of Revenue, *270* Ore. *737*, 530 P. 2d 88 (1974), 177 & 215.
Reynard v. City of Caldwell, 55 Idaho 342, 42 P. 2d 292, 296 (1935), 98.
Reynolds Metals Company v. Department of Revenue, 258 Ore. 116, 477 P. 2d 888 (1971), 177 & 215.
Rieck Ice Cream Co. Appeal, 417 Pa. 249, 209 A. 2d 383 (1965), 44.
Rosewood, Inc. v. Riley Garner, et al., 476 S.W. 2d 273 (1972), 259.
Russman v. Luckett, Ky., 391 S.W. 2d 694 (1965), 44.
Saint Germain Foundation v. Siskiyou County, 212 CA 2d 911, 28 Cal. Rptr. 393 (1963), 256.
Sam R. Cheedomelka vs. Board of Equalization of Dodge County, 192 N.W. 2d 403 (1971), 94.
Sarris v. Board of Assessors of Swampscott, 315 N.E. 2d 892 (1974), 107.
Schweizer v. Town of Pomfret, 134 Vt. 436, 365 A. 2d 134, (1976), 114.
Seagram's & Sons v. Tax Comm., N.Y.L.J., April 12, 1962, p. 14, 156.
Sierro Retreat v. Los Angeles County, 35 C 2d 755, 221 P. 2d 59 (1950), 257.
Servstation Realty Co. v. Board of Assessors, 392 N.Y.S. 2d 674 (1977), 197.
Shoppers World, Inc. v. Board of Assessors of Framingham, 348 Mass. 366, 203 N.E. 2d 811 (1965), 44.
Sigma Alpha Epsilon Fraternal Association v. Board of County Commissioners of Douglas County, 485 P. 2d 1297 (1971) 66 A.L.R. 2d 904 annotation, 258.
Sioux City and New Orleans Barge Lines, Inc. v. Board of Equalization of Douglas County, 185 N.W. 2d 866 (1971), 254.
Sioux City Bridge Co. v. Dakota County, 260 U.S. 441, 43 S.Ct. 190, 67 L.Ed. 340 (1923), 42.
Southern Railway v. Clement, 57 Tenn. App. 54 (1967), 44.
Springfield Marine Bank v. Property Tax Appeal Board, 44 Ill. 2d 428, 430, 256 N.E. 2d 334 (1970), 214.
State Bd. of Equalization and Assessment, 5 Op. Counsel SBEA No. 20 (1975), 255.
State Board of Tax Commissioners v. Valparaiso Golf Club, Inc., 330 N.E. 2d 394 (1975), 192.
State ex rel. Mitchell Aero, Inc. v. Bd. of Rev., 74 Wis. 2d 268, 246 N.W. 2d 521 (1976), 255.
State ex rel North Shore Development Co., et al. v. Axtel, 216 Wis. 153 26 N.W. 622 (1934), 27.
State ex rel. Park Plaza Shopping Center, Inc. v. O'Malley, et al., 59 Wash. 2d 217, 207 N.W. 2d 622 (1973), 93.
State ex rel. Russell v. LaManna, 498 S.W. 2d 891 (1973), 107.
Statler Industries, Inc. v. Board of Environmental Protection, 333 A. 2d 703 (1975) 261.
State v. Board of Tax Appeals, 175 Ohio 450, 195 N.E. 2d 908 (1964), 44.
Stephen and Stephen Properties Inc. v. State Tax Commission of Missouri, 499 S.W. 2d 798 (1973), 193.
Stieger v. Supervisor of Assessments of Howard County, Maryland Tax Court, Case N. 35 (1973), 97.
Supervisor of Assessments v. Middlebrook Home Owners Assn., Inc., Maryland Tax Court, Nos. 58 & 59 (June 9, 1976), 263.
Supervisor of Assessments of Anne Arundel County v. Bay Ridge Properties, Inc., 270 Md. 216, 310 A. 2d 773 (1973), 263.
Swan Lake Moulding Co. v. Dept. of Revenue, 478 P. 2d 393 (1970), 30 A.L.R. 361, 95.
Switz v. Township of Middletown, 23 N.J. 580, 130 A. 2d 15 (1957), 43.
Sword v. Low, 122 Ill. 487, 241.
Thiokof Chemical Corporation v. Peterson, 15 Utah 2d 355, 393 P. 2d 391 (1964), 253.
Tift vs. Tift County Board of Tax Assessors, 234 6th. 155, 215 S.E. 2nd 3 (1975), 286.
Town of Secaucus vs. Damsil, Inc. et al., 120 N.J. Super. 470, 295 A. 2d 8 (1972), 100.
Town of Sudbury v. Comm. of Corporations and Taxation, 366 Mass. 558, 321 N.E. 2d 641 (1974), 44.
Township of Hillsborough v. Cromwell, 326 U.S. 620, 623, 66 S.Ct. 53, 90 L.Ed. 358 (1946), 43.
Township of Sandyston v. Angerman, 134 Super. 448, 341 A. 2d 682 (1975), 254.

Index

Index

A